The Compendium of

FOREIGN TRADE REMEDY LAWS

Leonard E. Santos, Editor

with Stephen J. Powell and Mark T. Wasden

American Bar Association
Section of International Law and Practice

© American Bar Association 1998

ISBN: 1-57073-577-8

Printed in the United States of America
All Rights Reserved

Nothing herein contained shall be construed as representing the opinions, views, or actions of the American Bar Association unless the same shall have been first approved by the House of Delegates or the Board of Governors, or of the Section of International Law and Practice of the Association unless first approved by the Section or its Council.

Published under the direction of the Publications Committee of the Section of International Law and Practice.

Publications Committee Chair: Patrick M. Norton
Publications Director: Bill Bryan

Contents

Introduction v

Argentina 1
Australia 16
Brazil 37
Canada 56
Chile 85
Colombia 97
The Czech Republic 110
European Union 114
Guatemala 150
India 154
Japan 165
Korea 180
Malaysia 196
Mexico 216

New Zealand 236
Norway 246
Peru 255
Slovak Republic 267
South Africa 275
Switzerland 288
Taiwan 292
Thailand 314
Trinidad & Tobago 327
Tunisia 342
Turkey 350
Uruguay 371
Venezuela 384

About the Editors 413
About the Authors 415

Introduction

Since its inception in 1947, the General Agreement on Tariffs and Trade (GATT) has recognized, in Articles VI and XIX, three principal trade remedies—antidumping duties, countervailing duties, and "escape clause" measures. For most of the succeeding fifty years, these remedies were used mostly by producers in the developed countries such as the United States, Canada, and the European Union. This reflected, at least in part, the fact that by 1985, seven GATT negotiating rounds had reduced the average tariff (on non-agricultural products) in developed countries to 4.7 percent. At these levels, developed country producers turned to these trade remedies as a means of dealing with fairly and unfairly traded imports that they claimed contributed to their material injury, or the threat of such injury.

With the further tariff reductions negotiated in the Uruguay Round, producers in newly industrialized as well as developing countries have recognized that they cannot rely on high tariff barriers in their home countries to moderate the impact on domestic producers of international competition. Thus, many countries that had no trade remedy regime previously, or that rarely used these remedies, have implemented and given life to trade remedy laws. Antidumping and countervailing provisions have the added attraction of not requiring a country to grant compensation when such duties are imposed legitimately. It is fair to say that the enactment and use of trade remedies in the developing world may be one of the growth industries spawned by the Uruguay Round.

This Compendium contains chapters on twenty-seven countries, all of which, except Taiwan, are members of the World Trade Organization. Not all WTO members are included. The focus has been on the major trading nations, and a representative sampling of developing countries.

A review of the trade remedies described in the following chapters reveals great variations among countries in spite of the fact that the WTO imposes a discipline on the use of antidumping and countervailing duties. Textual differences between laws are amplified by differences in administrative structure and practice from country to country.

The development of trade remedy regimes in countries with little prior experience with these laws is an ironic corollary to the growing acceptance of international competition as an engine of economic growth and prosperity. This Compendium reflects the fact that, in most of the world, opening markets and freer competition have replaced import substitution and state-sponsored industries. It is a remarkable turn of events.

While this Compendium cannot substitute for counsel in the jurisdiction where a case is contemplated or filed, it is hoped that the reader will find this a useful introduction to the trade remedies of a particular country.

Special thanks in the preparation of this Compendium are due Stephen Powell and Mark Wasden. Both seasoned trade lawyers, their assistance in editing this volume was most welcome. Thanks also to the law firm of Perkins Coie and its staff, who helped produce this manuscript, particularly Joanne Fredette, Sheila Hawkins, and Linda Allen. Finally, it goes without saying that this Compendium would not have been possible without the distinguished foreign authors who contributed knowledge and time to this effort.

Leonard E. Santos
Perkins Coie
Washington, D.C.
December, 1997

Argentina

Osvaldo J. Marzorati
Allende & Brea
Buenos Aires, Argentina

HISTORY AND OVERVIEW OF TRADE REMEDY LAWS AND/OR REGULATIONS SINCE 1947

Discussion on the Country's Accession to GATT/WTO and Antidumping and Subsidies Codes

In November 1947, the Havana Conference of Trade and Employment approved the Charter of the International Trade Organization. The projected Organization was supposed to form a trilogy with the World Bank and the International Monetary Fund, with the common objective of dealing with the variety of problems that arose after World War II. However, the Charter was never ratified by a sufficient number of countries. During the Conference, Argentina held a position contrary to the principles shared by the industrialized countries, stating that the enforcement of such principles would generate an increasing rate of unemployment in those countries with less-developed industrial activity. As a result, Argentina did not approve the Charter.

Meanwhile, in an effort to stimulate the liberalization of international commerce, a group of twenty-three countries signed the General Agreement on Tariffs and Trade (GATT) that would be in full force as of January 1, 1948. After the failure of the Havana Conference, the GATT undertook the role originally meant for the International Trade Organization. Argentina joined the GATT in gradual stages, participating in only three of its eight rounds of international negotiation.

Argentina's first provisional accession occurred in 1960, during President Frondizi's Administration. Five years later, President Illia's Administration ratified that decision by Law No. 16,834. Both decisions meant an important step toward a new policy of integration within the international community. In 1968, after having participated in the Kennedy Round,

General Onganía's Administration issued Law No. 17,779, ratifying the agreements entered into in that meeting and subsequently incorporating Argentina in the GATT.

From 1973 to 1979, a new round of talks took place in Tokyo. Their main achievements were the agreement on significant tariff reductions, particularly those of industrialized products, and the creation of nine codes, four of which were approved by Argentina. The main purpose of the codes was to interpret and regulate certain GATT articles in order to limit the new methods of protectionism that spread around the world during that period of time. In 1992, Argentina ratified the Antidumping Code by Law No. 24,176.

In 1994, the Uruguay Round created the World Trade Organization (WTO), a supranational organization, and modified and enlarged many of the codes, including those on dumping and subsidies. Argentina was a key participant in the talks and subsequently implemented the agreement on dumping and subsidies.

Evolution of Trade Remedy Laws and Regulations

The first attempt at passing antidumping legislation in Argentina was Decree-Law No. 14.630, passed in 1944 and ratified by Law No. 13,892, that authorized the establishment of high tariffs to counteract dumping activities. The decree that regulated these activities limited the definition of dumping to those acts involving the "intention of depredating the national industry."

In 1963, Decree-Law No. 5,342 was passed, based on Article VI of the GATT, that referred to antidumping and countervailing duties. Similar to Decree-Law No. 14,630, the new decree authorized the imposition of antidumping and countervailing duties and required, for that purpose, the existence of both dumping or subsidies and injury. In fact, both decrees were hardly enforced because of their technical defects and because the tariff protection system that generally prevented the importation of like products (goods similar to those locally manufactured), the only ones that could actually cause injury.

Fifteen years later, Law No. 21,838, regulated by Decree 643/79, reflected the change in Argentina's economic policy. The economic opening of Argentina, coupled with the generalized reduction of import tariffs, increased the possibility of dumping activities and, therefore, made it necessary to improve the legislation. Law No. 21,838 was based on U.S., EC, and GATT antidumping rules. It introduced many improvements, such as the protection of the importer charged with dumping activities, the possibility of using several alternative parameters to establish the existence of dumping, and to differentiate between antidumping and countervailing duties and the rest of the import tariffs.

Law No. 22,415, passed in 1981, enforced the Argentine Custom Code (Código Aduanero de la República Argentina) that regulated dumping and subsidy activities under Sections 672 to 687. Law No. 24,176, passed in 1992 and regulated by Decree No. 2121/94, introduced both the Antidumping and the Subsidies and Countervailing Duty Codes. To enforce them, Decree No. 766/94 created the National Commission of Foreign Commerce (NCFC), whose administrative structure was created by Decree No. 2377/94.

Law No. 22,415's original text prescribed, in Section 2, the subsidiary applicability of the Customs Code's sections in reference to dumping and subsidies. However, Section 2 was subsequently vetoed by the Executive Power via Decree 1961/92. As a result, that section is now effectively invalidated.

In December 1994, Law No. 24,425 was approved at the conclusion of the Uruguay Round and the Marrakesh Agreement that created the WTO. Its Regulatory Decree has not been passed yet, but it is expected to be passed by the end of 1997. However, the Agreement on Safeguards, which permits temporary suspension of GATT concessions under limited circumstances, has been specifically implemented by Decree No. 1059/96, which was issued on September 24, 1996.

Summary Listing of Each Trade Remedy

There are two kinds of trade remedies, both regulated by Law No. 24,425: antidumping duties and countervailing duties. The usual practice followed by the Ministry of Economy is to apply Law No. 24,425 to those investigations initiated by petitions submitted after January 14, 1995; earlier investigations are still governed by Law No. 24,176.

Because the regulatory Decree of Law No. 24,425 has not yet been passed, Section 2 of Decree No. 710/95 has provisionally extended the applicability of Decrees No. 2121/94, No. 766/94, and No. 106/95, provided that they are not contrary to the contents of Law No. 24,425. Regulations under the new Law will be issued soon.

The petition to initiate an investigation of unfair practices must be submitted to the Undersecretariat of Foreign Commerce (SSFC), a division within the Secretariat of Commerce and Investments, which is a branch of the Ministry of Economy and Work and Public Services. The investigation to determine the legal basis for the imposition of antidumping or countervailing duties is then conducted by the Undersecretariat, which will determine the existence of dumping or of a subsidy. The National Commission of Foreign Commerce (NCFC) must determine the existence of any injury to national production. Finally, as a result of the former investigation, the Minister of Economy will, as appropriate, issue the order imposing provisional or definitive antidumping and countervailing duties.

ANTIDUMPING INVESTIGATIONS

Dumping Determination

Initiation of investigation

Pursuant to Law No. 24,425, which incorporates the Uruguay Round Agreements, the investigation that will determine the existence, level, and effects of alleged dumping is initiated either upon written request of the domestic industry or on its behalf.

The petition must include evidence of the existence of dumping, injury, and a causal relation between the dumped imports and the alleged injury.

To initiate the investigation, the petition should also include all reasonable available information relating to:

(i) petitioner's identity, volume and value description of national production of the like product (list of all known national producers of the like product is required when the petition is made on behalf of national production);

(ii) full description of the allegedly dumped product, name of the exporting country, identity of the known foreign exporter or producer, list of known importers;

(iii) information about the sale prices of the products subject to dumping, when they are locally consumed in the country of origin or exportation, as well as the export prices; and

(iv) information and evidence regarding the repercussions caused by the dumped imports on the local sale price of like products and effects on national production.

To be considered "national production," the petition has to be supported by national producers whose production represents 50 percent of the total production of the like product. No investigation will be initiated if support is given by less than 25 percent of the local producers of the like product.

Under special circumstances, the competent authority may initiate an investigation without previous written request of a private party if sufficient evidence of the above-mentioned requirements (dumping, injury, causation) exists.

Regulatory Decree No. 2121/94 of the old Law No. 24,176, still in full force and effect, states that the petition must be submitted with the Undersecretariat of Foreign Commerce who must serve notice on the National Commission of Foreign Commerce for the determination of the "national production" concept. Such notice must be served in order to formally accept the petition.

Timetable

Within thirty-five working days of acceptance of the petition, the SSFC must submit its conclusions regarding the initiation of an investigation to the Secretary of Commerce, who must make a final decision within ten working days.

In case of omission or mistake (discovered by the SSFC within thirty working days of submission), the petitioner is allowed to correct its petition within fifteen working days following notification.

The resolution related to the initiation of the investigation has to be published in the Official Gazette within ten working days following its adoption. According to the Antidumping Agreement, the submitted and accepted written request has to be provided to the authorities of the exporting country and to known exporting parties.

Interested parties (exporters, foreign producers, importers of an investigated product, and producers of the like product) that are involved in the investigation will have thirty working days (which may be extended) to answer any questions asked by the authorities.

Further investigations can be conducted by the authority either within the country or abroad if there exists the previous consent of the foreign country and the parties. Any information obtained will be made available to the interested parties within eight working days from its receipt, unless its confidentiality is established within five working days from the request.

As mentioned before, the SSFC determines the existence of dumping and the NCFC the existence of injury to national production.

Final results of the investigation are to be submitted to the Minister of Economy and Public Works and Services within one year of its initiation by the SSFC. The final determination is to be made within 120 working days from the preliminary determination and both findings have to be published in the Official Gazette. The Minister, based on preliminary or final determinations of the existence of dumping and injury, may then issue an antidumping order.

According to Art. 7 of the Antidumping Agreement, provisional measures

may be applied on the basis of affirmative preliminary determinations of dumping and injury. These measures are intended to prevent further injury during the investigation to the domestic industry and can only be applied if:
(i) an investigation has been initiated in accordance with the requirements of Art. 5 of the same agreement, the order is made public, and the interested parties have been able to present information and their argument;
(ii) the preliminary determination finds the existence of dumping and the related injury;
(iii) the competent authority considers that such measures are necessary to prevent injury during the investigation.

The provisional measure can take the form of an injunction granted upon a standing letter of credit or bond, or some suitable form of surety, and cannot exceed in general four months, or six months if the competent authority receives a request from exporters that represent a significant percentage of the merchandise under investigation. These periods can be six or nine months, respectively, when the authorities determine that a lower tariff than the dumping margin is sufficient to eliminate the injury. Provisional measures cannot be applied before sixty days have passed from the date of initiation of the investigation.

Any determination of dumping can be appealed to the Ministry or to the President of the Nation within ten working days following notification of such determination. The appeal does not suspend the execution of the challenged decision.

Although Art. 13 of the Antidumping Agreement has been implemented by Law No. 24,425, Decree No. 2121/94 does not expressly require an independent judicial review. However, Section 23 of Decree-Law No. 19,549, which applies to all administrative proceedings, implements the right of an independent judicial review of final administrative decisions. Nevertheless, this procedure has not been tested yet.

Access of parties to information developed in investigative proceedings

Unless classified as confidential, all parties have free access to the information submitted in an investigation. The parties may request confidential treatment based upon the special characteristics of the information provided (advantage to a competitor upon release of information, competitive harm to submitting party, etc.).

As mentioned above, any information obtained during an investigation is available to the interested parties within eight working days from its receipt, unless its confidentiality is established within five working days following the request for confidentiality. If confidential status is granted, the information is not attached to the public file and a nonconfidential summary of same must be submitted. The withdrawal of the information is permitted if confidential status is denied.

As foreseen by Art. 6 of the Antidumping Agreement, the SSFC and the Minister may base their determinations on confidential information that has not been seen by some of the parties. As a consequence, the determination based on confidential information shall not disclose any of said information but shall only refer to the nonconfidential summary provided together with it. Confidentiality will also be protected by the SSFC and the Minister during any administrative appeal.

Definitions

According to Law No. 24,425, a product will be considered as being dumped if its export price is less than the price of a like product destined for the local consumption of the export country in the ordinary course of trade.

Like product

Pursuant to Decree No. 2121/94, a "like product" is either an identical product—meaning "a product equal in every aspect"—to the product to which it is compared or, in case said identical product does not exist, any other product with very similar characteristics to the compared product.

Period of investigation

The period of investigation is the period which the authorities determine will best measure the existence of the alleged dumping. The final results of the investigation must be submitted to the Minister of Economy within one year of its initiation by the SSFC.

Related parties.

According to Section 14 of Decree 2121/94, parties are related if:
(i) one company directly or indirectly controls the other;
(ii) both companies are directly or indirectly controlled by a third company; or
(iii) both companies jointly and directly or indirectly control a third company.

In all cases, a company will "control" another company when the first one has the possibility of legally or effectively running the second company.

Calculation of dumping margins

Export price

According to Section 21 of Decree 2121/94, "export price" is the direct price of exportation, meaning the price actually paid or to be paid in a sale, trade, or exchange, related to the importation of the product into Argentina. In case the "export price" does not exist or is not reliable, the export price will be determined either on the basis of the price of the product when it is resold to an independent importer or on another reasonable basis.

Normal value

In accordance with Section 12 of Decree 2121/94, "normal value" is the price paid or to be paid for a like product when it is sold in the local market of the Country of origin or exported through an arm's length transaction. Transactions will be considered to be "arm's length" when:
(i) the price is not affected by any relation between parties, or
(ii) the price is not less than the cost of production.

Adjustments including those reflecting level of trade

Pursuant to Section 26, the comparison between the "normal value" and the export price will incorporate adjustments related to:
(i) level of trade, i.e. sales volume. A level-of-trade adjustment will not only be determined by the volume of sales but also by the subsequent commercialization in order to compare the normal value with the export price. The different levels within this commercialization will be taken into account;
(ii) physical differences between the product that is being investigated and the like product used to calculate the normal value;
(iii) discounts (for quantity). According to Art. 26d, adjustments in the framework of quantities have to be checked if it is a usual practice from the producers or exporters in the country of origin or export;
(iv) sale costs;
(v) warranty costs; and
(vi) costs of technical assistance.

Currency conversion

The currency exchange rate used for the comparison between the normal value and the export price will be the one that is in force on the day of the transaction used as the basis for such comparison. In Argentina, there is no direct provision or detailed definition for ignoring temporary fluctuations or sustained movements in currency exchange rates.

Nonmarket economy methodology

When the country of origin or exportation of the allegedly dumped products is characterized by a centrally planned economy, the normal value will

be determined in the most appropriate and reasonable manner, on the basis of one of the following standards:
(i) the local sale price or the export price of a like product from a third country that has a free market economy; or
(ii) the value determined for the like product in a third country that has a free market economy; or
(iii) the price paid or to be paid in Argentina for a like product, properly adjusted to include a reasonable margin of profit.

Price undertakings and other agreements to suspend investigations

Decree 2121/94 permits the submission to the authorities of any price agreement related to the product under investigation. The Secretary of Commerce and Investments will issue its resolution after considering the reports presented by the SSFC and the NCFC. The agreement must eliminate any injury caused to national production. In addition, the approval of the foreign government is required in order for the agreement to be enforceable. If accepted, the investigation will be suspended (it could also continue by request of the exporting party or if the authorities deem it convenient).

Effect of Antidumping Order

Effective date

According to Decree No. 2121/94, an antidumping order must be published in the Official Gazette in order to be effective.

Retroactivity

Retroactive application of antidumping duties (for a maximum of ninety days before the adoption of preliminary measures) can be imposed when the authorities conclude that:
(i) the importer should have known that the exporter or manufacturer was dumping and that said dumping would cause injury to the national production; and
(ii) the injury is caused by isolated dumping of such a magnitude that retroactive imposition of duties is necessary to prevent future dumping.

If the antidumping duty established in the final determination exceeds the amount of the preliminary duty, the difference will not be collected. However, if the amount of the preliminary duty is more, the excess will be refunded.

Duration

An antidumping duty can be applied for a maximum of five years counted from the final determination date. The final determination can be reviewed annually on petition being made by an interested party (Sec. 75, Decree 2121/94).

Enforcement, including measures to prevent circumvention of order

Upon publication of the antidumping duty order in the Official Gazette, the Minister of Economy and Public Work and Services must notify (within five working days) the National Customs Administration (NCA) of the final determination. The NCA, based on such final determination, is the authority in charge of collecting the amounts due within ten working days following the receipt of notification.

COUNTERVAILING DUTY INVESTIGATIONS

Subsidy Determination

Initiation of investigation

In accordance with Law No. 24,425, subsidy investigations are initiated upon written request of those representing national production of the affected product.

The petition must include evidence of the existence of a) a subsidy, b) injury, and c) causal relationship between the subsidized imports and the alleged injury.

To initiate the investigation, the petition should also include all reasonably available information related to:
(i) petitioner's identity, volume, and value description of the national production of the like product (listing of all known national producers of the like product is required when the petition is made on behalf of national production);
(ii) full description of the allegedly subsidized product, name of the exporting country, identity of the foreign exporter or producer, list of known importers;
(iii) evidence of existence, quantity, and the nature of the subsidy; and
(iv) evidence of important injury caused to national production by and because of subsidized imports.

To be considered "national production," the petition must be supported by producers whose production represents 50 percent of the total production of the like product. No investigation will be initiated if the support given is less than 25 percent of that total local production of the like product.

Under special circumstances the competent authority may initiate an investigation without previous written request if sufficient evidence of the above-mentioned requirements (subsidy, injury, causation) exists.

Regulatory Decree No. 2121/94 of the old Law No. 24,176, still in full force and effect, states that the petition must be submitted to the SSFC, which must serve notice to the NCFC for the determination of the "national production" concept. Such notice must be served in order to formally accept the petition.

Timetable

Within thirty-five working days of acceptance of the petition, the SSFC will submit its conclusions regarding the initiation of an investigation to the Secretary of Commerce, who in turn must make a final decision within ten working days.

In case of omission or mistake (discovered by the SSFC within thirty working days of submission), the petitioner is allowed to correct its petition within fifteen working days following notification.

The resolution related to the initiation of the investigation must be published in the Official Gazette within ten working days following its adoption.

Interested parties (exporters, foreign producers, importers of an investigated product, and producers of the like product) will have thirty working days (which may be extended) to answer any questions asked by the authorities.

Further investigations can be conducted by the authority either within the country or abroad if it has the previous consent of the foreign country and the parties. Any information obtained will be made available to the interested parties within eight working days from its reception, unless its confidentiality is established within five working days following the request.

The SSFC determines the existence of subsidies and the NCFC the existence of injury to national production.

Final results of the investigation are submitted to the Minister of Economy and Public Work and Services within one year from its initiation by the SSFC. The final determination is to be made within 120 working days from the preliminary determination and both have to be published in the Official Gazette. The Minister, based on preliminary or final determinations of the existence of a subsidy, can issue a countervailing duty order.

The provisional measures can take the form of an injunction granted upon a standing letter of credit or bond, or some suitable form of surety, and cannot exceed a period of four months. Provisional measures cannot be applied before sixty days have passed from the date of initiation of the investigation.

Any determination of a subsidy can be appealed to the Ministry or to the President of the Republic within ten working days following notification. The appeal does not suspend the execution of the decision.

Although Art. 23 of the Subsidy and Countervailing Measures Agreement has been implemented by Law No. 24,425, Decree No. 2121/94 does not expressly require an independent judicial review. However, Section 23 of Decree-Law No. 19,549, applicable to all administrative proceedings, implements the right of an independent judicial review of final administrative decisions. Nevertheless, this procedure has not been tested yet.

Access of parties to information developed in proceedings

The same rules apply as those described in antidumping proceedings.

Definitions

According to the Subsidies Agreement and Law No. 24,425, a subsidy exists if a benefit is granted when:
(i) there is a financial contribution from the government or any public authority of a party, such as:
   a) direct transfer of funds or obligations (donations, loans, capital contributions, loan guarantees);
   b) tax remissions or tax allowances;
   c) assets and services provided by the government;
   d) governmental financial aid, or any aid provided by a private company that would usually be provided by the government.
(ii) there is any form of income or price support as defined by Art. XVI of GATT 1994.

To be be subject to countervailing duties, a subsidy must be "specific" to an industry or group of industries within the jurisdiction of the production of the granting authority. To make such determination, the following principles are relevant:
(i)   There will be no specificity if objective criteria for the eligibility and amount of the subsidy is previously established by law, i.e., number of employees, size of the company.
(ii) There will be specificity if the subsidy is only available to certain industries or to industries located in a specific region.
(iii) If there are, nonetheless, reasons to believe that the subsidy is specific, other factors can be considered: the kind and number of compa-

nies to which the program is available, the amount of subsidies granted to certain companies, etc.

Green lighted subsidies (no action may be taken) include:
(i) non-specific subsidies; and
(ii) specific subsidies that comply with certain requirements, such as aid granted to research activities undertaken by industries or teaching institutions, aid for a depressed region of the Country, and aid for environmental development. The subsidy program must be notified to the WTO.

Calculation of subsidies

Under Decree 2121/94, which is still applicable, subsidies that are generally granted to any exports of the beneficiary industry are valued by calculating the ratio between the company's total sales and the specific sales of the product being investigated (Section 31 of Decree 2121/94). Likewise, the effect of the subsidy on the product's sales, during the period the subsidy was in effect, must be determined.

When a loan is granted under more favorable commercial conditions than those offered by the free market, loans must be classified as short- (less than two years) or long-term loans (in excess of two years) in order to calculate the value of the subsidy. Subsidies for short-term loans will be calculated as indicated above. Subsidies for long-term loans will be calculated according to the most appropriate financial method available to establish the real effect of the subsidy on the imported products (Sec. 32, Decree 2121/94).

Undertakings that may suspend an investigation

Decree 2121/94 permits the submission to the authorities of any price agreement related to the product under investigation. The Secretary of Commerce and Investments will decide whether to suspend the investigation after considering the reports presented by the SSFC and the NCFC. The agreement must eliminate any injury caused to national production. In addition, the approval of the foreign government is required in order for the agreement to be enforceable. If accepted, the investigation will be suspended (it could also continue by request of the exporting party or if the authorities deem it convenient).

Likewise, if the foreign government withdraws the subsidy, the investigation will be suspended.

Effect of Countervailing Duty Order

Effective date

According to Decree No. 2121/94, a countervailing duty order must be published in the Official Gazette in order to be effective.

Imported parts or components of a product to be assembled in Argentina can also be taxed if it is like a product subject to countervailing duties.

Retroactivity, if any

Retroactive application of countervailing duties (for a maximum of ninety days before the adoption of preliminary measures) can be authorized when the authorities consider it convenient to avoid future importations of the product under investigation (material injury caused by mass imports during a short period of time).

If the countervailing duty established in the final determination exceeds the amount of the preliminary duty, the difference will not be collected. If the amount of the preliminary duty is more, the excess will be returned.

Duration

A countervailing duty can be applied for a maximum of five years from the final determination date that imposed them. The final determination may be reviewed annually by a petition of the interested party (Sec. 75, Decree 2121/94).

Enforcement, including measures to prevent circumvention of order

Upon publication of the countervailing duty order in the Official Gazette, the Minister of Economy and Public Work and Services must notify (within five working days) the National Customs Administration (NCA) of the final determination. The NCA, based on such final determination, is the authority in charge of collecting the due amounts within ten working days following notification.

INJURY ANALYSIS

Material Injury

In accordance with Section 7 of Decree No. 2121/94, the determination of the existence of a material injury will be based on:
(i) the volume of the imports allegedly being dumped or subsided and their effect on the sale prices of the like products in the local market; and

(ii) the subsequent effects of those imports on national manufacturers of said products.

Threat of Material Injury

The determination of the existence of a threat of material injury will be based, among other things, on:
(i) the increase in participation of the investigated imports in the national market;
(ii) the overproduction or excess capacity or inventory of the product that is being investigated, in the country of origin or export, plus the possibility of its exportation to Argentina; and
(iii) the inventory of said product in Argentina, even if it has not yet been sold in the country .

Retardation of Industry

According to Section 10 of Decree 2121/94, a significant delay in the generation of national production can also be considered a form of "injury" if the investigated imports have caused a negative effect on the potential for such national production.

Australia

Matthew Kennedy
Clayton Utz
Sydney NSW, Australia

HISTORY AND OVERVIEW OF TRADE REMEDY LAWS AND REGULATIONS SINCE 1947

Australia was an original contracting party to the General Agreement on Tariffs and Trade (GATT) and accepted the protocol of provisional application on January 1, 1948. It was also a founding member of the World Trade Organization on January 1, 1995. Australia implemented the GATT Antidumping and Subsidies Codes in 1975, the Tokyo Round revisions in 1982, and both the WTO Antidumping Agreement and Agreement on Subsidies and Countervailing Measures on January 1, 1995.

International agreements, such as the GATT Codes and now the WTO Agreements, are part of Australian municipal law only to the extent that Parliament has implemented them. Domestic courts are only permitted to refer to them where the Australian laws that are intended to implement them are ambiguous.

Australia is a federation in which the federal government enjoys exclusive jurisdiction in the area of external trade. Trade remedies are therefore established under federal statutes and regulations, rather than those of the States and Territories.

Australia's first trade remedy law appeared in the Australian Industries Preservation Act 1906, which was replaced, in turn, by the Customs Tariff (Industries Preservation) Act 1921, the Customs Tariff (Dumping and Subsidies) Act 1961 and the Customs Tariff (Dumping and Subsidies) Act 1965.

Australia enacted the Customs Tariff (Antidumping) Act 1975 to enable it to sign the GATT Antidumping and Subsidies Codes, although some believed that the act failed properly to implement the codes. It was amended by the Customs Tariff (Antidumping) Amendment Act 1981 to implement the revisions to the codes agreed upon during the Tokyo Round. The procedural sections of that act have now been incorporated into the Customs Act 1901.

The economic recession of the late 1980s caused a large increase in the number of applications by the Australian industry for antidumping and countervailing measures. Various government reviews led to significant changes to the system. In 1988 the administration of both antidumping and countervailing investigations was divided between the Australian Customs Service (Customs) and the Antidumping Authority (ADA) as set out below. Changes from July 1992 reduced the maximum time for a prima facie decision by Customs concerning application acceptance, allowed Customs to consider material not contained in the application, extended the maximum period of measures, and permitted the ADA to order the continuation of measures when they expire. Changes from January 1, 1993 permitted interim duties to be imposed pending a final finding.

The legislation was amended most recently on January 1, 1995 to comply with the WTO Agreements. These changes affected many issues, including the definition of "countervailable subsidy," the procedure and requisite standing for applications, the assessment of dumping margins, the transparency of the system, and rules for interim duties.

The legislation requires the ADA, in exercising its powers, to have regard for the federal government's antidumping policy and Australia's GATT obligations, and prohibits the ADA from imposing duties to assist import competing industries in Australia or to protect industries in Australia from the need to adjust to changing economic conditions.[1]

The Full Court of the Federal Court has held that the scheme of the current legislation is both to protect Australian manufacturers from unfair international trading practices and to ensure that protective measures adopted by the imposition of duties do not unjustifiably impede international trade.[2] The Federal Court has also held that the latter of these objectives is not subsidiary or subordinate to the former objectives.[3]

Australian industry is critical of the time taken in antidumping and countervailing procedures. In 1996 the government announced a further review of procedures to investigate ways to "fast-track" them while still preserving the integrity and quality of decisions. The government has promised to reduce the length of investigations from 245 days to 155 days.

Antidumping measures may not be imposed on goods produced or manufactured in New Zealand (although countervailing measures may) due to the Australia and New Zealand Closer Economic Relations Trade Agreement.

The primary trade remedies available in Australia are antidumping duties and countervailing duties. The procedures applicable to both are set out in the Customs Act 1901 Part XVB, which is supplemented by the Customs Regulations. Duties may be imposed under the remaining provisions of the Customs Tariff (Anti-Dumping) Act 1975. Both antidumping and countervailing investigations are administered by Customs and the ADA. Customs' role is set out in the Customs Act 1901. It handles initial applications, conducts preliminary finding inquiries, and imposes provisional measures. The ADA's role is set out in the Antidumping Authority Act 1988. It reviews Customs' preliminary findings and makes final findings in the form of recommendations to the Minister responsible for Customs, currently the Minister for Small Business and Consumer Affairs, who imposes final measures.

Customs sanctions can be imposed under the Customs (Prohibited Imports) Regulations and Customs (Prohibited Exports) Regulations. These are administered by the Minister for Foreign Affairs and Trade.

ANTIDUMPING INVESTIGATIONS

Dumping Determination

Initiation of investigation

A person may request the publication of a dumping notice in respect of a consignment of goods that has been imported or is likely to be imported into Australia, where there is or may be established a domestic industry producing like goods and where there may be reasonable grounds to impose dumping measures in respect of the goods in the consignment.[4]

Any person who believes that there may be reasonable grounds to impose antidumping measures may make an application. The application must be made in the approved form, currently the Australian Customs Service "Application for Antidumping and Countervailing Duties." The application form requires information concerning the goods, the source of imports, export price, normal value, a comparison of the export price and normal value of weighted averages of each, injury and why the injury is material, a causal link between the dumping and material injury, and financial details of trading profit or loss in the goods. The applicant must lodge evidence of certain matters with the application, and may be required to provide evidence of other claims on the form later if an investigation is initiated. The application form can be either mailed, faxed, or lodged with a Customs dumping officer.

A foreign government may apply to Customs for antidumping duties in the same way as a private person or body where there is an industry in its country that produces or manufactures like goods for export to Australia that is suffering material injury from dumping of goods in Australia.[5] This procedure precedes the WTO Agreements and is rarely, if ever, used.

Timetable

Customs must make a prima facie decision whether or not to accept an initial application within twenty-five days.[6] If Customs rejects an application, a person may apply to the ADA for a review of the prima facie decision. The ADA must complete its review within sixty days and limit itself to the information that was available to Customs.[7] If the ADA decides that the application should have been accepted, Customs must then carry out a preliminary finding inquiry.

If Customs accepts an application, it initiates a preliminary finding inquiry which it must complete within 100 days, or 120 days if the matter is sufficiently complex. If the preliminary finding is positive, Customs will impose provisional measures. If the preliminary finding is negative, Customs will take no further action and a person may apply to the ADA for a review. The ADA must complete this review within sixty days, and if it decides that the preliminary finding should have been positive, the ADA will revoke Customs' preliminary finding and recommend provisional measures to the Minister.[8]

The ADA then begins a final finding inquiry which it must complete within 120 days. If the final finding is positive it will recommend final measures. The Minister responsible for Customs may impose measures immediately upon receiving a recommendation.

Participation of parties and their counsel

If Customs initiates a preliminary finding inquiry, it must give public notice of its decision in the federal government Gazette and Australian newspapers, setting out full particulars. It will also send a copy of the nonconfidential parts of the application to all known exporters of the goods and the governments of the exporting countries. If there are too many exporters, Customs can send copies to the governments of the exporting countries and each relevant trade association.

Customs invites all interested parties to make written submissions within forty days of the initiation of an investigation. It will then visit the applicant to verify the information contained in the application and may visit the applicant again to verify any further information which it provides later. Customs will conduct sales route inquiries and seek submissions from importers, domestic users, consumer organizations, and foreign manufacturers and exporters. Customs will usually request a meeting with each party that makes a written submission to verify the information that it has provided. Customs maintains offices at the Australian embassies in Washington DC, Tokyo, and Brussels where inquiries may be conducted.

All interested parties who make submissions and meet Customs dumping officers may be assisted by counsel. Frequently, the same consultant will assist both importers and foreign exporters in preparing written submissions and in conducting meetings with Customs.

The ADA must give public notice of initiation of a final finding inquiry.[9] It will review Customs' decision and may obtain further information and conduct further meetings. Interested parties also have the opportunity to make written submissions and meet the ADA's designated dumping officer during a final finding inquiry even if they chose not to cooperate with Customs' preliminary finding inquiry.

Access to information developed in proceedings

Customs and the ADA are each required to maintain a public record of all submissions received from interested parties and all relevant correspondence that they have with other parties in the course of an investigation or review, which all interested parties are entitled to inspect.[10]

If a person giving information, including the applicant, claims that the information is confidential or that its publication would adversely affect the person's business or commercial interests, the person must produce a summary of the confidential information containing sufficient detail to allow a reasonable understanding of the substance of the information without breaching the confidentiality or adversely affecting those interests. Customs will make that summary available to interested parties instead.[11]

A person is not required to produce a summary if he or she can satisfy Customs that there is no way a summary could be produced. If Customs disagrees and believes that the information is not confidential or would not adversely affect business or commercial interests, the person may insist on its claim, in which case the information will not become part of the public record and Customs may disregard it unless it can be demonstrated from some other source to be correct.

However, if a person claims that information that helps to ascertain the normal value, export price, or noninjurious price of goods is confidential, or that inclusion of that price or value in the public record would adversely affect the person's business or commercial interests, Customs and the ADA may omit it from a public notice imposing duty, but may notify the price or value to persons, on request, who would be affected by any review of the rate of interim or final duty on like goods.[12]

Definitions

Like goods

Like goods are goods that are identical in all respects to the goods under consideration or, although not alike in all respects, have characteristics closely resembling those of the goods under consideration.[13]

Investigation period

The investigation period is the period over which importations of goods will be examined to reach a preliminary finding.

Inquiry period

The inquiry period has a corresponding meaning during the final finding inquiry. Both will be specified in the public notice of the inquiry in each case.[14]

Domestic industry

The applicant must show that there is material injury to the domestic industry producing like goods, or that dumping is materially hindering the establishment of such a domestic industry. A domestic industry is one that carries out at least one substantial process of manufacture of the like goods in Australia.[15] The cost of Australian labor, materials, and factory overhead must represent at least 25 percent of the cost of manufacturing the like goods.

An application must be supported by a sufficient part of the domestic industry. This means that persons, including the applicant, who produce or manufacture like goods in Australia and who support the application must:

(i) account for more than 50 percent of the total production of like goods produced by those in the Australian industry that have either supported or opposed the application; and
(ii) account for not less than 25 percent of the total production or manufacture of like goods in Australia.[16]

Low volumes

Low volumes of sales of like goods for home consumption in a country of export may be disregarded in calculating the dumping margin on the basis that they do not permit a proper comparison. Low volumes are those sales of like goods by the exporter or another seller that amount to less than 5 percent of the volume of the goods that the exporter exports to Australia.[17]

Ordinary course of trade

Goods are not considered to be sold in the ordinary course of trade for the purpose of ascertaining the normal value where the weighted average selling price in the country of export or third country is less than the weighted average per unit costs for the sales in question, or the volume of sales in the country of export or third country that are below per unit costs represents 20 percent or more of the sales volume under examination, and it is unlikely that the seller will be able to recover the costs within a reasonable period.[18]

Arm's length

Australian law looks at whether a sale is at arm's length, rather than whether the parties are related. A sale is not considered to be at arm's length if the price is not the whole of the consideration, if the price is influenced by the relationship between buyer and seller or an associate of either of them, or if the buyer or an associate of the buyer will receive reimbursement. A sale may be at arm's length even if the importer sells at a loss in appropriate circumstances.[19]

If the parties are actually related, they may still be found to deal at arm's length. For example, in a case concerning canned ham from the Netherlands, the exporter was related to the sales company but its prices were still found to represent normal values. The parties maintained separate accounts, reported profits separately, and regularly reviewed prices, which reflected a fully absorbed cost with an additional percentage to cover variations in the buy-in cost of the raw material.[20]

Calculation of dumping margins

Export price

There are different means of calculating export price. Where the importer and exporter deal at arm's length, the export price is the price paid by the importer to the exporter, less transport charges and any other matter arising after exportation. If the exporter and importer do not deal at arm's length, but the importer and the first purchaser do and the goods are sold to the first purchaser in the same condition as that in which they were sold to the importer, the export price is the sale price to the first purchaser less prescribed deductions, such as duty, sales tax, and profit, as well as costs, charges, and expenses arising in relation to the goods after exportation.[21]

The meaning of "any matter arising after exportation" was considered in the case of clear float glass from Indonesia. The Australian importer placed orders to a Singapore company, which then placed orders to its partly owned Indonesian subsidiary that exported to Australia. The exporter invoiced the Singapore company for the clear float glass, freight, and a commission that it passed on to the importer. The commission arose on lodgment of the order by the Singapore company and was intrinsically linked with the order prior to exportation. It, therefore, did not arise after exportation and should have been calculated as part of the export price.[22]

Normal value

The normal value of goods exported to Australia is the price paid for like goods sold by the exporter at arm's length and in the ordinary course of trade for home consumption in the country of export. If like goods are not sold by the exporter, then normal value is the price paid to other sellers of like goods in the country of export.

A constructed value or the actual price of goods exported to an appropriate third country can be used to ascertain the normal value if the goods are sold in the home market in low volumes, or the situation of the market in the country of export makes it unsuitable for use.[23]

For instance, the price of goods sold in the home market was considered inappropriate in a case concerning sodium cyanide from Italy. The Court held that the normal value of the Italian goods should have been established by reference to the price at which they were sold in the United States, not the price in Italy. The price in Italy was abnormally high; sales there made up less than 10 percent of the exporter's total sales, and the sales were made to the electroplating and pharmaceutical industries over which the exporter had a virtual monopoly. However, its exports to the United States, like its exports to Australia, were to the gold mining industry, and exporters in the United States were found not to be dumping significant quantities of sodium cyanide in Australia.[24]

Adjustments to normal value

The normal value can be adjusted where it and the export price are ascertained from transactions that do not permit a fair comparison. Adjustments may be made to take account of the nature of the goods, sales volume, time of sale, invoice terms, level of trade, and other factors that could affect the price.

Dumping margins can be calculated either by comparing weighted average export prices with the weighted average of corresponding normal values, or by comparing export prices in individual transactions with the corresponding normal value, depending on the number of exporters and transactions involved and the feasibility of using each method. Both methods could be used in the same investigation, each one for different exporters, if considered appropriate. If the export prices differ significantly among different purchasers, regions, or periods so that these methods are inappropriate, the dumping margin can be calculated by comparing export prices in individual transactions with the weighted average of corresponding normal values.[25]

Sales not at arm's length

If neither the exporter and importer, nor the importer and first purchaser, deal at arm's length, the export price will be determined "having regard to all the circumstances," which means any reasonable manner.[26] This method was used in the case of clear float glass from China because the Chinese exporter also acted as an importer. An Australian company acted as its selling agent and charged a commission but did not purchase the goods. The ADA determined the export price by deducting the selling agent's commission, as well as the cost of overseas and Australian freight, marine insurance, customs duty, post and handling charges, and other costs incurred after exportation of the goods from the landed-duty-paid-into-store price. Under the usual method for parties dealing at arm's length, the ADA was not permitted to deduct the selling agent's commission. Nevertheless, the Court upheld the ADA's methodology because the export price, when determined 'having regard to all the circumstances' could be determined however the ADA reasonably chose.[27]

If sales in the country of export are not at arm's length, the normal value can be based on a constructed value or the actual price of goods exported to an appropriate third country.[28]

Currency conversion

Currency conversions used in comparing export prices and normal values are made "using the rate of exchange on the date of the transaction or agreement that, in the opinion of the Minister, best establishes the material terms of the sale of the exported goods."[29] The date on which the seller confirms an order is usually selected rather than the date of invoice. If the exporter used a forward rate of exchange, that rate may be used in converting currencies in the investigation. If there has been a sustained movement in a relevant foreign exchange rate, the rate of exchange in force on a given day may be used for up to sixty days. This can occur more than once in the same calculation if a sustained movement continues for more than sixty days. Short-term rate fluctuations may be disregarded.

Sampling

Investigations may be restricted to exporters who constitute a statistically valid sample of exporters where the number of exporters from a particular country is so large that it is not practicable to determine individual dumping margins for each of them.[30]

Constructed value

A constructed normal value is the sum of amounts determined to be the cost of production or manufacture of the goods in the country of export, plus the administrative, selling, and general costs that would have been associated with the sale if the goods had been exported and, in some cases, the profit on the sale.[31]

The cost of production will be determined by using the exporter's accounting records if they are kept in accordance with generally accepted accounting principles in the country of export and reasonably reflect the actual costs of producing the goods. Amortization, depreciation, and capital expenditure must be allowed for where appropriate, and adjustments must be made for nonrecurring items and start-up costs during the investigation period.[32]

Administrative, selling, and general costs and profit will primarily be determined using data relating to the production and sale of like goods by the exporter or another seller. This method permits some approximation of the actual cost, provided that there is sufficient information to make a determination. The statute does not necessarily require the costs to be calculated by reference to sales in the ordinary course of trade at arm's length because any distortion of price in such sales would presumably be offset by a distortion of profit.[33]

If it is not possible to use the primary method of determining these costs, there are alternatives available that identify the actual amounts for these costs incurred by selected exporters in the production and sale of the same general category of goods in the country of export, or a weighted average of the actual amounts incurred by selected exporters for the production and sale of like goods in the country of export.[34]

Non-market economies

Normal values for goods from nonmarket economies will usually be ascertained by reference to the normal value in a comparable third country with a market economy. The selection of a third country will be made according to similarities in the respective volumes of trade between it and Australia and between the country of export and Australia, per capita gross national product, and infrastructure development in the industry concerned. The normal value may be ascertained using any of the following methods:
- a value of like goods on the domestic market in the third country;
- a value of like goods exported from the third country;

- a constructed value of like goods in the third country; or
- a value of like goods produced and sold on the domestic market in Australia.[35]

Information provided by the applicant

Export prices and normal values can be determined based on all relevant information that has been supplied, which can include or consist solely of information supplied by the applicant provided that it is sufficiently reliable for a proper determination to be made.[36]

Price undertakings and other agreements to suspend inquiries

An exporter may offer an undertaking as to price or other conduct of its future trade in like goods in a particular way at any time before or after the imposition of measures. The Minister may also propose an undertaking to the exporter. Offers of price undertakings are considered by the ADA during its final inquiry, after which it recommends to the Minister whether to accept the undertaking and revoke the interim duty. In making its recommendation, the ADA must consider whether the undertaking would raise the price of the goods above the non-injurious price. It must give reasons if it refuses to accept an undertaking. The ADA may complete its inquiry even after it accepts a price undertaking, or it may suspend the inquiry. If it does not recommend measures, the exporter will be released from its price undertaking. If the ADA finds that measures are warranted, it may recommend that the Minister accept the price undertaking rather than impose duty.

Effect of Antidumping Notices

Effective date of measures

Measures apply from a specified date. They can only be imposed retroactively on goods for which securities for interim duty have already been taken. An exception to retroactivity applies if:

(i) goods are already entered for home consumption;
(ii) security for interim duty was or could have been taken on similar goods within ninety days; and
(iii) large quantities of the same kind of goods have been knowingly dumped in Australia in a short period and caused material injury to the domestic industry, or similar goods have been dumped and caused material injury on a number of previous occasions. An importer has a right to be informed and to comment prior to the imposition of retroactive measures.[37]

Provisional measures apply until the Minister makes a decision on the ADA's final findings. Final measures are imposed for five years or until revoked. The ADA gives public notice at least eight months prior to the expiration of final measures and interested parties may apply for the continuation of the measures for a further five years.[38]

Applicability of measures

Measures are usually imposed on certain goods exported by particular companies with a residual rate for other exporters from the same countries. Measures may also be imposed on certain goods from a particular country of export.[39]

Dumping duties

Interim duty is applied at the rate established by the inquiry. If the actual export price of a later consignment of goods is lower than the export price ascertained in the inquiry, the difference is added to the amount of duty payable.[40] When final measures are imposed, an importer may apply for reimbursement of excess duty paid until then. An importer may also apply for refunds of excess duty paid at the end of every sixth months after final measures are imposed if it can provide evidence that the rate of duty was too high in the actual circumstances and that it has overpaid duty of at least A$5000 during the relevant period. Customs must examine an application for a refund within 180 days.[41] No interest is payable on refunds.

Domestic industry usually monitors the market price of goods in order to ensure that measures are not circumvented. If it appears that a particular importer is selling at a loss, a person may request Customs to conduct a sales route inquiry, in which it will investigate the prices paid by an importer, the prices invoiced by the exporter, whether any rebate is received on the invoice price, and whether the importer is making a profit. It is more difficult to investigate "exporter hopping," where an exporter subject to measures uses another exporter not subject to measures to export goods. A completely new application for measures and a separate investigation are usually required if this occurs.

Residual exporters

Exporters who were not selected for the original investigation and new exporters are known as residual exporters. A residual exporter can apply for an accelerated review of measures insofar as it is affected by them. Customs may reject the application if the exporter was not selected for the original investigation because it refused to cooperate or is related to an exporter who was selected. Customs must recommend a final decision to the Minister within 100 days. While an accelerated review is being conducted, securities may be taken for interim duty but no interim duty can be collected in respect of consignments entered for home consumption during the review.[42]

Reviews

An affected party can apply for a review of provisional measures twelve months or more after they are imposed where one or more of the variable factors relevant to the determination of the measures has changed and a review is appropriate. An application supplying a statement of the variable factor that has changed and the amount of the change must be made on the approved form, and must be accompanied by supporting evidence. Customs must conduct the review within 100 days and recommend to the Minister whether to vary the rate of duty or not.[43] An affected party can apply for revocation of final measures at any time after they are imposed if the affected party can demonstrate that revocation is appropriate.

Parties affected by an antidumping decision, including a decision not to recommend or impose measures, may apply to the Federal Court of Australia for review under the Administrative Decisions (Judicial Review) Act 1977 on the grounds that the decision involved an error of law, or that it was completely unreasonable based on the facts.

Where a person appeals successfully against dumping measures, the order setting aside the measures will not necessarily take effect retroactively from the date the measures were imposed, nor order a refund of all duty paid up until that date. The person lodging the appeal can be required to show a positive reason why the order should take effect from the date that the measures were imposed.[44]

COUNTERVAILING DUTY INVESTIGATIONS

Subsidy Determination

Initiation of investigation

Countervailing investigations are initiated in the same way as antidumping investigations. The same approved application form must be used, but the section on subsidisation must be completed. The applicant must provide details and supporting evidence of the nature and title of the alleged subsidy scheme, the body that provides the subsidy, the manner in which the subsidy is paid, and the value of the subsidy when received and used by producers or sellers of the goods. It can be particularly difficult for the applicant to provide evidence of the value of the subsidy.

Timetable

Countervailing investigations are conducted by the same agencies and according to the same timetable as antidumping investigations. However, after receiving an initial application for countervailing measures, Customs must notify the governments from which countervailable subsides are alleged to have been received and give them a reasonable opportunity for consultations to arrive at a mutually agreed solution prior to making a prima facie decision to initiate a preliminary finding inquiry.[45] Customs must also notify the governments of the exporting countries and give them a reasonable opportunity for consultations, as their exporting industries will be affected by any measures.

Participation of parties and access to information developed in proceedings

The rules on participation of parties and their counsel, access of parties to information developed in proceedings, use of facts available, and opportunity to give undertakings are the same as those that apply in antidumping investigations.

Definitions

Subsidy

A subsidy is defined in detail to mean, basically, a financial contribution, income, or price support by a government of the country of export or country of origin of goods, or a private body carrying out a governmental function, in connection with the production, manufacture, or export of the goods that confers a benefit, either directly or indirectly, in relation to those goods. The definition includes direct transfers of funds, acceptance of liabilities, foregone revenue, and the supply or purchase of goods or services.[46]

In one case concerning frozen pork from Canada, countervailing measures were refused despite the existence of a whole range of farm stabilization programs and other subsidies provided by federal and provincial governments in Canada to grain and pig producers. It was found that market conditions prevented those producers from influencing the price of their output so that the benefits were not passed on in any significant way to the pork producers. It was also found that the subsidies did not cause any material injury to the Australian industry producing like goods.[47]

Countervailable subsidy

A countervailable subsidy is one that is "specific" unless it is excluded. A subsidy is considered specific where access to it is explicitly limited to particular enterprises or to those within a designated geographical region, where it is contingent on export performance, or where it is contingent on the use of domestically produced goods in preference to imported goods.[48]

Noncountervailable subsidy

A noncountervailable subsidy is one that is not specific or that is excluded. It will not be considered specific if access to it is established by objective economic criteria set out in legislation, and those criteria do not favor particular enterprises and are strictly adhered to in the administration of the subsidy.

A subsidy is excluded from countervailing measures if it falls within Article 8.2 of the WTO Agreement on Subsidies and Countervailing Measures, which covers certain assistance for research activities, assistance to disadvantaged regions, and assistance to comply with environmental requirements. A subsidy will also be excluded if it is a domestic support measure that meets the criteria or conditions set out in Annex 2 to the WTO Agreement on Agriculture.[49]

Calculation of subsidies

A direct financial contribution is always assumed to confer a benefit. Other forms of financial contribution, income, or price support are normally treated according to the guidelines below, but the amount of a benefit may be determined by a different method if these guidelines are inappropriate for some reason.[50]

A loan is assumed to confer a benefit if it requires repayment of a lesser amount than would be required for a comparable commercial loan. The difference that is not payable is treated as the amount of the subsidy. A loan guarantee is assumed to confer a benefit if, without the guarantee, the enterprise receiving the loan would have to repay a greater amount. The difference that is not payable, adjusted for any difference in fees, is treated as the amount of the subsidy. Equity capital is assumed to confer a benefit if the decision to provide the capital is inconsistent with the normal investment practice of private investors in the country concerned. The amount of the payment will be treated as the amount of the subsidy.

The provision of goods or services is assumed to confer a benefit if the goods or services are provided for less than adequate remuneration, and the purchase of goods or services is assumed to confer a benefit if the goods or services are purchased for more than adequate remuneration.[51] The difference from adequate remuneration in the light of prevailing market conditions in that country will be treated as the amount of the subsidy.

Undertakings that suspend inquiries

Undertakings may be given to prevent the imposition of countervailing duties just as in antidumping inquiries. In addition, the government of an exporting country may give an undertaking to review and change its countervailable subsidy so as to remove the material injury or threat of material injury to the domestic industry.

Effect of Countervailing Duty Notices

Countervailing duty notices are applied, enforced, and reviewed in the same way as antidumping notices. Countervailing and antidumping notices may also apply to the same goods at the same time in appropriate circumstances.

INJURY ANALYSIS

Investigation and Relation to Dumping and Subsidy Analysis

Applications for antidumping and countervailing measures must include information concerning the existence and cause of injury to a domestic industry. Measures cannot be imposed unless dumping or countervailable subsidies are causing, or threaten to cause, material injury to the domestic industry producing like goods. Customs and the ADA will investigate injury automatically once they have determined that imports have been dumped or have benefited from a countervailable subsidy. However, it is only the ADA, as part of its final inquiry, that ascertains the "noninjurious price" and that may recommend measures less than the dumping margin or amount of subsidy.

The noninjurious price is normally calculated based on free-on-board prices by determining an unsuppressed selling price at which the domestic industry would sell and then deducting all relevant costs that would be incurred by an importer; such as duty, sales tax, freight, selling expenses, and profit. The unsuppressed selling price is the notional price in Australia in the absence of dumped or subsidized imports. This can be determined, for example, by examining the price before dumping occurred, or ascertaining the domestic industry's cost of production or examining the price of goods from other countries of export.

If the noninjurious price is less than the ascertained normal value, then final dumping duties will be limited to the difference between the export price and the noninjurious price. If the noninjurious price is less than the ascertained amount of a countervailable subsidy and the export price, final countervailing duties will be limited in the same way. This ensures that duties are limited to those sufficient to remove the injury or recurrence of injury to the domestic industry producing like goods.[52]

Definitions

Domestic industry

The domestic industry producing like goods is defined only by the product involved and is not limited geographically to any particular geographical area within Australia. In one case, concerning cement clinkers, there was very little trade in clinker between the State of Western Australia and the remainder of Australia. The sole manufacturer in Western Australia applied for antidumping duties to be imposed on imports from Korea, all of which remained in Western Australia. No measures were imposed because the Australian clinker industry as a whole had not suffered injury, although the Western Australian industry might have.[53] Different parts of the domestic industry may suffer varying degrees of injury, but the industry overall must be affected. It is unusual for dumping or countervailable subsidies to cause material injury to certain parts of an industry but not others. In fact, where certain parts of an industry suffer material injury and others do not, it would normally suggest that dumping or countervailable subsidies are not the cause.

Like goods

The definition of like goods used in the injury assessment is the same as that used in assessing whether dumping has occurred. However, in addition, where the like goods are "close processed" agricultural goods, the industry producing upstream agricultural or horticultural goods will be treated as part of the domestic industry for the purposes of the injury analysis. This occurs where a substantial proportion of the upstream goods are devoted to processing the processed goods, and a substantial proportion of the processed agricultural goods are derived from the upstream goods. It must also be shown that the price of each is closely related or that the cost of the upstream goods is a significant part of the production cost of the processed agricultural goods.[54]

Investigation period

The investigation period for the determination of material injury usually begins at least twelve months earlier than the investigation period for dumping or ascertaining a countervailable subsidy, unless that is too long a time period and it would be unreasonable for companies to provide records for that earlier period. There is no mandatory limit to the investigation period for the determination of material injury.[55]

Material injury

Material injury is indicated both by the economic condition of the domestic industry and by recent trends. Relevant factors include loss of sales, loss of profits, loss of market share, price undercutting, price depression, price suppression, loss of production, reduced capacity utilization, reduced return on investment, reduced cash flow, reduced employment levels, and reduced ability overall.[56]

Injury must be material, not insubstantial or insignificant. In most cases it will be injury that is greater than that likely to occur in the normal ebb and flow of business uninfluenced by dumping or other prohibited anticompetitive practices.[57]

Threat of material injury

The threat of material injury is considered both when material injury has already occurred and when it has not. Measures may not be warranted if there is no longer a threat of injury. Conversely, a threat of material injury alone can warrant measures, including where dumping or countervailable subsidies are materially hindering the establishment of a domestic industry. Any such threat must be both foreseeable and imminent and established by reference to various factors including the likelihood of a substantial increase in dumped or subsidized imports.[58]

Cumulative effect

The cumulative effect of imports from different companies, different countries, or both may be considered in the investigation of injury, but only if appropriate in light of the conditions of competition between those goods and like goods produced domestically.[59]

Causation

Dumping or countervailable subsidies must cause the material injury to the domestic industry, or threaten to do so, before measures can be imposed.[60] For example, in one case the goods had been dumped, the dumping margins were very high, and the domestic industry producing like goods had suffered material injury. However, measures were not imposed because there was no causal link between the dumping and the material injury, nor was there any threat of further material injury. Although the sole domestic manufacturer of like goods was very unprofitable and prices had fallen, it had, during the investigation period, increased its sales and market share and improved its overall economic performance. The price of the imports to end-users was also consistently higher than the domestic product.[61]

The general rule is that the dumping or countervailable subsidies must be the only cause of the material injury. For example, in one leading case, it was concluded that material injury was caused by the relationship of domestic and foreign prices, the increasing utility of a substitute product, increased costs, and the general economic climate. Measures were, therefore, refused.[62] However, measures can be imposed if it can be shown that the dumping or countervailable subsidies have been the only cause of a quantified and discrete part of the material injury, although other factors caused the balance of it. In those circumstances, the measures will only remove the quantified and discrete part of the material injury caused by the dumping or countervailable subsidies.

CUSTOMS SANCTIONS

Australia imposes customs sanctions to fulfill its obligations under the United Nations Charter to implement resolutions of the Security Council.

Import prohibitions and restrictions may be imposed under section 50 of the Customs Act 1901. Export prohibitions and restrictions may be imposed under section 112 of the same Act. They are imposed in the form of Customs (Prohibited Imports) Regulations and Customs (Prohibited Exports) Regulations respectively. The regulations prohibit the import and export of goods originating in certain countries, and the export of goods, or certain types of goods, to certain countries without the Minister's authorization.

Customs sanctions are imposed by the Minister for Foreign Affairs and Trade. Other import and export restrictions to preserve public health and public order, maintain technical standards, and comply with the requirements of international commodity agreements are imposed by various other federal government Ministers. All regulations are published in the Australian Customs Notices in the federal government Gazette. There is no formal means for private persons to apply for such measures.

References

1. Antidumping Authority Act, 1988 § 10.
2. *ICI Australia Operations Pty Ltd v Fraser* (1992) 106 A.L.R. 257.

3. *Metal Manufacturers Ltd v. Comptroller-General of Customs* (Moore J, 13 April 1995).
4. Customs Act, 1901 § 269TB(1).
5. Customs Act, 1901 § 269TB(2).
6. Customs Act, 1901 § 269TC.
7. Antidumping Authority Act, 1988 § 8.
8. Antidumping Authority Act, 1988 § 8B.
9. Antidumping Authority Act, 1988 § 23.
10. Customs Act, 1901 § 269ZJ(1) and Antidumping Authority Act, 1988 § 23A(1).
11. Customs Act, 1901 § 269ZJ(2) and Antidumping Authority Act, 1988 § 23A(3).
12. Customs Act, 1901 § 269TG(3A).
13. Customs Act, 1901 § 269T.
14. Customs Act, 1901 § 269 TC(4) and Antidumping Authority Act, 1988 § 3(1).
15. Customs Act, 1901 § 269T(3).
16. Customs Act, 1901 § 269TB.
17. Customs Act, 1901 § 269TAC(14).
18. Customs Act, 1901 § 269TAAD.
19. Customs Act, 1901 § 269TAA.
20. Castle Bacon Pty Limited v. Comptroller-General of Customs (1995) 38 A.L.D. 230.
21. Customs Act, 1901 § 269TAB.
22. *Pilkington (Australia) Limited v. Antidumping Authority* (1995) 56 F.C.R. 424.
23. Customs Act, 1901 § 269TAC.
24. *Enichem Anic srl v. Antidumping Authority* (1992) 111 A.L.R. 178.
25. Customs Act, 1901 § 269TACB.
26. Customs Act, 1901 § 269TAB(1).
27. *Pilkington (Australia) Limited v. Antidumping Authority, supra, at n. 21*.
28. Customs Act, 1901 § 269TAC(2).
29. Customs Act, 1901 § 269TAF.
30. Customs Act, 1901 § 269TACB(8).
31. Customs Act, 1901 § 269TAC(2)(c).
32. Customs Regulation 180.
33. *Metal Manufacturers Limited v. Comptroller-General of Customs, supra, at n. 2*.
34. Customs Regulation 181.
35. Customs Act, 1901 § 269TAC(4).
36. Customs Act, 1901 §§ 269TAB(3) and 269TAC(6).
37. Customs Act, 1901 § 269TN.
38. Antidumping Authority Act, 1988 § 8A.
39. Customs Act, 1901 § 269TN.
40. Customs Tariff (Antidumping) Act, 1975 § 8(4).
41. Customs Act, 1901 § 269V.
42. Customs Act, 1901 §§ 269ZE-269ZH.
43. Customs Act, 1901 § 269Z.
44. *Wattmaster Alco Pty Ltd v. Button* (1986) 70 A.L.R. 330.
45. Customs Act, 1901 § 269TB.

46. Customs Act, 1901 § 269T.
47. Antidumping Authority Report no. 90: Review of negative preliminary finding concerning frozen pork from Canada (January 1993).
48. Customs Act, 1901 § 269TAAC.
49. Customs Act, 1901 § 269TAAC.
50. Customs Act, 1901 § 269TAAC(7).
51. Customs Act, 1901 § 269TACC(4).
52. Customs Act, 1901 § 269TACA; Customs Tariff (Antidumping) Act, 1975 § 8.
53. *Swan Portland Cement Ltd v. Minister for Small Business and Customs* (1991) 28 F.C.R. 135.
54. Customs Act, 1901 § 269T(4B).
55. Customs Act, 1901 § 269T(2AD).
56. Customs Act, 1901 § 269TAE.
57. *ICI Australia Operations Pty Limited v. Fraser* (1992) 106 A.L.R. 257.
58. Customs Act, 1901 § 269TAE.
59. Customs Act, 1901 § 269TAE(2C).
60. Customs Act, 1901 § 269TG.
61. Antidumping Authority Report No. 151 on reinforced wound closure strips from the United States (May 1996).
62. *ICI Australia Operations Pty Ltd v. Fraser* (1992) 106 A.L.R. 257.

Brazil

Maria Fernanda Pecora
Lilla, Huck e Malheiros
Sao Paulo, Brazil

HISTORY AND OVERVIEW OF TRADE REMEDY LAWS AND REGULATIONS SINCE 1947

Discussion of Country's Accession to GATT/WTO and Antidumping and Subsidies Codes

Brazil only recently implemented the General Agreement on Tariffs and Trade (GATT) as to antidumping and subsidies, by means of Decree No. 93,941, of Jan. 16, 1987 (Antidumping), and Decree No. 93,962, of Jan. 22, 1987 (Subsidies). At that time, Brazil did not introduce any modification to the terms of the GATT provisions. Despite the regulation, in practical terms these rules were not applied because Brazil had an economy closed to imports. Due to numerous restrictions on imports, dumping was not an issue in Brazil.

However, when president Fernando Collor de Mello took office, he implemented a new policy, which included the reduction of import taxes, the end of import quotas, and liberation of importation of about 3,000 products. As a result of the new policy, imports grew in Brazil, threatening Brazilian industries. Many of these imports entered Brazil with a price below normal value. The domestic industry was faced with a completely new situation—competition with foreign products. To compete, domestic industries had to evaluate their costs, their technology, and other factors that facilitate competition in a free market. On the other hand, in view of the new reality, mechanisms to protect the domestic industry were also evaluated. As a result, trade remedies, such as antidumping, antisubsidies, and safeguards regulations became a part of the Brazilian vocabulary.

After the Uruguay Round, and in view of the new Brazilian reality, Brazil reacted quickly to adjust its internal legislation to the new rules. In 1995, Brazil enacted:

(i) Decree No. 1,602, of August 23, which regulated the application of antidumping measures;
(ii) Decree No. 1,488, of May 11, 1995, which regulated the application of safeguard measures; and
(iii) Decree No. 1,751, which regulated the application of countervailing measures.

Discussion of Evolution of Trade Remedy Laws and Regulations

The crisis of the 1930s and World War II created difficulties with imports throughout the world, especially in Brazil. As a consequence, both domestic production and protectionism flourished.

Beginning in the 1950s, the Brazilian Government instituted a strict policy on imports, and created incentives for the incorporation of subsidiaries of multinational companies, for the purpose of creating specialized workers and a domestic industry. As a result, Brazil developed an industrial park, especially in the automobile and electronic sectors. For many years, Brazil basically exported primary products, such as coffee.

In the 1970s, in order to increase production and the surplus of the trade balance, the Brazilian government adopted a new policy that resulted in a substantial increase of exports of textile and metallurgic products. Later, with the oil crisis, more radical restrictions on imports were implemented. At that time, import of many products was forbidden, because of the lack of foreign currency. Foreign currency was used for the acquisition of oil, which nonetheless did not avoid a large foreign debt. In response, Brazil implemented a strong policy of import substitution.

As already mentioned, in 1987, Brazil ratified the GATT Antidumping and Subsidies Agreements, without elaborating on them by implementing legislation. However, as the Brazilian economy was effectively closed to foreign products, interest in these new agreements was not significant. In the 1990s, as Brazil shifted from a protectionist policy to an open-economy policy, allowing imports and reducing import barriers, and Brazilian producers started to feel the pressure of imports in the Brazilian market, the number of requests for investigations started to gradually increase. The Brazilian Government also had to face a new reality—the need to create a structure to respond to the growing number of trade remedy cases, which is, even now, in its infant stage.

Summary listing of each trade remedy, with corresponding statutory/regulatory references and agency responsible for administering

The provisions of Decree No. 1,602 establish that antidumping measures may be imposed as to the imports of primary or nonprimary products if there is dumping that causes injury to domestic industry, in accordance with investigations carried out under the Decree.

The Foreign Trade Office of the Ministry of Commerce, Industry, and Tourism *(Secretaria de Comércio Exterior–SECEX)* is the agency responsible for the administration not only of antidumping, but also of countervailing duty and safeguards cases. The investigation of all phases of dumping, countervailing, and safeguards (including the evaluation of injury) is carried out by the Technical Department of Commercial Interchange *(Departamento Técnico de Intercâmbio Comercial–DTIC)*, which is a division of SECEX. Provisional and definitive duties and the ratification of undertakings must be jointly approved by the Minister of Finance and the Minister of Commerce, Industry, and Tourism, by means of an order published in the Official Gazette. An order of the Ministers is based on the investigation and analysis carried out by DTIC.

Since 1987, Brazil has opened thirty-four antidumping and eight countervailing investigations, which resulted in one undertaking, seventeen investigations with imposition of definitive duties, and fourteen investigations without imposition of definitive duties. In most of the negative cases, Brazilian authorities did not impose antidumping measures because there was not enough evidence that the Brazilian market was actually injured or threatened with injury. In one specific case (metallic magnesium), the antidumping measure was withdrawn because the dumping practices were eliminated. In a few cases, there was not enough evidence that dumping had occurred. It is interesting to note that a great number of petitions do not lead to investigation, in view of the lack of information from the domestic industry. As a matter of fact, as the regulations are very recent, the domestic industry is not expert in the mechanisms of dumping, subsidies, and safeguard regulations, and is unfamiliar with how to present an adequate petition.

ANTIDUMPING INVESTIGATIONS

Dumping Determination

According to article 4 of Decree No. 1,602, the practice of dumping is considered to be the introduction of a product into the domestic market, including through drawback, at an export price that is less than normal value. Normal value is the price effectively charged for a like product in normal commercial transactions for consumption in the exporting country. Antidumping measures may be imposed as to primary or nonprimary products.

Initiation of investigation

An antidumping investigation may be initiated by petition or by the government on its own initiative. Usually, an investigation is initiated by petition of the domestic industry or on its behalf, in writing, according to the rules established by Decree No. 1,602 and SECEX.

Since 1987, Brazil has opened thirty-four investigations in connection with antidumping, all of them after a petition filed by the domestic industry or by entities representing the domestic industry.

By petition

In order to initiate an antidumping investigation in Brazil, the domestic industry must file a petition at SECEX, using the form provided by the agency. Besides proof of dumping, injury, and a causal connection between the two, the petition should contain:

(i) identification of the petitioner, including the volume and value of production of the domestic industry represented by the petitioner;

(ii) an estimate of the volume and value of total national production of the like product;

(iii) a list of known domestic producers that are not represented in the petition and an indication of the volume and value of their production;

(iv) a complete description of the product alleged to be imported under dumped prices, the country of origin or exporting country, and the identity of each known exporter;

(v) a complete description of the product manufactured by the domestic industry;

(vi) information on the sale price of the product when sold for consumption in the country of origin or exporting country, or to third parties (or in the alternative, the constructed value of the product);

(vii) information on the relevant exporting price, or on the price at which the product is sold to the first independent purchaser located in Brazil; and

(viii) information on the trends in the volume of imports, the effects of such imports on prices of the Brazilian like product, and the consequent impact on the domestic industry, evidenced by relevant data and indexes.

SECEX first analyses whether the petition complies with the agency's minimum requirements. Within twenty days after filing of the petition, SECEX must inform the petitioner if the petition was properly filed and SECEX will at this time request additional information, if necessary. Within ten days after a request for supplemental information, petitioner must submit the missing information to SECEX, which then has twenty days to examine the data and decide if an investigation should be opened.

By government

The Federal Government, in exceptional circumstances, may self-initiate an investigation, if there is sufficient evidence to establish dumping. The government of the affected country will be notified of these elements of proof before the investigation begins. Despite the legal provision, the Brazilian government has never initiated an *ex officio* dumping investigation.

Timetable

Once the petition is duly filed, SECEX will examine the information and the documents attached to the petition, and may request additional information. In this case, the term for delivery of the additional information shall be defined by SECEX in accordance with the nature of the required information. After receipt of additional information, SECEX has twenty days for analysis, after which it will reject the petition or open an investigation. If the petition is accepted, the petitioner has ten days to present a nonconfidential summary, one copy for each manufacturer or exporter and the government of the countries indicated. In case there are many manufacturers and exporters, the copies will be sent only to the government.

The information provided by the petitioner will be verified in order to decide if the investigation is necessary. The petition will be rejected if:
(i) there is insufficient proof of the existence of dumping or injury;
(ii) the petitioner is not or does not represent the domestic industry; or
(iii) the domestic producers that support the petition represent less than 25 percent of the domestic production of the alleged dumped product.

If the petition is considered to be in order, the investigation of dumping and its impact begins within thirty days after the publication in the Federal

Official Gazette of notice that the petition was properly filed. After publication, other parties have twenty days to request to participate in the proceeding. The foreign interested parties (governments excluded) will receive questionnaires and have forty days from transmittal of the questionnaires to return them. It is possible to extend this term by thirty days, if requested and accepted by SECEX. As the investigation begins, a complete copy of the petition, other than the confidential parts, will be furnished to the known exporters and producers and, if requested, it shall be available to any interested party.

Any interested party may request a hearing before SECEX at any time during the process. Also, at the end of investigation, SECEX may request a hearing on its own initiative. Five days before the hearing, the parties must present in writing the names of their representatives. One should note that, since Portuguese is the Brazilian official language, the hearing will be held in the Portuguese language (if in another language, a translator should be present). Fifteen days after the hearing, the parties must present written comments, also in Portuguese. Further, the information supplied orally by the parties must be provided to SECEX in writing within ten days after the hearing.

At least sixty days after the beginning of an investigation, provisional antidumping measures may be imposed, by means of an order jointly signed by the Minister of Finance and the Minister of Commerce, Industry, and Tourism. The provisional measures last from four to six months, at the discretion of SECEX. The investigation must end within twelve months after its initiation. If dumping does not exist, the proceedings terminate and there is reimbursement of any amounts deposited in response to provisional measures. If the investigation finds that there is no injury or threat of injury, the undertaking (see page 49) or provisional measures are suspended, as the case may be. If investigation finds the existence of dumping and injury, definitive antidumping duties may be imposed for future imports, also by means of an order jointly signed by the Minister of Finance and the Minister of Commerce, Industry, and Tourism. If there is an undertaking, SECEX will administer it.

In the case of a temporary change in market conditions, and provided that injury does not continue, SECEX may suspend the antidumping duties for one year, which may be extended for an equal period. Even if there is dumping and injury, the Ministry of Industry, Commerce, and Tourism and the Ministry of Finance may decide to suspend the application of the antidumping duties, based on national interest.

All definitive dumping duties are terminated no later than five years after application of the dumping duties or after the conclusion of the last revision that has taken into consideration dumping and consequent injury. Such termination is automatic. However, five months prior to the end of the five-year period, any interested party may request a hearing in order to argue for revision of the antidumping measures.

Participation of parties and their counsel

Interested parties are considered to be:
(i) domestic producers of the like product or its class;
(ii) importers of the product under investigation and associations of such importers;
(iii) exporters or international producers of the product; and
(iv) other domestic or international parties considered by SECEX to be interested parties.

All interested parties identified in a dumping investigation must be notified of the investigation and of the information required of them, and shall have the opportunity to present the elements of proof deemed to be pertinent to the investigation.

All interested parties will also receive questionnaires regarding the investigation, which they must answer within forty days from transmittal to them. This forty-day period may be extended for up to thirty days, if so requested. During the investigation, SECEX may request any information deemed to be necessary. If the parties refuse, or simply fail to furnish it within the established period, or impede the investigation, the investigation will be decided based on the best available information.

Domestic petitioners

The domestic petitioners have the right to present the petition and to ask for its revision, as well as to participate in the hearing.

Respondents, including industrial users

Anyone involved with the product alleged to be dumped is allowed to participate in the dumping investigation, including manufacturers, exporters, and importers. They also can participate in the hearing. Further, as interested parties include "other domestic or international parties considered by SECEX to be interested parties," it is possible that an industrial user of the product alleged to be dumped may participate in the investigation. In any case, it is up to SECEX to allow its participation.

Access to information developed

Non-proprietary information

All information, excluding confidential information, is given to the parties involved in the investigation and also to interested third parties. During the investigation, all information furnished by the parties must be verified by SECEX. If necessary and possible, the investigation can be conducted in other countries.

In practice, the Brazilian government still does not have a structure to allow it to conduct an extensive investigation abroad. However, resources are being devoted to this area in order to allow such investigation.

Business proprietary information

Information that is, by its nature, proprietary, or furnished by the parties on confidential grounds, will be treated as confidential and will not be disclosed without the express consent of the party that furnished it. Therefore, the information classified as confidential will not be available to the parties, but only to SECEX. Parties that furnish any proprietary information must inform SECEX of its confidential nature and must present an understandable extract of such proprietary information, or explain why such a nonproprietary summary is impossible.

SECEX will decide whether the information deemed to be confidential by its provider is actually of a confidential nature. If, according to SECEX, the information is not of a confidential nature, it will inform the provider that it intends to reveal the information to third parties. If the provider declines to permit such information to be presented to any of the parties, such information will simply not be considered in the analysis.

Further, if SECEX agrees that the information is of a confidential nature, the submitter must allow the extract of the information to be supplied to the parties to the process or give incontestable evidence of the accuracy of the information given, under penalty of the information not being taken into account in the analysis. Therefore, if an extract is not presented to all parties, the information cannot be considered by SECEX.

Parties to the dumping procedure only have access to the extract of the confidential information supplied by a specific party. Brazil has not yet reached a status where dumping issues have been decided by the courts. On the other side, there is no express rule as to the analysis of confidential information by the courts. However, as the dumping decree provides for the possibility of presenting confidential information, the courts must be bound to such secrecy, as well.

Definitions

Like products

Like products are deemed to be identical products, equal in all aspects to the product under examination. If there is no identical product, the like product shall be another product that, although not exactly equal in all aspects, presents very similar characteristics to the product being considered.

Period of investigation

The investigation starts with the acceptance of a properly-filed petition and should last for one year. In some cases, SECEX may investigate for an additional six months. The imports to be examined for the purposes of investigating the existence of dumping include the twelve months prior to the opening of the investigation. In exceptional circumstances, the period to be examined in the investigation of dumping can be less than twelve months, but never less than six months. In any case, the period to be examined for purposes of verifying if dumping occurred should be significantly representative to perform the analysis of export price, normal value, and corresponding adjustments.

Domestic industry and petition requirement for industry support

The domestic industry is all the domestic producers of the like product or the ones whose production constitutes a substantial part of national production. For this purpose, one should consider the producers of like or competitive products established in Brazil, or those whose joint production of like or competitive products correspond to a substantial proportion of the domestic production of said product. Producers that are related to exporters or importers shall not be considered as part of the domestic industry for purposes of investigating dumping.

Further, in some exceptional cases, the Brazilian territory may be divided into two different or more competing markets, in which case the domestic industry shall be considered as one of those markets. For this specific purpose, a regional market shall be considered a domestic market if the local producers sell all or most of their production in the same regional market, and if the demand of the market is not supplied, in substantial proportion, by producers of like products established in other parts of the territory.

The injury analysis is based on:
(i) volume and rate of increase of imports;
(ii) the part of the internal market accounted for by increasing imports;

(iii) import prices;
(iv) the consequent impact on producers of the domestic like products; and
(v) other factors (not related to increasing imports) that evidence injury.

Viability of markets

SECEX will normally consider the exporter's home market to be viable if the quantity of sales of like products for consumption in the internal market of the exporting country amounts to 5 percent or more of sales to Brazil of the relevant product. SECEX may accept a lower percentage if there is evidence that sales in the internal market are in a quantity sufficient to allow an adequate comparison.

Related parties

The domestic producers are considered to be related to the exporters or importers only in the following cases:
(i) if one of them controls, either directly or indirectly, the other;
(ii) both of them are controlled, either directly or indirectly, by a third party; or
(iii) they jointly control, directly or indirectly, a third party.

Calculation of dumping margins

The dumping margin is calculated as the difference between the export price and normal value. The basis for comparison shall be: (i) the average normal value and the average price in all comparable export transactions; or (ii) the normal value and the export prices ascertained in each transaction.

Usually the dumping margin is calculated separately for each known exporter or producer, but if there is an excessive number of exporters, producers, importers, or types of products under investigation, making individual margins impossible, the examination may be limited to a reasonable number of interested parties, by means of statistical sampling, based on the available information of the volume of exports from the country under investigation. Any selection shall have the consent of the interested parties. Individual margins may also be calculated for the producers and exporters that provide the necessary information in time to be considered in the investigation procedure (voluntary respondents) at the discretion of SECEX.

The comparison between normal value and export price must be made at the same level of trade. The interested parties shall be provided with the necessary information to make a fair comparison. Adjustments shall be made, on a case by case basis, to account for the differences in the sales conditions, taxes, quantities of products, and so forth.

Export price

Export price is the price paid or to be paid for the exported product to Brazil, free of taxes, discounts, and reductions directly related to the sales. If there is no export price, or if it is not certain, the export price could be determined by the first sale to an independent buyer, or on another reasonable basis, if the product is not sold to an independent buyer or if it is not sold in the same condition in which it was imported.

To arrive at an export price on a sale between the importer and the third party, the value of transportation, insurance, and other related costs, taxes, commissions, and a reasonable profit should be deducted from the price paid by the third party. Therefore, the export price is the price of the product as it is introduced into Brazilian commerce.

If there is no export price, or if the export price is unreliable, due to association or compensatory agreements between the exporter and the importer or a third party, the export price may be constructed from:
(i) the price at which the products were sold for the first time to an independent buyer; or
(ii) a reasonable basis, in case the products are not sold to an independent buyer or if they are not sold in the same condition as they were imported.

If product is not imported directly from the country of origin, but is exported to Brazil from a third intermediary country, the price at which the product is sold from the country that exported it to Brazil will be compared with the price in the exporting country. It is possible to compare the export price with the price in the country of origin if:
(i) there was only transit in the exporting country;
(ii) the product is not produced in the exporting country; or
(iii) there is no comparable price in the exporting country.

Normal value

Normal value is the price effectively charged for like products in the normal business transactions related to internal consumption within the exporting country. If there is no like product in the domestic market, or if the internal sales are not significant, the normal value will be based on the price of a like product in the export transactions to a third country, plus administrative and trade costs and profits.

Normal value is determined in the domestic market of the exporter country if sales there are at least 5 percent of the sales of the product in Brazil. Less than this percentage is permitted if it is established sufficient to permit an adequate comparison.

Adjustments, including those reflecting level of trade

For adjustment purposes, SECEX shall examine, on a case by case basis, depending on the specifications, differences that affect the comparison of prices, differences in the conditions of the sales, taxation, levels of trade, quantities, physical characteristics, and any other circumstances that can be shown to affect the comparison of prices. When several of those factors apply simultaneously, SECEX will avoid duplicating adjustments that have already been effected.

For purposes of determining the export price, which is the price effectively paid or to be paid for the exported products, free of taxes, discounts, and reductions directly related to the sale, SECEX shall also proceed with adjustments related to cost variations between importation and resale, including import tax, other taxes, and profits. If there are no sales of a like product in the domestic market or, due to the special conditions, the normal value shall be determined based on:

(i) the price of the like product for export to a third country, if the price is representative; or

(ii) the constructed value in the export country, plus administrative and selling costs and profit.

The export price and the normal value shall be compared based on sales effected at the same time. The interested parties will be advised by SECEX of the kind of information necessary to assure the fair comparison. SECEX will also consider the distribution cost paid by the exporter or by the producer during the investigation, if such distribution is traditionally used by the exporter or producer.

Treatment of sales through related parties

If sales are made from the producer to a related party, the export price may be constructed from:

(i) the price at which the products were sold for the first time to an independent buyer; or

(ii) a reasonable basis, in case the products are not sold to an independent buyer or if they are not sold in the same condition as they were imported.

Currency conversion

If the comparison of prices requires currency conversion, the exchange rate to be considered is the one in effect on the date of the sale, unless the sale in foreign currency occurs in future markets related to the export under examination, in which case the exchange rate used in the future sale shall be adopted. In normal situations, the date of the sale shall be that of the agreement, of the purchase order, or of the confirmation of the purchase order or invoice. Among these documents, SECEX will use the one that establishes the terms of the sale.

Exchange rate movement shall not be considered, and for investigation purposes, a period of less than sixty days shall be considered as necessary for the adjustments, by exporters, of their export price, so as to reflect relevant modifications that occurred during the dumping investigation period.

Sampling

As noted earlier, usually the dumping margin is calculated separately for each known exporter or producer, but if there is an excessive number of exporters, producers, importers, or types of products under investigation, making individualization impossible, the examination may be limited to a reasonable number of interested parties, by means of statistical sampling, based on the available information of the volume of exports from the country under investigation. Any selection shall have the consent of the interested parties. An individual margin may also be calculated, at the discretion of SECEX, for the producers and exporters that provide the necessary information in time to be considered in the investigation.

Cost of production and constructed value methodology

The constructed value is the cost of production plus a reasonable amount for administrative and selling costs and the profit, based on the production and sale of same category of products, in the domestic market, during normal commercial operations.

Nonmarket economy methodology

In the case of imports from countries with a nonmarket economy, where the prices are fixed by the government, if there are problems in establishing the comparable price, the normal value will be established by the constructed value of a like product of a third country with a market economy, or by the price within this economy, or by the price of this product when exported to other countries, or in any other reasonable way, including the price paid or to be paid for a like product in the domestic market, with adjustments for a reasonable profit. The interested parties will be informed immediately after the investigation begins of the third country to be used in the comparison and could give their opinion in the time permitted.

Use of facts available

If information requested by SECEX from the parties is not provided during the investigation, SECEX shall decide upon the information presented and facts available. For this purpose, SECEX shall consider the proprietary information given by the parties that is of a confidential nature, as long as the parties have also been provided with an extract of such information that can be revealed. Information considered by the parties as of a confidential nature, but not accepted as confidential by SECEX, shall not be revealed to third parties, but shall be treated as nonexistent for the purposes of the examination.

Price undertakings and other agreements to suspend investigations

The party alleged to cause dumping (exporters or foreign manufacturers) may present a price undertaking or agree to a price undertaking suggested by SECEX, after preliminary determinations of dumping and injury deriving from the dumping. SECEX may accept the undertaking presented by the party if convinced that it is sufficient to stop the dumping or the injury in the domestic industry deriving from the dumping. As a consequence of the undertaking, provisional and definitive antidumping duties would not be applied. In this case, the investigation continues in order to confirm the existence of dumping and injury to the domestic industry.

The exporters are not obliged to offer undertakings nor to accept them when offered by SECEX. SECEX may not accept an undertaking presented by exporters if it finds that the undertaking is not effective. In this case, SECEX shall explain its decision. As noted, the undertaking will not impede the continuation of the investigation, nor will it alter the preliminary determination reached by SECEX. Further, the exporters bound to the undertaking must inform SECEX, whenever requested, about their compliance with the terms accepted and must allow SECEX to verify the corresponding data, under the penalty of being considered in default of the terms of the undertaking.

In the case of a violation of the undertaking, or in the case of discontinuation of the investigation, SECEX may take the necessary steps to apply provisional antidumping measures, based on the best information available, and the investigation shall be reopened. The parties shall be notified about the termination of the undertaking and the provisional antidumping measures.

Effect of Antidumping Order

Effective date–Duration

A product will be subject to antidumping duties as long as there is the need to neutralize the injury or threat of injury caused by the dumping. All definitive dumping duties will be terminated within five years after application of the dumping order or after the conclusion of the last revision that has taken into consideration both dumping and consequent injury. Such termination is automatic. However, five months prior to the end of the five-year period, any interested party may request a hearing to argue the need for revision of the dumping measures.

Enforcement
After the investigation starts, SECEX must inform the Brazilian Federal Revenue (*Secretaria da Receita Federal*—SRF) to adopt the measures to enable, if SECEX's findings are affirmative, the application of antidumping duties. When an antidumping duty is applied to a product, it will be imposed, in addition to any tariff duty related to the importation, on the basis of the determined values on every import of the dumped product.

Procedures for new shippers
If an antidumping duty is ordered, new shippers will pay the same antidumping duty established by SECEX. No individual margin will be granted to new shippers.

Procedures for review and revocation of order
All definitive antidumping duties will cease five years after their application or after the most recent revision that considers both the dumping and its injury. This period can be longer if so requested by the parties for good cause. There can be revision of the antidumping determination by the interested party or by an Administrative entity, after at least one year from the date of the determination, presenting sufficient evidence that:
(i) there is no need to neutralize the dumping anymore;
(ii) the damage would not subsist; or
(iii) the antidumping duty is not sufficient to neutralize the effect of the dumping.

Antidumping duties can be suspended for up to one year, which may be extended if there are temporary changes in the market situation, and, therefore, the injury does not continue.

COUNTERVAILING DUTY INVESTIGATIONS

Subsidy Determination
Countervailing duties may be applied with the purpose of offsetting subsidies granted, either directly or indirectly, by the exporting country, for the manufacture, production, exportation, or transport of any product the ex-

portation of which to Brazil causes injury to the domestic industry.

The procedures and timetable applicable to countervailing duty investigations mirrors those applicable to antidumping investigations as described above.

Definitions

Countervailing subsidies

Specific subsidies are subject to countervailing duties. Subsidies are considered to be specific if:
(i) the government or legislation limits access to the subsidy to an enterprise or to a group of enterprises or industries, under the jurisdiction of such government;
(ii) the subsidy is limited to enterprises in a particular region;
(iii) there are linked subsidies.

Noncountervailable subsidies ("green light")

Subsidies not defined as specific are noncountervailable. There will not be countervailing duties imposed for subsidies for:
(i) research—excluding civil aircraft—if the subsidy does not exceed 75 percent of the costs;
(ii) to a particular region of the exporter country that needs the aid;
(iii) new environmental measures imposed by law.

Calculation of subsidies

In response to a countervailing duty petition, the amount of the subsidy will be calculated by unit of the subsidized product exported to Brazil. Loans, grants, and equity investments are not considered to be countervailable benefits, provided that the conditions for such transactions are at the market rate. However, if such loans or other indirect benefits are made on conditions that are not usually practiced in the market and benefit the company whose product is alleged to be subsidized, then such benefits shall be taken into account when deciding whether there is a subsidy.

Undertakings which suspend the investigation

The proceedings can be suspended, without the imposition of countervailing duties, if the government of the exporter country agrees to eliminate or reduce the subsidy, to adopt measures related to its effects, or if the exporter revises its export prices.

Effect of Countervailing Duty Order

Effective date–Duration
Countervailing duties will remain in effect as long as the product considered to be subsidized causes or threatens to cause injury to the domestic industry.

Procedures for review and revocation
Countervailing duties will remain in effect as long as there is the need to neutralize the subsidy that is causing injury. The duties will end in five years, unless extended, in order to prevent further injury. There will be a review, if requested by the interested party or government or by SECEX, on the anniversary of the imposition of countervailing duties.

INJURY ANALYSIS

Material Injury
Factors relevant to the material injury analysis include:
(i) the volume of subsidized or dumped imports: There are two tests in connection with the volume of imports:
   (a) the significance of the volume of imports (imports are insignificant if they represent less than 3 percent of imports of the like product, except for a country that, separately, represents less than 3 percent, but jointly with other countries represents more than 7 percent); and
   (b) a substantial increase in imports of the products, in absolute terms and in relation to production and consumption in Brazil;
(ii) the effects of imports on the price of like products in Brazil such as underselling or undercutting prices of the like product in Brazil or price depression. Those effects shall be examined on a case-by-case basis. In the case of imports of producers from more than one country, the effects of such imports shall be examined cumulatively if:
   (a) the dumping or subsidy margin in connection with each country is not *de minimis* and if the volume of imports from each country is not insignificant; and
   (b) the cumulative evaluation of the effects of the imports is appropriate in view of the competitive conditions between the imported products and the competition between imported products and the like domestic product; and

(iii) the consequent impact on the domestic industry: evaluation of all applicable economic factors and indexes that are related to the relevant industry (including real or potential decrease of sales, profits, output, market share, productivity, and income from investments, in addition to other factors that affect the domestic price).

Threat of Material Injury

Factors relevant to a determination of threat of material injury include:
(i) the increase of imports of dumped or subsidized products, indicating possible substantial increase of such imports;
(ii) production capacity of the producer;
(iii) imports that have the effect of reducing the domestic price or restricting the increase of such price; and
(iv) inventory of investigated products.

OTHER TRADE REMEDIES

Safeguards

Decree No. 1,488, of May 11th, 1995, establishes the conditions for the application of safeguard measures. According to this Decree, safeguards in connection with imports may be imposed if imports of such products increase in such quantities (in absolute or relative terms) and under such conditions as to cause or threaten to cause serious injury to the domestic industry producing like or competitive products. The safeguard investigation is conducted by SECEX and application of measures is imposed by means of an order jointly signed by two State Ministers: the Minister of Finance and the Minister of Commerce, Industry, and Tourism.

The request for imposition of safeguard measures may be presented by: (i) SECEX; (ii) any Federal Government agency; (iii) companies or entities representing companies that produce products that compete with the imported product. The application of safeguards measures is based on a form, with sufficient evidence, that shows an increase of imports, serious injury or threat of serious injury caused by imports, and the relationship between the two circumstances.

The decision to open an investigation is published in the Official Gazette, and interested parties shall be heard within thirty days from such publication. Interested parties must submit evidence and give their opinion on the other parties' allegations. Also, SECEX will consult with the foreign governments with a substantial interest as exporting countries.

Provisional safeguard measures may be imposed in critical situations, where delay of application of definitive measures may cause serious injury that may be difficult to remedy. Provisional safeguard measures shall be applied after evidence is produced of an increase in imports that caused or is threatening to cause serious injury to the domestic industry, and shall not last for more than 200 days. In the case of provisional measures, there will be imposed an *ad valorem* rate, or a specific rate, or a combination of both; or provisional deposits may be withheld or deposited as a bond, for return in case definitive measures are not imposed on imports of the products in question, whatever their origin.

Timetable

Safeguard decisions must be made within 130 days of initiation, except in complex cases in which a decision may be postponed for two months.

Remedies

Measures may take the form of an ad valorem tariff rate, or a specific rate, or a combination of both; quantitative restrictions; or a reduction in the volume of imports based on recent import volumes.

The Brazilian government may enter into agreements with interested countries to distribute the quotas. If this is not possible, there shall be separate quotas for each country. The term of definitive quotas should be sufficient to prevent or remedy injury, provided it does not exceed four years, including the term of provisional measures. Safeguard measures may be extended, not exceeding ten years total, including the term of provisional measures. After one year of application of safeguards measures, there is a progressive liberalization of the quotas or other import restrictions.

For safeguard measures exceeding three years, SECEX will investigate the actual effects of definitive measures and suggest revocation if the domestic industry is not complying with the adjustment program. There shall be no application for extension until safeguard measures have been in effect for two years. In the case of safeguard measures that last for more than four years, the period for application of new safeguard measures shall be equal to half of the period of the previous safeguards term.

Safeguard measures shall not be applied to developing countries when:
(i) their share of imports are not greater than three percent of total imports of the like product; and
(ii) participation of all developing countries with individual shares less than three percent do not exceed 9 percent in total for the product in question.

Canada

Peter A. Magnus
Smith Lyons
Ontario, Canada

HISTORY AND OVERVIEW OF CANADIAN TRADE REMEDY LAWS*

Canadian Accession to GATT/WTO and to GATT Codes

Canada is an original member of the World Trade Organization as a signatory of the WTO Agreement, as well as having been an original contracting party of the GATT 1947.

Canada was also party to the original GATT Antidumping Code of 1967 (the 1967 GATT Code)[1] and to its successor code in 1979 (the 1979 GATT Antidumping Code),[2] as well as to the 1979 GATT Code on Subsidies and Countervailing Duties.[3]

Canada's status as an original adherent to all of these instruments is reflective of the longstanding Canadian position that the country's interests are best served by a rules-based international trading system. This position, in turn, reflects the extent to which the wealth of the Canadian economy depends on trade: about one-quarter of Canadian GDP is generated by exports.

Evolution of Canadian Trade Remedy Laws

Canada was the first country to institute an antidumping system.[4] Until 1969, Canada's antidumping provisions contained no injury test. Dumping duties were imposed if a domestic producer could establish that imported goods were goods of a "class or kind made in Canada"[5] and the administering authority, the Department of National Revenue (generally referred to as Revenue Canada), established that the imported goods were being dumped.[6] As a signatory to the 1967 GATT Code,[7] Canada under-

---

*This chapter reflects the state of anti-dumping law in Canada to January of 1997.

took to incorporate an injury test in its antidumping legislation. The revised antidumping legislation, the *Antidumping Act*,[8] came into force on January 1, 1969. Revenue Canada continued to determine whether imported goods were being dumped. However, a new quasi-judicial body reporting directly to Parliament, the Antidumping Tribunal,[9] was formed to assess the question of material injury[10] to production in Canada.

An extensive review of Canadian trade remedy law was initiated by the federal government after the coming into force of the 1979 GATT Antidumping Code. The government issued a discussion paper in 1980[11] that proposed in particular another overhaul of Canadian antidumping legislation.[12]

The review eventually led to the replacement of the *Antidumping Act* of 1969 by the *Special Import Measures Act*[13] (*SIMA*), which came into force on December 1, 1984. *SIMA* also updated and consolidated Canadian countervail law, which was previously contained in regulations made pursuant to the *Customs Tariff*. Under *SIMA*, the Antidumping Tribunal (which by this time also had responsibility for injury determinations in countervail cases) was renamed the Canadian Import Tribunal and subsequently the Canadian International Trade Tribunal (CITT).[14]

SIMA, along with regulations made pursuant to it, remains the basic Canadian antidumping and countervail legislation. It is noteworthy that neither the Canada-U.S. Free Trade Agreement of 1988 (the FTA), nor the North American Free Trade Agreement (NAFTA) between Canada, Mexico, and the United States, which came into force on January 1, 1994, led to changes to the substance of the legislation in terms of such basic matters as its general application to all products and countries, and its provisions regarding initial determinations of dumping, subsidy, and injury. It was a Canadian objective in the negotiation of the FTA to include provisions to tighten or even eliminate the application of trade remedy actions between the two parties.[15] Such an approach was unacceptable to the U.S. However, it was agreed that the FTA would require a new system whereby the final determinations of dumping, subsidy, and injury by the domestic authorities of each party to the FTA, with such determinations still made according to each party's domestic laws, would be subject to review by panels consisting of trade experts from each country.[16] This system was continued under NAFTA.

As contemplated by Article XIX of the GATT 1947, Canadian trade law contains an "escape clause" in the form of administrative authority to apply surtaxes and import controls even where imports are not dumped or subsidized. Unlike antidumping and countervail, the FTA and NAFTA have required limitations on the operation of safeguard measures vis-à-vis imports originating in Mexico and the U.S.

Summary of Canadian Trade Remedies

Antidumping and countervailing duty regimes

Antidumping and countervailing duty regimes are imposed pursuant to *SIMA* and the Special Import Measures Regulations[17] (the Regulations). Apart from a period of provisional duty, liability for antidumping and countervailing duties (sometimes referred to as "special duties") arises only after an injury determination made by the CITT in relation to the production in Canada of like products. The amount of any special duty applicable to a particular imported product is determined by officials of Revenue Canada. Revenue Canada is also the federal government department responsible for the Canadian Customs Service and, as such, enforces the payment of all duties, regular customs duties, and special duties alike.

Under *SIMA*, the authority to initiate a dumping or subsidy investigation formally rests with the Deputy Minister of National Revenue, who is the operational head of Revenue Canada. In practice, however, such decisions are made by officials of the Antidumping and Countervailing Directorate within Revenue Canada.

Safeguard regime

Canadian safeguard measures principally include the authority for the imposition of surtax pursuant to the *Customs Tariff*,[18] the withdrawal of certain tariff preferences (also pursuant to the *Customs Tariff*), and the imposition of import controls pursuant to the *Export and Import Permits Act*.[19] The imposition of safeguard measures is generally preceded by an inquiry conducted by the CITT pursuant to the *Canadian International Trade Tribunal Act*,[20] although some safeguard measures may also be implemented by order of the federal cabinet on the basis only of a report by the Minister of Finance.

ANTIDUMPING INVESTIGATIONS

Dumping Determination

Initiation of investigation

By petition

The antidumping process normally begins with the filing by a private party of a petition (the Canadian terminology is a "complaint") with Revenue Canada alleging injury to a Canadian industry caused by imports of dumped

goods. Once a complaint is determined to be properly documented, i.e., sufficient information exists upon which Revenue Canada can decide to initiate (or, for that matter, not to initiate), a decision will be made whether to initiate a formal investigation of dumping.[21] An affirmative decision to initiate a dumping investigation will be made if:
- there is evidence that goods have been dumped,[22] and
- the evidence discloses a reasonable indication that the dumping has caused, is causing, or is likely to cause material injury to the production in Canada of like goods sufficient to enable such an opinion to be formed.[23]

In the event of a Revenue Canada decision not to initiate on the basis of no apparent injury, the complainant can request that the CITT advise whether in its view (as the body specialized in matters related to injury) the evidence provided to Revenue Canada discloses a reasonable indication of material injury.[24] If the CITT confirms the view of Revenue Canada, the complaint comes to an end. Revenue Canada may also refer this threshold injury question to the CITT of its own motion. If the CITT advises that there is *prima facie* evidence of injury, Revenue Canada must initiate a formal dumping investigation.[25] The CITT can only be asked to render its advice on the question of *injury*. In the event of a Revenue Canada decision not to initiate on the basis of no apparent *dumping*, there is effectively no challenge available to the complainant.[26]

If Revenue Canada initiates an investigation, any party formally notified (for example, importer, exporter, government of country of export) may request the CITT to advise on the existence of *prima facie* evidence of injury.[27] In this case, the CITT renders its advice after examining the record upon which Revenue Canada arrived at the decision to initiate without holding any hearings.[28] Meanwhile, the Revenue Canada dumping investigation continues. If the CITT advises that, in its view, the evidence placed before Revenue Canada does not disclose a reasonable indication of material injury, the Revenue Canada dumping investigation must be terminated immediately by Revenue Canada.[29]

By government

SIMA provides for the initiation of an investigation by Revenue Canada without the prior submission of a complaint by a private party.[30] However, this procedure has rarely been used and it is doubtful that it would be used in the absence of a pre-existing complaint concerning related products or concerning other source countries in relation to the same product.[31]

Timetable

SIMA provides tight deadlines for each step of an antidumping investigation.

Step	Maximum number of days
Determination by Revenue Canada that complaint is properly documented[32]	21 days
Decision by Revenue Canada to initiate investigation after receipt of properly documented complaint	30 days
Response by CITT to any request concerning sufficiency of prima facie evidence of injury	30 days
Duration of investigation after initiation and prior to issuance of preliminary determination of dumping[33]	90 days
Final determination of dumping	90 days
Recalculation of duties after injury finding	180 days

Participation of parties and their counsel

Domestic petitioners

Domestic complainants are generally assisted by either trade lawyers and/or trade consultants in the preparation of a dumping complaint, including the numerous discussions with Revenue Canada that generally occur prior to the complaint being accepted as properly documented. Once an investigation is initiated, counsel for domestic complainants has little more to do with Revenue Canada.

Domestic and foreign respondents

Revenue Canada treats the filing of a dumping complaint as confidential. As such, exporters and importers whose interests are potentially affected by the dumping complaint may remain unaware of the existence of the complaint until a formal dumping investigation is announced by Revenue Canada. However, the government of the exporting country is notified of the receipt of a properly documented complaint.

Once an investigation is initiated, those importers and exporters with a stake of any significance in the proceedings usually engage counsel. Initially, counsel assist in the preparation of responses to the questionnaires issued to importers and exporters after initiation. As discussed below, the role of counsel is necessarily limited in the Revenue Canada phase of an investigation by the lack of access to the confidential submissions of other parties.

Access to information developed in proceedings

Nonproprietary information

Nonconfidential summaries of submissions to Revenue Canada by complainants, exporters, and importers are publicly available after initiation of an investigation.

Business proprietary information

SIMA appears to contemplate the adoption by Revenue Canada of procedures paralleling those employed by the CITT, discussed in the "Access to Information Developed in Proceedings" section of Injury Analysis, below, to enable independent counsel representing parties opposite in interest to have access to the confidential portions of all submissions to Revenue Canada by the complainant, exporters, and importers.[34] However, the confidential portions of submissions to Revenue Canada remain essentially inaccessible even to independent counsel due to Revenue Canada's current administrative practices.[35] As a result there is effectively no basis upon which counsel (on either side of the proceedings) can develop effective counter-representations to submissions by a party opposite in interest at the preliminary stage.

However, Revenue Canada's statements of reasons issued in connection with initiation and the preliminary determination of dumping have become much more detailed, providing parties with a significantly improved understanding of the investigation process leading up to the final determination.

Definitions

Like products

As noted in the "Normal Value" section below, the normal value of exported goods is determined in the first instance on the basis of the selling price of "like goods" in the home market of the exporter. "Like goods" are defined in *SIMA* "in relation to any other goods" (i.e., the class formulated by Revenue Canada) as:
(i) goods that are identical in all respects to the other goods; or
(ii) in the absence of any goods described in paragraph (i), goods the uses and other characteristics of which closely resemble those of the other goods.[36]

Revenue Canada formulates the class of goods that becomes the subject of the dumping investigation. The class of goods thus formulated is not, however, necessarily synonymous with the specific goods that have actually been imported.

Due to the rather limited consideration of injury to production in Canada of like goods during the Revenue Canada phase of an investigation, consideration of what constitutes like goods is generally more problematic in the injury phase of the investigation before the CITT discussed in the "Like Products" section of Injury Analysis below.

Period of investigation

SIMA does not prescribe a period of investigation (POI). Prior to amendments to *SIMA* to implement various provisions of the WTO Agreement relating to trade remedies, periods of investigation had been as short as two months. Given the new requirements to examine the profitability of sales in the home market over a period of at least six months, it is expected that a POI of six months for an exporter will become the norm.[37]

Requirement of support for complaint by domestic industry

Complainants are not required to be producers in Canada of like goods.[38] However, *SIMA* provides that an investigation may not be initiated unless the complaint is supported by domestic producers of like goods representing at least:
(i)   50 percent of the production of all producers who have indicated either support or opposition to the complaint; and
(ii) 25 percent of total production of the like goods in Canada.[39]

Related parties

For the purposes of the required support of the domestic industry for a complaint, described in the immediately preceding section, *SIMA* provides that the domestic industry may be defined to exclude a domestic producer who is a related party of an exporter or importer of the product in issue. *SIMA* contains a detailed definition of a related party, based on control of one by another.[40]

Calculation of dumping margins

Export price

Export price is defined as the lesser of:
- the exporter's sale price; or
- the importer's purchase price.

In both cases, the sale and purchase price take into account deductions which insure a proper comparison of price at an ex-factory level.[41]

In specific circumstances, Revenue Canada can disregard the export price that would otherwise be determined. These circumstances include:
- non-arm's length sales[42] between exporters and importers that are related;[43] and

- arm's length sales that involve a compensatory arrangement.[44]

Export price is then established by reference to the first arm's length sale in Canada by the importer less:
- all costs, charges, and expenses incurred between the exporter and the first arm's length sale by the importer; plus
- an amount for profit by the importer.[45]

The determination of the costs, charges, and expenses incurred between the exporter and the first arm's length sale by the importer necessarily includes an allocation of the selling, general, and administrative expenses incurred by the importer with respect to its sales of the like goods.

Revenue Canada determines the amount of profit to be attributed to the importer by undertaking a survey of the profit on like goods (or on goods of the same general category) earned on arm's length sales by vendors in Canada who are at the same trade level as the importer under investigation. These vendors could include Canadian producers and other importers. Current Revenue Canada administrative practice is to establish a period of review for determining the profitability of other vendors falling within the time frame chosen as the period of investigation for determining whether dumping has been occurring.

The calculation of export price is also affected by certain additional adjustments:
- Sales on credit terms: In the case of sales on credit terms (other than cash discounts), a specific methodology is established for determining the discount rate to be used in determining the value of such credit terms.[46]
- Exporter providing benefit on resale: Where the exporter provides any benefit on the resale of the goods in Canada (for example, by way of rebate, service, other goods, etc.), the export price is reduced by an amount to reflect the value of the resale benefit.[47]
- Indemnification agreements: *SIMA* provides a general antiavoidance provision[48] that requires the export price of any goods be further reduced by the amount of any indemnity, payment, or reimbursement to the importer of any antidumping duties.

Normal value

SIMA provides two basic methodologies for the determination of normal value:
- by reference to home market sales; and
- by reference to constructed cost.

In general terms, the home market selling price approach entails, as a first step, establishing the price level at which the exporter freely sells like goods in the ordinary course of trade during a specified period to customers in its home market who are at the same or substantially the same trade level as the importer.[49] The price used is the weighted average price of sales made during the period of investigation specified by Revenue Canada.[50] A number of conditions must be satisfied for the home market selling price methodology to be applied, including, in particular, a sufficient number of profitable sales.[51]

Adjustments

After a home market selling price is derived, differences in terms and conditions of sale, taxation, and other differences relating to price comparability between the sale of the goods to the Canadian importer and the domestic sales by the exporter are then taken into account. This second step involves making adjustments to the home market price to calibrate for differences in comparability with the export sale for such factors as trade level, quantity, quality (including structure, design and material), transportation, and differences in terms of payment.[52] In addition, the home market price is reduced by any taxes or duties not borne by the exported goods. The resultant price, the normal value, is the benchmark against which the comparison is made to the ex-factory price at which goods are being exported to Canada.

Treatment of sales through related parties

The home market sales under consideration must be at arm's length, or in other words to customers who are not associated with the exporter. An "associated person" is defined as including at least a 5 percent equity interest (direct or indirect) between the exporter and the customer.[53] Sales between the exporter and persons associated with the exporter are therefore excluded by Revenue Canada in determining normal value under this methodology.

Cost of production methodology

If the conditions for the use of the home market selling price as normal value are not satisfied, the cost of production methodology is to be used.

In general terms, the constructed cost approach requires an identification of all costs incurred by the exporter with respect to the goods in question. Revenue Canada's practice is to use a fully allocated basis upon which to establish the constructed cost.[54] In establishing the constructed cost of the goods, the exporter is required to include the cost of production of the goods as well as an amount for selling, general, and administrative expenses for goods being exported to Canada. A profit margin is then attributed to the resulting constructed cost at the level of profit made by the exporter[55] on home market sales of like goods or, alternatively, goods of the same general category. The profit used is the weighted average profit, which is considered to include sales of like goods made at a loss as long as the sales show a net profit.

Nonmarket economy methodology

The treatment presently accorded a nonmarket economy ("NME") continues, in practice, to be somewhat arbitrary. As a result, Canadian dumping investigations against NMEs have tended to result in margins of dumping that generally do not reflect the level of economic development of the NME producer.

The general approach in NME cases is for Revenue Canada to identify as a surrogate a third country in which an exporter is prepared to provide Revenue Canada, on a courtesy basis, with information sufficient to permit normal values to be established for the NME exporter by applying either of the conventional normal value methodologies. The record of Canadian NME dumping investigations reflects an understandable lack of success on the part of Revenue Canada in soliciting the cooperation of an exporter in a surrogate country whose economy would reflect a level of economic development comparable to the NME under investigation.[56]

Revenue Canada has also been reluctant to treat all the countries in Eastern Europe, the former Soviet Union, and the PRC, as market economy countries. In order to consider a change in its traditional position vis-à-vis a country that has in the past been treated as an NME, Revenue Canada has insisted on the submission of very detailed questionnaires about such matters as government involvement in the export process. This has proved in practice to be a high hurdle to cross, given the costs involved relative to the size of the Canadian market for the producer in question.

Use of facts available

Where normal value and/or export price cannot be determined for an exporter because sufficient information has not been furnished or is not available, they are determined by means of a Ministerial specification.[57] This means that the Minister of National Revenue, acting on the advice of officials, specifies the normal value and/or export price on the basis of the best information that is available. Normally, the specification would be the highest margin of dumping found for any exporter or country on the basis of the information available.

Price undertakings

SIMA provides for the suspension of a dumping investigation where undertakings are accepted by Revenue Canada from exporters or govern-

ments of the source countries of the allegedly dumped goods, in which a commitment is made either to revise the price at which the subject goods are sold, or to cease dumping the goods. Revenue Canada may accept a price undertaking with respect to dumped goods, provided that:
- the undertaking will eliminate the margin of dumping, or any material injury the dumping is likely to cause;
- the undertaking will not cause prices of the subject goods to increase beyond the estimated margin of dumping;
- a preliminary determination has been made; and
- Revenue Canada considers the undertaking practicable to administer.[58]

The practicability of administering an undertaking will vary with the number of exporters or countries involved, the complexity of the product (number of product lines, anticipated volume and ease of identification), as well as the frequency of price changes. Revenue Canada appears to be open to accepting undertakings notwithstanding that a fairly high degree of administrative complexity may be involved.

An undertaking is subject to a "sunset" provision requiring a review after five years, although it can be renewed for one further five-year period. An undertaking that is not renewed automatically expires, thereby bringing the dumping proceeding to an end. Undertakings may be terminated if a violation occurs, or if new circumstances arise that affect the usefulness of the undertaking.

Effect of Antidumping Order

Effective date

A Revenue Canada preliminary determination results in the immediate imposition of provisional antidumping duties on imports of the goods in question. Such provisional dumping duties, based on the estimated margin of dumping, remain in effect for the following 120 days.[59]

An injury decision by the CITT, following a preliminary determination of dumping by Revenue Canada, results in imports of the affected goods being assessed a dumping duty to the extent that the export price of the goods in question is less than the normal value. If the CITT makes a finding of no injury, or of threat of injury only, then any duties collected during the provisional period are refunded.

A CITT injury decision, and thus the ongoing collection of dumping duty, expires five years after the date of the decision unless the CITT carries out a review, discussed in "Procedures for review and revocation of order" below, and determines that its injury decision should remain in effect.

Scope determination

Antidumping duties in the provisional period are collected in relation to the class of imported goods as defined by Revenue Canada. The CITT injury finding may be in relation to that class, or a narrower class of goods.[60] If the CITT narrows the class of goods through exclusions, then any duties in relation to excluded goods that were collected in the provisional period are refunded.

Enforcement and anticircumvention

Antidumping duties are enforced at the border in the first instance by Canada Customs, which is part of the same government department (Revenue Canada) that houses the Antidumping and Countervailing Directorate. Canada Customs enforces the normal values and export prices that are determined by the Directorate.

There are few specific anticircumvention rules in Canada. Rather, antidumping duties are enforced through the wide discretion that Revenue Canada has to determine who is the exporter and importer, and thus to determine on what basis export price and normal values will be calculated. The discretion over the determination of who is the importer allows Revenue Canada, in practice, to ensure that there is an entity in Canada liable for payment of any dumping duty.

Procedure for new shippers

New shippers may contact Revenue Canada prior to shipment of goods subject to dumping enforcement and request that normal values and export prices be calculated for the products in question, to enable the shipment to take place at an export price that is not less than normal value.

Procedures for review and revocation of order

As noted, a CITT injury decision, and thus antidumping enforcement, expires after five years unless the CITT undertakes a review prior to expiry and determines that its injury decision should remain in effect. The issue in any review hearing conducted by the CITT is whether, if the injury finding were removed, a resumption of dumping would be likely to occur with attendant consequences of material injury to the production in Canada of like goods. The CITT is also empowered to vary or alter a finding of injury that has previously been made.

There are no mandated time frames within which Revenue Canada must undertake an administrative review of normal values and export prices. Revenue Canada's internal guidelines call for an administrative review to be undertaken at least once in any twelve-month period.

COUNTERVAILING DUTY INVESTIGATIONS

Subsidy Determination

As is evident from the discussion below, in general the scheme in *SIMA* for a subsidy or countervailing duty investigation mirrors that of an antidumping investigation discussed in Part II above. As a practical matter, Canadian experience has been that most subsidy cases have also involved an allegation of dumping and thus the investigations have been joined from the outset. However, subsidy cases, with or without an accompanying dumping allegation, have been relatively rare in Canada.

Initiation of investigation

Subsidy investigations are initiated in the same fashion and are subject to the same injury standards as antidumping investigations outlined above: investigations begin either after acceptance of a complaint filed by private parties or through self-initiation by Revenue Canada. In either case, there must be at least a reasonable indication of material injury.

Timetable

The timetable for a subsidy investigation is the same as that of a dumping investigation, outlined above.

Participation of parties and their counsel

The participation of parties and their counsel in a subsidy investigation is subject to the same limitations as that of a dumping investigation.

Access to information developed in proceedings

Unlike in a dumping investigation, a copy of the nonconfidential version of the complaint in a subsidy investigation is provided to the government of the exporting country as soon as the complaint is considered to be properly documented. This effectively enables representatives of that government to make submissions directly to Revenue Canada prior to the initiation of a subsidy investigation if that government wishes to do so. Other considerations with respect to access to information are the same as those for a dumping investigation.

Definitions

The portions of *SIMA* concerning countervailing duties were extensively revised in 1994 as part of Canada's implementation of its obligations under the WTO Agreement. Thus the definitions of subsidy-related concepts found in *SIMA* and the Regulations closely follow the definitions contained in the WTO Agreement, but there is as yet little Canadian caselaw or administrative decisions interpreting most subsidy-related definitions.

Countervailable subsidies

Under *SIMA*, all subsidies to foreign producers are *prima facie* countervailable.

SIMA provides a detailed framework to determine what constitutes a "financial contribution" for the purposes of the definitions of "subsidy,"[61] and then defines "subsidy" in terms of a "financial contribution" to foreign producers conferred by a foreign government.[62] Part of the text of the definition of "subsidy" in *SIMA* refers specifically to the text of the WTO Agreement.

Noncountervailable subsidies

Under *SIMA*, countervailing duties may not be levied against a "nonactionable subsidy."[63] Included in the definition of the latter is a subsidy that is "not specific."[64] Subsidies for industrial assistance and regional development are also included in the definition of "nonactionable subsidy." Excluded from the definition of "nonactionable subsidy," and thus countervailable, is a "prohibited subsidy," which is defined principally as an "export subsidy."[65]

Application to nonmarket economies

Although *SIMA* contains a specific provision for nonmarket economies with respect to the calculation of normal value in the dumping context, there is no similar provision in the context of subsidies. In any event, because of Revenue Canada's propensity to find high margins of dumping in the case of complaints against nonmarket source countries,[66] complainants have little incentive to take on the greater complexity of a subsidy allegation and have generally not done so. However, as noted, the Regulations contain detailed provisions concerning the manner in which a subsidy is to be calculated. They provide that where a government has supplied goods or services in relation to subsidized goods, the fair market value of those goods or services may be attributed for the purposes of calculating the amount of subsidy.[67]

Calculation of subsidies

Treatment of loans, grants, and equity investments

The Regulations contain detailed provisions for calculating the amount of subsidy on goods in relation to grants,[68] loans at a preferential rate,[69] loan guarantees,[70] and equity investment by government.[71] Generally, the amount of subsidy in relation to such benefits is to be determined by allocating the subsidy to the goods on the basis of "generally accepted accounting principles," with the amount of each benefit determined on the basis of its fair market value.

Effect of privatization

Neither *SIMA* nor the Regulations contain any specific provisions with respect to the effect of privatization in the subsidy context,[72] although the rules concerning the types of benefits discussed above would undoubtedly come into play.

Allocation of subsidies over time

The references to "generally accepted accounting principles" in the Regulations would appear to be the only specific provisions concerning the calculation of the amount of subsidy in relation to the allocation of subsidies over time.

Use of facts available

Where sufficient information has not been provided or is not available to determine the amount of subsidy pursuant to the legislative scheme, it is determined by means of a Ministerial specification. This means that the Minister of National Revenue, acting on the advice of officials, specifies the amount of subsidy on the basis of information available.

Undertakings

SIMA provides for the termination of a subsidy investigation and thus the nonapplication of countervailing duties when there is an acceptable undertaking from exporters and/or the source country to price the product at a level that would eliminate either the amount of subsidy or injury in Canada.[73] The provisions are the same as those applicable to the acceptance and administration of undertakings in the dumping context.

Effect of Countervailing Duty Order

The effect of a countervailing duty order is exactly the same as the effect of an antidumping order, substituting where necessary "amount of subsidy" for "margin of dumping," "countervailing duty" for "antidumping duty," etc.

INJURY ANALYSIS

Initiation of Investigation

SIMA requires that Revenue Canada determine that there is a "reasonable indication" of injury before a dumping investigation is initiated; parties may request that the CITT rule on the existence of such *prima facie* evidence. However, the latter step is optional and *ex parte*. The formal and more elaborate injury investigation that must be carried out by the CITT is initiated when Revenue Canada makes a preliminary determination of dumping.

Timetable and Relation to Dumping and Subsidy Analysis

The CITT must make its determination as to the existence of injury within 120 days of Revenue Canada's issuance of a preliminary determination of dumping and/or subsidy. The CITT makes its determination after engaging in a process of information-gathering that culminates in a public hearing. Since Revenue Canada is required to issue a final determination of dumping and/or subsidy within 90 days of the issuance of its preliminary determination, this means in practice that the CITT's public hearing begins in the normal course just after the issuance of Revenue Canada's final determination. However, if Revenue Canada concludes in its final determination that there is no dumping, the CITT investigation is terminated.[74]

Participation of Parties and their Counsel

Domestic petitioners

Domestic complainants are generally represented by experienced trade lawyers and/or consultants throughout the CITT injury investigation. Often one group of counsel will represent all complainants, even where the complainants are domestic competitors.

Domestic and foreign respondents

Importers and exporters with a stake of any significance in the outcome of a dumping or subsidy case usually engage counsel when Revenue Canada initiates an investigation. Most of those parties will also participate at least to some extent in the injury investigation before the CITT.

Access to Information Developed in Proceedings

Nonproprietary information

The CITT endeavors to make its processes as transparent as possible, and thus all nonproprietary (referred to in Canada as "nonconfidential" or "public") information filed in a dumping or subsidy case is available for public inspection as soon as it has been assembled by CITT staff. Parties are required to file nonconfidential summaries of all filings for which confidentiality is claimed.[75]

Business proprietary information

Counsel for all parties before the CITT in principle have access to the confidential filings and *in camera* oral testimony of all other parties. However, such access is subject to those counsel being "independent"[76] and residents of Canada, and having filed undertakings that they will not disclose the confidential information of other parties to anyone, including of course, their clients.

Definitions

Domestic industry

SIMA provides an explicit definition of "domestic industry" for the purposes of the CITT's injury determination: "The domestic producers as a whole of the like goods or those domestic producers whose collective production of the like goods constitute a major proportion of the total domestic production of the like goods."

It has been held that "major proportion" does not require at least 50 percent of the domestic producers, or any mathematical formulation; rather, domestic industry has been interpreted to mean those producers whose output is "significant."[77]

Domestic production for export has not been included within the meaning of "domestic industry."[78]

SIMA incorporates the two exceptions for the definition of domestic industry permitted by the WTO Agreement, namely that for related producers and regional industries. Thus "domestic industry" in a particular case may be defined to exclude those domestic producers who are related to importers or exporters of dumped goods.[79] In addition, where production and sales of the product in question are concentrated in a particular region of Canada, "domestic industry" may be defined as the industry of that region alone.[80]

Like products

Under Canadian law, Revenue Canada formulates the class of goods that becomes the subject of the dumping investigation. The class of goods thus formulated is not, however, necessarily synonymous with the specific goods that have actually been imported.

The task of the CITT at the injury stage of an investigation is to ascertain whether "material injury" has been caused, or is threatened, by the class of dumped or subsidized goods as defined by Revenue Canada, to the domestic producers of "like goods." Thus, the CITT determines the Canadian industry producing goods *like* the class of imported goods subject to investigation.

The first comprehensive treatment in Canada of what constitutes "like goods" occurred in the *Steam Traps* case:

> It appears to the Tribunal that the question of whether goods are "like" is to be determined by market considerations. Do they compete directly with one another? Are the same consumers being sought? Do they have the same end-use functionally? Do they fulfill the same need? Can they be substituted one for the other?[81]

The "functional similarity" test that the CITT has used in the construction of "like goods" has been upheld by the Federal Court of Appeal.[82]

Period of investigation

For its injury investigation, the CITT is not obligated to use the same period of investigation used by Revenue Canada for its dumping investigation, and in fact the CITT usually looks at a much broader period. Nothing in *SIMA* actually requires the CITT to look at any particular length of time. Although questionnaires sent by the CITT to manufacturers and importers prior to the public hearing request data in relation to changes in selling price and so on over a particular period, this does not prevent the parties from presenting evidence concerning a longer or shorter period.

Material injury

Canadian trade remedy legislation has never contained a definition of "material injury." However, amendments to *SIMA* introduced as part of the WTO implementation in 1994 provide that the government may prescribe by regulation factors that "may be considered" in determining whether dumping or subsidizing has caused injury or threatens to cause injury.[83] Prescribed factors include the following:

- actual and potential volume of the dumped or subsidized goods;
- effect of the goods on domestic prices;
- impact of the goods on the domestic industry, including output and profits; and
- any significant increase of imports into Canada of the goods.[84]

Threat of material injury

As an alternative to finding that the dumped or subsidized goods have "caused injury," SIMA provides that the CITT may find that the imported goods are "threatening to cause injury."[85] To make such a finding, the CITT must determine that the circumstances which would cause injury are "clearly foreseen and imminent."[86]

If the CITT makes a finding of threat of injury only, then antidumping or countervailing duties are payable only from the date of the finding; any duties paid by importers during the provisional period are refunded.[87]

Other injury findings

The CITT may also make injury findings in relation to retardation, massive importation, and public interest. It has done so rarely.

SIMA defines "retardation" as "material retardation of the establishment of a domestic industry."[88] The CITT's ability to base an injury finding on "retardation" constitutes an exception to the normal requirement that a finding be made in relation to existing production in Canada.

Under certain conditions, the CITT may also make a finding that the dumped or subsidized goods constituted a "massive importation" into Canada. In such a case, extraordinary antidumping or countervailing duties may be collected retroactively for the ninety-day period prior to the date of Revenue Canada's preliminary determination.[89]

Finally, where the CITT makes an injury finding, it may recommend to the government that the imposition of the full amount of antidumping or countervailing duties "would not or might not be in the public interest."[90]

OTHER TRADE REMEDIES

History and Rationale

Apart from the application of antidumping and countervailing duties, two other trade remedies have long existed in Canadian law: surtax and import controls. They have been employed most frequently, although not exclusively, in response to potentially disruptive seasonal agricultural products from the United States.

Canadian safeguard measures were designed to ensure compliance with Article XIX of the GATT 1947. Thus they have generally only been imposed after a federal tribunal has concluded, upon an inquiry initiated by the federal government, that certain imported goods are causing or threaten to cause serious injury to Canadian producers. The responsibility for holding such inquiries was consolidated in the newly-created CITT in 1989. At the same time, a right of direct access for private parties to request such an inquiry was introduced into Canadian trade law.[91] Previously, such an inquiry could only be initiated at the request of the Minister of Finance.

With the coming into force in 1989 of the Canada-US Free Trade Agreement, followed by NAFTA in 1994, escape clause mechanisms and limitations unique to the member countries of those agreements were introduced.

Procedures

A safeguard action against particular imports is generally preceded by an inquiry at the CITT concerning the existence of serious injury or threat of such injury posed by the imports to production in Canada. Such an inquiry may be initiated either by order of the Minister of Finance, or upon the filing of a complaint by domestic producers.[92]

The process required of producers for a safeguard inquiry to be initiated and pursued by the CITT is in some ways a combination of what a complainant must do with both Revenue Canada and the CITT to pursue a dumping or subsidy complaint. A complaint filed with the CITT must contain certain details concerning production, market share, prices, etc.[93] The CITT then determines if the complaint is properly documented, and considers whether the evidence in the complaint discloses a reasonable indication of injury. If so, a public notice of the initiation of an inquiry will be issued. The inquiry process includes the filing of briefs and the holding of a public hearing. A report to the government will then be prepared and issued publicly.

Administrative Framework

The CITT may recommend the imposition of a surtax, quota, or a combination of the two in the form of a tariff-rate quota. It is then up to the federal cabinet to decide what action to take on the report. Surtaxes would be imposed under the authority of the *Customs Tariff* and administered by the customs arm of Revenue Canada. Permits in relation to quotas on imports would be administered by the Department of Foreign Affairs and International Trade pursuant to the *Export and Import Permits Act*.[94]

Timetable

The *CITT Act* provides the following deadlines for the processing of a safeguard complaint by a domestic producer:

Step	Maximum number of days
Decision by CITT that complaint received is properly documented	21 days
Decision by CITT that there is reasonable indication of serious injury from imports, and thus inquiry should be initiated	30 days
CITT conducts inquiry, including public hearing, and issues report	180 days

There is no time limit on government action to implement safeguard measures in response to a report.

Remedy

The procedures described above apply to the "basic" safeguard measures contemplated by the WTO Agreement on Safeguards, i.e., surtax and quotas. It is noteworthy that, pursuant to Canada's obligations under NAFTA, safeguard measures may not be applied against imports from a NAFTA country unless it has been determined that those imports are contributing "importantly" to the injury.[95] The procedures described above also apply to the operation of the special safeguard measures permitted by NAFTA in the form of a suspension in the reduction of customs duties provided under the Agreement.[96] There are also special provisions in the *Customs Tariff* allowing for the temporary "snap-back" of customs duties and other measures on certain NAFTA-origin fruits and vegetables and textile and apparel products.[97]

References

1. B.I.S.D. (15th Supp.) at 24 (1968) "The Kennedy Code."
2. B.I.S.D. (26th Supp.) at 171 (1978-79) "Revised Antidumping Code."
3. B.I.S.D. (26th Supp.) at 56 (1978-79) "Subsidies and Countervail Measures Code."
4. See an *Act to Amend the Customs Tariff*, 1897, S.C. 1904, c. 11, s. 19. The general principles applicable in the period before the 1969 amendments were set out in section 6 of *the Customs Tariff*, R.S.C. 1952, c. 20 and the regulations passed pursuant to section 6.
5. Subsection 6(1), *Customs Tariff, ibid*. In theory, once dumping was established, dumping duties were imposed automatically. However, it had to first be established that the goods were of a "class or kind" made in Canada, which in turn required that the quantity of such goods produced in Canada was equal to at least 10 percent of Canadian consumption (Order in Council, P.C. 1618, July 2, 1936). There were many complaints from producers about the practical difficulties involved in obtaining a ruling and, on the other hand, from Canada's trading partners about the automatic imposition of dumping duties. See Rodney de C. Grey, *The Development of the Canadian Antidumping System* (Montreal: Private Planning Association, 1973), 19-22.
6. The lack of an injury test was permitted under the GATT since Canada's antidumping statute was already in place when it joined the GATT in 1947. This meant that Canada's existing antidumping provisions were "grandfathered," such that Canada was not required to adhere to the requirement of Article VI of the GATT 1947 that "material injury" to a domestic industry be shown prior to the imposition of antidumping duties.
7. B.I.S.D. (15th Supp.) at 24 (1968) "The Kennedy Code."
8. R.S.C. 1970, c. A-15, as amended by R.S.C. 1970 (2nd Supp.) cc. 1, 10 and S.C. 1970-71, cc. 43, 63.
9. ADA, ibid., subsection 21(1). When SIMA, infra note 13, came into force, the Antidumping Tribunal was renamed the Canadian Import Tribunal.
10. On January 1, 1989, as a result of the Canadian International Trade Tribunal Act, R.S., 1985, c. 47 (4th Supp.), as amended, subsection 3(1), the function of the Canadian Import Tribunal was amalgamated with other Canadian trade boards and this plenary jurisdiction over trade-related matters was given to a new panel called the Canadian International Trade Tribunal.

    A number of provisions in the ADA made reference not only to the concept of "material injury" but also to the concept of "material retardation" of the establishment of production in Canada of like goods. The same is true of the successor legislation, SIMA. In accordance with general usage in the field, "material injury" is understood here to include the concept of "material retardation."
11. Government of Canada, Department of Finance, *Proposals on Import Policy: A Discussion Paper Proposing Changes to Canadian Import Legislation* (Ottawa: July, 1980) (the "White Paper").

12. The key recommendations in the White Paper affecting antidumping law were:
    - to establish stricter time limits in antidumping proceedings, in part by making dumping investigations and injury inquiries coincide to a greater degree;
    - to permit price undertakings;
    - to permit the use of a "basic price system" in certain circumstances; and
    - to incorporate the new definition of "regional industry" found in the 1979 GATT Code.
13. R.S.C. 1985, c. S-15, as am. R.S.C. 1985, c. 23 (1st Supp.); R.S.C. 1985, c.1 (2nd Supp.), ss. 197-212, 213(3); R.S.C. 1985, c. 47 (4th Supp.), s. 52; S.C. 1988, c. 65, ss. 22-45; S.C. 1990, c. 8, ss. 69-73; S.C. 1993, c. 44, ss. 201-223; S.C. 1994, c. 13, s. 7(1)(j); S.C. 1994, c. 47, s. 144-189.
14. In 1988, the Canadian Import Tribunal was amalgamated with other federal boards responsible for various international trade matters (such as tariff classification) to form the Canadian International Trade Tribunal. Revenue Canada remained responsible for dumping and subsidy determinations.
15. Article 1906 of the FTA states the intention of both parties to phase out the antidumping and countervailing duty rules under Chapter 19 and replace them with a new system within five to seven years. This goal was later abandoned, and the rules were incorporated permanently into Chapter 19 of NAFTA. Jon R. Johnson, in *The North American Free Trade Agreement: A Comprehensive Guide*, offers several possible explanations as to why Canadian negotiators accepted this result (pp. 512-513):

    First, the panel review process established under FTA Chapter 19 functioned better than expected and protected Canadian interests in a number of significant respects. Second, the introduction of some definition of countervailable or actionable subsidies set out in the *Agreement on Subsidies and Countervailing Measures* (the "1994 Subsidies Code") partially addressed Canadian concerns in this area. Third, it was probably unrealistic to expect the U.S. Congress in 1993 to approve any regime that restrained the application of U.S. trade remedy laws more than is done by NAFTA Chapter 19.

    NAFTA Article 1902 states that each Party reserves the right to apply its antidumping law to goods imported from the territory of any other Party, and that each Party further retains the right to modify its antidumping laws subject to a series of conditions to which the amending Party must adhere.
16. Pursuant to FTA Art. 1904.11, a party could opt for domestic judicial review in respect of a definitive decision if neither party requested a panel within the thirty-day time limit in 1904.4.
17. SOR/84-927 as amended.
18. R.S.C. 1985, c. 41 (3rd Supp.), as am. Section 59.1 authorizes the Governor in Council to issue an order subjecting goods to a surtax as a result of a report from the Minister of Finance or an inquiry of the Canadian International Trade Tribunal under ss. 20 or 26 of the Canadian International Trade Tribunal Act.
19. R.S.C. 1985, c. E-19, as amended.
20. R.S.C. 1985, c. 47 (4th Supp.), as amended.

21. *SIMA* s. 31(1).
22. *Ibid.*, s. 31(1)(a).
23. *Ibid.*, s. 31(1)(b).
24. *Ibid.*, s. 33(2).
25. *Ibid.*, s. 31(8).
26. The decision to initiate is an administrative act and does not determine the rights or interests of the person being investigated. A question of procedural fairness does not arise, and the action of the Deputy Minister is not reviewable. See *Hyundai Motor Co. et al. v. A.G. Can. et al.*, [1988] 1 F.C. 333 (F.C.T.D.).
27. *SIMA* s. 34(1)(b).
28. *Ibid.*, s. 37.
29. *Ibid.*, s. 36. See *Steel Wool in Pad Form from the United States* (Advice, September 13, 1988).
30. *Ibid.*, s. 31(1).
31. See *Photo Albums with Self-Adhesive Leaves from Thailand and the Philippines* (SOR, July 10, 1990); *Certain Hot Rolled, Heat Treated Carbon Steel Plate from the United States et. al.* (SOR, September 8, 1992); *Certain Hot-Rolled Carbon Steel Plate, Heat Treated or Not from Italy, Korea, Spain and Ukraine* (SOR, October 18, 1993).
32. *SIMA* s. 2(1) "properly documented"; s. 32. This deadline is probably of little relevance. Complaints are, in practice, often informally submitted in draft form first and are not "formally" submitted until Revenue Canada indicates that the most recent draft would be considered to be properly documented.
33. Pursuant to *SIMA* s. 39, the Deputy Minister may extend the investigation to 135 days. Section 40 ensures that time does not run when the Tribunal is considering a request to provide advice.
34. *SIMA* ss. 83 to 87.
35. See *R.W. Patten Distributors Ltd. v. Canada (Deputy Minister of National Revenue)*, [1995] F.C.J. No. 864 (QL). This was an application for judicial review of a decision of the Deputy Minister (DM) taken prior to the preliminary determination in the *Sugar* case, in which the DM denied the applicant access to confidential information appearing in a report prepared by Revenue. In dismissing the application, the court held that the DM had, in exercising his discretion, judged that the information already provided to the applicant was sufficient to allow the applicant to make proper representations. To interfere with the DM's decision would have been to judicialize the investigative process and unnecessarily hamper the investigative process established by Parliament.
36. *SIMA* s. 2(1). It is evident that the Canadian definition of "like goods" closely parallels the 1979 GATT Code's definition of "like product." However, the definition in *SIMA* goes further than the 1979 GATT Code (as does the definition in the U.S. statute), by referring not only to characteristics which closely resemble the goods being investigated but to "uses" as well.
37. The rules for determining normal value stipulate that a period of sixty days will apply in respect of domestic sales (*SIMA* s. 15(d)), but that a period of six months will apply in respect of a determination of profitability (*SIMA* s.16(2)(b)).

38. Complaints filed by industry associations and other entities have resulted in the initiation of investigations on numerous occasions. See *Sour Cherries* (SOR, June 22, 1988), *Fresh, Whole, Delicious Apples* (SOR, July 8, 1988), *Women's Leather Boots and Shoes* (SOR, August 25, 1989), *Machine Tufted Carpeting* (August 6, 1991), *Christmas Trees* (SOR, November 15, 1991), *Fresh Iceberg (Head) Lettuce* (SOR, June 8, 1992), *Black Granite Memorials* (SOR, December 22, 1993), *Dry Pasta* (SOR, August 30, 1995).
39. *SIMA* s. 31(2). These precise requirements were introduced into *SIMA* as part of the amendments which took place as a result of the *World Trade Organization Agreement Implementation Act*, S.C. 1994, c. C-57.
40. *Ibid.*, ss. 2(1) "domestic industry," 31(4) and (5).
41. *Ibid.*, ss. 24 to 30.
42. *Ibid.* Subsections 2(2) and (3) define "associated person" as including as little as a 5% equity interest (direct or indirect) between the exporter and importer.
43. *Ibid.*, subparagraph 25(b)(i).
44. *Ibid.*, subparagraph 25(b)(ii).
45. *Ibid.*, ss. 25(c)-(d).
46. *Ibid.*, s. 27.
47. *Ibid.*, s. 28.
48. *Ibid.*, s. 26.
49. *Ibid.*, s. 15.
50. The Deputy Minister may also use the price at which like goods were sold in any sale during the sixty-day period specified in s. 15(d) where the Deputy Minister is of the view that the price is generally representative of the sale prices of like goods sold during the period: *SIMA* s. 17(b).
51. *SIMA ss.* 15-18.
52. *SIMA* Regulations ss. 20–25.1.
53. *Ibid.*, paragraph 16(2)(b).
54. Revenue Canada's practice of using a fully allocated cost appears to be based on (*SIMA*) Regulation subparagraph 11(a)(i) which requires the inclusion of all costs "attributable to, or in any manner related to, the production of the goods." See the Binational Panel Review decision and reasons in *Gypsum from the United States of America* (BNP Secretariat File No. CDA-93-1904-01) at pages 28 and 29, where the panel indicates the following in relation to s. 11 of the *SIMA Regulations*:

   In our view, the only reasonable interpretation of the relevant provisions of SIMA and SIMA Regulations is that, in calculating normal values on a constructed-value basis, the costs to which the profit margin is to be added are what are commonly called "fully distributed" or "total" costs. For whatever reason and however incurred, the interest expenses in question ... became part of the actual costs of the corporation, and are 'attributable' ... The statutory direction that 'all other costs' are to be allocated indicates that every type of corporate expenditure, no matter how extraordinary or unrelated to production, is to be allocated to all products in some fair way.

55. Or another exporter of like goods in the same country: *SIMA* Regulations, subparagraph 9(1)(b)(iii).
56. See *Absorption-type Refrigerators from Poland* (SOR, April 19, 1989); *Portable File Cases from China* (SOR, February 5, 1996).
57. *SIMA* s. 29.
58. *SIMA* s. 49(1).
59. *SIMA* s. 42(1)(b) contemplates the imposition of retroactive antidumping duties in situations where a complainant successfully establishes a case of massive dumping. The elements of s. 42(1)(b) necessary for a finding of massive dumping were set out by the panel in *Photo Albums from Indonesia, Thailand and the Philippines* (NQ-90-003) at pages 13 and 14:

... the Tribunal [must be] satisfied that, either:
(a) there has occurred a considerable importation of like goods,
(b) that were dumped,
(c) which dumping has caused material injury (or would have caused material injury except for the application of antidumping measures),
(d) material injury has been caused by reason of the fact that the dumped goods
  (i) constitute a massive importation into Canada, or
  (ii) form part of a series of importations into Canada, which in the aggregate are massive and have occurred within a relatively short period of time, and
(e) it appears necessary to the Tribunal that duty be assessed on the imported goods in order to prevent the recurrence of that material injury;
or
(f) the importer of the dumped goods was or should have been aware that the exporter was practicing dumping and
(g) that the dumping would cause material injury, and
(h) material injury has been caused by reason of the fact that the dumped goods
  (i) constitute a massive importation into Canada, or
  (ii) form part of a series of importations into Canada that in the aggregate are massive and have occurred within a relatively short period of time, and
it appears necessary to the Tribunal that duty be assessed on the imported goods in order to prevent the recurrence of that material injury.

The Tribunal took the view that the necessary elements for a finding of massive dumping were reflected in the record, and retroactive duties were imposed. As a matter of public policy, this provision seeks to "deter...not only the importation of dumped goods from the subject countries, but also, the switching 'en masse' of those importations to other dumped sources . . . " thereby defeating *SIMA*. Massive dumping findings are rare. In *Caps, Lids and Jars* (NQ-95-001), the Tribunal was not convinced that the marked increase of imports of subject goods in the first half of 1995 warranted a finding of massive dumping. In any case, the Tribunal was of the view that such a finding was not necessary to prevent a recurrence of injury in the future. The Tribunal also declined to find massive dumping in *Dry*

Pasta from Italy (NQ-95-003), noting that such a finding was unlikely given that it had not found injury or the threat of injury.
60. See discussion of "like products" at IV.E, *infra*.
61. SIMA s.2(1.6), defining financial contribution for the purposes of the definition of "subsidy."
62. *Ibid.*, s. 2(1) "subsidy."
63. *Ibid.*, s.30.4(3): An amount of subsidy shall not include any amount that is attributable to a nonactionable subsidy.
64. *Ibid.*, s.2(1) "nonactionable" (a).
65. *Ibid.*, s.2(1) "prohibited subsidy" and "export subsidy."
66. See II.A.6.6 and 6.7, *supra*.
67. *SIMA Regulations* ss. 35.2, 36.
68. *Ibid.*, ss. 27 (SOR/95-26, s. 17) and 27.1 (SOR/95-26, s. 6).
69. *Ibid.*, ss. 28-30.
70. *Ibid.*, s. 31.1
71. *Ibid.*, s. 35.1
72. Nor has the issue of the effect of privatization in relation to such subsidies arisen in any recent subsidy cases.
73. *SIMA* ss. 49-54.
74. *Ibid.*, s. 41(1)(b).
75. *Canadian International Trade Tribunal* Act R.S.C., 1985, c.47 (4th Supp.) as amended., s. 46(1)(b).
76. *Ibid.*, s. 45(4)—"counsel," in relation to a party to proceedings, includes any person, other than a director, servant or employee of the party, who acts in the proceedings on behalf of the party.
77. In some cases, "domestic industry" has been interpreted as less than one-half of Canadian production. In *Stainless Steel Bars from India* (NQ-90-002), there was only one producer of the subject goods in Canada, and therefore that producer was considered to constitute the domestic industry. In *Lint Rollers from the United States of America* (NQ-90-004), one producer out of a total of four was held to constitute the domestic industry alone given that it was the largest producer of the subject goods in Canada.
78. *Cars Produced by or on Behalf of Hyundai Motor Co.* (CIT-13-87, Finding, March 23, 1988).
79. *SIMA* s. 2(1) "domestic industry" and s. 2(1.2). See *Gasoline Powered Chainsaws from the Federal Republic of Germany, U.S.A. and Sweden* (CIT-2-87), in which a majority of the Tribunal was not prepared to exclude the complainant or another company that joined the complainant, notwithstanding that both were at the time owned by a parent company responsible for more than half the dumped goods entering Canada. The majority stressed the discretionary nature of the exclusion provision in Article 4(1)(I) and said such an exclusion "would not only deny the existence of a domestic industry and deprive domestic producers of their right of protection . . . but it would also not recognize the realities of the interaction and competition among multi-national enterprises . . . ."

80. *SIMA* s. 2(1.1). In *Beer from the United States of America for Use or Consumption in the Province of British Columbia* (NQ-91-002), the Tribunal found that the complainants constituted a separate regional industry. The data showed that the combined sales of beer of the two largest complainants amounted to 95 percent of their total domestic sales. All of the domestic sales of the third and much smaller complainant were made in British Columbia. Further, the evidence showed that shipments of domestic production by the complainants to other provinces was minimal, and that demand for beer in British Columbia was not supplied by producers elsewhere in the country. Therefore, British Columbia was considered an isolated market and its beer production a regional industry. In *Fresh, Whole, Delicious Apples* (CIT-3-88), British Columbia was not considered a regional market since the producers in that province engaged in national marketing, and competed directly with American apples in the Ontario market. Further, it was found that the Ontario apple industry suffered material injury as well as, though to a lesser extent than, the industry in British Columbia.

81. *Steam Traps, . . . Produced by or on Behalf of Sarco Co. Inc., Allentown, Pennsylvania, United States of America* (ADT-10-76).

82. *Sarco Canada Limited* v. *Antidumping Tribunal*, [1979] 1 F.C. 247 (C.A.). In this case it was common ground that the complainant's goods were in fact not "identical in all respects" (paragraph 2(1)(a) of the ADA) to the dumped class of goods. Thus the Court of Appeal went on to consider whether the complainant's goods "closely resembled" the exported goods, as required by paragraph 2(1)(b) of the ADA's definition of "like goods":

In my view, in defining "like goods" the respondent was required to consider all of the characteristics or qualities of the goods, and not restrict itself to a consideration of something less than the totality of those characteristics. Accordingly, if the record disclosed that the Tribunal had restricted itself to "market considerations" in defining "like goods" I would agree with counsel for the applicant that the Tribunal had erred in law...Thus, while it seems evident that the Tribunal ascribed more weight to the question of functional similarity than to the other characteristics in defining "like goods," I am not able to say that it did not consider those other characteristics.

For recent appeals to the Tribunal which consider the meaning of "like goods," see *Madison Industrial* v. *Deputy M.N.R.* (1991), 5 T.T.R. (300) and *Fletcher Leisure Group Inc.* v. *Deputy M.N.R.* (AP-90-23 and AP-90-127, March 19, 1993), appealed successfully to the Federal Court of Appeal (October 28, 1996, A-320-93) returning the matter to the CITT for redetermination (the Tribunal erroneously took sales of goods to domestic customers which "closely resemble" goods sold to an associated domestic purchaser as being sales of like goods for the purposes of a section 15 calculation of normal value).

83. *SIMA* s. 97.

84. *SIMA Regulations*, s. 37.1.

85. *SIMA* s.42. Subparagraph 42(1)(a)(i) directs the Tribunal to inquire as to whether the dumping or subsidizing of the subject goods "has caused injury...*or* is threat-

ening to cause injury... ." In *Caps, Lids and Jars*, the Tribunal determined that this language requires it to make a finding in relation to past injury, or threat of future injury, but not both. In other words, the Tribunal need only proceed to consider the threat of future injury should it fail to make a finding of past injury. An application for judicial review challenging this alternative finding approach was filed with the Federal Court but later discontinued in March, 1996.

86. *Ibid.*, s.2 (1.5).
87. *Ibid.*, s. 8(2).
88. *Ibid.*, s. 2(1) "retardation."
89. *Ibid.*, s. 42.
90. *Ibid.*, s.45. See *Grain Corn* (Report on Public Interest, October 20, 1987), *Beer from the United States of America for Use or Consumption in the Province of British Columbia* (PI-91-001, November 25, 1991), *Preformed Fibreglass Pipe Insulation from the United States of America* (PB-93-001, January 28, 1994), *Caps, Lids and Jars* (PB-95-001), and *Refined Sugar* (PB-95-002). In *Sugar*, the Tribunal noted that the object in a public interest determination was to balance the various interests that would be affected by the imposition of duties. In the present case, the interests of the domestic industry and the sugar beet growers were balanced against those of the industrial users, resellers and consumers. This exercise was informed by the relevant provisions of the GATT and WTO, and the primary objective of SIMA, being the protection of the domestic industry from dumped and/or subsidized imports that have caused or are threatening to cause material injury. In assessing the impact of the imposition of duties, the Tribunal considered evidence of modest margin and volume increases experienced by the domestic industry, the relatively high price of raw sugar from the U.S. in comparison to the world price, and the relative bargaining power of the industrial users in relation to the domestic producers.
91. *Canadian International Trade Tribunal* Act R.S.C., 1985, c.47 (4th Supp.) as amended., ss. 23(1)-23(1.1). The right of private parties to request an inquiry existed previously for textile and clothing products.
92. *Ibid.*
93. *Canadian International Trade Tribunal Regulations*, s. 5(4) (SOR/93-600, s. 3; SOR/95-12, s. 3).
94. R.S.C. 1985, c. E-19, as amended.
95. *NAFTA*, Art. 801 and Art. 805 "contribute importantly."
96. Article 801.1 of *NAFTA* indicates that bilateral actions between Canada and the U.S. will continue to be governed by Chapter 11 of the *FTA*. Chapter 11 indicates that the right to initiate an action without the consent of the target country expires at the end of 1998, except for textile and apparel goods. As between Canada and Mexico, the right to initiate an action without consent expires at the end of 2003 pursuant to the definition of "transition period" under *NAFTA*, Art. 805.
97. *Customs Tariff*, R.S.C. 1985, c.41 (3rd Supp.), as am., ss. 60.2-60.4.

Chile

Raúl Santa Maria
Claro Y Cia
Santiago, Chile

HISTORY OF TRADE LAWS AND/OR REGULATIONS SINCE 1947

Before Law No. 18,525 was enacted in 1986, Chile had no regulations on antidumping or countervailing duties, even though Chile has been a member of the General Agreement on Tariffs and Trade (GATT) since 1949.

Notwithstanding the foregoing, there did exist traditional legal provisions that, to some extent, established procedures and created instruments aimed at attacking unfair trade practices without, however, defining them as dumping, subsidies, or otherwise. As discussed below, these traditional regulations reflected two main principles: international reciprocity and protection of the domestic industry.

Law No. 4,321

Article 15 of Law No. 4,321 of 1928 set forth a minimum tariff, which was applicable to goods imported from nations that applied to Chilean goods an equal minimum tariff and that did not:
(i) increase tariffs on products exported from Chile;
(ii) make tariffs applicable to the products that were exempt from tariffs;
(iii) offer exceptional tariff reductions on similar products from other countries; or
(iv) prevent the importation of domestic fruits and products by means of any restrictive measures.

The same provision established that, otherwise, the President of the Republic would have the right to apply to products imported from such countries a surcharge of up to 50 percent on the duties set forth in the tariff schedule, or to impose an ad-valorem tax of up to 15 percent on goods exempt from tariffs or from an equivalent specific duty. Similarly, the President of the Republic was given the right to apply, should the national interest require, a temporary and exceptional reduction of tariffs that could not go below 25 percent of the tariffs established in the tariff schedule. Furthermore, the President of the Republic was authorized to increase by up to 35 percent the tariffs on products that were similar to those produced or manufactured in Chile, where Chilean production was able to satisfy Chilean domestic demand for the product. This authorization was subordinated to the regulations that were issued in each case in order to regulate the price of such products.

It is apparent from the description above that Chilean law granted the President of the Republic the right to determine those situations in which there was no reciprocity in international trade, or in which the interest of the domestic economy might be affected by imports, or in which Chilean production was able to satisfy domestic demand. The investigation into these situations, which the President of the Republic carried out through the Ministry of Finance, could include dumping, unfair competition, subsidies, distortions of the world economy, and other unspecified situations.

Law No. 13,305

Under Section IV of Law No. 13,305, enacted in 1959, the President of the Republic is authorized to increase by up to 50 percent the tariffs imposed on the importation of products that compete with Chilean products deemed essential for public health. The same section authorizes the President of the Republic to suspend or reduce tariffs imposed on the importation of such goods if they are in short supply.

Law No. 16,464

Article 185 of Law No. 16,464, enacted in 1966, abrogated the tariff schedule established by Law No. 4,321 with a tariff schedule based on the guidelines of the Brussels Council on Customs Cooperation. In addition, Article 186 gave the President of the Republic the right to release, suspend, or reduce, in accordance with the nation's needs, tariffs, taxes, and other encumbrances imposed by the Chilean Customs Service. Finally, Article 188 provided that the President of the Republic would put into effect the new customs tariff schedule. In the exercise of this right, the President of the Republic issued the Executive Decree No. 10 of 1967, which set forth the new customs tariff schedule based on the one adopted by the Brussels Council on Customs Cooperation signed by Chile. Section 2 of the new customs tariff schedule bases valuation of goods on "normal price," which is the price at which these goods might have sold to an independent purchaser under free market conditions. This concept is known as the "Brussels Value," which presupposes independence between seller and purchaser and free market conditions for the transaction. The Brussels Value applied by Law No. 16,464 includes all behavior that could affect the free market, such as subsidies and dumping.

Notwithstanding the foregoing, these provisions do not establish specific procedures or remedies for taking action against unfair trade, except for those cases that may qualify as crime or fraud, and that result in damage to the State by reducing the revenues obtained from customs duties.

Decree-Law No. 211

Decree-Law No. 211, issued in 1973, established certain rules for the defense of free competition. Article 1 of the Decree provides that any person who individually or collectively carries out or enters into any act or agreement aimed at preventing free economic competition, whether domestic or related to international trade activities, will be punished with a medium-term prison sentence ranging from sixty-one days to five years. To date, this provision has not been applied to unfair foreign trade practices.

Law No. 18,525

In 1986, Law No. 18,525 was enacted. Article 6 of Law No. 18,525 defines "Customs Value." This definition expands on the concept of "Brussels Value" contained in existing law, and is used in proceedings on dumping, subsidies, and other unfair trade practices. In fact, Article 6 provides that whenever a sale is carried out under free market conditions, the "Customs Value" thereof shall be determined based on the transaction price, that is, on the real price paid or payable for the goods when such goods are sold for importation into the country. In addition, Article 6 provides that a transaction is carried out under free market conditions when the buyer and seller are independent of each other; the purchase price of the goods is the only payment due by the buyer; and there exists between them and their associates no commercial relationship other than that created by the sale of the relevant goods or products. For this purpose, two individuals or entities are commercially related if one of them has an interest in any kind of business carried out by the other, or if both have a common business interest, or if a third party has a direct or indirect business interest in each of them.

Three types of issues arise under the definition of "Customs Value:"

Goods whose customs value declared is not real

If the customs value declared by the interested parties is not real, due to the fact that the price of the goods has been distorted because of the lack of real independence between the buyer and the seller in accordance with the above-mentioned terms, the law grants the National Customs Service the right to establish such value, taking into account the elements of the sale or transaction that are inconsistent with the concept of a free market. In accordance with this procedure, the National Customs Service must establish the real value of the goods, taking into consideration the customs value of identical goods, or if these are not available, of similar goods sold at the same commercial level as those goods that are being valued. To make such determination, the Service may also take into consideration reports issued by manufacturers, or it may request background information from domestic or foreign public organizations. The values thus established will constitute the base for the application of tariffs.

Goods whose normal transaction prices have suffered temporary reduction

Law No. 18,525 grants the President of the Republic the right to establish a minimum customs value (*Valores Aduaneros Mínimos*) for those goods that, owing to circumstantial effects of international markets, are subject to a temporary reduction in their normal transaction prices, causing actual or imminent serious injury to domestic production.

In these instances, although there may be no collusion between buyer and seller aimed at altering the "customs value" of the products, and there may be no subsidies or other practices affecting free market conditions, there may still exist temporary circumstances, such as an overproduction or oversupply of certain goods, which create a temporary reduction in their normal transaction prices.

Goods whose entry into the country causes injury

The President of the Republic may apply tariff surcharges of 3, 5, 8, 10, 12, 15, 18, 20 or 24 percent as antidumping duties or countervailing duties on the importation of goods whose entry into the country causes severe current or imminent injury to domestic production, when the goods are imported at reduced prices as a consequence of artificial practices in their respective markets.

The establishment of a minimum "customs value" or the application of surcharges by the President of the Republic, must be effected after the issuance of a report by a special committee, the National Commission, created for this purpose.

The National Commission is in charge of investigating price distortions in imported goods. This commission is composed of the National Economic Prosecutor, who acts as chairperson; two representatives of the Central Bank of Chile, who are appointed by the Bank's Board of Directors; and one representative each from the Ministry of Finance, the Ministry of Agriculture, and the Ministry of Economy, all of whom are appointed by a resolution that is published in the Official Gazette. The Commission is also composed of the National Director of Customs, and a representative of the Ministry of Foreign Affairs.

DUMPING INVESTIGATIONS

Antidumping investigation procedures are provided for by Article 11 of Law No. 18,525, as complemented by Executive Decree No. 575, issued by the Ministry of Finance and published in the Official Gazette of August 20, 1993.

Application

In accordance with the provisions of Article 10 of Executive Decree No. 575, any interested party—individual or entity—may report to the Commission any price distortions in imported goods. For these purposes, the interested party must submit an application to the President of the Commission, and fill in the form provided by that office. The applicant shall provide the following information:
- Evidence of price distortion: Price distortions in imported goods may be caused, *inter alia*, by subsidies or dumping. The term subsidy refers to any direct or indirect bounty or grant that a government gives or may have given for the manufacture, production, or exportation of a product in its country of origin or exportation, including any special subsidy given for the transportation of these goods, any internal price support, or the forgiveness or noncollection of public taxes that would have been applicable otherwise.

    Products are dumped when they have been brought into the country at a price that is below normal market price. Thus, dumping exists when the export price to Chile is lower than the comparable price, in the course of normal business operations, of a similar product sold in the exporting country under competitive market conditions.

When similar products are not sold in the course of normal business operations in the domestic market of the exporting country, or when a special situation in that market, such as low sales volumes, does not allow an adequate comparison, the dumping margin is established by making a comparison with:
  (i) the comparable price of a similar product when exported to a third country, provided that such price is representative; or
  (ii) the cost of production of the goods in the country of origin plus a reasonable amount assigned to administrative, sales and any other costs, and profits.
- Evidence of current or imminent injury, or threat of serious injury, to domestic production; and
- Demonstration of a cause-effect relationship between imports and the alleged injury.

Initiation

Once the application has been submitted, the technical department of the Commission must certify the circumstances of the price distortion and immediately inform the applicant of the results in writing. A report regarding the price distortion must be submitted to the Commission on the next working day after the certification.

The Commission may also decide to carry out an investigation on its own initiative. In this case, once the Commission has obtained all relevant data, it will act in accordance with the same procedure established in the case of an investigation initiated by report.

Any application that does not comply with the requirements established in the law will be returned by the technical department to the party concerned within a period of ten working days following the submission thereof. Any disputes that may arise with regard to the return of the data appearing in the application must be resolved by the President of the Commission, who will make a final decision.

In accordance with the terms of Article 12, the Commission will decide whether to initiate an investigation within five working days following the formalization of the report, which will be published in the Official Gazette. This publication will contain an excerpt of the data contained in the report, including:

- the date of submission of the relevant report;
- the goods or products identified in the report and their corresponding tariff schedule;
- identification of the petitioner(s);
- identification of the manufacturers, exporters or importers of the goods;
- the country of origin of the relevant goods;
- a description of the unfair trade practice used or a statement of the measure that resulted in the relevant price distortion;
- a preliminary analysis of the factors that would contribute to damage to domestic production;
- the Commission's statement of whether an investigation has been undertaken; and
- the address of the technical department wherein any interested party may file statements regarding the report or request a hearing.

Consultations With Third Countries

The Commission shall inform the Foreign Affairs Ministry of any report requesting an investigation so that the Ministry can notify the relevant countries of the products that are to be investigated.

Submission of Information

Within a period of thirty days from the date of publication of the notice of investigation in the Official Gazette, the Commission must receive from the technical department all the information that the parties or any interested third party may consider relevant to submit for investigation, and request any other additional information it deems necessary.

Decision on the Part of the Commission

Within a period of ninety days from the date of publication of the notice of investigation in the Official Gazette, the Commission must issue a ruling based on the information it has received and the investigations it has conducted. Should the Commission find, on the basis of the examined data, the existence of price distortions relating to the imported goods, and that these distortions cause serious injury to domestic production, it will so state in the resolution it issues on the subject, as well as recommend the establishment of a minimum custom value, referred to in Article 9 of Law No. 18,525, or a tariff surcharge referred to in Article 10 thereof. In any case, the measure recommended may not exceed the margin of the price distortion. Should the Commission determine that the information examined is not sufficient to prove the existence of distortions in the price of imported products, or that these distortions do not have the requisite injurious effect, it will issue a corresponding resolution ending the investigation.

Presidential Decision

A resolution of the Commission that establishes the existence of price distortions relating to the imported good shall be sent to the President of the Republic through the Minister of Finance, who will also inform the Commission of the final decision made by the President of the Republic. The Commission will make available to any interested parties an excerpt of the resolution, once the corresponding decree is published in the Official Gazette.

Provisional Measures

Before issuance of the resolution referred to in the preceding section, the Commission may, at any stage of the investigation, and within a period of sixty days following the opening of the proceedings, request through the Minister of Finance that the President of the Republic establish a provisional minimum customs value or surcharge according to sections 9 and 10 of Law No. 18,525, whenever necessary to avoid or prevent any injury to domestic production.

The surcharge or minimum customs value applied in accordance with the preceding paragraph will be imposed for a period not to exceed the date of the issuance of the final decision. Payment, should the provisional measure remain valid, is due on the date of the relevant Import Statement (*Declaración de Importación*).

An excerpt of the resolution issued by the Commission will be provided to interested parties after the decision of the President of the Republic regarding the application of provisional measures has been published in the Official Gazette. This excerpt will contain a summary of the conditions that the Commission has considered to reach a preliminary decision regarding the existence of a price distortion and the damage or threat of damage to domestic production caused thereby.

If the Commission decides, once the investigation is concluded, that there is no price distortion regarding the goods for which provisional measures were requested, or that the distortions do not cause current or imminent damage to domestic production, the Commission may request the President of the Republic to revoke such measures. An excerpt of the resolution issued by the Commission will be made available to the interested parties once the decision of the President of the Republic has been published in the Official Gazette. This excerpt will contain a summary of the conditions that the Commission has considered in modifying or suspending the provisional measures. In fact, the Commission may, at any time, request through the Minister of Finance that the President of the Republic suspend or modify any provisional measures.

Once the Commission has issued its ruling, the persons who might have suffered the effects of provisional measures that have been revoked or modified may seek compensation for the amounts paid or the amounts paid in excess, if there is no distortion in the price of the goods for which a provisional measure was requested, or if the existing distortion was considered not a cause of serious, current, or imminent injury to domestic production.

The amounts subject to restitution accrue regular interest. The right to refund must be exercised within a ninety-day period from the date on which the restitution was made mandatory.

Duties, taxes, and other tariffs that result from provisional surcharges are imposed by means of depositing the percentage that should be applied in the import declaration and the amount to be paid on the payment receipt. This amount will be the result of adding the tariff surcharge to the custom value to be applied to the corresponding item.

Should a refund of duties and other tariffs that result from the provisional minimum customs value or surcharge be applicable, the importer must submit a written application to the Regional Director or Customs Director General to whom the respective declaration was submitted, enclosing an authorized copy of the corresponding Import Declaration.

SUBSIDY INVESTIGATIONS

Executive Decree No. 3,567 of January 30, 1981, which approved the Subsidies Code, Executive Decree No. 300 of the Ministry of Foreign Affairs of January 13, 1981, which enacted the same Code and the Agreement on Interpretation and Application of Articles VI, XVI, and XXII of the GATT, are all enforceable in Chile. In fact, the criteria listed in the Subsidies Code for establishing whether a particular governmental action qualifies as an unfair trade practice is applicable in Chile, not only with respect to Chile's relations with other signatory countries, but also internally, because the criteria constitute a law of the Republic and, as such, are enforceable at the domestic level.

Criteria for the Appraisal of Subsidy Claims

The Subsidy Commission created by Executive Decree No. 3,567 adopted certain criteria regarding the appraisal of subsidy claims. These criteria are still in force, notwithstanding the fact that such commission was replaced by the Commission created by Section 11 of Law No. 18,525.

The procedure for investigating the existence of subsidies with respect to imported goods is regulated by Article 11 of Law No. 18,525 and Executive Decree No. 575 issued by the Ministry of Finance, published in the Official Gazette of August 20, 1993. Thus, the procedure is identical to the procedure applicable to investigations regarding other price distortions.

Types of Export Subsidies

A subsidy is any measure, adopted by a relevant government or organization, that grants special benefits to a company or industry that directly or indirectly results in the increase of the export of a given product or in the decrease of the import of such product.

Export subsidies include, among others, the following:
- governmental incentives for exportation, which may consist of direct transfers from the State to the exporter in relation to the exporter's export performance. In many cases, the subsidy involves a refund of indirect taxes or of customs duties; nevertheless, the subsidy normally corresponds to the previously-fixed tariff percentage, which may not have a direct relation to the taxes levied or the duties actually paid by the exporter.

    This category also includes the supply, whether by the government or by an agency thereof, of imported or domestic products or services for use in the production of exported goods on terms more favorable than those applied to the supply or production of similar or competitive products or services.
- credit incentives for exports at preferential interest rates that are lower than those normally found on the international market; and
- tax incentives such as direct tax exemptions, refunds of indirect taxes in an amount that exceeds the sums actually collected when the products are sold in the domestic market, or refunds of import duties exceeding the amount of money actually earned on the exportation of primary products that are incorporated to the exported product.

ELEMENTS OF INJURY ANALYSIS

Volume

With respect to the volume of imported products, it is important to consider whether there has been a dramatic increase in absolute terms, in relation to similar domestic production or in relation to apparent domestic consumption.

Upon analyzing the effect of importation on national demand and consumption, the degree of competition in the domestic market should be considered. Also to be considered is whether the increase in importation has caused a reduction in domestic production or prevented the establishment of a new domestic industry.

Effect on Prices

With respect to the effect on prices for similar domestic products, the following issues must be considered:
(i) whether the price of the imported product under investigation is significantly lower than the price of the similar domestic product; or
(ii) whether exports have caused a reduction in the prices of similar domestic products or prevented a significant increase in the price of such products that otherwise would have occurred.

Effect on Domestic Product

With respect to the appraisal of the effect of the imported product on domestic production, an investigation of all the factors and relevant economic indices that influence that production must be undertaken, including:
(i) the actual or eventual decrease in production, sales, market participation, benefits, productivity, performance of investments, or the use of installed capacity;
(ii) the factors that have important effects on domestic prices; and
(iii) the actual or eventual adverse effects on cash flow, assets, employment, salaries, growth, capital availability, and, in the case of agriculture, if there has been an increase in the cost of governmental support programs.

In addition, the analysis must consider other factors that might affect domestic production and cause injury, but that might not be attributable to the existence of subsidized or dumped imports. These factors may include the volume and prices of fairly-traded imports, variations in consumption structure, reduction of demand, restrictive commercial practices of the foreign and domestic producers, competition between foreign and domestic producers, and evolution of technology.

THREAT OF INJURY

The existence of a threat of injury must be proven based on facts and not simply on allegations, conjecture, or remote possibilities. The circumstances that would cause injury must be clearly foreseen and imminent. Consequently, there should be convincing evidence that, in the near future, there will be a substantial increase in the importation of dumped or subsidized products, which will have a significant effect on domestic prices and production.

Colombia

Gabriel Ibarra
Castro Escobar & Ibarra Abogados
Bogotá, Colombia

HISTORY AND OVERVIEW OF TRADE REMEDY LAWS AND/OR REGULATIONS SINCE 1947

Discussion of Country's Accession to GATT/WTO and Antidumping and Subsidies Code

Subsidies code

Colombia's participation in the GATT was approved by Law No. 49 of 1981, thereby making applicable the provisions contained in Article VI of the GATT. In 1990, Colombia attempted to adhere to the Antidumping (AD) and Countervailing Duty (CVD) Law, but the United States resisted this attempt and entered into negotiations with Colombia to obtain certain commitments from Colombia.

As a result, Colombia signed a guarantee by which it incurred the following obligations:
(i) to eliminate the interest benefits that were being granted to exporters through Proexpo;[1]
(ii) to adjust CERT[2] methodology; and
(iii) to eliminate the Replacement Programs for machinery.

Antidumping law

Colombia adhered to the norms of the GATT Antidumping Code in 1993. This agreement was never ratified by the Colombian Congress.

Nevertheless, Colombia subscribed to the new GATT/WTO Agreement with the approval of Law 170 of 1994.

Discussion of Evolution of Trade Remedy Laws and/or Regulations

Taking into account the policy of protectionism in effect until 1990, Colombia was never concerned with adopting antidumping mechanisms. Business was conducted by means of licenses and high customs duties.

With the adoption of the economic opening, the Colombian government issued Law 1500 of 1990, which was Colombia's first regulation concerning antidumping and countervailing duties. Responsibility for the application of this law is placed in the hands of the Foreign Trade Ministry and the Colombian Foreign Trade Institute (INCOMEX).

Decree 299 of 1995 is the antidumping and countervailing duty statue in effect at the present time. In addition to the antidumping and countervailing duty law, Law 7 of 1991 creates the framework law for foreign trade, and confers upon the government the power to regulate the protection of national producers against unfair international trade practices. Colombian antidumping and countervailing duty law is applicable to those goods imported from countries outside the Andean Group.[3]

In the case of merchandise entering Colombia from other member countries of the Andean Group, Decision No. 283 of the Cartagena Pact takes priority over national legislation and is administered by the Cartagena Agreement Board.

The competent authority for performing antidumping or countervailing duty investigations is INCOMEX, through its Trade Practices Division, which determines the existence of dumping or of countervailable subsidies, injury or threat of injury, and the causal link between them. Once INCOMEX completes its investigation, it convenes the Trade Practices Committee to report on the conclusions of the investigations.[4] The Trade Practices Committee must take into account the opinion of the Superintendence of Industry and Commerce (Colombian Governmental Anti-Trust Agency) concerning the effect of the trade remedy on competitive conditions in Colombia. Once the Committee issues its decision, the Foreign Trade Ministry is charged with its implementation.

ANTIDUMPING AND COUNTERVAILING DUTY INVESTIGATIONS

Determination of Dumping or Subsidy

Initiation of investigation

The procedure may be initiated by the administrative authority on its own initiative or by request of the petitioning party.

INCOMEX is responsible for initiating an investigation when requested to do so by national producers representing the domestic producers affected by importation of similar products made within twelve months of the request.

The petition must, at a minimum, contain the following:
(i) identification of the petitioner;
(ii) description of the merchandise;
(iii) listing of countries of origin (exporting countries);
(iv) listing of name and place of residence of importers and exporters;
(v) description of exportation prices—market value;
(vi) description of the "dumping;" and
(vii) description of injury or threat of injury.

No countervailing duty investigation has been initiated in Colombia.

Participation of parties and their counsel

Domestic petitioners

The petitioning parties may participate:
(i) directly throughout the investigation;
(ii) through an association of producers; or
(iii) through an attorney at law.

Domestic respondents, including industrial users

Domestic producers are notified through public notice of the initiation of the investigation and have forty days to submit any information they consider pertinent to the investigation.

Foreign respondents

Within seven days of the initiation of the investigation, a copy of the notice of initiation, together with questionnaires, must be sent to the exporters. These questionnaires must be returned within forty days of transmittal and must be submitted in Spanish, either directly or through counsel.

In countervailing duty investigations, INCOMEX must give governments of the countries whose products are under investigation the opportunity to consult for up to thirty days in order to clarify the facts of the case and to reach a mutually satisfactory solution.

Access to information developed in proceedings

Nonproprietary information

Consistent with Colombian law generally,[5] the AD/CVD statute provides interested parties unrestricted access to the public case-file and a photocopy of any document contained therein may be requested.

Business proprietary information

Pursuant to Article 43 of Law 299, all the documents submitted as confidential by the authorities, the petitionaries or by the interested parties, will be segregated in a separate file from the public file. Nonconfidential summaries of confidential information must be included in the public case-file. If INCOMEX believes that information for which confidential treatment is requested does not qualify as confidential, it may request the supplier of such information to relinquish its confidentiality.

Under Colombian law, there is no provision, as in the United States, for restricted access to confidential information, through Administrative Protective Order; consequently, in Colombia, counsel may not have access to the confidential information.

Definitions

Like product

The definition of a "like product" conforms in general terms to that established by the GATT.

Even though there are general criteria to determine a product's similarity to another product, Colombia has not established a detailed classification system. Therefore, the question of a given product's similarity must be considered on a case-by-case basis. INCOMEX has been quite strict in some cases, and very lax in others.

Length of investigation

INCOMEX has a maximum limit of eight months from the date of publication of the notice of initiation to conclude its investigation.

Domestic industry and petition requirements for industrial support

An antidumping or countervailing duty petition must be supported by a majority of the domestic industry affected by dumped or subsidized products imported within the twelve months prior to the filing of the petition.

The petitioning parties must meet the following criteria:
(i) They must represent 25 percent of the national production in terms of the volume of production of the identical or like product.
(ii) At least 50 percent of the domestic producers of said product must support the petition.

Related parties

Parties are deemed to be related where:
(i) One company controls the other company directly or indirectly.
(ii) Both companies are directly or indirectly controlled by a third party.

(iii) Both companies control a third party directly or indirectly, provided that the parties do not engage in arm's length transactions with each other.

Countervailable subsidies

An import is considered to have been subsidized when the production, fabrication, transportation, or exportation of that product, or of its raw materials and inputs, has received, directly or indirectly, any kind of premium, assistance, award, stimulus, or incentive from the government, or governmental entities, of the country of origin or exportation.

Noncountervailable subsidies (green light)

GATT standards are applicable to "green light" subsidies, which are not further defined under Colombian law.

Calculation of dumping margins or subsidies

GATT definitions are applicable to the calculation of export price and normal value in antidumping investigations and to the analysis of subsidies.

The following are elements of the antidumping methodology:

Adjustments to export price

(i) expenses incurred by the exporter, taking into account the conditions agreed upon with the buyer for the delivery of the product (FOB, CIF, etc.);
(ii) direct expenses for guarantees, technical assistance, and other post-sales services; and
(iii) expenses that represent commissions paid for the sales in question as well as amounts paid in salaries to full-time sales personnel.

Adjustments to normal value

(i) adjustments for differences in product characteristics; and
(ii) import duties or indirect taxes that must be paid on a similar product and on the materials that have been physically incorporated into said product, when it is destined for consumption in its country of origin or exportation, and which are not paid or refunded when the product is exported to Colombia.

Adjustments for sales expenses

(i) expenses for transportation, insurance, maintenance, unloading, and the costs of accessories needed to transfer the product from the exporter's warehouse to the first unrelated buyer;

(ii) wrapping and packaging expenses;
(iii) credit expenses;
(iv) commissions paid on the sales in question and salaries paid to full-time sales personnel; and
(v)   direct expenses incurred in supplying guarantees, technical assistance, and other post-sales services.

Currency conversion

The investigation will rely on the average exchange rate for the national currency during the period of investigation.

Sampling

There is no established methodology for sampling and, consequently, general accounting rules are used.

Nonmarket economy methodology

The surrogate country analysis is used in the case of antidumping investigations of imports from a nonmarket economy. In such cases, normal value is established by the price of a similar product sold for consumption in a surrogate market economy. The investigative authority may also use any other system it chooses.

In a case involving imports of phosphoric acid from the People's Republic of China, the United States was chosen as the substitute surrogate country, for the following reasons:
(i) The United States is a market economy.
(ii) The United States is one of the chief producers of phosphoric acid in the world; thus U.S. prices reflect economies of scale.

Use of facts available

Colombian authorities will rely on facts available pursuant to GATT rules when they are unable to obtain timely or adequate information from the parties. Information for which confidential treatment is requested but not granted will not be relied upon in an investigation. Whenever INCOMEX is unable to verify information provided by a respondent, INCOMEX will rely on facts available which, absent evidence that is inaccurate, means the information contained in the petition.

Price undertakings and other agreements to suspend investigation

During the investigation, the competent authority of the country of origin or exportation, or the producers or exporters of such country, may propose a revision of the export price or even a suspension of exportation to Colombia.

The following offers will not be considered:
(i) those that do not include the relevant information and a verification authorization to enable Colombian authorities to fulfill their responsibilities; and
(ii) those that offer quantitative limitations.

Effect of Antidumping or Countervailing Order

Effective date
Retroactivity, if any

Although GATT norms apply, there are no cases in Colombia in which duties have been applied retroactively.

Duration

An antidumping duty will remain in effect for a maximum period of five years, unless the conditions giving rise to the duty persist beyond that period.

Enforcement, including rules to prevent circumvention or orders

The application of an antidumping duty is carried out through the National Customs and Duties Department.

Antievasion measures provide that when an antidumping duty is imposed upon a product, said duty should include the parts, pieces, or components destined for assembly or finishing in Colombia, if it can be established that these pieces will in any way serve in the manufacture of products similar to products that have duties imposed upon them.

INJURY ANALYSIS

The analysis of dumping or subsidies and of injury are performed simultaneously by the same administrative authority—INCOMEX.

OTHER TRADE REMEDIES

Safeguard measures

Law 809, enacted in 1994, is Colombia's first law and provides for safeguard measures. A safeguard measure applicable to a product imported from a member country of the Andean Pact must be approved by the Cartagena Agreement Board.

Applications for safeguard measures must meet the following requirements:

(i) The petitioners must represent a substantial part of the national production of the product in question.

(ii) There must be a substantial increase in the importations of said product and serious injury to national production.

(iii) Massive quantities of said importations must constitute the main cause of serious injury to national production.

In contrast to the antidumping procedures, in the case of safeguard application, it is not necessary that the imported product be identical or similar to the domestic product; it must simply be directly competitive.

Safeguard measures are considered by INCOMEX. Once the investigation is completed, INCOMEX provides its conclusions and recommendations to the Committee of Foreign Trade, Customs and Duties.[6] The Foreign Trade Board of Directors makes the final decision.

A provisional safeguard measure may be applied if justified by critical circumstances. To date, provisional safeguard measures have been imposed on rice from Vietnam and Venezuela, propylene from Ecuador, steel bars from Venezuela, footwear from the PRC, and textiles, clothing, triplex, and "agglomerates" (a special kind of tightly packed wood) from countries of the Andean Pact.

Colombia's safeguard measures are under review for possible reform.

Remedy

The safeguard measure consists of a customs duty imposed upon the imported product determined to be the cause of the injury.

Only in exceptional circumstances may a quantitative restriction be imposed upon the importation of said product as a measure necessary to avoid the serious injury to the national production.

References

1. Proexpo was a Colombian entity whose function was to promote exports.
2. The certificate of reimbursement tributary (CERT), created by Law 48 of 1983 as an instrument of support for exporters, includes two objectives:
    a. To stimulate exports through the reimbursement of sums equivalent to all or a proportion of indirect taxes, rates, and contributions paid by the exporter; and,
    b. To promote, based on the value exported, those activities that tend to boost the volume of exports.

3. The Andean Group consists of Colombia, Venezuela, Ecuador, Bolivia, and Peru, although in April, 1997, Peru announced its intention to withdraw from the Andean Group.
4. The Trade Practices Committee is composed of the Foreign Trade vice president who serves as chairman, the Director of the Colombian Foreign Trade Institute (INCOMEX), a delegate from the Foreign Trade Board of Directors, the Ministry's General Director of Negotiations, the Viceminister or assistant director from the entity most closely related to the affected products, and one of the advisors from the Foreign Trade Board of Directors.
5. Article 74 of the National Constitution provides that all persons have a right to access documents in administrative proceedings, except in cases established by law.
6. The members of the Board of Directors of Foreign Trade are the President of the Republic, the Foreign Relations Minister, the Finance and Public Credit Minister, the Agriculture Minister, the Economic Development Minister, the Foreign Trade Minister, the Mines and Energy Minister, the Chief of the National Planning Department, the Director of the Banco de la República, the Director of the Foreign Trade Bank of Colombia–BANCOLDEX, and the board counsel.

Table 1. Colombian Antidumping Cases

COUNTRY	PRODUCT	PROVISIONAL MEASURES/AMOUNT OF DUTY	DEFINITIVE MEASURE/AMOUNT OF DUTY
Germany	Electric Lead Accumulators	The continuation of the investigation was ordered without the imposition of provisional duties.	The investigation was completed, and the request for the imposition of definitive antidumping duties was denied.
United States	Polypropylene-Homopolymer	The equivalent of the difference between the base price (US $549.9/ton) and the declared FOB/ton, price, without exceeding the dumping margin (US $64.56).	The equivalent between the base price (US $549.29/ton) bulk FOB and the declared FOB/ton, price, bulk, without exceeding the dumping margin estimated at US $142.08/ton, bulk.
Holland	Compound Fertilizers NPK 10-30-10	The continuation of the investigation was ordered without the imposition of provisional duties.	The investigation was completed, and the request for the imposition of definitive antidumping duties was denied.
Mexico	Corn Derivates: 1. Starches and Feculas 2. Liquid Glucose	1. The equivalent to the difference between the base price (US $288.04/ ton) and the declared FOB/ton price, without exceeding the dumping margin (US $66.62/ton). 2. The equivalent of the difference between the base price (US $353.46/ton) and the declared FOB/ton price without exceeding the dumping margin (US $75.73/ton).	
Cuba	Steel Bars	The continuation of the investigation was ordered without the imposition of provisional duties.	The investigation was completed without the imposition of definitive antidumping duties.
Belgium	Coffee Grade Fertilizers NPK 17-6-18-2	The equivalent of the difference between the base price (US $160.95/ton) and the declared FOB/ton price, without exceeding the dumping margin (US $64.56/ton).	The equivalent of the difference between the base price (US $160.50/ton) and the declared FOB price.
Belgium*	Orthophosporic Acid	The equivalent of the difference between the base price (US $847.93/ton) and the declared FOB/ton price, without exceeding the dumping margin (US $309.76/ton).	The equivalent of the difference between the base price and the declared FOB/ton price, as long as the base price be greater than the declared price.
United States*	Orthophosporic Acid	The equivalent to the difference between the base price (US $866.73/ton) and the declared FOB/ton price, as long as the base price be greater than the declared price.	1. The difference between the base price (US $639.15/ton) and the declared FOB/ton price multiplied by 1.3 2. The result of multiplying the FOB value by FMC Corp. 8.51% Monsanto Chemical 20.83% Transmarketing Houston 37.30%, Other Exporters 24.33%.
United States	Ethyl Acetate	The equivalent to the difference between the base price (US $676.38/ton), and the declared price, without exceeding the dumping margin (US $478.24/ton).	The equivalent to the difference between the base FOB price (US $792.85/ton), bulk, and the declared price without exceeding the dumping margin (US $478.24/ton).
United Kingdom	Chromite Plats	The continuation of the investigation was ordered without the imposition of provisional duties.	The investigation was completed, and the request for the imposition of definitive antidumping duties was denied.
United States	Chromite Plats	The continuation of the investigation was ordered, without the imposition of provisional duties.	The equivalent to the difference between the base price (US $649.28/ton) and the declared FOB/ton, price without exceeding the dumping margin (US $650.52/ton).
Vietnam	Whitened or Semiwhitened Rice	The continuation of the investigation was ordered, without the imposition of provisional duties.	The investigation was completed, without the imposition of definitive antidumping duties.

*These cases are the subject of review, based in Article 26 that states that an antidumping or countervailing duty may remain in force for a maximum period of five years, provided that the causes which originally gave rise to the measures persist (sunset review).

Table 2. Colombian Safeguard Cases

PRODUCT	COUNTRY OF ORIGIN	REQUESTED BY	DECISION
Rice	Vietnam	Fedearroz	The maintain the safeguard measure for the period necessary to avoid serious injury to national rice production and will be reviewed before July 6, 1995.
Rice	Venezuela	Initiated by the Administrative Authority	To suspend importation of products originating and or coming from Venezuela classified in the following customs subdivisions 1006109000, 1006)9)0000, 30, 40.
Corrugated Steel Bars	Venezuela	FEDEMETAL on behalf of ACERIAS PAZ DEL RIO S.A., SIMESA, SIDEBOYACA, SIDEMUÑA, SIDELPA.	The safeguard measure was not adopted.
Footwear	China, Taiwan, Vietnam North Korea	CORNICAL on behalf of STANTON & CIA. S.A., PANAM COLOMBIA S.A., CIA. DE PRODUCTOS GRIULLA S.A., CIA MANUFACTURERA MANISOL S.A., CROYDON S.A.	Additional customs duties of 93% on importations of Customs Division 64.01, originating from China and Taiwan. Additional customs of 71% on importations from customs Division 64.03 (1)0000, 19, 30, 40, 51, 59, 91 originated from China, Taiwan, North Korea or Vietnam. Additional Customs duty of 134% on importations originating from China, Taiwan or North Korea.
			6404(11)0000 and 19. Additional Customs Duties of 134% on importations of Customs Division 6404200000 originating from China, Taiwan or North Korea. Additional Customs duties of 108% on importations from China, Taiwan or North Korea in Customs Division 64.05.
Polypropylene Sacks	Ecuador	ACOPLASTICO on behalf of CIA. DE EMPAQUES S.A., SACOS DE COLOMBIA LTDA, CIPLAS S.A., INDUSTRIAS KENTY SORRENTO S.A.	Incomex submits the final technical report to triple A Committee (4-6-94).
Polypropylene Sacks	Ecuador	On the petition of the Foreign Trade Ministry	Incomex submits the final technical report to triple A Committee (3-5-96).
Textiles Clothing and Footwear	China	Economic Development Ministry	40% additional customs duties on products from particular customs divisions.
Plywood and Aglomerados	Member Countries of The Andean Group	PIZANO S.A. and TABLEMAC S.A.	Provisional safeguard duties imposed.

Figure 1. Colombian Antidumping Investigation Timetable Law 299.1995

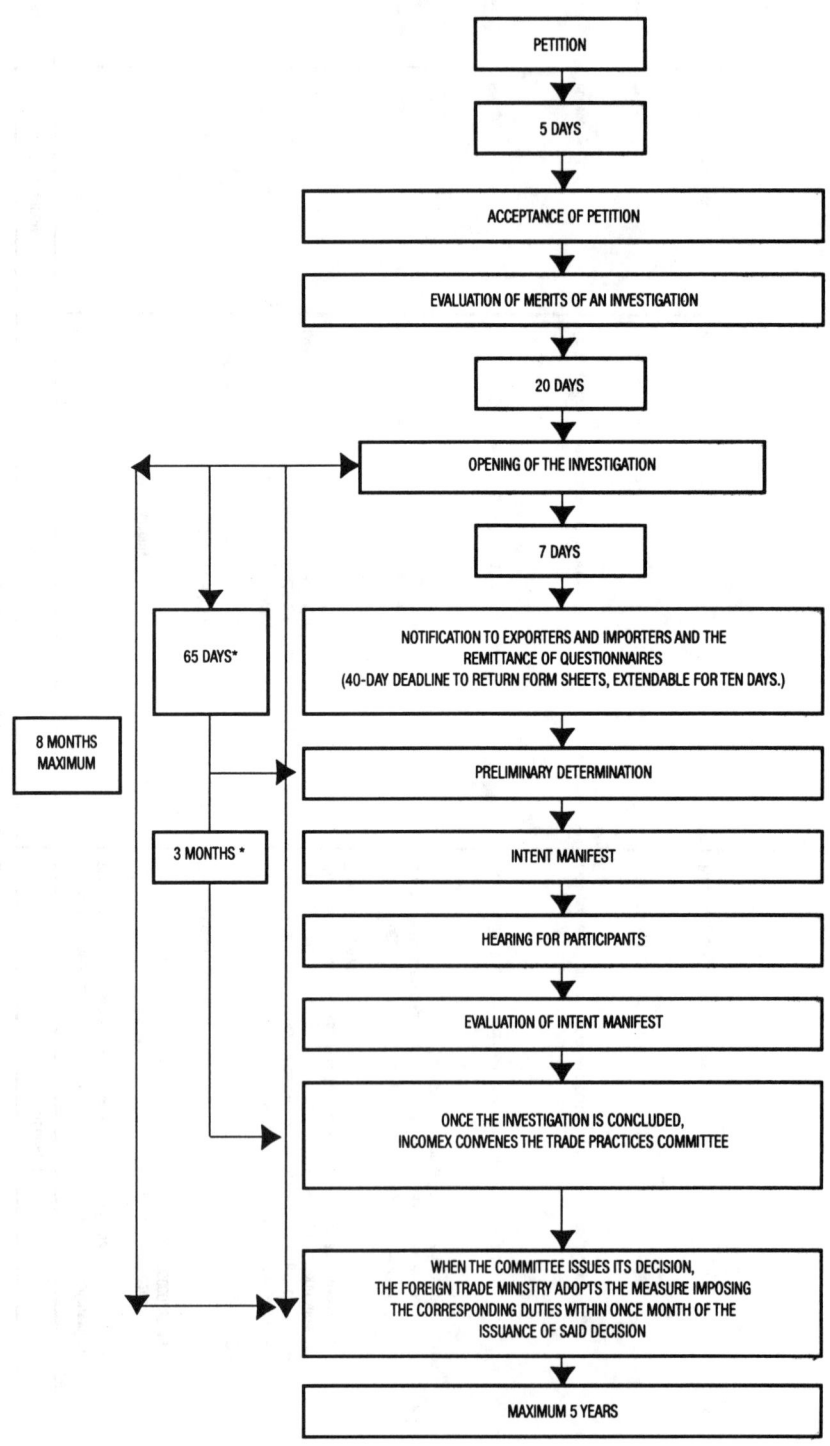

* Extendable for one month.

Figure 2. Countervailing Duty Investigation Timetable

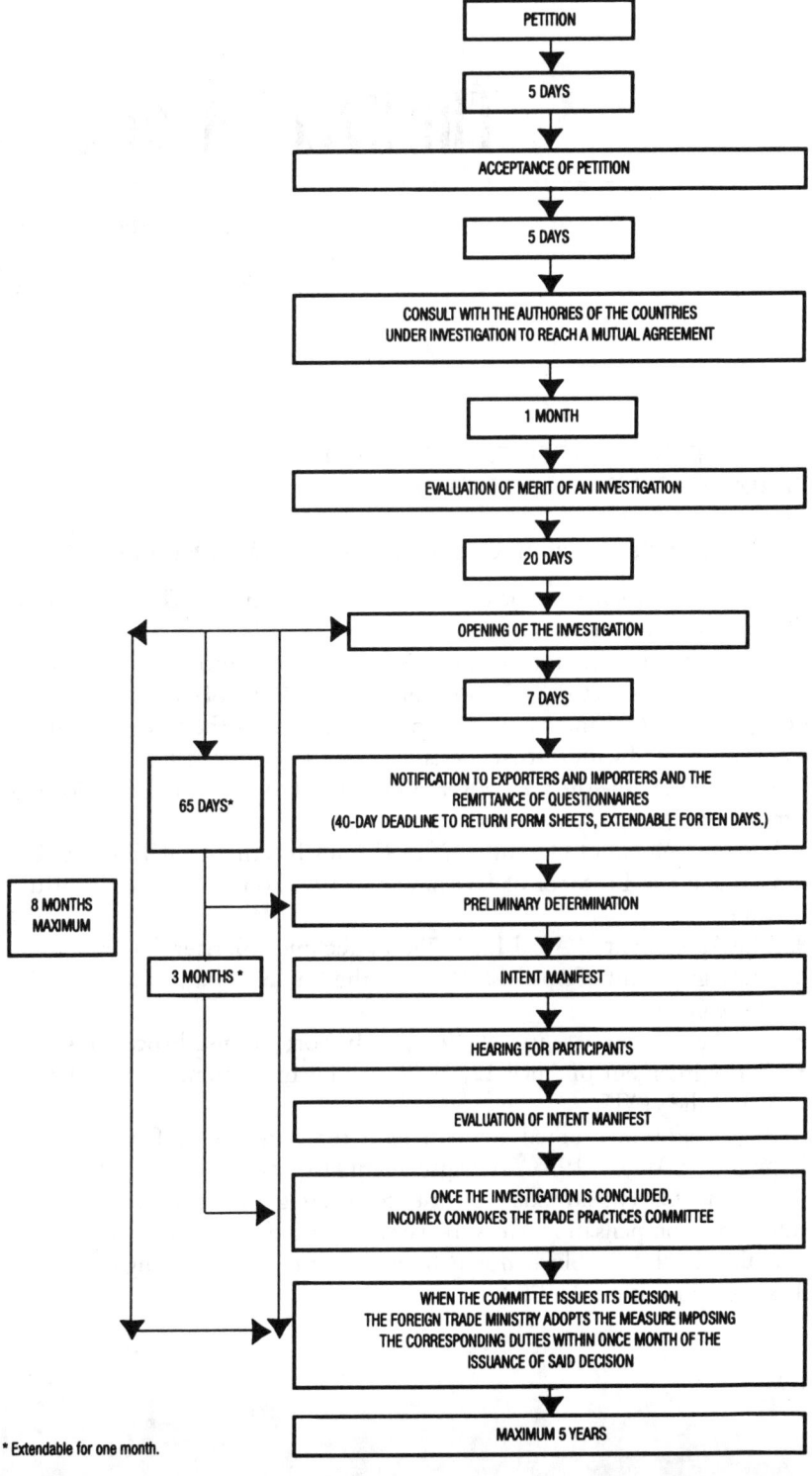

* Extendable for one month.

The Czech Republic

Ralf Thaeter
Gleiss Lutz Hootz Hirsch & Partners
Prague, Czech Republic

THE GENERAL AGREEMENT ON TARIFFS AND TRADE (GATT) IN THE CZECH REPUBLIC

GATT and the Former Czechoslovakia/Czech Republic

The former Czechoslovakia was a founding member of GATT, and GATT entered into force in Czechoslovakia on April 20, 1948.

Following the division of the federation, the Protocol of the Czech Republic's accession to GATT was signed. This Protocol entered into force on April 15, 1993, and the rights and obligations of the Czech Republic were constituted with retroactive effect from January 1, 1993.

At the same time the Czech Republic applied to accede to the following agreements:
- The Agreement of December 20, 1973, for International Trade in Textiles and the Protocol of December 9, 1992, on the extension of the same;
- The Agreement of April 12, 1979, on Technical Barriers to Trade;
- The Agreement of April 12, 1979, on the Implementation of Article VI of the GATT;
- The Agreement of April 12, 1979, on Import License Procedures; and
- The Agreement of April 12, 1979, on the Implementation of Article VII of the GATT.

All the aforementioned agreements entered into force for the Czech Republic on May 1, 1993. Any agreements to which the Czech Republic (the former Czechoslovakia) had not acceded (e.g. the Agreement on Subsidies and Compensation Measures) entered into force on January 1, 1995 after the Czech Republic had signed the convention establishing the World Trade Organization (WTO).

Unlike GATT, the WTO is formed on the basis of a single obligation of the member states. An exception is made in the case of four multilateral agreements, i.e. on trade in civil aircraft, beef, dairy products, and public contracts, which have only been signed by some countries. The Czech Republic is not party to these four agreements.

GATT Antidumping and Antisubsidy Provisions

During the Kennedy Round of the multilateral trade negotiations (1964-1967), discussions focused on matters of customs and antidumping policy. One of the results of these negotiations was the Agreement on the Implementation of GATT Art. VI (the so-called "antidumping code" from the Kennedy Round). A basic obligation of the parties to the antidumping code includes conformity of national laws to the antidumping code. The antidumping code came into force in the former Czechoslovakia on August 28, 1980.

In 1979, simultaneously with the reform of the antidumping code, the code on subsidies and compensation measures (the Agreement on the Interpretation and Implementation of Arts. VI, XVI, XXIII of GATT) was adopted. The former Czechoslovakia did not sign this Agreement because of its "discriminatory nature." In particular, the "discriminatory nature" referred to the fact that this Agreement permitted a finding of subsidies for goods imported from socialist countries based on the fact that the prices of the imported goods were lower than the prices for similar goods in the importing country.

By signing the Convention Establishing the WTO, the Czech Republic has also acceded to the new versions of the antidumping code and the code on subsidies and compensatory measures.

Because of an exception for countries in the process of transition from a centrally-planned economy to a free-market economy, the Czech Republic has seven years from the effective date of the Convention Establishing the WTO to eliminate the prohibited subsidies.

Antidumping and Antisubsidy Procedures in the Czech Republic

To date the Czech Republic has not enacted an antidumping or antisubsidy law, although this was provided by the antidumping code agreed during the Kennedy Round. For this reason, no antidumping or antisubsidy proceeding is available with respect to imports of foreign goods into the Czech Republic.

The only provisions of domestic legislation that permit the imposition of antidumping and compensatory duties are § 54 of Customs Act No. 13/1993 Collection of Laws. However, they have not yet been applied because of the absence of procedural rules.

The Ministry of Industry and Trade and the Ministry of Finance of the Czech Republic have been charged with the task of drafting the antidumping law and the antisubsidy law, respectively.

TRADE LAW OF THE EUROPEAN UNION IN THE CZECH REPUBLIC

The Association Agreement between the Czech Republic and the EC, also known as the Europe Agreement, came into force on April 1, 1995. Even before this effective date, the section relating to trade and commerce, including the antidumping and antisubsidy provisions, was implemented by way of a December 1991 interim agreement.

Following the conclusion of the Europe Agreement and the Interim Agreement, the former Czechoslovakia/Czech Republic was no longer classified as a state-trading country, but as a free-market economy.

The Interim Agreement provided for the establishment of a Joint Committee, which is to be informed about the dumping practices immediately after the opening of an antidumping procedure against exports from the former Czechoslovakia/Czech Republic. This provision was also adopted in the Europe Agreement with the Czech Republic.

Current practice goes beyond the scope of the Europe Agreement. The Czech Republic is now officially informed about alleged Czech dumping practices before the antidumping proceeding is instituted. The Czech Republic's proposal concerning the application of the so-called consultation mechanism before the opening of cost-intensive investigations was also adopted. As a consequence, there is presently only one EU proceeding pending against exports of Czech goods.

Other Protective Measures

Three agreements were concluded between the EC and the former Czechoslovakia on the basis of so-called "autolimitation." These agreements fixed the conditions for access of Czech goods to EC markets. The goods concerned were textiles, iron and steel products, and mutton.

With the entry into force of the Interim Agreement (March 1, 1992), the quantitative import restrictions on goods originating in the former Czechoslovakia that had hitherto applied in the Community were lifted, as were measures having a similar effect. With the Europe Agreement the liberalization policy was continued.

The quantitative restrictions in force in the former Czechoslovakia for the entry of goods originating in the Community were also abolished on March 1, 1992, with the exception (identified in Appendix VIII to the Europe Agreement) of those for uranium ore and uranium concentrates, natural and enriched uranium, and waste paper.

These quantitative restrictions will be progressively abolished between now and January 1, 2001. Imports into the Czech Republic are governed by Import Regulation No. 560/1991 Collection of Laws as amended by Regulation No. 156/1996 Collection of Laws relating to Law No. 42/1980 Collection of Laws on economic relations with foreign countries. Trade in agricultural products is another exception to the otherwise liberal principles laid down by the Europe Agreement.

The introduction of new protective measures between the EU and the Czech Republic is possible only in exceptional cases (Arts. 25-29 of the Europe Agreement). Before new protection measures are introduced, however, the Association Council is obliged to seek a mutually acceptable solution.

European Union

Clive Stanbrook
Stanbrook & Hooper
Brussels, Belgium

HISTORY AND OVERVIEW OF TRADE REMEDY LAWS IN THE EU

Evolution of Trade Remedy Laws

The six original Member States of the European Community signed the Treaty of Rome in March 1957. It soon became clear that, even among the Member States, a very different approach had been taken to antidumping legislation. The three Benelux countries, for example, had never introduced antidumping provisions in the proper sense, but relied upon general safeguard clauses. This diversity in the antidumping policies of the Member States would inevitably have distorted the customs union and the principles of free movement of goods that was due to be realized at the end of the transitional period (July 1, 1968).

Article 113 of the Treaty of Rome provided that from the end of the transitional period, a Common Commercial Policy should be established "based upon uniform principles, particularly in regard to changes in tariff rates, the conclusion of tariff and trade agreements, the achievement of uniformity in measures of liberalization, export policy, and measures to protect trade such as those to be taken in the case of dumping and subsidies."

In advance of the end of the transitional period, the Community adopted common rules on antidumping and countervailing practices. These have been amended many times and are now to be found in Regulation 384/96[1] ("the anti-dumping regulation") and Regulation 3284/94[2] ("the subsidy regulation").

This article draws from material in "Dumping and Subsidies" which was co-authored by Clive Stanbrook QC and Philip Bentley QC. Published by Kluwer Law 1996.

Over this time the Community has grown from the original six to fifteen[3] Member States, now called the European Union. Some countries obtained transitional derogations in respect of certain trade remedy laws. However, these have all now expired.

In Europe, trade remedies (to the extent that Member States had them before they joined the EU) have historically been perceived as a part of governmental policy, thereby subject to rules of good governance and rather weakly supervised by the courts under the general principles of Administrative law. This contrasts with the position in the United States where elaborate due process rules, intended to defend the rights of the parties, were implemented more or less from the outset.

Early antidumping and countervailing practice in the European Community was characterized by the absence of proper rules for transparency, disclosure, or due process. Many cases were dealt with by way of undertakings, a procedure that facilitated early termination of cases and enabled the Commission, the administrative agency, to operate with far fewer officials in comparison to the staffing levels in the United States.

With the evolution of the international rules on antidumping practice, and the concern to ensure due process for parties within the EU, the rules in the EU have become much more similar to those in the United States. There are now, for example, strict time limits, more elaborate rules on disclosure and confidentiality, clearer provisions on reviews, and the European Court will tend to exercise a greater level of supervision than before.

The current Community rules on antidumping and countervailing practices were transposed almost word for word from the new WTO Agreement. There are some notable differences, the most obvious being in the area of circumvention. Here the Community, having suffered an adverse finding in a dispute panel before the Uruguay Round, has nevertheless retained circumvention rules supposedly amended to accommodate the principles behind the adverse finding.

From a procedural point of view, the imposition of strict deadlines for the completion of investigations has been the justification for a very substantial increase in the number of EU officials dealing with antidumping proceedings. Another significant development has been the reorganization of the antidumping unit and the separation of the responsibilities for investigating injury and assessing dumping. This latter change should guarantee a more impartial and detached handling of the cases.

The number of appeals to the European Court have increased dramatically, particularly since the responsibilities for hearing appeals was transferred to the new Court of First Instance in Luxembourg.[4] This Court has been prepared to go much further into the details of antidumping cases and is more willing to interfere with the Community Authorities' conclusions.

Before embarking upon a step by step summary of the EU's trade rules, it is important to have in mind an overview of the framework of the European Union. For historical reasons there are differences in the role of the Commission when dealing with coal and steel products covered by the Treaty of Paris (ECSC Treaty) as opposed to all other products covered by the Economic Community established by the Treaty of Rome (EEC Treaty). At this stage the Uruguay Round amendments have been implemented with respect to all non-coal and steel products and it is anticipated that two Commission Decisions covering these products will be forthcoming, which would substantively reflect almost exactly Council Regulations (EC) Nos. 384/96 and 3284/94.

Trade Remedies Today

Trade Barriers Regulation

The Trade Barriers Regulation provides for an investigation procedure based upon the antidumping procedures. The Commission performs much the same role and a special department within the Commission has the responsibility for Regulation (EC) No. 3286/96 of the Trade Barriers Regulation body (TBR).[5] This provides for a Community mechanism for responding to any illicit commercial practice with a view to removing any resulting injury and to ensure the effective exercise of the Community's rights under international trade rules.

The objective behind the adoption of this Regulation is similar to that of section 301 of the U.S. Trade Act of 1974. However, it leads to a rather more subdued and cautious outcome.

Where a TBR complaint is substantiated, the EU must first comply with any international procedure for consultation or the settlement of disputes laid down by the WTO Agreement or any other international agreement to which the Community is a party.

Only after this has taken place may the EU retaliate. Retaliation can take the form of:
- suspension or withdrawal of any concessions resulting from any commercial policy negotiation;
- the raising of existing customs duties or the introduction of any other charge on imports;
- the introduction of quantitative restrictions or any measures modifying import or export conditions or otherwise affecting trade with the third country concerned.

Surveillance and safeguard measures

There are four Regulations under which surveillance or safeguard measures may be adopted outside the scope of countervailing or antidumping proceedings. In all four cases the Commission is the investigator and regulatory authority.

These are:
(i) Regulation (EC) No. 3285/94 on common rules for imports,[6] which lays down the conditions in which surveillance or safeguard measures may be adopted with regard to products other than textiles originating in countries other than those to which Regulation (EEC) No. 519/84 applies;
(ii) Regulation (EC) No. 519/94 on common rules for imports from certain third countries,[7] which lays down the rules for surveillance and safeguard measures with respect to products (other than textiles) originating in countries which are not members of the World Trade Organization;
(iii) Regulation (EC) No. 517/94 on common rules for imports of textile products from certain third countries not covered by bilateral agreements, protocols or other arrangements, or by other specific Community import rules;[8] and
(iv) Regulation (EC) No. 517/94 on common rules for imports of textile products from certain third countries with whom bilateral agreements or protocols have been entered into.

Agricultural products

Although agricultural products can be the subject of antidumping or countervailing actions, no action has ever been taken under these provisions. Instead, reliance is placed upon the fairly draconian protective measures implemented under the Common Agricultural Policy.

Unfair pricing practices in the maritime sector

Rules that are essentially similar to those in antidumping proceedings have been adopted and are applied under Council Regulation (EEC) No. 4057/86[9] to unfair pricing practices of third countries in the field of maritime transport and Council Regulation (EC) No. 385/96 on the injurious pricing of vessels.[10] The Commission is the agency with the regulatory responsibility.

ANTIDUMPING AND COUNTERVAILING PRACTICE IN THE EU

Administering Authorities

The Commission

The European Commission is the executive body, a sort of civil service. However, it is the primary initiator of policy in the Community and its role is, therefore, much greater and more political than a normal executive body.

It is collegiate in nature with twenty members, one for each country and two for the largest countries (see note 13). Its members (Commissioners) are nominated by national governments and appointed by common accord amongst the Member States and take an oath to put the institutions of the Community before national allegiances. The meetings of the Commission are presided over by the President, currently Jacques Santer, former Prime Minister of Luxembourg.

The Commission of the European Communities has the responsibility for administering antidumping cases. It decides whether a case should be opened in the first place. The Commission is the investigator and, subject to consultation only with another body, can impose provisional duties, accept undertakings, or terminate without protective measures. The other Institution involved in the administrative side of antidumping and countervailing practice is the Council.

Within the Commission each Commissioner has a portfolio. Trade protective measures, including antidumping and countervailing actions, fall within the portfolio of the Commissioner responsible for the common commercial policy and relations with OECD and WTO, currently Sir Leon Brittan.

The Commission is divided up into various Directorates General (DGs). The Directorate General responsible for antidumping and countervailing measures is DGI. Within DGI, Directorate C deals with dumping itself and Directorate E deals with injury findings, Community Interest, all countervailing matters, and other commercial policy instruments. Each of these directorates has about 130 people, of which there are some eighty officers.

The legislative function of the Commission differs, depending on whether the products involved fall under the EC or ECSC Treaty. In the case of ECSC products, i.e., basic coal and steel products, the Commission has the role of "High Authority,"[11] or supreme legislator. Thus, in the ECSC area the Commission adopts the basic antidumping and countervailing legislation and also the measures imposing final, definitive duties. For all other products, the EC regime applies. Here the Commission is not the supreme legislator; its legislative powers are limited to accepting undertakings and imposing provisional duties, while it has no power to order the definitive collection of such duties.

The ultimate legislative authority for definitive action in relation to EC products rests with the Council, although the Council can only act on a proposal from the Commission. This division of responsibilities reflects the delicate political considerations often involved in EC antidumping and countervailing proceedings. It is, however, modified in practice because the Commission works closely with the Member States through their representatives on the Advisory Committee.

In the period 1989 to 1995 the Commission's Antidumping and Antisubsidy Unit was handling between seventy-eight and 103 antidumping cases per year, the peak being in 1990. In 1995 the number of cases being handled was ninety-eight.[12]

The Council

The Council is generally the ultimate legislative body in the Community. It is the vehicle within which all Member States are represented through their government. It is based in Brussels alongside the main Commission building.

It is the Council that imposes duties and collects provisional duties. However, it may only do so in accordance with a proposal from the Commission. This unusual division of responsibilities reflects the balance of power and competence between the two Institutions in the EU.

For antidumping purposes, it is important to be aware of the voting procedures. The Council may act either by way of simple majority, qualified majority or unanimity, depending on the type of proposal that is put before it.

Simple majority

As the name suggests, each Member State has one vote and a simple majority is achieved when at least eight of the fifteen vote together. Most antidumping matters are subject to this procedure.

Qualified majority

A qualified majority is made up of sixty-two votes out of a total of eighty-seven.[13]

Unanimity

There are no circumstances when an antidumping measure need be determined by a unanimous vote.

The duties are, of course, collected by the Member States' national customs authorities. They have no discretion in the matter; therefore implementation is automatic.[14]

The Antidumping Committee (Advisory Committee)

There is also a further body, the "Advisory Committee," often referred to as the "Antidumping Committee." This Committee comprises one member from each country, usually from the appropriate national Department of Trade, with the representative from the Commission as the Chairman. It acts as a sort of go-between in the interaction between the Council and the Commission. This Committee must be consulted at certain stages of the proceedings and, as a practical matter, is kept informed of developments in the various cases. It usually meets each month to conduct its business. In cases of urgency, however, it can be consulted in writing.

There are, however, certain stages of a proceeding at which the Commission is required to consult formally with the Committee. These are before:
- deciding whether the initiation of a proceeding is warranted;[15]
- accepting undertakings;[16]
- imposing a provisional duty (although in very urgent cases, the consultations may take place after the duty has been imposed);[17]
- proposing to the Council the imposition of a definitive duty;[18]
- deciding to open an investigation to review antidumping or countervailing measures;[19]
- deciding on the grant or refusal of a refund of a duty;[20]
- deciding to terminate proceedings without the adoption of protective measures;[21]
- applying provisional duties in a case where an undertaking has been withdrawn or breached;[22]
- opening an investigation into the question of whether antidumping duties have been absorbed;[23] (The analogous problem involving countervailing duties is handled by an ordinary review, the opening of which also requires consultation of the Committee);[24]
- opening an investigation into circumvention of duties;[25]
- issuing a certificate that importation does not amount to circumvention of duties;[26]
- deciding to suspend duties;[27] and
- taking any steps to register imports.[28]

The Commission is not required to consult the Committee before proposing to the Council that a provisional duty be definitively collected. The rationale for this is presumably that the Committee was consulted when the provisional duty was instituted.

The Advisory Committee's role is purely consultative. However, in two cases under the EC regime, the Committee has the power to require the Commission to refer the matter to the Council. First, if the Commission intends to terminate a proceeding without protective measures, it must consult the Advisory Committee and may terminate the proceeding if no objection is raised by a Member State representative. If a Member State objects, the Commission must submit a proposal to the Council that the proceeding be terminated and the proposal is regarded as having been adopted if the Council does not, within one month, decide otherwise than by qualified majority.[29] Second, the same procedure applies if the Commission has received undertakings that it considers acceptable, and wishes to terminate the investigation without the imposition of provisional or definitive duties.[30]

In ECSC matters, the Commission is the High Authority and adopts all measures itself. The role of the Advisory Committee in ECSC matters is to ensure that the Commission is properly appraised of the views of the Member States. In EC matters, the role of the Advisory Committee has a different significance since it is the Council that adopts (or tacitly approves) any definitive action on a proposal from the Commission. It is reasonable to suppose that the views expressed by Member States' representatives in the Committee will be the same as the views of the Member States' representatives in Council. Thus, in EC matters, the Commission will treat the views expressed in the Advisory Committee as an indication as to whether, at the end of the day, the Council will agree to definitive action. For ease of presentation, our discussion of decision-making is limited to EC procedure, but the reader should remember that the institutional procedures for adopting decisions in ECSC cases are different.

Procedure

Initiation of Investigation

All antidumping and countervailing investigations in the EU commence with a written complaint. The complaint must contain sufficient evidence of dumping or subsidization and resulting injury and must be submitted on behalf of a "major proportion" of the Community industry. This has now been defined to require formal support of complainants representing at least 25 percent of total production of the like product in the Community provided a larger percentage does not expressly oppose the complaint.[31]

The Commission may consider a complaint in respect of injury to a certain region within the EU provided (i) the producers within such a market sell all or almost all of the production in that market and (ii) the demand in that market is not to any substantial degree supplied by producers located elsewhere in the EU.[32]

In regional cases however, before antidumping duties can be considered that would affect the whole of the EU, the exporters must be given an opportunity to offer an undertaking in respect of the region concerned.[33]

Finally, domestic producers may be excluded from the definition of Community industry if they are themselves importers or perhaps related or controlled by foreign exporters.[34] The definition of Community industry may exclude Community producers who are themselves importers of allegedly dumped product or who are related.[35]

In theory a case may be initiated merely on the evidence submitted by a Member State. In practice this has never happened.

Investigation Period

In practice, in the EU, the investigation period or reference period, is nearly always twelve months, ending immediately prior to the initiation of the proceeding.

Timetable

The European Union adopted strict time deadlines in antidumping and subsidy proceedings in 1994. The first of these relates to the initiation.

Once the complaint is filed, the Commission is required to decide within forty-five days whether there is sufficient evidence to open an investigation. If it considers that there is sufficient evidence it must initiate an investigation within that period.[36] If the Commission fails to open a proceeding the decision may be challenged before the Court of First Instance.

When a case is initiated a notice is published in the Official Journal of the EU. From this point on, certain time limits are provided for by Regulations (EC) No. 384/96 and (EC) No. 3284/94:

- parties receiving questionnaires are given thirty (+7) days in which to reply;[37]
- where the exporters are in a nonmarket economy country, the parties to the investigation have ten days in which to comment on the proposed choice of analogue country;[38]
- parties are given fifteen days in which to provide sufficient information to enable a representative sample to be taken. In cases where the Commission decides to have recourse to sampling a decision must be taken within twenty-one days of initiation;[39]
- the Commission must decide whether or not to impose provisional duties within nine months of initiation of the investigation; and

- the Council must take definitive action within thirteen months of initiation for countervailing proceedings, or fifteen months from initiation for antidumping proceedings.

Although Regulations (EC) No. 384/96 and (EC) No. 3284/94 do not so provide expressly, it is generally accepted that the Commission may set *ad hoc* time limits whenever it makes a specific request for information. In making such requests the Commission must respect the general principles of good administration and reasonableness.

Participation of Parties and their Counsel

There are three categories of potential participants in EU antidumping and countervailing proceedings. The first category covers those entitled to inspect the nonconfidential file and take a full part in the proceedings. This is limited to the complainant, the importers, and the exporters known to be concerned, as well as the representatives of the exporting country.

Since the Uruguay Round, the right to consult the nonconfidential file has been extended to users and consumer organizations. There are special provisions dealing with the rights of this category of participants to make representations.[40] Significantly, these rights do not extend to the full right to disclosure given to the first category.[41]

The Commission is also required to provide a hearing for any "interested party likely to be affected by the result of the proceeding." This description clearly includes parties that would not fall within either of the above two categories. In practice, the Commission will listen to parties who are not entitled to consult the nonconfidential file.

There are no restrictions on who may represent parties in antidumping or countervailing proceedings before the Commission. The Regulations provide that a complaint may be submitted by "Any natural or legal person, or any association not having legal personality."[42] However, if there is an appeal to the European Court of Justice from any Commission decision, representation before that tribunal will be restricted to EU qualified lawyers.

Use of facts available

The Commission has no power to subpoena witnesses, to enter premises, or to require the production of documents. If parties fail or even refuse to cooperate in an investigation, they cannot be penalized. In this respect trade remedy investigations are very different from those in antitrust procedures.

However, where a party does not cooperate in the investigation, the Commission is entitled to make provisional or definitive findings, affirma-

tive or negative, on the basis of the facts available. The following are deemed to constitute noncooperation:[43]
- where an interested party refuses access to information;
- where an interested party does not provide necessary information within the time limits as provided by Regulation (EC) No. 384/96 or Regulation (EC) No. 3284/94;
- where an interested party significantly impedes the investigation; and
- where an interested party has supplied false or misleading information.

Access to information developed in proceedings

The Commission maintains a full file containing all the information collected. It also compiles a nonconfidential file. The parties to an antidumping proceeding together with any users and consumers association are entitled to access to the nonconfidential file.

Confidentiality

It is clear that the Commission could not carry out its investigations effectively if parties to a proceeding were not guaranteed that the confidentiality of information supplied by them would be respected. Commission officials are under a general duty not to disclose information of the type covered by the obligation of professional secrecy, in particular, information about enterprises, their business relations, and their cost components.[44] Regulations (EC) No. 384/96 and (EC) No. 3284/94 build on this principle by specifying that information supplied for the purposes of antidumping or countervailing investigations shall be used only for the purpose for which it is requested.[45] This provision would also preclude information received during an antidumping or countervailing investigation from being passed on to the Commission's Competition Directorate, (DGIV), to be used in an investigation into possible breaches of articles 85 and 86 EC.

Confidential information is defined as information the disclosure of which is likely to have a significantly adverse effect upon the supplier or the source of such information.[46] It is implicit in this definition that information will not be confidential if it is in the public domain. Regulations (EC) No. 384/96 and (EC) No. 3284/94 require that any request for confidential treatment of information must indicate why the information is confidential. It must also be accompanied by a nonconfidential summary of the information or, if this is not possible, by a statement of the reasons why the information is not susceptible of being summarized in a nonconfidential way.[47] If, however, information is submitted on a confidential basis and the Commission concludes that the information is of a nature which does not warrant confidential treatment, the information will be disregarded unless the supplier is willing to make the information public.[48]

In recent years the Commission has been taking a strong line on nonconfidential summaries. It now requires all documents submitted to be accompanied at the same time by a nonconfidential summary. It has also required that nonconfidential summaries provide meaningful summary information in contrast to showing merely a lot of blank spaces. As a result, lawyers and advisors are now obliged to pay greater attention to the preparation of nonconfidential summaries.

Obligation to disclose

Once provisional measures have been adopted, the complainants, importers, exporters, and their representative associations, as well as representatives of the exporting country, may request disclosure of the details underlying the essential facts and considerations on the basis of which such measures have been imposed. Requests for such disclosure should be made in writing immediately after the imposition of the provisional measures, although it is prudent to make a formal request at the time of submitting one's response to the questionnaire. Upon receiving such request the Commission is obliged to make disclosure in writing of such details as soon as possible thereafter.[49]

Where requests for provisional disclosure have been made before the provisional measures were adopted, the Commission's practice is to address disclosure letters to the parties in question on the same day as, or within one or two days of, the publication in the *Official Journal* of the regulation imposing the provisional measures. The Commission's disclosure letter usually sets a time limit of one month for the submission of observations. Moreover, the regulation imposing the provisional duties usually states the same time limit within which any interested party may submit comments on the regulation.

The purpose of final disclosure is to enable the parties to comment on the essential facts and considerations on the basis of which it is intended to recommend the imposition of definitive measures, or the termination of an investigation or a proceeding without the adoption of measures. At this stage it is important that both the parties concerned and the Commission pay attention to those facts and considerations that are different from those used to justify the adoption of any provisional measures.[50] Requests for final disclosure must be made no later than one month after publication of the provisional duty. Where no provisional duty is imposed, the Commission is obliged to provide the parties concerned with the opportunity to request final disclosure within reasonable time limits.[51] Once again the

Commission is obliged to make disclosure in writing, this time no later than one month prior to the definitive decision, or, where the decision is to be taken by the Council, no later than one month prior to the submission of the Commission's proposal for definitive action.[52] Where the Commission is unable, i.e., cannot reasonably be expected, to disclose certain facts or considerations at this time, it must disclose them as soon as possible thereafter.[53]

The time limit for making representations in reply to final disclosure may not be less than ten days but may be longer if the disclosure takes place sufficiently in advance of the latest date for submission of a proposal by the Commission.[54]

Sampling

Where there is a large number of either transactions or parties, the Commission may restrict its investigation to a sample. The selection of the sample should, if possible, be adopted in agreement with the parties concerned. As a practical matter, the selection needs to be made as quickly as possible at the outset of the proceedings. Parties are given fifteen days in which to make their views known and the Commission must take a decision in the next six days, giving a total of twenty-one days. The Commission will regard any company that fails to provide the initial information that it needs for the purposes of choosing the sample as noncooperating and will make it the subject of the highest ascertained duties.[55]

Determination of Dumping

Export price

The export price is defined as "the price actually paid or payable for the product when sold for export from the exporting country to the Community."

The term "the price actually paid or payable" means that a sale made but not paid for within the reference period would fall within the scope of the investigation. The Community Authorities also regard goods exported to the Community under inward processing rules to be covered by the term "sold for export." As a result, these transactions are included in the calculation of the export price. Nevertheless, inward processing operations will be exonerated from any antidumping duties.

When it is not possible to use an actual price either because there is for some reason no such price or because the price must be regarded as unreliable because of an association or compensatory arrangement between the respective parties, a constructed price may be used.

The aim of a constructed price is to obtain an objective measure of the export price charged by the exporter in place of relying on the exporter's invoice. The Commission will, therefore, look for the first price at which the product is sold to an arm's-length buyer. The constructed price will then be calculated by working back from this sale, deducting all the costs involved. These include the following:
- usual transport, insurance handling, loading, and ancillary costs;
- customs duties, any antidumping duties, and other taxes payable in the importing country by reason of the importation or sale of the goods; and
- a reasonable margin for overhead and profit and/or any commission usually paid or agreed.

Occasionally, there may be no onward sale to an independent buyer; for instance, when the imports are processed into another product. In this case the Commission must still calculate an export price, but it may use "any reasonable basis."

Normal value

The normal value is usually calculated by reference to the sales of the like product made to independent customers in the ordinary course of trade in the country of export.[56]

There must be a sufficient number of these sales made in the country of export to be representative. The Community Authority will not generally accept sales for this purpose if they fall below 5 percent of the total sales exported to the EU.

Sales may not be considered to be made "in the ordinary course of trade" if they are sold at a loss and:
- such sales are made at prices that do not provide for recovery of all costs within a reasonable time; and
- such sales occur in substantial quantities within an extended period of time.[57]

In the case of sales not made at arm's-length, Regulation (EC) No. 384/96 provides that prices charged between parties that appear to be associated or to have a compensatory arrangement with each other may be considered as being in the ordinary course of trade and may be used to establish normal values only if it is determined that the prices are not affected by the relationship.[58] The Community authorities first have to identify the facts that show that the parties appear to be associated or to have a compensatory relationship. Once this occurs, it is for the exporter to show that the prices are not affected by the relationship.

Finally, an alternative normal value construction will have to be used if, due to the particular market situation, sales on the domestic market do not permit a proper comparison. In the case of nonmarket economics, for example, when prices are not a function of normal market forces, a different approach is adopted.

There are two alternative methods of calculating normal value for exports from a market economy country:
(i) the price of export sales to third countries; or
(ii) the constructed value.

Either may be used, but in practice the constructed value is almost always used, probably because if a product is dumped in the Community, it is quite likely to be dumped also in third countries.

The constructed value is computed by calculating the costs of production of the company concerned in the country of origin and by adding a reasonable amount for selling, general and administrative costs, and a figure for profit.

Where the exporter makes more than one product and an allocation of costs is required, the Regulation provides the following rules for so doing:

- Costs shall normally be calculated on the basis of records kept by the exporter provided that such records are in accordance with the generally accepted accounting principles (GAAP) of the country concerned and it is shown that the records reasonably reflect the costs associated with the production and sale of the product under consideration.[59]
- In the absence of a more appropriate method, preference shall be given to the allocation of costs on the basis of turnover.[60]
- The exporter may produce evidence on the proper allocation of costs, e.g., the allocation on some basis other than turnover, and the Community Authorities must give due consideration to such evidence provided it is shown that such allocations have been used historically by the exporter.[61]
- Costs allocations shall be adjusted appropriately for those nonrecurring items which benefit future and/or current production.[62]
- Adjustment shall be made for start-up costs incurred during the investment period.[63]

The addition of a reasonable amount for sales, general and administrative expenses, and profits is based upon:

- actual data pertaining to production and sales, in the ordinary course of trade, by the exporter or producer under investigation;
- the weighted average of the actual amounts determined for other exporters or producers subject to investigation in respect of production and sales of the "like product" in the domestic market of the country of origin;

- the actual amounts applicable to production and sales, in the ordinary course of trade, of the same general category of products for the exporter or producer in question in the domestic market of the country of origin; or
- any other reasonable method, provided that the amount for profit so established shall not exceed profit normally realized by other exporters or producers on sales of products of the same general category in the domestic market of the country of origin.

Nonmarket economy methodology

Article 2(7) of Regulation (EC) No. 384/96 provides that nonmarket economy countries include those to which Regulation (EC) No. 519/94 applies.[64] The list is not exhaustive, and each country has to be assessed in the light of its particular economic situation.

In the case of nonmarket economy countries, the Community Authorities have a choice of any one of four approaches to the calculation of the Normal Value:
(i) the domestic price in a market economy third country;
(ii) the price for exports from such a third country to other countries, including the Community; or
(iii) the constructed value[65] in such a third country.

If none of the first three measures of normal value provides a reasonable basis, the Community Authorities may use the price actually paid or payable in the Community subject to suitable adjustment.

The most commonly used calculation is that based upon the prices or costs in an analogue country. There are no guidelines as to the choice of the analogue country except that the Community Authorities are required to act in a reasonable and appropriate manner. Nevertheless, the European Court has reviewed the exercise of the discretion.[66]

Assessment of Subsidy

In the EU, pursuant to WTO obligations, a countervailing duty may be imposed to offset any subsidy granted, directly or indirectly, for the manufacture, production, export, or transport of any product whose release for free circulation in the Community causes injury. Consistent with the position with respect to antidumping duties, it must also be shown that it is in the overall Community interest to adopt protective measures.

Definition of subsidy

The definition of a subsidy has been transposed word for word from the Subsidies Agreement.

To be countervailable a subsidy must:
- involve a financial contribution by government;
- confer a benefit on the recipient;
- be specific within the meaning of the Subsidies Agreement; and
- not be in the category of noncountervailable subsidies set out in the Subsidies Agreement.

Calculation of a subsidy

Article 4(1) of Regulation (EC) No. 3284/94 provides that the amount of the countervailable subsidy shall be calculated in terms of the benefit conferred on the recipient, which is found to exist during the investigation period. Article 4(2) of Regulation (EC) No. 3284/94 provides guidance in assessing the following four types of case.

In the first case, where government or a public body provides equity capital to a company on terms that would not be acceptable by investors in the market, the amount of the benefit to the recipient is the value of the use of the capital, less the remuneration paid by the firm in the form of dividends, if any. In the second case, where government or a public body makes a loan to a firm and the interest and other fees and commissions payable by the firm for the loan are less than the amount that the firm would have had to pay for a comparable commercial loan obtained on the market, the amount of the subsidy is the difference between the interest, commissions, and fees that would have been paid on the commercial market and the amount actually paid. Equally, where government or a public body provides a loan guarantee so that a firm is able to borrow money on the commercial market on terms that are less onerous than if it did not have the guarantee, a benefit is conferred. The amount of the benefit is the difference between the interest, commissions, and fees that the firm would have had to pay without the benefit of the guarantee and the amount actually paid. Lastly, where government or a public body provides goods or services to a firm against payment of a price or a fee that is less than a proper market price, the amount of the subsidy will be the difference between the market price and the price actually paid. Conversely, where government or a public body purchases goods or services from a firm for more than a proper market price, the amount of the subsidy is the difference between the price actually paid and the market price.

Article 4(3)(a) of Regulation (EC) No. 3284/94 requires that the amount of the subsidy be determined per unit (e.g., per ton or per item) of the subsidized product exported to the Community. This implies that any countervailing duty should usually be determined per unit, e.g., per ton or per item, of the exported product. However, where the subsidy is not granted by reference to quantities manufactured, produced, exported, or transported, in effect then the countervailing duty can be expressed as a percentage of the value.

It is clear that where a grant is bestowed specifically for the purchase of costly items of capital equipment, the benefit flowing from that grant should not be allocated entirely to the year of receipt of the grant. Article 4(3)(d) of Regulation (EC) No. 3284/94 provides that where the subsidy can be linked to the acquisition or future acquisition of fixed assets, the amount of the countervailable subsidy shall be calculated by spreading the subsidy over the normal depreciation period for the assets in question. Any subsidy which is linked to the acquisition of nondepreciating assets is a grant for an indefinite period, and so must be treated as an interest free loan[67] and treated accordingly.

Where a subsidy cannot be linked to the acquisition of fixed assets, the general rule is that the amount of the benefit actually received during the reference period is to be taken as the total subsidy received during that period.

The net amount of a subsidy may not be equal to the gross amount paid. It may be, for example, that to obtain the subsidy it would be necessary to pay an application fee or incur other costs to qualify for, or receive the benefit of, a subsidy. In such cases, the amount of the fee or other costs are deductible from the gross amount of the subsidy to arrive at the countervailable amount.[68] Likewise, a deduction will be made for any export taxes, duties, or other charges levied on the export of the product to the Community, specifically intended to offset the subsidy.[69]

Injury

Before either antidumping or countervailing measures can be applied in the EU, it must be shown that material injury has been suffered by the Community industry and that this injury was caused by the dumped or subsidized import complained of.

However, in the EU it is not sufficient merely to ascertain the existence of material injury, it must also be quantified. This further step is required because the level of the duty in the EU must not exceed what is necessary to remove the injury found to exist.

Definition of injury

The definition of "injury" encompasses the following three categories:
(i) material injury to the Community industry; or
(ii) threat of material injury to the Community industry; or
(iii) material retardation of the establishment of a Community industry;[70]

The common theme is that the actual or threatened injury or the retardation should be "material." The requirement that the actual or threatened injury or the retardation should be material has existed since the beginning of the GATT,[71] and the Community regulations have used the same term.

Actual material injury

No definition of "material" is provided in Regulation (EC) No. 384/96 or Regulation (EC) No. 3284/94. It would, in any event, be very difficult to achieve a definition because the scope of injury will change in different cases, and between one industry and another. The term material should be looked at in conjunction with the French version "préjudice important," which gives perhaps a better flavor of the concept. Its limits are difficult to determine in practice. There can be no question of establishing, for example, threshold levels of import penetration, above which material injury would automatically be found to exist.

It would seem that its effect is certainly to exclude action taken in circumstances involving short term temporary price fluctuations, or sales of end of season goods, out of date stock, or short-term dumping for the purpose of ensuring market entry.[72]

The factors that are generally considered in an assessment of injury are set out in Regulation (EC) No. 384/96 and Regulation (EC) No. 3284/94. This list is illustrative only, although most injury issues can be seen to fall under one heading or another:
- in the process of recovering from the effects of past dumping or subsidization;
- the magnitude of the margin of dumping or the amount of countervailable subsidies;
- actual and potential decline in sales and development in market shares;
- profits, return on investment, cashflow, and the ability to raise capital or make investments;
- productivity, utilization of capacity, and output; or
- inventories, employment, wages, and growth.

In any given case, the evidence of injury will be reflected in a number of categories. Some may point toward injury and some may not. Ultimately, the issue is decided by balancing all the factors together and arriving at a conclusion.

Threat of material injury

In practice, the EU Authorities are very reluctant to act on the basis of a threat of material injury. Only in one case has an antidumping proceeding been initiated on the basis of an allegation of threat of injury,[73] and in no case have definitive measures been taken exclusively on this basis.

Regulation (EC) No. 384/96 and Regulation (EC) No. 3284/94 set out a list of the factors which, *inter alia*, should be considered in making a determination regarding threat of injury:
- a significant rate of increase of dumped or subsidized imports into the Community market indicating the likelihood of substantially increased imports;
- freely disposable capacity of the exporter or an imminent and substantial increase in capacity of an exporter indicating the likelihood of substantially increased dumped or subsidized exports to the Community market, taking into account the availability of other export markets to absorb any additional exports;
- whether imports are entering at prices that would, to a significant degree, depress prices or prevent price increases that otherwise would have occurred, and would probably increase demand for further imports; and
- inventories of the product being investigated.

Material retardation

The question of material retardation has never been a decisive factor in any of the decided cases in the Community. Neither Regulation (EC) No. 384/96 nor Regulation (EC) No. 3284/94 specify any special factors that justify a finding of material retardation of a Community industry, so one can only presume that the general factors listed above are to be used. For example, the presence of low-priced, dumped or subsidized imports will make it difficult for a new investor to obtain the optimum volume and prices to generate the profits necessary to justify the capital investment, whether made by providers of equity or loan capital. Many complaints have referred to such problems but these have been peripheral matters.

To consider the possibility of material retardation, the Community Authorities would, at the very least, require very convincing evidence that an industry was at an advanced stage of planning—for example, that premises were available or were in the process of being acquired and that finance and the necessary technology were available.

Causation

The Community Authorities' analysis is intended to go beyond the mere coincidence of imports and a deteriorating situation in the Community industry. For this purpose, the extent of undercutting, pricing behavior, similarity of sales channels, common customs, and customer loyalty all serve to prove or to disprove the causal link.

Injury caused by other factors such as volume and prices of imports that were not dumped or subsidized, or contraction in demand that individually or in combination also adversely affected the Community industry, must not be attributed to the dumped or subsidized imports.[74] Regulations (EC) No. 384/96 and (EC) No. 3284/94 set out what appears to be a non-exclusive list of other factors which, if they are present in any case under investigation, must be examined by the Community Authorities. The Community Authorities must ensure that the injury caused by these other factors is not attributed to the dumped or subsidized imports. These include, *inter alia:*[75]

- volume and prices of imports not sold at dumped or subsidized prices;
- contraction in demand or changes in the pattern of consumption;
- trade restrictive practices of and competition between third country and Community producers;
- developments in technology and productivity of the Community industry; and
- export performance of the Community industry.

The Lesser Duty Rule

The level of duties imposed must be less than the margin of dumping or subsidization if a lesser duty would be adequate to remove the injury to the Community industry.

Regulation (EC) No. 384/96 and Regulation (EC) No. 3284/94 make this a mandatory rule.[76] If the Community Authorities fail to consider the possibilities of imposing a lesser duty, the measures will be annulled.[77] Implementation of this rule requires sophisticated calculations, which inevitably lead to debate between the Community Authorities and the parties concerned. A duty is in general considered to remove injury if its effect is to raise prices of the imported product to a level that does not cause injury to the Community producers.

Community Interest

In practice, once it is shown that there has been dumping or subsidization and that injury has been caused, duties will normally follow. In the United States, they follow automatically. However, in the EU, there is one further condition that has to be satisfied. This condition is known as the "Community interest test" and requires that it be shown that "the Community interest calls for intervention to prevent such injury."

There do not appear to be any limits to the interests that may be taken into account. However, the appreciation of these various interests must be balanced against each other and considered as a whole. Article 21 of Regulation (EC) No. 384/96 provides examples of the more obvious interest groups, which are the domestic industry, the users or processors, and the consumers.[78] Other interests that have been considered by the Community Authorities in the past include: maintaining conditions of competition in the Community market; trade relations with other countries; component suppliers to the domestic industry; and employment in the distribution network.

For the Community Authorities to decide not to impose measures they must, in the words of article 21 of Regulation (EC) No. 384/96, *"clearly conclude that it is not in the Community Interest to apply such measures."*[79] Article 21(1) of Regulation (EC) No. 384/96 requires the Community Authorities to give "special consideration" to the need to eliminate the trade distorting effects of injurious dumping and the need to restore effective competition. Apart from this, there is no other indication as to how the Community Authorities should approach their task. However, both these factors favor the Community industry. The application of the Community Interest test is, therefore, a balancing of competing interests, with the interests of the Community industry being given special weight. In practical terms, Community Interests are normally equated with the Community industry's interests, so there is a presumption in favor of the introduction of measures. This approach corresponds closely with the policy adopted by the Community Authorities in the past and, if maintained, will mean that Community Interest will only interfere with the imposition of duties in the most exceptional of cases.[80]

Antidumping and Countervailing Measures

Undertakings

One of the features that distinguishes the Community's practice in antidumping and countervailing matters from the practices of the other major trading nations that are active in this field is the frequency with which the Community Authorities terminate investigations with the acceptance of undertakings from exporters.

Undertakings that may be accepted are those that lead to an increase in prices or a cessation of imports at dumped prices and that satisfy the Commission that the dumping or the subsidy or the injurious effects thereof are eliminated.[81] Where the exporter sells through a related importer in the

Community, the undertaking must extend to the resale prices of that importer.[82]

In countervailing cases the undertaking must be one whereby the government of the country of origin or export agrees to eliminate or limit the subsidy or take other measures concerning its effects,[83] or where the exporter agrees to revise its prices or to cease exports to the Community as long as such exports benefit from countervailable subsidies, so that the injurious effects of the subsidies is eliminated. As with the lesser duty rule, action pursuant to an undertaking must not be more than is necessary to remove dumping or subsidization or the injurious effects thereof.[84]

It is a normal requirement of any undertaking that the exporter supply the Commission regularly with information relevant to the fulfillment of the undertaking. This normally takes the form of a requirement to report periodically on export prices to the Community. If an exporter fails to comply with such a requirement, it will be regarded as having violated the undertaking.[85] Regulations (EC) No. 384/96 and (EC) No. 3284/94 contain new rules on action that the Commission can take if an undertaking is withdrawn or violated: it may impose provisional duties or it may make a proposal to the Council that definitive duties be imposed. The choice between these two alternatives depends on what happened in the investigation during which the undertakings were accepted. If the investigation was concluded and a final determination of dumping (or subsidization) causing injury was made, the Commission may simply propose to the Council that definitive duties be imposed on the basis of the facts established during the earlier investigation.[86] If the earlier investigation was not concluded, the Commission will have to open a new investigation to determine the margin of injurious dumping or subsidization. Pending the outcome of that investigation, it may impose provisional measures.

Antidumping and countervailing duties. General–retroactivity

Antidumping or countervailing duties are imposed by regulation in Community matters, and by decision in ECSC matters. They are, therefore, directly applicable in all Member States without the need for any implementing legislation in the Member States. A Regulation (EC) or Decision (ECSC) imposing duties must indicate, having due regard to the protection of confidential information, the names of the exporters, if practical, the countries involved, a description of the product and a summary of the material facts and considerations relevant to the dumping (or subsidization) and injury determinations.[87]

Where the dumping or subsidy margins are *de minimis*, no duties or measures may be adopted. For dumping purposes, margins below 2 percent are *de minimis*,[88] whereas, for countervailing purposes, margins of less than 1 percent are *de minimis*.[89]

Three different types of duty have been applied by the Community:
(i) *ad valorem*;
(ii) minimum price; and
(iii) specific duties, e.g., thirty-three ECU per unit of product.

Which of these types of duty is appropriate must be determined on a case-by-case basis.

When imposing the duty, the Commission or the Council must state expressly that they have considered whether a lesser duty would serve to remove injury. Thus, for example, the Court annulled the definitive duties imposed in *UAN fertilizer from the United States* because the Commission had failed to state that it had examined whether a duty less than the dumping margin would suffice to eliminate injury.[90] This is another situation where Community practice differs considerably from the practice in the United States, where duties must eliminate the full amount of the dumping margin or subsidy once injury has been established.

Retroactivity

Antidumping or countervailing duties may not normally be imposed or increased retrospectively and, in normal situations, apply only to goods entered for Community consumption after the entry into force of the duties. There are, however, certain exceptional circumstances in which duties may be imposed on products that were entered for consumption after initiation of the investigation and not more than ninety days before the imposition of provisional duties.

These circumstances are the following:
- for dumped products, where there is a history of injurious dumping or where the importer was, or should have been, aware that the exporter dumped and that such dumping would result in injury and, in addition to the level of imports that caused injury during the investigation period, there is a further substantial rise in imports which, in the light of its timing and volume and other circumstances, is likely to undermine seriously the remedial effect of the definitive dumping duty to be applied;[91] or
- for subsidized products, where injury that is difficult to repair is caused by massive imports, in a relatively short period, of a product benefiting from export subsidies bestowed inconsistently with the GATT 1994 Subsidies Agreement, and where, in order to prevent a recurrence of such injury, it is necessary to impose countervailing duties retrospectively.[92]

In the case of breach of (or withdrawal from) an undertaking the Community Authorities may also impose duties retroactively to the date of violation, subject to a maximum retroactivity of ninety days.[93] Under the old Regulation, this power was restricted to violation of undertakings. (EC) No. 384/96 and (EC) No. 3284/94 have now extended this to the withdrawal from undertakings. The first case in which this power was invoked related to the withdrawal from an undertaking by two companies in *Ferro-silico-manganese from Russia*.[94]

The Commission has never yet imposed duties retroactively. However, in *Urea from USSR*, the Commission published a notice to the effect that it had been requested by the complainants to impose duties retroactively and was considering acceding to that request.[95] There was nothing in the legislation requiring the Commission to publish such a notice. Doubtless the Commission considered that the principles of good administration and the protection of the rights of the defense obliged it to publish the notice. Under Regulations (EC) No. 384/96 and (EC) No. 3284/94 a requirement of registration of imports replaces the need to publish such a notice.

Provisional duties

Where the Commission's preliminary investigation shows the existence of dumping or subsidization and there is sufficient evidence of injury caused by the dumping or subsidization, and where the interests of the Community call for intervention to prevent injury being caused during the proceeding, the Commission may impose a provisional antidumping or countervailing duty.[96] This may be done at the Commission's initiative or at the request of a Member State.

Provisional duties may not, in any event, be imposed earlier than sixty days from initiation of the proceedings, and must be imposed no later than the expiration of nine months from the initiation of the investigation.[97] The effect of the imposition of a provisional duty is that goods covered by the duty cannot be entered for consumption in the Community without the importer providing security for the amount of the duty. This security normally takes the form of a banker's bond. Whether or not such securities will finally be collected depends on a subsequent decision of the Council, containing its definitive conclusions, made after the Commission has completed its investigation.

Provisional duties may be imposed for either six-month or nine-month periods. However, where provisional duties are applied for only six months, they may be extended for a further three. The extension of the six-month period or the initial extended nine-month provisional duty can only be applied if exporters representing a significant proportion of the trade involved so request, or, if such exporters do not object after the Commission publishes a notice of its intention to do so.[98]

In the case of subsidies, provisional countervailing duties have a fixed duration of four months and cannot be extended.[99]

The amounts secured by way of provisional duties can be collected only to the extent that the Council so decides. If the Council decides on the collection of only a portion of the provisional duty, the remainder must be returned to the importers.[100]

Registration of imports

The GATT 1994 Antidumping Agreement provides that provisional measures may take the form of a provisional but immediate duty or, preferably, a security—by cash deposit or bond—equal to the amount of the antidumping duty provisionally estimated. It also provides that the "withholding of appraisement is an appropriate provisional measure, provided that the normal duty and the estimated amount of the dumping duty be indicated and as long as the withholding of appraisement is subject to the same conditions as other provisional measures."[101] Withholding of appraisement means literally that the Customs withholds determining the level of duty until a later date. Regulation (EC) No. 384/96 and Regulation (EC) No. 3284/94 describe this procedure as "registration." The Commission may decide to impose registration measures by regulation after consultation with the Advisory Committee. The regulation introducing registration must specify the purpose of the action and, if appropriate, the estimated amount of possible future liability. The maximum duration of registration measures is nine months. Registration measures may be adopted in any case in which the Community industry produces sufficient evidence to justify such action.[102]

Regulation (EC) No. 384/96 provides expressly for use of the registration procedure in the following cases:
- where a newcomer antidumping review is opened. The purpose of registration is to allow the newcomer's products to be imported into the Community without payment of the general residual antidumping duty, with duty being paid retrospectively to the date of initiation of the review once the results have been determined;[103]
- where an antiabsorption review is opened and the investigation involves a re-examination of normal values. The purpose of registration is to ensure that the Community can collect any extra duties that may become payable as a result of the re-examination of normal values;[104]
- where an anticircumvention investigation is opened. The purpose of registration here is to ensure that, if it is determined that duties have

been circumvented, they can be recovered retrospectively to the date of initiation of the investigation. Importers may apply to the Commission for a certificate that the import of particular goods does not constitute circumvention. If, upon examination of the facts, the Commission decides, after consulting the Advisory Committee, that circumvention is not occurring in particular circumstances, it must issue a certificate to this effect and the imports will be free from registration requirements;[105] and
- where it is intended to impose duties retroactively.[106]

Suspension of measures

Prior to Regulation (EC) No. 384/96 and Regulation (EC) No. 3284/94, there were no express provisions in Community legislation that allowed antidumping and countervailing measures to be suspended.[107] In theory, the only possibility was to repeal them as the result of an interim review. The review mechanism is not particularly flexible. If, as a result of the investigation, it is found that antidumping or countervailing measures are still warranted, the Commission has no choice but to propose to the Council that they be continued. Equally, once measures have been repealed, it is not possible to reinstate them without the initiation of new proceedings.

Now these Regulations (EC) No. 384/96 and (EC) No. 3284/94 provide that measures may be suspended in the Community Interest.[108] Certain procedural safeguards must be respected before antidumping or countervailing measures are suspended. The Commission must be satisfied that market conditions have *temporarily* changed to an extent that injury would be unlikely to resume as a result of the suspension. Second, the Community industry must be consulted and its comments must be taken into account. Third, the Commission must consult the Advisory Committee. Where these conditions are satisfied, the Commission may grant a suspension for a period of nine months. The period may be extended by a further twelve months, but only by the Council acting by a simply majority on a proposal from the Commission.

Circumvention Proceedings

In 1990, the EU's anticircumvention legislation was condemned by a GATT Panel.[109] No specific guidance was given on anticircumvention rules in the Uruguay Round. The Community therefore amended its approach, now contained in article 13 of Regulation (EC) No. 384/96, and enabled antidumping duties that have already been instituted to be extended to imports from third countries of like products or parts thereof, when circum-

vention of the measures is taking place. There are four conditions to be satisfied:
(i) a change in the pattern of trade between third countries and the Community;
(ii) practices, processes, or works for which there are insufficient cause or economic justification other than the imposition of the duty;
(iii) the remedial effect is being undermined; and
(iv) there is dumping in relation to the normal values previously established for the "like products."

These conditions are dealt with in more detail in the Regulation.[110]

Refunds and Reviews

Once definitive measures have been adopted, that is not necessarily the end of the exporters' or the complainants' procedural rights. Antidumping or countervailing duties can be reviewed in certain circumstances at the request of either the exporters or the complainants.[111] Furthermore, the importers may apply for a refund where the duty collected exceeds the actual dumping margin or the amount of the subsidy.[112]

Refunds of duties

After the conclusion of an investigation and the imposition of a definitive antidumping or countervailing duty, the dumping margin or the amount of the subsidy may change. In the case of dumping, this could come about, for example, because of a reduction in normal value, an increase in export price, or an alteration in exchange rates. In the case of subsidies, it could happen because a subsidy program was terminated or changed.

Where the amount of the duty collected exceeds the dumping margin or the amount of the subsidy, Regulations (EC) Nos. 384/96 and 3284/94 enable the importer to claim a refund of all or part of the duty paid, and establish a procedure for the processing of such claims. A refund procedure is not a forum for challenging the regulation imposing the duties in the first place[113] and, thus, the principle that duties are chargeable remains intact.

Review Procedures

There are four types of review procedure to be examined:
(i) interim review;[114]
(ii) review at the request of a newcomer;

(iii) five-year review; and
(iv) review when there is evidence that duties are being absorbed.

We will first examine the provisions of Regulation (EC) No. 384/96 on reviews of antidumping duties before looking at the differences that exist in reviews of countervailing duties.

Interim review

A review may be held at any time at the request of a Member State or on the initiative of the Commission.[115] Any interested party may also request a review but, in this case, it must submit evidence of changed circumstances and at least a year must have elapsed since the adoption of the measures that it wishes to have renewed.[116]

Where the Commission decides to reopen the investigation, article 11(5) of Regulation (EC) No. 384/96 requires that the procedure applicable to original investigations be followed. Thus, the Commission sends questionnaires to the exporters or to the exporting country and also to the complainants. It investigates dumping by reference to a period of not less than six months immediately prior to the opening of the proceeding and it investigates injury resulting from the dumping. It must hear interested parties, grant importers, exporters, or representatives of the exporting country access to the nonconfidential file, etc.

Newcomer review

As stated above, a person who did not produce or export during the original investigation period is not able to apply for a refund because there is no established basis for the calculation of the dumping margin. Consequently, the Commission decided, as a matter of policy, to open review proceedings in respect of producers who "are newcomers to the market, and who did not export during the reference period." The first of such so-called "newcomer" reviews was held in 1990, and fifteen newcomer proceedings had been opened by the end of 1995.[117]

A "newcomer" review is concerned only with the technical question of the determination of the dumping margin of a particular exporter. If the newcomer considers that the findings on injury should also be reviewed, it must prove that there has been a change in circumstances and request an interim review.

In making its request for a review, the newcomer must produce adequate proof:
- that it did not export to the Community during the period of the inquiry;
- that it began to export after that period;

- that it is not related to any of the companies covered by the initial investigation.[118]

A newcomer review is not possible when the original antidumping duties were determined by taking a sample of exporters.[119]

Five-year review

The five-year review or sunset clause was introduced for the first time by Regulation (EEC) No. 2176/84 and now exists in modified form in article 11(2) of Regulation (EC) No. 384/96. The basic principle is that antidumping or countervailing duties and undertakings should lapse after five years from the date on which they entered into force. However, if the measures have already been subject to review, the five-year period runs from the most recent review. A notice of impending expiration should be published in the *Official Journal* at an appropriate time in the final year of the period of application of the measures.

A five-year review under article 11(2) can be opened by the Commission, on its own initiative, or at the request of Community producers. In the case of a request by Community producers, it must contain sufficient evidence that expiration of the measure would be likely to lead to a continuation or recurrence of dumping and injury. Article 11(2), second paragraph, of Regulation (EC) No. 384/96 provides that such a likelihood may, for example, be indicated by:
(i) evidence of continued dumping and injury;
(ii) evidence that the removal of injury is partly or solely due to the existence of measures; or
(iii) evidence that the circumstances of the exporters, or market conditions, are such that they would indicate the likelihood of further injurious dumping.

If the Community producers wish to lodge a request for a review, they must do so no later than three months before the end of the five-year period.[120] The Commission must give the representatives of the exporting country and the Community producers the opportunity to amplify, rebut or comment on the matters set out in the review request.[121]

The review is conducted in the same way as an interim review under article 11(3), and the outcome of the review can either be a refund, maintenance or amendment of the existing measures. The Commission is obliged to publish a notice to this effect in the Official Journal.[122]

Absorption of duties

Once the antidumping duty has been imposed, it may be the case that the exporter absorbs the cost instead of passing it on, thereby circumventing the purpose of the duty. The absorption of antidumping duties can take many forms: reductions in the export price, direct compensatory payments to the importer, reductions in the prices of other goods purchased by the importer, and payments for such services as advertising expenses and other expenses previously paid by the importer. When this occurs, the antidumping duty may be recalculated.[123]

The Commission can reopen the investigation where the Community industry submits sufficient information showing that the antidumping measures have not led to any movement, or sufficient movement, in resale prices or subsequent selling prices in the Community.[124] The purpose of reopening the investigation, as opposed to opening a new investigation, is to reassess the export prices and recalculate the dumping margins. Thus, where it is found that export prices have fallen since the reference period, whether such fall occurred before or after the imposition of duties, the dumping margin may be recalculated based on the lower prices. Exporters, importers and Community producers must be given the opportunity to clarify the situation with regard to resale prices and subsequent selling prices.[125] It would be a defense for the exporters or importers to show that there were objective market reasons beyond their control as to why prices did not rise as a result of the imposition of duties.

References

1. OJ L56, 6.3.96, p. 1
2. OJ L349, 31.12.94, p. 22
3. Austria, Belgium, Denmark, Finland, France, Germany, Greece, Ireland, Italy, Luxembourg, Netherlands, Portugal, Spain, Sweden, United Kingdom
4. OJ L66, 10.3.94, p. 29
5. OJ L349, 31.12.94, p. 71
6. OJ L349, 31.12.94, p. 53; amendments in OJ L67, 10.3.94, p. 89 and OJ L55, 11.3.95, p. 1
7. OJ L67, 10.3.94, p. 89
8. OJ L67, 10.3.94, p. 1
9. OJ L378, 31.12.86, p. 14
10. OJ L56, 6.3.96, p. 21
11. Now called "the Commission," see article 7, ECSC as amended by article H(1) of the Treaty on European Union
12. These statistics are taken from the Fourteenth Annual Report from the Commission to the European Parliament on the Community's Anti-dumping and Anti-subsidy Activities, 1995 COM(96)146, 8 May 1996

13. Each Member State has a weighted vote as indicated in the chart below.

Member State	Votes in the EU Council	European Commissioners	Members of the European Parliament
Belgium	5	1	25
Denmark	3	1	16
Germany	10	2	99
Greece	5	1	25
Spain	8	2	64
France	10	2	87
Ireland	3	1	15
Italy	10	2	87
Luxembourg	2	1	6
Netherlands	5	1	31
Austria	4	1	21
Portugal	5	1	25
Finland	3	1	16
Sweden	4	1	22
UK	10	2	87
Total	87	20	626

14. "purely automatic and, moreover, in pursuance not of intermediate national rules but of Community rules alone," Case 113/77, *NTN Toyo Bearing Company, Ltd. and others v Council*, [1979] ECR 1185
15. Regulation (EC) No 384/96, article 5(9); Regulation (EC) No 3284/94, article 7(13)
16. Regulation (EC) No 384/96, article 8(5); Regulation (EC) No 3284/94, article 10(5)
17. Regulation (EC) No 384/96, article 7(4); Regulation (EC) No 3284/94, article 9(4)
18. Regulation (EC) No 384/96, article 9(4); Regulation (EC) No 3284/94, article 11(6)
19. Regulation (EC) No 384/96, article 11(6); Regulation (EC) No 3284/94, article 13(12)
20. Regulation (EC) No 384/96, article 11(8), fourth sub-paragraph; Regulation (EC) No 3284/94, article 13(17)
21. Regulation (EC) No 384/96, article 9(2); Regulation (EC) No 3284/94, article 11(2)
22. Regulation (EC) No 384/96, article 8(10); Regulation (EC) No 3284/94, article 10(10)
23. Regulation (EC) No 384/96, article 12(1)
24. Regulation (EC) No 3284/94, article 13(8)
25. Regulation (EC) No 384/96, article 13(3); Regulation (EC) No 3284/94, article 14(2)
26. Regulation (EC) No 384/96, article 13(4); Regulation (EC) No 3284/94, article 14(3)

27. Regulation (EC) No 384/96, article 14(4); Regulation (EC) No 3284/94, article 15(4)
28. Regulation (EC) No 384/96, article 14(5); Regulation (EC) No 3284/94, article 15(5)
29. Regulation (EC) No 384/96, article 9(2); Regulation (EC) No 3284/94, article 11(2)
30. Regulation (EC) No 384/96, article 8(1); Regulation (EC) No 3284/94, article 10(1). As to the difference between termination of the investigation and termination of the proceeding
31. Regulation (EC) No 384/96, article 5(4); Regulation (EC) No 3284/94, article 7(8)
32. For conditions to qualify for regional protection see Regulation (EC) No 384/96, article 4(1)(b); Regulation (EC) No 3284/94, Article 6(1)(ii)
33. Regulation (EC) No 384/96, article 4(3); Regulation (EC) No 3284/94, article 6(3)
34. Regulation (EC) No 384/96, article 4(2); Regulation (EC) No 3284/96, article 6(2)
35. Regulation (EC) No 384/96, article 4(1)(a); Regulation (EC) 3284/94, article 6(1)(a)
36. Regulation (EC) No 384/96, article 5(9); Regulation (EC) No 3284/94, article 7(13)
37. Regulation (EC) No 384/96, article 6(2); Regulation (EC) No 3284/94, article 8(2)
38. Regulation (EC) No 384/96, article 2(7)(b)
39. Regulation (EC) No 384/96, article 17(2); Regulation (EC) No 3284/94, article 18(2)
40. Regulation (EC) No 384/96, articles 6(7) and 21; Regulation (EC) No 3284/94, articles 8(7) and 22
41. Regulation (EC) No 384/96, article 20; Regulation (EC) No 3284/94, article 21
42. Regulation (EC) No 384/96, article 5(1), first subpara; Regulation EC No 3284/94, article 7(1)
43. Regulation (EC) No 384/96, article 18(1); Regulation (EC) No 3284/94, article 19(1)
44. Article 214 EC; Article 47 ECSC
45. Regulation (EC) No 384/96, article 19(6); Regulation (EC) No 3284/94, article 20(6)
46. Regulation (EC) No 384/96, article 19(1); Regulation (EC) No 3284/94, article 20(1)
47. Regulation (EC) No 384/96, article 19(2); Regulation (EC) No 3284/94, article 20(2)
48. Regulation (EC) No 384/96, article 19(3); Regulation (EC) No 3284/94, article 20(3)
49. Regulation (EC) No 384/96, article 20(1); Regulation (EC) No 3284/94, article 21(1)
50. Regulation (EC) No 384/96, article 20(2); Regulation (EC) No 3284/94, article 21(2)

51. Regulation (EC) No 384/96, article 20(3); Regulation (EC) No 3284/94, article 21(3)
52. Note that Regulation (EEC) No 2423/88, article 11(6), required that the proposal for definitive action be submitted to the Council at least one month prior to expiry of the provisional duties, but this statement has been dropped from Regulations (EC) No 384/96 and (EC) No 3284/94
53. Regulation (EC) No 384/96, article 20(4); Regulation (EC) No 3284/94, article 21(4)
54. cf. Regulation (EC) No 384/96, article 20(5); Regulation (EC) No 3284/94, article 21(5)
55. See Article 17, Regulation (EC) No 384/96 and Article 18, Regulation (EC) No 3284/94.
56. See generally Article 2, Regulation (EC) No 384/96.
57. Regulation (EC) No 384/96 article 2(4)
58. Regulation (EC) No 384/96, article 2(1)
59. Regulation (EC) No 384/96, article 2(5)
60. Regulation (EC) No 384/96, article 2(5), second subparagraph, second sentence. Allocation in proportion to turnover was the general rule under all the regulations pre-GATT 1994, see e.g. Regulation (EEC) No 2423/88, article 2(11)
61. Regulation (EC) No 384/96, article 2(5), first sentence
62. Regulation (EC) No 384/96, article 2(5), second subparagraph, last sentence
63. Regulation (EC) No 384/96, article 2(5), third subparagraph
64. Albania, Armenia, Azerbaijan, Belarus, the People's Republic of China, Estonia, Georgia, Kazakhstan, North Korea, Kyrgyzstan, Latvia, Lithuania, Moldova, Mongolia, Russia, Turkmenistan, Ukraine, Uzbekistan, Vietnam.
65. Although Regulation (EC) No 384/96 does not define the constructed value, this term must be taken to mean the costs of production plus a reasonable margin for SG&A and profits
66. See Paintbrushes from the Peoples' Republic of China, T-167/94, Detlef Nölle v Council, 18 September 1995
67. Regulation (EC) No 3284/94, article 4(3)(d), second subparagraph
68. Regulation (EC) No 3284/94, article 4(3)(b)(i)
69. Regulation (EC) No 3284/94, article 4(3)(b)(ii)
70. In shorthand, practitioners often refer to "actual injury", "threat of injury" and "material retardation." The word "actual" is used to contrast with "threat"
71. See the GATT, article VI(6)(a)
72. This last example was provided by the Commission in its Eleventh annual report to the European Parliament on the Community's antidumping and subsidy activities (1992), COM(93)516, at p. 8
73. DRAMS from Japan, OJ L193, 25.7.90, p. 1
74. Regulation (EEC) No 2423/88, article 4(1)
75. Regulation (EC) No 384/96, article 3(7); Regulation (EC) No 3284/94, article 5(7)
76. Regulation (EC) No 384/96, article 9(4); Regulation (EC) No 3284/94, article 11(6)

77. Case 53/83, Allied Corp v Council, [1985] ECR 1621, paragraph 19
78. See also Regulation (EC) No 3284/94, article 22
79. In the case of countervailing measures the word used is safely; Regulation (EC) No 3284/94, article 22
80. Although the reasoning is now more extensive, the position substantively is much the same as in 1990 when one experienced commentator wrote "the expectation seems to be that the Commission applies the clause only in exceptional cases and generally in response to political pressure.", Klaus Stegemann, Anti-dumping policy and the consumer, Journal of World Trade, (1985), Volume 19
81. See Ammonium nitrate from Russia, OJ L198, 23.8.95, p. 13
82. Ferro-silico-manganese from Russia, OJ L248, 14.10.95, p. 56, recital (7)
83. e.g. Women's shoes from Brazil, where Brazil imposed a compensatory export tax, OJ L327, 14.11.81, p. 39
84. Regulation (EC) No 384/96, article 8(1); Regulation (EC) No 3284/94, article 10(1)
85. Regulation (EC) No 384/96, article 8(7); Regulation (EC) No 3284/94, article 10(7)
86. Regulation (EC) No 384/96, article 8(9); Regulation (EC) No 3284/94, article 10(9)
87. Regulation (EC) No 384/96, article 14(2); Regulation (EC) No 3284/94, article 15(2). The strict text seems to suggest that either the names of the exporters or the names of the countries involved must be published. Since duties are imposed against imports from defined countries, the countries will always be identified
88. Regulation (EC) No 384/96, article 9(3), see, for example, Polyester Yarns from Indonesia, OJ L118, 25.5.95, p. 1
89. Regulation (EC) No 3284/94, article 11(3); the 1 per cent figure is increased to 2 per cent or 3 per cent for certain developing countries. For an old example of de minimis margins, see Stainless steel bars from Brazil, OJ L139, 5.6.80, p. 30
90. Case 53/83, Allied Corporation and others v Commission, [1985] ECR 1621
91. Regulation (EC) No 384/96, article 10(4)(b)
92. Regulation (EC) No 3284/94, article 12(4)
93. Regulation (EC) No 384/96, article 10(5); Regulation (EC) No 3284/94, article 12(5)
94. OJ L18, 24.1.96, p. 1
95. OJ L42, 12.02.87, p. 25
96. Regulation (EC) No 384/96, article 7(1); Regulation (EC) No 3284/94, article 9(1)
97. Regulation (EC) No 384/96, article 7(1); Regulation (EC) No 3284/94, article 9(1)
98. Regulation (EC) No 384/96, article 7(7)
99. Regulation (EC) No 3284/94, article 9(7)
100. Regulation (EC) No 384/96, article 10(3); Regulation (EC) No 3284/94, article 12(3)
101. GATT 1994 Anti-dumping Agreement, article 7.2

102. Regulation (EC) No 384/96, article 14(5); Regulation (EC) No 3284/94, article 15(5)
103. Regulation (EC) No 384/96, article 11(4), third sub-paragraph
104. Regulation (EC) No 384/96, article 12(5)
105. Regulation (EC) No 384/96, article 13(4)
106. Regulation (EC) No 384/96, article 10; Regulation (EC) No 3284/96, article 12
107. But it has suspended countervailing duties when adequate protection was already offered by anti-dumping duties. See, for example, Iron and Steel sheets and plates from Brazil, OJ L205, 29.7.83, p. 29
108. Regulation (EC) No 384/96, article 14(4); Regulation (EC) No 3284/94, article 15(4)
109. Panel Report on EEC Regulation on Imports of parts and Components ("Screwdriver case") adopted 16th May 1990, GATT Doc. L6657 of 22nd March 1990.
110. Regulation (EC) No 384/96, article 13(2)
111. Regulation (EC) No 384/96, article 11(1) and (3); Regulation (EC) No 3284/94, article 13, paragraphs 1 to 13
112. Regulation (EC) No 384/96, article 11 (8); Regulation (EC) No 3284/94, article 13, paragraphs 14 and 18
113. Case 312/84, Continentale Produkten Gesellschaft Ehrhardt-Renken (GmbH & Co) v Commission, [1987] ECR 841; Case T-169/94, PIA Hi-fi Vertriebs GmbH v Commission, 27 June 1995
114. In theory it would also be possible to circumvent the rules by increasing prices to the importer who applied for a refund but decreasing prices to the importers who did not cooperate. However, such a course of action would disrupt the market and, therefore, is unlikely to be followed by the exporters
115. Regulation (EC) No 384/96, article 11(3)
116. Regulation (EC) No 384/96, article 11(3)
117. Fourteenth Annual Report from the Commission to the European Parliament on the Community's Anti-dumping and Anti-subsidy Activities, 1995, COM(96)146, 8 May 1996
118. Regulation (EC) No 384/96, article 11(4), second paragraph, cf. Synthetic polyester fibres from Romania, Taiwan, Turkey, Serbia, Montenegro and Macedonia (ex Yugoslavia), OJ L306, 22.10.92, p. 1, recital (55); See also the following cases, Ferro Silicon from Brazil, OJ L118, 25.5.95, p. 7, Synthetic fibres of polyester yarn, OJ L262, 1.11.95, p. 28
119. Regulation (EC) No 384/96, article 11(4), last sentence
120. Regulation (EC) No 384/96, article 11(2)(c)
121. Regulation (EC) No 384/96, article 11(2), third subparagraph
122. Regulation (EC) No 384/96, article 11(2), fourth subparagraph
123. Regulation (EC) No 384/96, article 12. Additional duties were imposed and the anti-dumping duty recalculated in *Electronic weighing scales from Singapore*, OJ L307, 20.12.95, p. 30
124. Regulation (EC) No 384/96, article 12(1)
125. Regulation (EC) No 384/96, article 12(2)

Guatemala

Eduardo Mayora Alvarado
Mayora & Mayora
Guatemala City, Guatemala

HISTORY AND OVERVIEW OF TRADE REMEDY LAWS AND/OR REGULATIONS SINCE 1947

Since 1947, Guatemala's legal history with respect to trade remedies can be traced to two events: (1) the entry of Guatemala into the Central American Common Market as a result of the treaty, *Tratado General de Integración Económica Centroamericana* (TIECA), of December 13, 1960, and (2) the opening of the Guatemalan economy and its participation in the globalization of the world's economy, which includes the ratification of the General Agreement on Tariffs and Trade (GATT) and the World Trade Organization Agreement (WTO).

It is substantially accurate to say that prior to 1960 there were no trade remedies specifically established by legislation. Naturally, the general civil, criminal, and commercial law provided for remedies relating to commercial transactions, although these remedies did not particularly focus on the international dimension of the commercial transactions. These remedies continue to exist and they cover a wide range of matters including intellectual property, noncompetitive practices, fraud, deceitful practices, etc.

Because the TIECA was conceived to generate industrial growth within the member states, through both the promotion and the protection of regional industry, the general focus of the treaty is directed more toward repressing smuggling and false declarations as to the origin and manufacturing of products.

In summary, since 1947 to the present, the regulation of foreign trade in Guatemala can be divided into three major periods:
(i) 1947 until 1960, when the Central American Common Market was established;

(ii) 1960 to approximately 1974, when the Central American Common Market was affected by major regional political and global economic phenomena; and finally,
(iii) from 1974 until the present, which has been a period of economic opening and entry of Guatemala into the global economy.

During this latter period, the Central American Market has taken a new view, directed basically toward the creation of a customs union agreement as a means to establishing a regional free trade zone, ultimately connected with the NAFTA system. Concomitantly, and perhaps more importantly, during this period, as indicated above, Guatemala has participated actively in the Uruguay Round, ratifying both GATT and the Final Act Embodying the Results of the Uruguay Round of Multilateral Trade Negotiations and the Marrakech Agreement Establishing the World Trade Organization (WTO).

ANTIDUMPING INVESTIGATIONS

Initiation of Investigation

As indicated above, there is no *corpus* of national legislation on antidumping, but only the legal rules and remedies derived from the GATT and the WTO agreements. This notwithstanding, and to the extent that, as regards international trade, it would not be considered to have been abrogated by the GATT and the WTO agreements, the Penal Code of Guatemala does include in article 341, 4 a provision making dumping a criminal act.

This provision states that, the sale of goods of any kind, below cost, intended to prevent free competition in the market can be punished with imprisonment from six months to three years plus a fine of up to approximately US $1,000.00.

Quite obviously, there are serious conceptual problems with the manner in which this provision reads. For example, the concept of "cost" can be construed in many different ways, particularly in the international trade area. Unfortunately, there are no rulings of the Supreme Court (the only Court that may establish precedent) clarifying the meaning of this concept. Similarly the meaning of the phrase "intention to prevent free competition" also has not been interpreted by the Court.

It is also important to note that, according to general principles of Guatemalan Law, civil damages stemming from criminal activities can be sought both within criminal procedure or separately.

The reason that there are no jurisprudential developments relating to dumping stems, to a large extent, from the fact that there is no governmental agency responsible for pursuing these particular cases. The Ministry of Economy has a general duty to supervise the functioning of the economy and to prevent monopolistic actions from affecting the market. But these general duties have been primarily interpreted as relating to the fixing of certain prices for basic commodities and products, rather than a formal investigation into possible dumping activities.

In addition, although it has always been theoretically feasible to initiate criminal prosecution with respect to dumping, the cost of criminal litigation, in comparison with its anticipated benefits, is rather high. This is to say that criminal litigation is lengthy, complex, highly formalistic, and very unpredictable.

Since 1992, however, there have been important changes to Guatemala's criminal procedure with the introduction of a new Code of Criminal Procedure. Under the new Code, the General Attorney's Office is responsible for the prosecution of criminal violations. At this point it is still too early to tell whether criminal violations involving dumping and other monopolistic activities will develop within the General Attorney's Office.

In summary, there is no particular agency in charge of investigating dumping activities, although it is clear that with the ratification of the GATT and the WTO agreements there is a growing awareness of the use of trade remedies.

Participation of Parties and Their Counsel

As indicated above, because there are no extended administrative and/or civil procedures and remedies to combat dumping practices, the Guatemalan national legislation does not extend beyond article 341, 4° of the Penal Code and the possible legal consequences in terms of civil damages, which consist of actual losses and reduction of income. Therefore, the participation of the parties in this type of proceeding would be that applicable to any criminal procedure, which, as indicated above, results from a new Code modeled, to an important extent, after the German Code.

COUNTERVAILING DUTY INVESTIGATIONS

It follows from our comments above that there are no countervailing rules and procedures, other than those derived from the GATT and WTO rules, that Guatemala has incorporated as national law by means of the ratification of both agreements. It is important to mention, however, that the implementation of the national agencies in charge of the enforcement of the rules and procedures of the said international agreements is now in progress. In addition, the Ministry of Economy has begun consultations and studies to determine to what extent it is required or convenient to develop a national set of rules and procedures to provide for countervailing and other related matters.

A CURRENT CASE

The only antidumping case brought in Guatemala was filed by a local cement plant with the Ministry of Economy to obtain the imposition of antidumping duties (both provisional and definitive). The procedures followed by the Ministry tracked the GATT and WTO rules fairly closely and the investigation was conducted by an agency under the Ministry of Economy, although it is not clear that this Ministry could be considered beyond doubt to be the competent authority. The filing was made against a Mexican producer of cement on the grounds that its sales of virtually the same product in Mexico were made at substantially higher prices than in Guatemala. The Ministry found this to be the case and therefore issued a fairly long ruling on August 16, 1996 (published in the Official Gazette on August 28, 1996), whereby a 38.72 percent antidumping import duty was imposed on the Mexican producer's cement exports to Guatemala.

India

V. Lakshmi Kumaran
Lakshmi Kumaran & Sridharan
New Delhi, India

HISTORY OF INDIAN TRADE REMEDIES

India enacted national legislation effective January 1, 1995, to give effect to India's obligation under the WTO.

India, though a founding Member of the GATT, did not have any legal provision to investigate the dumping of goods and to levy antidumping duty thereon. The Indian Customs Tariff Act of 1975 was amended for the first time in 1982 with the addition of three new Sections, 9, 9A, and 9B, empowering the Central Government to take measures against subsidized or dumped imports by levying countervailing or antidumping duties if such imports caused or threatened to cause material injury to the domestic industry. These amendments came into force on September 2, 1985. With these amendments, Indian legislation was brought into conformity with the GATT Antidumping Code. The Customs Tariff (Identification, Assessment, and Collection of Duty or Additional Duty on Dumped Articles and Determination of Injury) Rules of 1985 were published to implement this law. Similarly, the Customs Tariff (Identification, Assessment, and Collection of Duty or Additional Duty on Bounty Fed Articles and Determination of Injury) Rules of 1985 were adopted in respect of subsidized articles. These enactments remained only in the Statute Book until 1993.

The high tariff rates prevailing in India until 1993 effectively ensured that dumping did not cause injury to any Indian industry. It was only with the liberalization of the Indian economy, started in about mid-1991, that the tariff rates started coming down. Even in 1991, the maximum tariff rate of about 85 percent effectively protected the domestic industry from dumping. Since 1993, Indian tariffs have fallen continuously, and currently the maximum tariff rate is 50 percent. The effective and average rate is much less, around 25 percent, and consequently Indian industry is forced to compete with international suppliers. Petitions for antidumping investigations and for the levy of antidumping duties started flowing in a small way in 1993/1994 and currently a number of products are the subject of antidumping investigation. Even so, the number of such requests is not large (about ten to fifteen). India is new to the detailed antidumping procedures and domestic industry is becoming attuned to the requirements.

ADMINISTRATION OF ANTIDUMPING LAWS

The Indian Ministry of Commerce is the primary agency for antidumping investigations. A senior official of this Ministry has been named as the Designated Authority. He is assisted by experts in the field of antidumping laws and in accounting and economic laws.

In line with the commitment under the Uruguay Round, India had amended its earlier laws to give effect to the provisions agreed upon in the Uruguay Round. The Customs Tariff (Identification, Assessment, and Collection of Antidumping Duty on Dumped Articles and for Determination of Injury) Rules of 1995 and the Customs Tariff (Identification, Assessment, and Collection of Countervailing Duty on Subsidized Articles and for Determination of Injury) Rules of 1995 have been enacted and are in force since January 1, 1995. A new section 9C has been added providing for an appeal of the determinations made by the Designated Authority.

The Designated Authority, based on its investigation, submits recommendations to the Central Government on the issues of dumping, injury, and the causal relationship between the two. The imposition of antidumping duty is implemented by the Ministry of Finance by the issuance of Notifications under the Customs Tariff Act and the implementation is effected by the Customs Department.

The Designated Authority has been entrusted with the following duties:
- to investigate the existence, degree, and effect of any alleged dumping in relation to importation of any article;
- to identify the article liable for dumping duty;
- to submit its findings, provisional or otherwise, to the central government;
- to recommend the date of commencement of duty and the amount which, if levied, would be adequate to remove injury; and
- to review the need for continuance of such duty.

ANTIDUMPING INVESTIGATIONS

Dumping Determination

Initiation of Investigations

Rule 5 of the Dumping Rules empowers the Designated Authority to self-initiate an investigation if it is satisfied from the information received from the Commissioner of Customs or from any other source of the existence of sufficient evidence as to justify the initiation of an investigation. The Rules also empower the Designated Authority to initiate an investigation upon receipt of a written application by or on behalf of a domestic industry.

Timetable

The regulations have not laid down any time table for initiation and completion of an antidumping investigation. However, the designated authority adheres to an internally set schedule.

Preliminary screening

The application is scrutinized to see if it provides adequate evidence for initiation. If the evidence is not adequate, then a deficiency letter is issued, normally within twenty days of the receipt of the application.

Initiation

When the Designated Authority is satisfied that there is sufficient evidence in the application of dumping and material injury caused thereby, a Public Notice is issued initiating an antidumping investigation. The Public Notice is published in the Gazette of India.

The Designated Authority notifies the government of the exporting country before it proceeds to initiate the investigation.

The initiation notice will be issued normally within forty-five days of the date of receipt of the application.

Preliminary finding

The Designated Authority will proceed expeditiously with the conduct of the investigation and shall, in appropriate cases, make a preliminary finding of dumping, injury, and the causal link, and provide the main reasons behind the determination. The preliminary finding will normally be made within 120 days of the date of initiation.

Provisional duty

A provisional duty not exceeding the margin of dumping may be imposed on the basis of the preliminary finding.

The provisional duty can be imposed only after the expiration of sixty days from the date of initiation of the investigation.

The provisional duty will remain in force for a period not exceeding six months, which may be extended to nine months.

Final determination

The final determination is normally made within 150 days of the date of the preliminary determination.

Disclosure of information

The Designated Authority will inform all interested parties of the essential facts that form the basis for his decision before the final finding is made.

Statutory time limit

The normal time allowed by the statute for conclusion of the investigation and submission of the final finding is one year from the date of initiation of the investigation. The above period may be extended by the Central Government by six months.

Participation of parties and their counsel

Under Rule 6, which deals with "principles governing investigations," the Designated Authority is required to issue a Public Notice wherever it decided to initiate an investigation and to determine the existence, degree, and effect of any alleged dumping. A copy of this Public Notice is sent to known exporters of the article alleged to have been dumped, the Government of the exporting country concerned, and other interested parties.

An "interested party" has been defined to include an exporter or a foreign producer or the importer of the article under investigation, or a trade or business association, a majority of the members of which are producers, exporters, or importers of such articles, the Government of the exporting country and a producer of a like article in India or a trade/business association, a majority of the members of which produce the like article in India. The Rules also require the Designated Authority to provide an opportunity to the industrial users of the article under investigation and to representative consumer organizations in cases where the article is commonly sold at the retail level. Thus, the domestic petitioner, respondents including industrial users and consumers, and foreign respondents are given full opportunity to present information in writing, to participate in public hearings held by the Designated Authority, to put forth their views, and to meet the objections of the other parties face to face. The parties are permitted to be represented by counsel.

Access to information developed in proceedings

The Designated Authority is required to make available a copy of the application and other evidence presented by one interested party to the other parties so long as they are provided to the Designated Authority on a nonconfidential basis.

Any information provided to the Designated Authority on a confidential basis by any party may not be disclosed to any other party without the specific authorization of the party providing the information, if the Designated Authority is satisfied that it is confidential. The Designated Authority may request the parties who submit confidential information to furnish a nonconfidential summary thereof or a statement of reasons as to why such summarization is not possible.

If the Designated Authority is not satisfied that confidential treatment is warranted, or if the provider of information is not willing to disclose it in a generalized form, then such information may be disregarded.

Unlike the United States, where the confidential information of one party is made available to the counsel for other parties under an administrative protective order, in India, confidential information is not available to the other party. The nonconfidential summary alone is made available.

Definitions

The definition of "like product" reflects the GATT definition. The definition in the Dumping Rules, however, refers to it as "a like article." A like article means an article that is identical or alike in all respects to the article under investigation or, in the absence of such an article, another article that, although not alike in all respects, has characteristics closely resembling those of the article under investigation.

There is no accepted definition of the term "period of investigation." The period of investigation is decided by the Designated Authority with reference to the information made available in the petition filed by the domestic industry and normally covers a period ranging from six months to one year prior to the initiation of the investigation.

A dumping investigation can, normally, be initiated only upon receipt of a written application by or on behalf of the "domestic industry." Domestic industry means the Indian producers as a whole of like goods or those whose collective output constitutes a major proportion of total Indian production.

The Indian Law provides that producers who are related to the exporters or importers or are themselves importers of the allegedly dumped goods *shall be deemed not to form part of the domestic industry*.

In order to constitute a valid application, the following two conditions have to be satisfied:

(i) The domestic producers expressly supporting the application must account for not less than 25 percent of the total production of the like product by the domestic industry.

(ii) The domestic producers expressly supporting the application must account for more than 50 percent of the total production of the like product by those expressly supporting and opposing the application.

Indian law appears to depart markedly from the definition of "domestic industry" in Article VI of the GATT. Article 4.1 (i) of the GATT Code provides that the term "domestic industry" *may* be interpreted as referring to the rest of the producers where producers are related to the exporters or importers or are themselves importers of the allegedly dumped product. Indian law, however, provides no such discretion. The law uses the term "shall" and provides that producers who are related to the exporters or are themselves importers of the allegedly dumped product shall not be deemed to form part of the domestic industry.

Calculation of dumping margins

The provisions in the GATT Antidumping Code in regard to export price, normal value, adjustments necessary to make these two comparable, treatment of sales through related parties, currency conversion, sampling, cost of production and constructed value methods and use of facts available (best information assessment) have been incorporated in Annex-1 of the Rules.

Nonmarket economies

The legislation does not contain any specific provision for determination of normal value in the case of imports from nonmarket economy countries. In the absence of any latitude given under the Customs Tariff Act for determination of normal value in the case of nonmarket economy countries, the practice has been to learn from the experience of other countries like the United States, the EU, and Australia, among others. In particular, the EU Regulation No. 2423 of 1988, Section 773(c) of the U.S. Tariff Act of 1930 and Section 5(3) of the Australian Customs Tariff Act are being followed.

Price undertakings

Provision for termination of an investigation or suspension thereof on the basis of price undertakings has been provided under Rule 15 of the Rules. Rule 15 reflects the corresponding provisions in Article VI of GATT 1994. The Designated Authority has been empowered to accept or refuse any such price undertaking and to consider practicability or other administrative aspects before accepting a price undertaking. In practice, this provision has not been put to use so far.

EFFECT OF ANTIDUMPING ORDER

Effective Date—Retroactivity

The Act provides for levy of an antidumping duty retrospectively, where:
- there is a history of dumping that caused the injury or the importer should have been aware that the exporter practices dumping that would cause injury; and
- the injury is caused by massive dumping, in a relatively short time, which is such as to seriously undermine the remedial effect of the antidumping duty.

Such retrospective application will not go beyond 90 days before the date of imposition of provisional duty. Further, no retrospective application prior to the date of initiation of the investigation is possible.

Duration—Review and Appeal

An antidumping duty imposed under the Act will be in for effect for five years from the date of imposition, unless revoked earlier.

The Designated Authority shall also from time to time review the need for the continued imposition of the antidumping duty, based on information received by the Authority. A review shall also follow all the procedures prescribed for an investigation. The Designated Authority is also required to carry out a review for determining new margins of dumping for any new exporter or producer from a country that is subject to antidumping duties, provided that these exporters or producers are new and are not related to any of the exporters or producers who are subject to an antidumping duty on the product.

Appeal

An appeal may be filed with the Customs, Excise, and Gold (Control) Appellate Tribunal within 90 days of the date of the order. An appeal of a dumping or subsidy determination or review thereof has been provided for in Section 9C of the Customs Tariff Act of 1975. Every such appeal should be filed within 90 days of the date of order under appeal. In view of the importance attached to this subject, such appeals are to be heard by a Bench consisting of three Judges, one of whom must be the President of the Tribunal.

Levy of Antidumping Duty — Whether It Should Be the Full Margin or Less

Section 9A of the Customs Tariff Act provides for the levy of an antidumping duty not exceeding the margin of dumping. Dumping Rule 4(d) requires the Designated Authority to recommend the amount of an antidumping duty that, if levied, would be adequate to remove the injury to the domestic industry. Pursuant to these provisions, the Designated Authority has been determining the dumping margin and the injury margin in each case and recommending the lesser of these two margins. The injury margin is the difference between the fair selling price of the article to the domestic industry and the landed cost (including customs duty) of the dumped imports. The determination of fair selling price is bound to become a bone of contention and also vests the Designated Authority with significant discretion.

MATERIAL INJURY AND CAUSAL LINK

Unlike the United States, where the dumping and injury determinations have been entrusted to different agencies, in India the Designated Authority is responsible for both. Consequently, information on the initiation of an investigation, the timetable for completing the investigation, participation of interested parties, access to information, and so forth outlined earlier are equally applicable to the injury determination. In fact, in India the dumping, injury, and the causal link between dumping and injury are taken up simultaneously for investigation.

PROBLEMS AND ISSUES

Because the application of Indian antidumping law is relatively recent, a number of issues are being dealt with for the first time.

Nonmarket Economies

Many of the petitions received by the Designated Authority in the Ministry of Commerce in the initial stages involved chemicals from China. Importation of Isobutyl Benzene (IBB), Tri-Methoxy Benzaldehyde, Dead-Burnt Magnesite, Theophylline and Caffeine, were some of the items that were alleged to be dumped in India from China. Both the Designated Authority and the domestic industry faced considerable difficulty with regard to *prima facie* evidence of the normal value of the products in China. Indian law does not have any specific provisions on nonmarket economies. Nonetheless, the concept of surrogate country was used in most of these cases. The petitioners treated India itself as a surrogate country and provided *prima facie* evidence of dumping with reference to the cost of production of the product in India, adjusted for any known differences. In the absence of a response or other cooperation from the Chinese exporters, most of these petitions were decided on the basis of best available information. In a recent case on the alleged dumping of Low Carbon Ferro Chrome (LCFC) from China, the Designated Authority used Zimbabwe as the surrogate country.

Domestic Industry—Monopoly

In a few cases, the domestic industry alleging dumping happened to be monopoly manufacturers. Bisphenol-A and Nitrile Butadiene Rubber are two cases where the domestic supplier was a monopoly supplier. Even in the absence of a response from the exporters, arguments were exchanged between the petitioners and the Indian importers of the product, who argued that the domestic industry was a monopoly supplier and should not be allowed to obtain an antidumping duty. Although the monopoly status of the petitioners proved irrelevant to the determination of dumping, the monopoly issue did make it difficult to evaluate the factors affecting competition within the domestic industry.

Fair Selling Price

Indian law provides for the levy of an antidumping duty equal to or less than the dumping margin. To determine whether a margin less than the dumping margin would be sufficient to remove the injury, the Designated Authority calculates what is called the fair selling price to the domestic industry. This fair selling price is compared with the landed price (inclusive of Customs duty) of the imports and the difference, if any, is treated as the injury margin. If such injury margin is less than the dumping margin, then the antidumping duty is restricted to such injury margin. The calculation of fair selling price has posed considerable problems in determining the optimum cost of production and the optimum level of capacity utilization plus reasonable profit. The Authority does not disclose the methodology used for arriving at the fair selling price and, hence, considerable litigation is expected on this score. In the case of imports of Nitrile Butadiene Rubber from Japan, an appeal has already been filed against the antidumping order questioning , *inter alia*, the fair selling price determined by the Authority.

International Price

One other argument put forth in a number of investigations was that there was no dumping as the export prices to India were comparable to the export prices of the product to other countries. The argument was that the export prices are international prices prevailing in the world market and, hence, there cannot be an allegation of dumping.

Period of Investigation (POI)

The determination of the POI may also become a bone of contention in antidumping investigations in the years to come. There are no guidelines on how the POI is to be set and what should be the length of POI. To cite an example, an investigation has been initiated in September 1996 wherein the POI has been set as the six month period, April-September 1995. The propriety of fixing a POI ending one year prior to the date of initiation is being questioned. There have also been instances when the POI has included an eighteen-month period.

Like Product

Like product is also likely to become a contentious issue. For example, Bisphenol-A was alleged to be produced in two grades, namely, epoxy grade and polycarbonate grade. Similarly, in the case of Dead-Burnt Magnesite from China, where the manganese content varies from 88 percent to 99 percent, it was argued that there should be as many like products as there are goods. In both the cases, the Designated Authority did not agree with the contentions and treated all grades of Dead-Burnt Magnesite and Bisphenol-A as one like product.

COUNTERVAILING DUTY MEASURES

Section 9 of the Customs Tariff Act, 1975 provides for the levy of a countervailing duty on subsidized articles. The Section defines subsidy in terms identical to Article I of the Agreement on Subsidies and Countervailing Measures adopted in the Uruguay Round of Negotiations. The Government has framed the Subsidy Rules of 1995 by incorporating relevant articles of the GATT Agreement.

There have been no countervailing duty investigations in India.

Japan

Yasuhide Watanabe
Nagashima & Ohno
Tokyo, Japan

HISTORY AND OVERVIEW OF TRADE REMEDY LAWS AND/OR REGULATIONS SINCE 1947

Japan's Accession to GATT/WTO and Antidumping and Subsidies Codes

When the GATT was established in 1947, Japan was under the control of the occupation forces. Although the United States always supported the participation of Japan in GATT, Japan could not achieve this status until September 10, 1955, due to the strong opposition of other member countries. Japan acceded to the old GATT Antidumping Code and Subsidies Code established as a result of the Tokyo Round in 1979, and drastically amended its relevant laws and regulations in 1980. Thereafter, trade remedy laws in Japan have been amended from time to time to reflect respective changes in international agreements. The most recent amendments were passed in the Diet in December 1994 and became effective on January 1, 1995 in coordination with Japan's accession to the Marrakech Agreement establishing the World Trade Organization (WTO Agreement).

Discussion of Evolution of Trade Remedy Laws and/or Regulations

Basically, trade remedy laws in Japan stipulate the fundamental rules contained in the then-current international agreements, including the Agreement on Implementation of Article VI of the General Agreement on Tariffs and Trade 1994 (GATT Antidumping Code) and the Agreement on Subsidies and Countervailing Measures (Subsidies Code). The relevant cabinet orders, which stipulate the procedures for the implementation of the laws, and the guidelines for procedures relating to antidumping duties and countervailing duties have also been amended to conform to changes in the relevant laws. The relevant Japanese law, cabinet orders, and guidelines incorporate only a portion of the GATT Antidumping Code and the Subsidies Code. Where the law, orders, or guidelines are silent, it is widely interpreted that the international agreements are directly applicable to such areas. Because the guidelines state that the internationally-established interpretation should be taken into consideration in the implementation of the relevant international agreements, some commentators justify the direct application of the international agreements based on such statement. However, the guidelines have no legal binding effect and such justification is not considered to be dispositive.

In Japanese history, there are only two cases where antidumping duties have been imposed: against ferro-silico-manganese originating in China in February 1993 and against cotton yarn originating in Pakistan in August 1995. The reasons why trade remedies, especially antidumping duties, are rarely used in Japan are unclear. One commentator has stated that the strong international competitive power of Japan and the allegedly closed Japanese market might have hindered the submission of antidumping claims, and the reportedly high government standards regarding the submission of supporting materials might have discouraged potential applicants.

Summary Listing of each Trade Remedy

Antidumping Duty:	Article 8 of Customs Tariff Law; Cabinet Order relating to Antidumping Duty; Guidelines for Procedures relating to Countervailing and Antidumping Duties
Countervailing Duty:	Article 7 of Customs Tariff Law; Cabinet Order relating to Countervailing Duty; Guidelines for Procedures relating to Countervailing and Antidumping Duties
Emergency Duty:	Article 9 of Customs Tariff Law; Cabinet Order relating to Emergency Duty
Retaliatory Duty:	Article 6 of Customs Tariff Law; Cabinet Order relating to Retaliatory Duty
Counter Duty:	Article 9 of Customs Tariff Law; Cabinet Order relating to Emergency Duty
Restriction on Importation:	Article 52 of Foreign Exchange and Foreign Trade Control Law; Cabinet Order relating to Import Trade Control

ANTIDUMPING INVESTIGATIONS

Dumping Determination

Initiation of investigation

By petition

Interested parties for a domestic industry may request the imposition of antidumping duties. A petition must be filed with the Planning and Legal Division of the Customs and Tariff Bureau, Ministry of Finance, and must demonstrate the importation of a dumped product and material injury therefrom to either a domestic industry or the establishment of a domestic industry by including sufficient evidence supporting such facts. Japan's two antidumping cases were initiated by the entrepreneurs' associations in the relevant industries.

Interested parties for the domestic industry may include:
(i) domestic producers of the like product (or an association thereof, a majority of the members of which are domestic producers of the like product) whose total output of the like product constitutes 25 percent or more of the total domestic production thereof; or
(ii) labor unions, the direct or indirect members of which are engaged in the manufacture of the like product, where the total number of such members constitutes 25 percent or more of the total members of the labor union.

Although based on the GATT Antidumping Code, which also provides a 25 percent threshold as a requirement for the initiation of an investigation, the above 25 percent threshold is a requirement for the filing of a petition in Japan. The criteria contained in the GATT Antidumping Code that requires 50 percent support of those expressing an opinion regarding a petition is not a necessary prerequisite for filing a petition in Japan.

By government

The government may initiate an investigation where there is sufficient evidence indicating the importation of a dumped product and material injury to a domestic industry. The relevant laws use in many cases the term "government" without specifying a particular authority. As mentioned below, although the Minister of Finance plays the primary role, the Minister of International Trade and Industry and other ministers having jurisdiction over the industry concerned may discuss the issue. However, there is no predetermined authority in charge of antidumping matters. Accordingly, the term "government" is used in this article unless a particular authority is specified in the relevant laws.

Timetable

Within approximately two months of the filing of a petition, the Minister of Finance, the Minister of International Trade and Industry, and the minister having jurisdiction over the industry concerned will decide, after consultation, whether or not to initiate an investigation.

Promptly after deciding to initiate an investigation, the Minister of Finance will notify those parties who are directly interested in the following information: the description, name, type, model, and features of the product; similar details regarding the suppliers or supplying country of the product subject to the investigation; the date on which the investigation is initiated; the duration of the investigation; a summary of the matters subject to the investigation; and the deadline for submitting evidence. Notice to, or a presentation of the full text copy of the petition to, the affected government contained in the GATT AD Code is not provided for. The Minister of Finance will also place a public notice in the official gazette.

Directly interested parties are exporters or importers of the product being investigated, an association thereof (in which a majority of the direct or indirect members are suppliers or importers of the investigated product), and the petitioners in the investigation. Additionally, the Minister of Finance will notify the Special Duty Group of the Customs Tariff Council that an investigation has been initiated. (The Customs Tariff Council engages in the investigation and deliberation of important matters concerning the customs rate. The Minister of Finance must consult with the Customs Tariff Council when imposing, changing, or abolishing duties, including antidumping duties, or taking a provisional measure. The Special Duty Group handles such matters. However, the Customs Tariff Council is not involved in the actual antidumping investigation.)

Investigations are conducted by investigation teams composed of a certain number of officials of the Ministry of Finance, the Ministry of International Trade and Industry, and the ministry having jurisdiction over the industry concerned.

No sooner than sixty days from the date of the initiation of an investigation, the government may impose a provisional duty or issue an order to deposit a security in lieu thereof if it is presumed that the importation of the dumped product and the material injury to the domestic industry exist based on sufficient evidence (in the case of the violation of an undertaking, the best information available) and it is deemed necessary to protect such domestic industry. Because no provisional measure has ever been taken, it is not clear which factors would necessitate the protection of a domestic industry. However, if the government has accepted a price undertaking by an exporter whereby the export price is increased so that the antidumping margin is offset, or if an applicant for the imposition of the antidumping margin has withdrawn its application, the need to protect the domestic industry would diminish.

A provisional measure, in principle, may last for no more than four months. However, such period may be extended to six months if:

(i) the government announces that it will consider imposing an antidumping duty that is less than the dumping margin (in such cases the government requires more time to determine whether or not such antidumping duty may eliminate damages); or

(ii) an exporter of the product, who is responsible for approximately 50 percent of the exports of such product, requests the extension of the period in advance.

An exporter may have an incentive to request an extension because, as mentioned below, the imposition of an antidumping duty is retroactive to the end of the period during which the provisional measure was taken, but the amount of the antidumping duty may not exceed the amount of the provisional measure. If both (i) and (ii) are met, the period may be extended up to nine months. The maximum period of nine months is intended to be consistent with that of the GATT Antidumping Code.

In principle, investigations are concluded within one year after they are initiated. Such period may be extended by up to six months if special reasons warrant such an extension. The Minister of Finance will inform directly interested persons of the important facts on which the decision is based well before the final decision.

The Minister of Finance will, after issuing a referral to the Customs Tariff Council, levy the antidumping duty by issuing a cabinet order. He shall also inform the directly interested parties of the details regarding the facts identified during the investigation and of the final decision. At the same time, the Minister will publish such facts and final decision in the official gazette.

Participation of parties and their counsel

Domestic petitioners

During an investigation, the government makes various inquiries by sending written questionnaires, holding hearings, conducting on-site verifications, and/or holding meetings between parties with adverse interests. Interested parties may submit evidence and testify and exchange views with opposing interested parties.

Domestic respondents, including industrial users

Industrial users of the investigated products and, if the investigated products are commonly sold at the retail level, the principal consumers associations may, within a specified duration of the investigation, provide in writing to the Minister of Finance any relevant information.

Foreign parties

Taking the procedures in the two antidumping precedents into consideration, it is likely that a substantial portion of the materials, including a questionnaire to which a respondent must respond within a limited time period, will be sent to the respondent in Japanese only. Considering the time necessary to translate various documents into English and respond to various technical inquiries with careful consideration, the timely involvement of Japanese counsel would be quite important. Unlike the GATT Antidumping Code, there is no allowance providing for a minimum of thirty days to reply to a questionnaire.

Access to information developed in proceedings

Nonproprietary information

Prior to the deadline designated by the Minister of Finance in the notice and the official gazette concerning the initiation of an investigation, interested parties may have access to the evidence provided by the petitioner and relevant persons during the investigation, except for evidence that is by nature confidential or provided by the interested parties with the request that it be treated as confidential.

Business proprietary information

The Minister of Finance must allow interested parties to have access to submitted documents and evidence, except for that which is to be treated as confidential in nature or has been submitted by the relevant parties as such. Such access is allowed upon the application of an interested party.

A petitioner or an interested party may request confidential treatment for business proprietary information by presenting evidence substantiating that such information is worthy of confidential treatment. Unlike the GATT Antidumping Code, there is no provision in Japanese law defining "confidential information." If confidential treatment is deemed to be appropriate, the Minister of Finance may request the applicant to submit a nonproprietary summary of the proprietary information involved. If the applicant fails to submit the summary to the Minister of Finance and does not withdraw the request for confidential treatment, the Minister of Finance is not required to investigate such information.

Definitions

Like products

Unlike the GATT Antidumping Code, there is no provision defining "like product."

Period of investigation

This period is one year in principle, but it may be extended an additional six months if necessary for special reasons.

Domestic industry and petition requirement for industry support

Domestic industry means the producers in Japan whose collective output of the like products constitutes 50 percent or more of the total domestic production of the like product.

Viability of markets

Although the cabinet order allows the use of an export price or a constructed value for a normal price when the sales volume of the like product is low, there are no statutory standards equivalent to the 5 percent standard provided in the GATT Antidumping Code by which market viability is tested.

Related parties

Related parties include the producers who:
(i) directly or indirectly control suppliers or importers of the imported products under investigation, are directly or indirectly controlled by such suppliers or importers, have common direct or indirect control over a third party with such suppliers or importers, or are under the direct or indirect common control, along with such suppliers or importers, of a third party (unless such relationships do not cause the producer to behave differently from any other producer); or
(ii) have imported the products within the six-month period prior to the date of the application for the investigation or, if the investigation was initiated by the government, the date of initiation of the investigation (unless the quantity of such importation was small).

Item (ii) above is limited to the six-month period prior to the antidumping investigation because it is not appropriate to deem a producer who imported the like product substantially prior to the investigation a related party. Unlike the GATT Antidumping Code under which the related parties *may* be excluded from the scope of the domestic industry, under the cabinet order, the related parties *must* be excluded from the scope of the domestic industry.

Calculation of dumping margins
Export price
In principle, the export price is the selling price for the exported products. However, if no such selling price exists or it is deemed improper to use such selling price because the exporter of the product is associated with the importer (including any transferee of such products in Japan), the export price shall be calculated on the basis of the price for domestic sale at which the imported products are first resold to any person who is not associated with any of the exporters or the importers of such products. When the price for domestic sale is the price at which the imported products are sold after having been processed as raw material, the value added by such production shall be deducted from the sale price. Although it is generally interpreted that "associated with" includes not only a capital relationship, such as a parent and a subsidiary or that between a headquarters and a branch, but also a compensatory arrangement, no statutory criteria have been provided to help determine whether or not an exporter and an importer are "associated." In addition, there are no statutory provisions regarding the calculation of the added value or the profit deduction.

Normal value
In principle, the normal value is the price of the like product, in the ordinary course of trade, destined for consumption in the country of origin of the imported products.

In cases where the normal value in the preceding paragraph is not available or where it is deemed inadequate to use such normal price because of the particular market situation of the supplying country or because of the low volume of sales of the like product in the supplying country, normal price may be either:
(i) the selling price of the like product for export to any country other than Japan from the country supplying the imported product being investigated; or
(ii) the cost of the production of the imported product plus normal profits and the administrative, selling, and general costs for the like product produced in the country of origin.

No preference for either of these two methods is stated in the relevant regulations nor has one been announced by the government.

Adjustments, including those reflecting level of trade
To obtain the normal value, necessary adjustments are made for the differences in price resulting from differences in transaction stages, quantity, or any other conditions affecting price, such as the difference in the quality of the product, payment terms, quality guarantee, and sales conditions including after-sale-service and taxation.

Nonmarket economy methodology
In cases where the supplying country of the imported goods is a nonmarket economy country, normal price may be the price of the like product, in the ordinary course of trade, destined for consumption in a comparable country with economic development that is closest to the supplying country of the imported product; the selling price of the like product for export from such country; or the costs of production of the like product in such country plus normal profits and administrative, selling, and general costs of the similar product.

Price undertakings and other agreements to suspend investigations
The exporter of the product under investigation may offer the government its undertaking to revise the prices of such product so that the injurious effect of the dumping of such product on the domestic industry is eliminated. In the alternative, the exporter may cease exporting such product. The exporter is permitted to offer an undertaking after an investigation has been initiated. The government may accept such an offer of undertaking as long as the effective term thereof is five years or less. The government may then suspend or terminate the investigation unless the exporter wishes to complete the investigation.

Effect of Antidumping Order

Effective date
An antidumping order is issued in the form of a cabinet order and the effective date thereof is provided therein. In the two antidumping precedents, both of the dates of promulgation thereof were the effective dates of the antidumping order.

Retroactivity
If a provisional measure was taken and the products specified thereby were imported during the periods set forth below, an antidumping duty may be imposed that shall not exceed the amount of the provisional duty or the amount of security that has been ordered to be deposited. If the amount of

the antidumping duty under the antidumping order exceeds that under the provisional measure, the difference will be reimbursed.

Retroactive duties are imposed for the following periods:
(i) if the provisional measures were imposed, for such period;
(ii) if an undertaking was violated, for the period commencing on the date that is ninety days before the date on which the provisional measures were taken or the date of the violation of the undertaking, whichever is later, and ending on the date immediately preceding the date of ordinary final measures; and
(iii) if substantial dumping occurred, for the period commencing on the date that is ninety days before the date on which the provisional measures were taken or the first date of the investigation, whichever is later, and ending on the date immediately preceding the date of ordinary final measures.

Duration

The duration of an antidumping order is provided for in the relevant cabinet order thereof. There is a sunset clause under which the maximum duration of the antidumping order is five years.

Scope determination

The antidumping order must include the following information:
(i) the description, type, model, and features of the affected products;
(ii) the supplier or supplying country;
(iii) the duration of the antidumping order (and the date of termination if the antidumping order is to be terminated);
(iv) the facts identified in the investigation and conclusions obtained therefrom, other than in cases where the specified duration has already expired;
(v) the products concerned and reason for determination (if the provisional duty is imposed); and
(vi) any other relevant matters.

There is no statutory provision allowing outside parties to narrow the scope of the antidumping order by seeking to limit the kinds of products that are subject to the order.

Enforcement, including rules to prevent circumvention of orders

Under the Customs Law, a person who imports products to which a customs charge should be assessed (including antidumping duties) without paying such charges through fraud or any other unlawful act shall be subject to imprisonment with labor for up to five years and/or a fine of up to five million yen. If such importation is made by a representative, an agent or an employee of a corporation or other legal entities within the scope of his/her duty or with respect to assets thereof, such corporation may also be subject to a fine of up to five million yen. With respect to anticircumvention measures, there is no statutory provision.

Procedures for new shippers

New shippers (persons other than those who imported the products during the investigation period and related parties in cases where the antidumping duty is imposed by specifying the supplying country) may submit to the government evidence indicating that the amount of the antidumping duty imposed on the product of such new shippers should be different from the amount of the actual dumping margin of such product and request the government to modify or abolish the antidumping duty to be imposed upon the relevant product. The government may impose an antidumping duty on the specified supplier or supplying country (i.e., the exporting country and/or the country of origin). In the latter case, the "all other" rate is applied.

Procedures for review and revocation of order

A supplier of the product or its association, an importer thereof or its association, or interested parties for the domestic industry may submit to the government evidence concerning the existence of a change in circumstances and apply for a review of:
(i) antidumping duties imposed on a new supplier;
(ii) antidumping duties that had been based on a change in circumstances after the initial imposition;
(iii) whether or not the period of imposition should be extended, or
(iv) the undertaking.

If the amount of the collected antidumping duty exceeds the dumping margin, the relevant importer is entitled to a refund of the amount in excess of the dumping margin without interest upon request by submitting sufficient evidence therefor.

There is no statutory provision providing for a judicial review.

COUNTERVAILING DUTY INVESTIGATIONS

Subsidy Determination

Initiation of investigation

Timetable

Participation of parties and their counsel

Domestic petitioners

Domestic respondents, including industrial users

Foreign respondents

Access of parties to information developed in proceedings

Nonproprietary information

Business proprietary information

With respect to the above matters, the provisions of the Customs Tariff Law and its ordinance are similar to those for antidumping. Please note, however, that the period of the provisional measure for the countervailing duty may not exceed four months.

Definitions

Countervailable subsidies

Section 7.2 of the Customs Tariff Law provides that "subsidies" mean those provided for in Article 1 of the Subsidies Code, except for those that are not subject to the countervailing duty in accordance with Article 13 of the Agreement on Agriculture and Sections 8.1 and 8.2 of the Subsidies Code. Accordingly, a "red light," "yellow light," or "green light" will be assigned to each of the subsidies in accordance with the Subsidies Code. Due to lack of precedent, what specific kinds of subsidies fall under "red light," "yellow light," or "green light" subsidies is unclear.

Noncountervailable subsidies ("green light")

Please see the preceding item.

Undertakings that suspend investigation

Undertakings in countervailing duty investigations are similar to undertakings in antidumping duty investigations.

Effect of Countervailing Duty Order

Effective date
Retroactivity, if any
Duration
Scope determinations
Enforcement, including measures to prevent circumvention of order
Procedures for review and revocation

With respect to the above matters, the provisions of the Customs Tariff Law and its ordinance are similar to those for antidumping.

INJURY ANALYSIS

With respect to injury analysis, there are no special statutory provisions.

OTHER TRADE REMEDIES

History and Rationale

As emergency measures to restrict importation, the Customs Tariff Law and its relevant cabinet orders provide for the imposition of the emergency duty, the retaliatory duty, and the counter duty. The Foreign Exchange and Foreign Trade Control Law and its relevant cabinet orders provide for the imposition of a limit upon the quantity of certain imported products. However, none of these remedies has ever been used.

Procedures

Emergency duty

If, as the result of a decline in the price of a product in a foreign country or of unforeseen circumstances, the drastic increase in the importation of such product causes or threatens to cause serious injury to the domestic industry of the like or competitive products, the government may commence an investigation. Only the government may initiate the investigation. The investigation shall be completed within one year, provided that it may be extended if deemed necessary for special reasons. The government may undertake provisional measures for a period not exceeding 200 days before

the completion of the investigation. The government may take preventive measures by either:
(i) imposing a duty in an amount equal to or less than the amount corresponding to the difference between the normal customs value of said product and the wholesale price in Japan of like or similar products minus an amount for normal customs; or
(ii) withdrawing or modifying a tariff concession made under the Agreement on Safeguards (Safeguards Code).

The period for the imposition of a duty shall be four years or less, including the period for the provisional measure. The period may be extended, but it may not exceed eight years. The measurements taken in the extended period may not be more restrictive than those taken during the period before extension.

Retaliatory duty

If it is considered necessary to protect interests accrued to Japan directly or indirectly under the WTO Agreement or attain the objectives thereof, the government may impose a duty of an amount equal to or less than the customs value of the relevant product after specifying the country and product, subject to the approval of the Dispute Settlement Body or the Committee on Subsidies and Countervailing of the WTO, as the case may be.

Counter duty

If any foreign country has taken emergency measures under the GATT Antidumping Code or Safeguards Code without first obtaining the necessary agreements or holding any conference in advance thereunder, except for the case where such emergency measures were taken as a result of a drastic increase in the importation of the relevant product in the country in question and more than three years have not elapsed since such measure was taken, the government may impose a duty in an amount equal to or less than the relevant customs value, or impose a duty by suspending the application of the relevant tariff concession.

Restriction of importation

In approving or confirming an import or import quota allocation, the Minister of International Trade and Industry may attach conditions with regard to the period during which the import is to be affected, place of origin, shipment area, and other matters relating to the import if he deems it necessary to do so for the sound development of foreign trade.

Administrative Framework

The emergency duties are imposed by the Minister of Finance, while restrictions on importation are implemented by the Minister of International Trade and Industry. In the case where the import of a particular product causes or threatens to cause serious injury to a domestic industry, in theory, either of the measures under the Customs Tariff Law or the Foreign Exchange and Foreign Trade Control Law may be taken. It is conceivable that an adjustment as to the measure to be taken may be made among two Ministers and the minister having jurisdiction over the relevant industry based on mutual consultation.

Timetable

The investigation for an emergency duty, in principle, will be completed within one year, provided that such period may be extended if necessary for special reasons. With respect to other emergency measures, there are no statutory provisions concerning the procedures for such measures.

Korea

Mr. Dae Yun Cho
Kim & Chang
Seoul, Korea

HISTORY AND OVERVIEW OF TRADE REMEDY LAWS AND/OR REGULATIONS SINCE 1947

Discussion of Country's Accession to GATT/WTO and Antidumping and Subsidies Codes

Korea first acceded to the GATT in April 1967 and to the GATT Subsidies Code in June 1980, after which it ratified the GATT Antidumping Code in February 1986. Korea was an active party in the Uruguay Round negotiations and, with the entry into force of the WTO Agreement and the GATT 1994, became a chartered member of the WTO in 1995.

Discussion of Evolution of Trade Remedy Laws and/or Regulations

Antidumping and countervailing duties were first introduced in Korea in 1963. Korea's antidumping and countervailing laws and safeguard measures were introduced in modern form in 1967, the year Korea joined GATT.

Few trade remedy actions were taken prior to the late 1980s, which was about the time when the Korean Trade Commission (KTC) was established. Since 1986, as many domestic industries have grown and replaced foreign suppliers, antidumping cases and safeguard measures began to emerge in Korea. After twelve years of experience, the Korean government is facing more restraints in triggering safeguard measures, although antidumping cases are increasing very rapidly and now total thirty-five cases to date. By contrast, not a single countervailing duty case has ever been initiated in Korea.

Korean laws on antidumping and countervailing duties and safeguard measures generally are in compliance with the respective WTO codes and are similar to the legislation in countries with advanced trade remedy laws. Hence, a causal connection is required between the injury and either the dumping, subsidy, or increased imports. In determining causation, the KTC will review, inter alia, whether the dumped import was sold at a price lower than that of the domestic product in the Korean market during the investigation period and whether there were any other reasons for the deterioration of the domestic industry. In addition, as a final element for trade remedies, further consideration is to be given to whether or not it is worthwhile to protect the domestic industry by way of imposition of a remedy or sanction.

Summary listing of each trade remedy, with corresponding statutory/regulatory references and agency responsible for administering such remedy

Antidumping and countervailing measures, including provisional and final measures and the acceptance of undertakings, are administered by the Minister of Finance and Economy (MOFE) based on investigations conducted by the KTC with respect to both dumping/subsidy and injury to the domestic industry. Effective January 1996, the authority to investigate dumping/subsidy was also transferred from the Korean Customs Service to the KTC, which, although under the Korean Ministry of Trade, Industry, and Energy, is designed to be an independent quasi-judicial organization.

The relevant laws and regulations related to antidumping duties in Korea are Article 10 of the Customs Act, Articles 4-2 through 4-15 of the Presidential Decree of the Customs Act, and the Enforcement Regulations thereunder.

The relevant laws and regulations related to countervailing duties are also the Customs Act (Article 13), its Presidential Decree, and the Enforcement Regulations. In fact, Article 4-25 of the Presidential Decree of the Customs Act stipulates that most of the provisions applicable to antidumping duties under the same Decree are to be applied *mutatis mutandis* to countervailing duties.

Certain provisions of the WTO Antidumping and Subsidies codes are not fully reflected in these laws and regulations. However, it should be noted that under the Constitutional Law of Korea, international norms generally recognized and treaties concluded and promulgated in accordance with the Constitutional Law have an effect that is equivalent to domestic law. Hence, in the event that the domestic laws do not address any mandatory provisions of the relevant WTO codes, the Korean Constitutional Law may arguably entitle the interested parties to rely on the pertinent provisions of the WTO codes as directly applicable to actual cases.

Safeguard measures, including provisional ones, may be imposed by the MOFE (in the event of services, by a competent ministry and authority) in accordance with KTC's recommendation based on its investigation with respect to the serious injury to the domestic industry at the request of an interested party or the competent ministry or authority. The relevant laws and regulations related to safeguard measures are Chapter Four of the Foreign Trade Act and Article 12 of the Customs Act, Articles 61 through 82 of the Presidential Decree of the Foreign Trade Act, and the KTC Regulations.

ANTIDUMPING INVESTIGATIONS

Dumping Determination

Initiation of investigation

By petition

A petition for an antidumping duty may be filed with the KTC by an interested party in the relevant domestic industry (a manufacturer or an association of manufacturers). The petition should present sufficient evidence demonstrating the presence of dumping and injury caused thereby. A domestic manufacturer will have standing as an interested party if its production of products concerned constitutes a major portion of domestic production. However, a manufacturer who has imported dumped products or has a special relationship with the exporter and/or importer of the dumped products may lose its standing as an interested party.

By government

An antidumping investigation may also be commenced at the request of the minister of the competent ministry supervising the relevant domestic industry. The ministry-initiated investigation does not require any elements additional to those required by the investigations initiated by petition.

Timetable

When the petition is filed, the KTC must notify the MOFE, the minister of the competent ministry, and the government of the country(ies) exporting the subject products. The KTC must decide whether or not to initiate an investigation and report its decision to the MOFE within one month after the date of filing of a petition. The KTC will reject the petition if there is insufficient evidence of dumping and the injury caused thereby; a de minimis dumping margin; a negligible import volume; a lack of standing; or a failure to meet other requirements. The MOFE then announces its decision in the *Official Gazette* with detailed information, including the period of investigation and the names of exporters involved.

After the initiation of the investigation, the KTC investigates and determines the existence of dumping and whether a dumped import causes or threatens to cause material injury to a domestic industry, or causes material retardation of the establishment of a domestic industry.

The preliminary investigation must be completed no later than three months from the date of initiation of the investigation. If the preliminary investigation indicates that dumped imports have caused injury and that provisional measures are deemed necessary, provisional measures may be imposed by the MOFE in the form of a provisional antidumping duty or provision of security, within one month from MOFE's receipt of KTC's report.

The final investigation must be completed no later than three months from the date of the preliminary investigation. During the period of final investigation, if the foreign government and respondents concerned agree, KTC investigators will conduct on-the-spot investigations. For certain complex cases or with a reasonable request from the parties concerned, a one-month extension may be granted for the preliminary and/or final investigation.

Participation of parties and their counsel

Domestic petitioners

The KTC sends questionnaires to the domestic petitioners and may conduct investigations of petitioners' manufacturing facilities. The petitioners and their counsel are entitled to participate in the proceedings by attending public hearings to present their opinions; submitting briefs and evidence; and obtaining copies of briefs and evidence presented by other interested parties.

Domestic respondents, including industrial users

The KTC also sends questionnaires to the domestic respondents, including exporters' agencies, importers, and industrial users. These domestic respondents are allowed to participate in the proceedings by submitting briefs and evidence and obtaining copies of briefs and evidence presented by other interested parties. Due to the limited time of hearings, however, the domestic respondents must obtain a prior approval from the KTC to attend public hearings and present their opinions.

Foreign respondents

The KTC sends questionnaires to the foreign respondents, including manufacturers and exporters, and would conduct on-the-spot investigations (verification), subject to consent by the respondents and the authorities of the exporting country. The rights of defense are fully recognized, thus foreign respondents and their counsels are entitled to participate in the proceedings by attending public hearings to present their opinions; submitting briefs and evidence; and obtaining copies of briefs and evidence presented by other interested parties.

Access to information developed in proceedings

Nonproprietary information

Once the investigation begins, and the public notice to that effect is published in the Government Gazette, the interested parties are entitled to and, subject to a written request, are actually freely allowed access to, any non-proprietary information, and to obtain a copy of briefs and evidence presented by other interested parties.

None of the information developed in the proceedings, whether business proprietary or not, may be used for purposes other than the subject investigations and rulings.

Business proprietary information

When submitting data and information, interested parties are allowed to designate the relevant portion thereof as business confidential with justified reasons and request the KTC to treat them as business proprietary information. The KTC may dismiss the request, in whole or in part, if it deems such request inappropriate or unjustified, judging from the industry practice. In practice, however, the KTC would usually accept such a request, if the requesting party agrees to submit a separate version to the other interested parties, containing a summary of the business confidential information withheld.

There is no protective order or equivalent mechanism recognized under the Korean judicial system. Under the circumstances, once the information is submitted as business confidential and so recognized by the KTC, neither an interested party nor its counsel would be allowed access to such information.

Under the KTC's internal regulations, confidential information is supposed to be disclosed to the relevant counsels; however, that procedure is not currently practiced in Korea. Moreover, no appeal of a KTC determination has ever taken place in Korea, but if there were such an appeal, then the parties might theoretically obtain confidential information. Generally speaking, the KTC is required to reject a confidential submission if it is not accompanied by a public version that may be seen by all the parties. However, if a public version is not submitted, then whether or not a confidential submission actually will be rejected is not certain - there is no precedent on this point.

Definitions

Like products

Like products are defined as products that are identical in all respects (except for minor differences in appearance), such as physical characteristics, quality, and consumer reputation or, in the absence of such identical products, ones most similar that, although not alike in all respects, have characteristics, composition, and functions closely resembling, and that may be interchangeably used with, the article subject to an investigation.

Period of investigation

Generally, the period of investigation for dumping is six or twelve months prior to the initiation of investigation.

Domestic industry and petition requirement for industry support

A petition is deemed to have been filed by or on behalf of a domestic industry if the domestic producers who support the petition account for more than 50 percent of the like products produced by the members of the domestic industry expressing either support for or opposition to the petition; and those domestic producers expressing support for the petition account for at least 25 percent of the total domestic production of the like products. If such standard is not satisfied, the petition shall be rejected without commencement of an investigation.

Viability of markets

If the home market sales in the exporting country constitute less than 5 percent of the sales to the importing country, such sales shall not be a basis for calculating normal value, unless the evidence demonstrates that the sales at a percentage lower than 5 percent can provide a basis for the price comparison.

Related parties

Related parties are defined as those having special relationships as enumerated by the Presidential Decree of the Customs Act. One example that is most relevant for a foreign exporter/domestic importer relationship is 5 percent or more of the ownership or management control of the respective companies. Other examples include: the purchaser and seller are officers and managers in mutual business; the purchaser and seller have an employment relationship; and the purchaser and the seller are directly or indirectly managed by an identical third person.

Calculation of Dumping Margins

Export Price

The export price is normally the purchase price as recognized on the basis of records. In the event there is no export price or the export price is not reliable due to the presence of affiliation or a compensatory arrangement between the exporter and the importer or a third party, the export price may be constructed on the basis of the price at which the imported products are first resold to an unrelated buyer, or if the products are not resold to an unrelated buyer, or not resold in the conditions as imported, on such reasonable basis as the KTC may determine.

Normal value

The normal value for a product is determined, in principle, by the domestic market price of the product in the exporter's home country. However, if the sales volume in the home country (excluding sales at prices below the cost of production and sales to persons having a special relationship with the exporter) is small, then either the representative and comparable export price to a third country or a constructed value determined by the KTC will be deemed to be the normal value.

Where sales below cost constitute no less than 20 percent of the volume sold in the domestic (or third country) market and the sales, excluding the sales below cost, cannot provide for the recovery of costs within a reasonable period of time, such sales below cost shall not be a basis for calculating normal value.

Adjustments, Including those reflecting level of trade

For the purposes of calculating the dumping margin, the export price to Korea and the normal value will be adjusted to ex-factory price, and the percentage of the dumping margin will be calculated as follows:

$$\frac{\text{Adjusted normal value - Adjusted export price}}{\text{Adjusted export price (CIF basis)}} \times 100$$

Korean law provides a general requirement that comparisons be fair and provides specific requirements to achieve this fairness, including requirements that comparisons be made at the same level of trade, normally at the ex-factory level, and between sales made as concurrently as possible. In addition, differences in physical characteristics, quantity, conditions and terms of sale, taxation, fluctuations of the exchange rate, and so forth, may also be considered for adjustment under certain conditions.

Treatment of sales through related parties

If the products are sold through related parties and are not resold to an independent buyer, or are not resold in the same condition in which they were imported, the export price shall be the price calculated after taking into account the costs incurred between the importation and resale, plus reasonable profits.

Currency conversion

When the price comparison requires a conversion of currencies, such conversion shall be made using the foreign exchange rate on the date of sale. Foreign exchange fluctuations may be recognized as a price adjustment factor only if there is a sustained movement of the rate in a certain direction.

Sampling

If there is a large number of exporters or products subject to investigation, the investigation may be limited to using statistically valid sampling methods including the volume of imports. An individual rate should be calculated for exporters who voluntarily provide information. An "all-others" rate for exporters that are not individually investigated shall be a weighted average rate of all exporters examined.

Cost of production and constructed value methodology

The constructed value shall be the amount of the costs incurred in the normal production process in the country of origin plus the selling, general and administrative costs and profit. The amount for profit shall not exceed the profits normally realized on the sales of products of the same general category in the domestic market of the country of origin.

Nonmarket economy methodology

If the product is imported from a country in which the economy is state-controlled and where nonmarket conditions prevail, the KTC will determine the normal value on the basis of either the price of the like product that is sold for consumption in a market economy country other than Korea or exported to a third country, or on the basis of the constructed value. However, if the nonmarket economy country is in transition to a market economy, the KTC may recognize the home market price of that nonmarket economy country for calculating normal value.

Use of facts available

All verifiable information that is appropriately submitted so that it can be used in the investigation without undue difficulties and that is supplied in a timely fashion will be taken into consideration by the KTC. If a party fails to supply or refuses to provide the requisite information or impedes the investigation or the information is otherwise unverifiable, the KTC may make determinations on the basis of the facts available.

Price undertakings and other agreements to suspend investigations

In cases where the exporter of a product offers undertakings to increase its price or to cease exports, and where such undertakings are accepted by the MOFE, the investigation will in principle be suspended or terminated without imposition of antidumping duties. Undertakings may only be accepted after an affirmative determination of the preliminary investigation of dumping and injury.

Effect of Antidumping Order

Effective date

Retroactivity, if any

Antidumping duties, whether provisional or final, will in principle apply to products imported after the respective determinations are made.

However, where a final determination of material injury (but not of a threat thereof or of the material retardation of the establishment of an industry) is ascertained or, in the case of a final determination of a threat to an industry, where the effect of the dumped imports would have led to material injury but for the application of provisional measures, an antidumping duty may be levied retroactively for the period during which the provisional measures have been applied. In addition, a final antidumping duty may be levied on products that were imported not more than ninety days prior to the date of application of the provisional measures if it is necessary to impose retroactively the antidumping duties to prevent a recurrence of injury caused by massive importation in a relatively short period of time and if there is a history of dumping that caused injury, or the importer was, or should have been, aware of the presence of dumping and injury caused thereby. If the retroactive imposition does not apply, the provisional antidumping duties paid shall be refunded to the importers.

Duration

The antidumping duty imposed or the undertakings, unless otherwise fixed, shall be terminated no later than five years from such imposition or enforcement. However, if the contents are modified as a result of a review, such five-year period will commence on the date of such revision.

Scope determination

If an affirmative determination is made with respect to both the injury and dumping, the MOFE will decide whether the imposition of an antidumping duty is necessary for the protection of the domestic industry and the appropriate amount of duty based on the result of the final determinations. An antidumping duty will be imposed in the form of a duty rate or a minimum import price. If the minimum import price method is chosen, the difference between the actual import price and the minimum import price will be the amount of the antidumping duty payable by importers. Since the so-called "lesser duty rule" is applied in Korean antidumping procedures, the actual amount of antidumping duty may be lower than the final dumping margin.

There is no separate proceeding to determine whether a particular product is included within the coverage of an order. Ordinarily, the MOFE sends to the Korean Customs Service (KCS) the necessary information, such as the country of origin and the model or grade of the products concerned to identify the dumped products, and authorizes the KCS to establish detailed criteria, as appropriate, to implement MOFE's decision.

Enforcement, including rules to prevent circumvention of orders

Antidumping duties are imposed with respect to the products from a dumping country upon ascertainment through a certificate of origin. If the product is imported from a third country, other than the dumping country, by way of transshipment or repacking, or if there is no local industry manufacturing the like products in such third country, the product is deemed to be imported from the dumping country. Otherwise, Korean antidumping laws do not provide anticircumvention provisions.

Procedures for new shippers

If new shippers can show that they are not related to any of the exporters or manufacturers in the exporting country who are subject to antidumping duties, the KTC must initiate and conduct new shipper reviews for calculating individual dumping margins on an accelerated basis.

Procedures for review and revocation of order

If the MOFE deems it necessary or if the interested parties or the competent ministry supervising the relevant domestic industry so requests, an administrative review may be conducted. Under the Korean proceedings, there are four kinds of reviews: changed circumstances administrative review; sunset review; annual review; and refund review.

The review investigation shall be concluded within six months (or, if extended, an additional four months) from the initiation of the review and the imposition of final measures must be concluded within one month (or, if extended, an additional twenty days) from the conclusion of the investigation.

Although it is not entirely clear, provisional or final antidumping measures may also be subject to judicial review under the general judicial review system for administrative actions. Up to now, however, no case has ever been brought before the courts.

COUNTERVAILING DUTY INVESTIGATIONS

Contrary to the rapid development of antidumping cases, a countervailing duty case has yet to be seen in Korea. The MOFE retains the authority to implement all countervailing measures, including provisional and final measures, as well as to administer the acceptance of undertakings, on the basis of investigations conducted by the KTC. However, neither the MOFE nor the KTC has promulgated any independent policy or detailed regulations by which to exclusively regulate countervailing duties. Instead, the rules that govern countervailing duty are parallel to those that govern antidumping duty and continue to be the authoritative body of law, thus the involved parties will have to consult the antidumping regulations should countervailing duty cases arise in the future. The reader may thus refer to the corresponding sections under the heading of antidumping in the absence of any contrary indication.

Subsidy Determination

The rules relating to the initiation of an investigation, its timetable, participation of parties, their access to information, and the effect of an order in subsidy investigations are the same as in dumping investigations.

Definitions

Countervailable subsidies

Any benefit conferred by a financial contribution by a government or any public body within the exporting country is deemed a subsidy, if such subsidy is specific to an enterprise or industry or group of enterprises or group of industries in accordance with the standard set out in the Enforcement Regulations of the Customs Act. Except for those subsidies that are made noncountervailable by the Enforcement Regulations of the Customs Act, any subsidy or bounty provided overseas, directly or indirectly, with respect to the manufacture, production, or exportation of a class or kind of merchandise imported, or sold for importation, into Korea is countervailable. If a subsidy is provided to or used by a limited number of particular enterprises, or if a subsidy is provided to a limited area, such subsidy is deemed to be specific.

Noncountervailable subsidies ("green light")

Regardless of specificity, subsidies for research, regional development and environmental protection as may be so recognized by international treaties are nonactionable.

Calculation of Subsidies

Treatment of loans, grants, and equity investments

In the case of equity investments, the subsidy is the difference between the amount to be generated by such equity participation and the amount that may be generated in the ordinary pattern of investment. In the case of loans, the subsidy is the difference between the amount that the firm receiving the loan pays on the government loan and a comparable commercial loan that the firm could actually obtain on the market. In the case of an outright gift of money, the subsidy is the entire amount of such gift. In the case of the supply or purchase of goods or services in the form of grants, the subsidy is the difference between the selling/purchase price and market value. This is a theoretical question and not enforced in practice. In addition, it may be noteworthy that "grant" does not necessarily connote an outright gift of money.

Effect of privatization

Korean law provides an additional broad criterion to calculate the amount of subsidy, which contemplates adherence to standards recognized by international treaties, in terms of the benefit actually conferred on the firm.

Otherwise, there is no express provision on the point.

Undertakings that suspend investigation

Both the government of the export country and the MOFE may propose undertakings to eliminate or reduce the subsidy concerned or to take appropriate measures to eliminate the injurious effect on the domestic industry caused thereby. With the consent of its government, the exporter of a product may also offer undertakings to revise its price to such an extent as to eliminate the injurious effect on the domestic industry caused by the subsidy concerned. If such undertakings are accepted by the MOFE, the investigation will in principle be suspended or terminated without imposition of countervailing duties. Undertakings may only be accepted after an affirmative preliminary determination of subsidy and injury.

INJURY ANALYSIS

As discussed above, Korea now operates under a unitary system rather than a bifurcated system for investigation and rulings. The KTC simultaneously conducts the dumping/subsidy investigation and injury analysis under identical procedures. The reader may thus refer to the corresponding section under the heading of antidumping in the absence of any contrary indication.

Definitions

Domestic industry

Domestic industry means the domestic producers as a whole of a like product, or those producers whose collective output of the like product constitutes a major proportion of the total domestic production of the product at issue.

Period of investigation

Generally, the period for the investigation of injury is the period between the date three years preceding the initiation of investigation and the date for the final determination of injury so long as any relevant information is available.

Material injury

A determination of injury shall be based on positive evidence and involve an objective examination of both the volume of the dumped imports and the effect of the dumped imports on prices in the domestic market for like products, and the consequent impact of these imports on domestic producers of such products. To determine the presence of material injury, among other things, the volume of the dumped product, the price of the imported product, and various economic indices for the domestic industry (e.g., shipments, profit, production capacity, capacity utilization, inventory, and so forth) will be evaluated with respect to the investigation period. The KTC will consider, as one of the major factors, the magnitude of the dumping margin in determining the impact of dumped imports on the domestic industry. The KTC will cumulate the impact of imports from multiple countries that are simultaneously subject to investigation.

Threat of material injury

A determination of a threat of material injury shall be based on facts and not merely on allegation, conjecture, or remote possibility. The change in circumstances that would create a situation in which the dumping would cause injury must be clearly foreseen and imminent. To determine the presence of threat of material injury, the possibility of substantial increase in the import of the product (production capacity and utilization rate in the exporter's country), the possibility of price depression or suppression of price increases (trends in the import price and the Korean market price, and so forth) and other economic indices will be evaluated.

Other injury findings

The criteria for material retardation of the establishment of the domestic industry are far from being clearly established. In light of some recent cases, one possible criterion is to measure whether the profit of the domestic industry is below the proper level of profit that the domestic industry would have reached but for the dumped import.

OTHER TRADE REMEDIES (SUCH AS ESCAPE CLAUSE, NATIONAL SECURITY EXEMPTION AND CUSTOMS SANCTIONS)

History and Rationale

There are other trade remedies contemplated by Korean laws, such as safeguard measures, retaliatory duty, adjustment duty, special escape clause with respect to agricultural, forestry and livestock products, and allocation duty. In addition, Korean laws empower the relevant authorities, including the KTC and the customs authority, to take appropriate measures to effectively control and counter unfair trade practices. However, except for safeguard measures, the other measures are seldom used, if at all.

Safeguard measures, including provisional ones, may be imposed by a competent ministry and authority in accordance with KTC's recommendation based on its investigation with respect to the serious injury to the domestic industry at the request of an interested party or the competent ministry or authority. Safeguard measures may be taken only if a subject product is imported into Korea in such increased quantities, absolute or relative to domestic production, and under such conditions as to cause or threaten to cause serious injury to the domestic industry that produces like or directly competitive products. Under the same conditions, the Foreign Trade Act also provides remedies to the same effect with respect to the increased foreign supply of trade and distribution related services and to the import of products in infringement of intellectual property rights and/or computer programming rights protected under Korean law.

Procedures

A petition for an investigation of injury due to the rapid increase of foreign products may be filed with the KTC by an interested party in the relevant domestic industry (a manufacturer or an association of manufacturers) or a competent ministry or agency. The petition should present sufficient evidence demonstrating the presence of the increased imports and the injury caused thereby. A domestic manufacturer/service provider will have standing as an interested party if its production/market share of involved products/services constitutes 20 percent or more (in the event of agricultural, forestry and fishery products, manufacturers of such products in the number of five persons or more) of domestic production/supply of services. However, a manufacturer which has imported a sizable amount of the subject products may lose its standing as an interested party in the domestic industry.

Administrative Framework

The Korean Government will notify promptly the WTO Committee on Safeguards of Korean laws and regulations and administrative procedures relating to safeguard measures as well as any modifications thereto. The KTC will immediately notify the WTO Committee on Safeguards upon initiating an investigation, finding serious injury or threat thereof caused by increased imports, and taking a decision to apply or extend a safeguard measure. The Korean Government will provide adequate opportunity for prior consultations with the WTO member countries having a substantial interest as exporters of the product concerned. The Korean Government will also make proper notification prior to taking a provisional safeguard measure, and consultations shall be initiated immediately after such measure is taken.

Timetable

The KTC must decide whether or not to initiate an investigation in conjunction with the head of the relevant ministries and agencies within one month from the date of filing of a petition. The KTC will reject the petition if there is lack of sufficient evidence of the injury. The KTC announces its decision in the *Official Gazette* and, if it decides to investigate the injury, the KTC may create a special task force to conduct such investigation, using government officers, industry experts, and other professionals.

The investigation must be completed no later than 120 days after its initiation. During the course of the investigation, if it is revealed that increased imports have caused serious injury and provisional measures are deemed necessary, provisional measures may be recommended by the KTC to be implemented by the relevant ministries and agencies. For certain complex cases or with a reasonable request from the parties concerned, the investigation period may be extended for up to 120 days. If the KTC determines that there has been serious injury to the domestic industry, it may recommend to the relevant ministries and agencies within forty-five days from the date of such decision that certain remedial actions be taken for a certain period.

Remedy

Remedies may include restrictions on import volume; an increase in the applicable tariff rate; industry support, including vocational training and preferential purchase of domestic goods; implementation of an industry rationalization plan; and others as contemplated by the Presidential Decree of the Foreign Trade Act. These measures will be applied only for a certain period of time and to the extent necessary to prevent or remedy serious injury and to facilitate adjustment. In principle, the period for remedies may not exceed four years.

Malaysia

Quay Chew Soon
Skrine & Co.
Kuala Lumpur, Malaysia

HISTORY AND OVERVIEW OF TRADE REMEDY LAWS AND/OR REGULATIONS SINCE 1947

Malaysia's Accession to GATT/WTO and Antidumping and Subsidies Codes

Malaysia acceded to GATT in 1957 and has since sought to enact legislation that is consistent with the said agreement to deal with dumping and subsidies. Malaysia has also acceded to the WTO Agreement and is in the process of conforming its legislation to the WTO Agreement.

The Evolution of Trade Remedy Laws and Regulations in Malaysia

In 1959, the Customs (Dumping and Subsidies) Act was enacted to cover the areas of dumping and subsidies. The aforesaid Act has now been repealed and replaced by the Countervailing and Antidumping Duties Act 1993, which is discussed below.

Summary of Trade Remedy Laws and Agencies Responsible for Administering the Same

Countervailing and Antidumping Duties Act 1993[1] ("Act")

In the Explanatory Statement ("Explanatory Statement") to the Bill introducing this Act, the Malaysian Government ("Government") stated that it was its intention to improve the provisions for overcoming unfair trade practices relating to the dumping and subsidization of merchandise imported into Malaysia and that the new legislation would authorize the imposition and collection of antidumping and countervailing duties to offset such activities that have caused or are threatening to cause injury to the domestic industry.

Countervailing and Antidumping Regulations 1994[2] ("Regulations")

The Regulations were promulgated pursuant to the powers conferred upon the Minister of International Trade and Industry ("Minister") by section 50 of the Act. The basic provisions stipulated in the Act are amplified by the implementing Regulations.

It must be noted that the Act and the Regulations will only be applicable when a relevant international obligation exists between Malaysia and the interested foreign government. In this regard section 43 of the Act provides:

> (1) When no applicable international obligation on countervailing and antidumping duties exist between Malaysia and the interested foreign government:
> (a) countervailing and antidumping duties may be imposed without regard to an investigation referred to in sections 4 and 20; and
> (b) the Government shall be entitled to use any administrative and legal definition, methodology and procedure it deems appropriate, with regard to the investigations."

In the Explanatory Statement, the Government stated that the principle of minimum treatment that was provided for in the Bill was not intended to extend to parties if the country in which they operate have no relevant international obligations to Malaysia. Thus, the procedure established by the Act and Regulations will only be applicable to interested parties from other GATT countries or nations that have relevant trade agreements with Malaysia.

ANTIDUMPING INVESTIGATIONS

Dumping Determination

Initiation of investigation

By petition

Antidumping investigations are covered by Part III of the Act and are conducted by the Ministry of International Trade and Industry. Section 20 of the Act provides that a request for an antidumping duty investigation may be submitted by a producer,[3] producers, or an association on behalf of the domestic industry producing such product.

The Regulations provide that the Petitioner is required to supply, to the extent that it is reasonably available to the Petitioner, *inter alia*, the following particulars:

(i) the identity of the domestic industry on behalf of which the petition is being submitted and where the same is being made on behalf of regional producers, information and details to support the carrying out of the investigation on a regional basis;

(ii) a detailed description of the merchandise including its technical characteristics and uses. Also to be included is its current Malaysian customs tariff classification;

(iii) the name of the country in which the subject merchandise is being produced and any intermediate country through which it is imported;

(iv) the name and address of each party the Petitioner believes is selling the merchandise at below the normal value;

(v) factual information relevant to the calculation of the normal value and export price of the merchandise;

(vi) the volume of the merchandise imported into Malaysia during the most recent two-year period and any other period that the Petitioner believes is more representative or, if the merchandise was not imported into Malaysia during the two-year period, information as to its likelihood of sale in Malaysia;

(vii) the identity of any party that is importing or likely to import the subject merchandise;

(viii) evidence of injury to the domestic industry; and

(ix) in circumstances where the Petitioner believes that the injury would be difficult to repair, evidence that such injury is being caused by massive imports of the subject merchandise in a short period of time and there is a history of dumping that caused injury, or that the importer was or should have been aware that the exporter practices dumping and that such dumping would cause injury.

In relation to the evidence of injury to domestic industry, the Petitioner is required to include factual information on relevant economic factors and indices that have a bearing on the condition of such domestic industry such actual and potential decline in output, sales, market share, profits, productivity, returns on investments, factors affecting domestic prices, actual and potential negative effects on cash flow, inventories, employment, wages, growth, ability to raise capital, and investment.

The Government is required, within the period prescribed in the Regulations, to review the petition and other available information and determine whether in fact there is sufficient evidence to warrant an investigation and whether such an investigation would be in the public interest.

Section 20(4) of the Act provides that where the Government determines that sufficient evidence does not exist to warrant an investigation or that such an investigation would not be in the public interest, the Government shall publish a notice[4] stating the reasons for its determination not to initiate an investigation.

Under section 20(5) of the Act, if the Government determines that sufficient evidence does exist to warrant the initiation of an antidumping duty investigation and that such investigation is in the public interest, the Government shall notify the appropriate interested parties and publish a notice of initiation of investigation.

By Government

Section 20(6) of the Act authorizes the Government to initiate an antidumping duty investigation on its own accord where it has sufficient evidence that:
(i) the export price of the subject merchandise is less than its normal value;
(ii) there is material injury or a threat of the same to the domestic industry in Malaysia by reason of the subject merchandise;
(iii) the subject merchandise will materially retard such industry in Malaysia.

Where the Government decides to initiate an investigation pursuant to Subsection 20(6), it is required to notify the appropriate interested parties and publish a notice of initiation of investigation.

Timetable

The Act does not of itself stipulate time periods for the various events, but such deadlines are prescribed by Regulations. A summary of the salient time periods is set out in Appendix A.

Participation of parties and their counsel

The Act and the Regulations do provide "interested parties" with an opportunity to present their case. Section 38 of the Act provides:
"All interested parties in a countervailing or antidumping investigation shall be given notice of the information required by the Government and opportunities to present all evidence they consider relevant."

An "interested party" is defined in section 2 of the Act as:
(a) a producer, exporter, or importer of the subject merchandise;
(b) a trade or business association of which a majority of its members are

producers, exporters, or importers of the subject merchandise;
(c) the government of a country in which the subject merchandise is produced or from which it is exported;
(d) a producer of the like product in Malaysia; or
(e) a trade or business association of which a majority of its members produce a like product in Malaysia;

Neither the Act nor the Regulations expressly confer a right on the parties to be represented by counsel or to an oral hearing, but in practice, interested parties can be represented by counsel.

Section 38(1) of the Act stipulates that the Government shall give notice to all interested parties of the information required by the Government and opportunities to present all evidence they consider relevant.

Furthermore, regulation 37(3) stipulates that where an interested party intends to submit information orally, the oral submissions must be reduced to writing and submitted to the Government within seven days of the date of the oral submission.

Access to information developed in proceedings

The Malaysian legislation draws a distinction between confidential and nonconfidential information. The Act and Regulations seek to balance the competing interests of providing interested parties with as much information as necessary on the one hand and protecting confidential information on the other.

Section 38(2) of the Act provides that:

> The Government shall, whenever practicable, provide an opportunity for all interested parties to see information submitted that is not confidential that is relevant to the presentation of their case.

Section 39 of the Act deals with the issue of confidential information from interested parties and provides that:

(1) Any information that is by its nature confidential, or any information that is provided on a confidential basis by parties to an investigation, shall for good cause shown, be treated as such by the Government.
(2) The confidential nature of a document shall not be used as a reason for refusing to provide it to the Government.
(3) The government shall be responsible for ensuring the confidentiality of such documents.
(4) Confidential information shall not be disclosed without specific written permission from the party submitting the confidential information.
(5) The Government shall require parties providing confidential

information to furnish nonconfidential summaries that are sufficient in detail to permit reasonable understanding of the substance of the confidential information.
(6) In the event, that such information is not susceptible of summary, a statement of reasons why summarization is not possible shall be provided.
(7) The Government may disregard information presented if:
 (a) the Government finds that a request for confidentiality under subsection (1) is not warranted and the supplier of the information nevertheless is unwilling to make the information public;
 (b) the nonconfidential summaries as required under subsection (5) are not in sufficient detail; or
 (c) the reasons given for not providing nonconfidential summaries under subsection(6) are not deemed adequate and the party supplying the information nevertheless refuses to provide nonconfidential summaries.

It is clear from the foregoing that an interested party does not have an unrestricted right to have access to information that is developed in the proceedings but the Government is obliged to provide parties with access to nonconfidential information that is relevant to the presentation of their case whenever practicable.

In circumstances where interested parties are uncooperative and refuse access to, or otherwise do not provide, necessary information within a reasonable period or significantly impedes an investigation, then the Government is entitled to make a preliminary and final determination of either subsidization or dumping on the basis of the facts available.

Definitions

Like product

Like product is defined in section 2 of the Act as:

> ... a product that is identical or alike in all respects to the subject merchandise, and may include any other product that has physical, technical or chemical characteristics, applications or uses that resemble those of the subject merchandise as the Government deems appropriate

Period of Investigation

See Appendix A.

Domestic industry and petition requirement for industry support

"Domestic industry" is defined in section 2 of the Act as:
 (a) the domestic producers as a whole of the like product;
 (b) the domestic producers whose collective output of the like product

constitutes a major proportion of the total domestic production of those products; or

(c) regional producers of the like product,

but does not include:

(a) domestic producers who are related to the exporters or importers, or are themselves importers, of the subject merchandise or a like product from other countries unless otherwise determined by the Government.

(b) domestic producers who produce the like product primarily for export unless otherwise determined by the Government;

Related parties

Subsection 2(5) of the Act provides that parties are deemed to be related if:

(a) one of them directly or indirectly controls[5] the other;
(b) both of them are directly or indirectly controlled by a third party; or
(c) together they directly or indirectly control a third party, unless there are grounds for believing that such related parties will not behave differently from non-related parties."

Calculation of dumping margins

Export price

Export price is defined in section 17 of the Act as:

(1) The export price shall be the price actually paid or payable for the subject merchandise.
(2) In cases where it appears that the exporter and the importer or a third party are related, or that there is a compensatory arrangement between the exporter and the importer or a third party, or that for other reasons the price actually paid or payable for the subject merchandise is unreliable, the export price may be constructed on the basis of the price at which the subject merchandise is first resold to an independent buyer, or if the subject matter is not resold to an independent buyer, or not resold in the condition imported, on any reasonable basis.
(3) If the export price is constructed as described in subsection (2), allowance shall be made for all costs incurred between importation and resale.

Normal value

Normal value is defined in section 16 of the Act as the comparable price actually paid or payable in the ordinary course of trade for comparable merchandise sold for consumption in the domestic market of the exporting country. When there are no sales in the domestic market of the exporting country, or when such sales do not permit a proper comparison, normal value shall be either:

(i) the comparable price actually paid or payable in the ordinary course of trade for comparable merchandise exported to any third country or countries; or
(ii) the constructed value of the subject merchandise, determined by adding cost of production and a reasonable margin of profit.
(iii) Whenever there are reasonable grounds for believing or suspecting that the prices at which comparable merchandise is actually sold for consumption are less than the cost of producing that merchandise, sales at such prices may be considered as not having been made in the ordinary course of trade.

The section also provides that the cost of production is to be computed on the basis of all fixed and variable costs of materials and manufacturing in the ordinary course of trade in the exporting country, plus a reasonable amount for selling, administrative, and other general expenses.

In circumstances where the sales are not considered as having been made in the ordinary course of trade, the normal value may be determined on the basis of:

(a) the remaining sales in the domestic market made at a price that is not less than the cost of production, provided that such remaining sales are in sufficient quantities;
(b) the remaining sales in the third country market made at a price that is not less than the cost of production, provided that such remaining sales are in sufficient quantities; or
(c) the constructed value as described above.

Section 16 of the Act also states that for the purpose of determining normal value, transactions among related parties, or among parties that appear to have compensatory arrangements with each other, may be considered as not being in the ordinary course of trade, unless the Government is satisfied that the price and costs involved are comparable to those involved in transactions among parties that are not related or do not have compensatory arrangements.

Further, regulation 26 of the Regulations also provide that for the purpose of determining normal value under section 16 of the Act, the Government will normally examine any sale of the comparable merchandise in the domestic market of the exporting country during the six-month period preceding the initiation of an investigation or any additional or alternative period that the Government deems relevant or necessary if such sales permit a proper comparison.

However, regulation 16 of the Regulations also states that sales of comparable merchandise in the domestic do not permit a proper comparison where:

(a) the quantity of merchandise sold for consumption in the domestic market during the period being examined is so small in relation to the quantity sold for exportation to Malaysia or to total export that it is an inadequate basis for the normal value of the merchandise; or
(b) the sales in the domestic market are not in the ordinary course of trade.

Adjustments, including those reflecting level of trade

Section 18 of the Act and the Regulations provide for various adjustments to be made.

In relation to the calculation of export price under Section 17 of the Act, regulation 30 of the Regulations provides that the Government will make an adjustment in that it will deduct the amount of any antidumping duty that the producer or reseller:

(a) has paid directly on behalf of the importer; or
(b) has reimbursed to the importer.

Further, to ensure a fair comparison between the normal value and the export price of a merchandise, section 18 of the Act and more particularly regulation 32(1) of the Regulations authorizes the Government to make reasonable allowances for:

(a) transport expenses such as freight, shipping, insurance, or other similar expenses to ensure the prices are comparable normally at an ex-factory level;
(b) differences in the physical characteristics of merchandise compared if the Government is satisfied that the amount of any price difference is wholly or partly due to such physical differences;
(c) a bona fide difference in the selling conditions of the sales compared if the Government is satisfied that the amount of any price difference is wholly or partly due to such differences in the selling conditions such as commissions, credit terms, guarantees, warranties, technical assistance, and servicing;
(d) the differences in selling costs incurred by the producer or seller, but only to the extent that such costs are assumed by the producer or seller on behalf of the purchaser.

The Government will also calculate normal value and export price based on:

(i) comparable quantities of merchandise;
(ii) sales at the same commercial level of trade.

If the quantities or the levels of trade are not comparable or different, and the Government is satisfied that the amount of any price difference is wholly or partly due to such difference, the Government may make a reasonable allowance for the difference.[6]

The Government may also make any other adjustments it deems necessary to ensure a fair price comparison.[7] Consideration will be given to all discounts and rebates, including deferred discounts if they are directly linked to the sales under consideration and supported by sufficient evidence as prescribed.[8]

Treatment of sales through related parties

Section 16(6) of the Act provides that in determining normal value, transactions among related parties or among parties that appear to have compensatory arrangements with each other may be considered as not being in the ordinary course of trade and may be disregarded,[9] unless the Government is satisfied that the price and costs involved are comparable to those involved in transactions among parties that are not related or do not have compensatory arrangements.

Cost of production and constructed value methodology

Section 16(2) of the Act[10] provides that:

> Where there are no sale in domestic market of the exporting country or when such sales do not permit a proper comparison, normal value shall be either:
> (a) the comparable price actually paid or payable in the ordinary course of trade for comparable merchandise exported to any third country or countries; or
> (b) the constructed value of the subject merchandise, determined by adding cost of production and a reasonable margin of profit.

Subsection 16(4) provides that the cost of production shall be computed on the basis of all fixed and variable costs of materials and manufacturing in the ordinary course of trade in the exporting country, plus a reasonable amount for selling, administrative, and other general expenses.

In relation to the constructed value of a subject merchandise, regulation 29(1) provides that it shall be the sum of:

(a) the cost of materials and of fabrication or other processing method employed in producing such or similar merchandise;
(b) an amount for general expenses, which is equal to the actual expenses

incurred on sales of the general class or kind of merchandise; and
(c) an amount for profit, which is equal to:
   (i) the actual profit earned by the exporter;
   (ii) an amount usually earned by the producers in the same country of exportation on sales of the same general category; or
   (iii) any other reasonable method of calculating profit.

Nonmarket economy methodology

"Nonmarket economy country" is defined in section 2(1) to mean "any foreign country that the Government determines does not operate on market principles of cost or pricing structures."

Regulation 33 of the Regulations provides that where the country of origin of the subject merchandise is a nonmarket economy country, the Government shall:
(b) in the case of dumping, calculate the normal value of the subject merchandise based on-
   (i) the prices of comparable merchandise sold in the ordinary course of trade in a surrogate country;
   (ii) the cost to make and sell comparable merchandise in the ordinary course of trade in a surrogate country;
   (iii) the prices of comparable domestically produced merchandise sold in Malaysia in the ordinary course of trade; or
   (iv) any other appropriate method.

Price undertakings and other agreements to suspend investigations

Section 27(1) of the Act provides that an investigation may be suspended at any time if undertakings are accepted by the Government. However, before the acceptance of the undertakings, section 27(2) requires the Government to determine if such undertakings

(a) will eliminate the dumping margin or the injurious effects caused by the subject merchandise;
(b) can be monitored effectively; and
(c) are in the public interest.

The undertakings may be accepted by the Government at two stages:

(i) prior to the preliminary investigation; or
(ii) after the preliminary investigation.

In the first case, the Government shall suspend the investigation and publish a notice stating the reasons for the acceptance of such undertakings. In the latter case, the Government shall further:

(a) suspend the investigation;
(b) suspend any provisional measures applied under section 24 of the Act and release all or part of the security required by such measures as the Government deems appropriate;
(c) publish a notice stating the reasons for the suspension of the investigation and actions under paragraph (b).[11]

However, section 27(5) of the Act provides that even after the acceptance of the undertakings, the investigation may be completed upon the written request of the interested foreign government or if the Government so decides. Once the Government completes the investigation pursuant to section 27(5), the undertakings shall either:

(i) remain in effect consistent with the provisions of the Act, if an affirmative determination is made; or
(ii) lapse, if a negative determination is made, unless the negative determination is due in large part to the existence of the undertaking, in which case the undertaking shall be maintained consistent with the provisions of the Act.

A suspended investigation may be resumed at any time if the Government determines that the undertakings accepted no longer meet the requirements of section 27(2) of the Act or there is a material violation of the undertakings.

By virtue of regulation 18(2)(b) of the Regulations, the Government may accept the following forms of undertakings:

(i) the exporters agree to revise their prices to eliminate the injurious dumping; or
(ii) the Government of the exporter country or the exporters agree to take such other action so as to eliminate the injurious effects of the dumping.

Effect of Antidumping Order

Effective date

Retroactivity, if any

The Act is silent with regard to the retroactive imposition of the antidumping order. However, regulation 14(1) of the Regulations permits a petitioner to make a written request[12] to the Government at any time prior to thirty days of the final determination for the retroactive imposition of countervailing and antidumping duties. It therefore appears that the Minister may make a retroactive imposition of such duties.

Duration

According to section 28(6) of the Act, unless the Government determines on the basis of an administrative review that there is good cause for the continued imposition of such duties, antidumping duties shall not be collected on imports made after five years from the date of publication of the notice of the final determination under section 25.

Procedures for Review and Revocation of Order

Administrative reviews and appeals are governed by Sections 28 and 29 of the Act and Part VI of the Regulations.

Section 28(1) of the Act empowers the Government to conduct an administrative review if the Government determines that such review is in the public interest, after being informed by an appropriate interested party or otherwise obtained information, that:

(a) the dumping margin has changed substantially;
(b) a refund of an antidumping duty is no longer necessary;
(c) the imposition of an antidumping duty is no longer necessary;
(d) an undertaking is no longer necessary or should be modified; or
(e) an antidumping duty that is required to be terminated pursuant to section 28(6) of the Act should be maintained.

Pursuant to sections 28(1) and (3) of the Act, regulation 34(1) further provides that such administrative review shall be undertaken only after one year has lapsed from the date of publication of the decision of which the review is sought. Moreover, such review shall be completed within 180 days.[13] On completion of the administrative review, the Government shall publish a final administrative review determination, stating reasons for its determination.

By virtue of section 29(1) of the Act, the appropriate interested parties also has the right to appeal to the Tribunal[14] against:

(a) an affirmative or negative final determination under section 25; or
(b) any final administrative review determination under subsection 28(4).

However, such an appeal must be filed within fourteen days from the date of the notice of the final determination under section 25 or final administrative review administrative determination under section 28(4).

COUNTERVAILING DUTY INVESTIGATIONS

Subsidy Determination

Initiation of investigation

By petition

In general, the requirements of a countervailing duty petition are similar to those of an antidumping petition. Countervailing duty investigations may be initiated by petition or by the government.

Timetable; participation of parties and their counsel; access to information developed in proceedings

These provisions are the same as in relation to antidumping investigations.

Definitions

Countervailable subsidies

Subsidies are defined in part V of the Regulations. Section 24 of the Regulations state that the following forms of financial benefit or contributions shall be considered as a subsidy by the Government:

- (i) where Government practice involves a direct or potential direct transfer of funds or liabilities;
- (ii) where Government revenue that is otherwise due, is foregone or not collected;
- (iii) where the government provides goods or services, other than general infrastructure, or purchases goods;
- (iv) where the Governments makes payments to a funding mechanism or directs a private body to carry out one or more of the type of functions mentioned in paragraphs (i) (ii) (iii) that would normally be vested in the Government and the practice does not defer from practices normally followed by Governments; or
- (v) where there is any form or income or price support.

If no cash flow effect can be calculated the Government may make an estimate of the financial benefit.

Noncountervailable subsidies ("green light")

Not specifically provided for.

Application to non-market economies

By virtue of regulation 33 of the Regulations where the country of origin of the subject merchandise is a nonmarket economy, the Government shall deem the amount of subsidy to be the difference between the ex-factory price of the like product sold by domestic manufacturers in the Malaysian market and the ex-factory price of the subject merchandise imported from the nonmarket economy country.

Calculation of subsidies

Regulation 25 of the Regulations states that the basis for calculation of subsidy and the principles which will be adopted by the Government in doing so, are as follows:

(i) The Government will calculate the total subsidy provided with respect to the subject merchandise during the designated period of investigation;
(ii) The Government will regard a subsidy to be received at the time when there is a cashflow effect on the enterprise, industry or exporters receiving the subsidy. However, if this methodology will significantly distort the subsidy level, the Government may use any other reasonable method to determine when the subsidy is received;
(iii) The Government will either calculate the entire subsidy received by the enterprise, industry, or exporters as to be expended in a single year or on an annual basis for two or more years, as it deems appropriate;
(iv) The Government will allocate the subsidy to those products to which the subsidy is associated;
(v) The Government will calculate a weighted average subsidy applicable to the product on a countrywide basis;
(vi) The amount of subsidy shall be determined per unit on an ad valorem basis or on any other reasonable basis;
(vii) The Government may subtract the amount of any application fee, deposit, or similar payment paid to qualify for, or to receive, the subside and export taxes, duties, or other charges collected on the export of the merchandise to Malaysia specifically intended to offset the subsidy received.

Undertakings that suspend the investigation

Section 12(1) of the Act provides that an investigation may be suspended at any time if undertakings are accepted by the Government. The undertakings required for the suspension of a countervailing duty investigation are similar to those for the suspension of an antidumping investigation.

Regulation 18 of the Regulations provides that the Government may accept the following forms of undertakings in relation to a countervailing duty investigation:

(i) The Government of the exporting country agrees to eliminate, offset or limit the subsidy.
(ii) The exporters agree to renounce the subsidy.
(iii) The exporters agree to revise their prices to eliminate the injurious effect of the subsidy.
(iv) The Government of the exporting country or the exporters agree to take other action to eliminate the injurious effect of the subsidy.

Effect of Countervailing Duty Order

Effective date
Retroactivity, if any
The Act is silent with regard to the retroactive imposition of the countervailing duty order. However, regulation 14(1) of the Regulations permits a petitioner to make a written request[15] to the Government at any time prior to thirty days of the final determination for the retroactive imposition of countervailing duties. It therefore appears that the Minister may make a retroactive imposition of such duties.

Duration
According to section 13(6) of the Act, unless the Government determines on the basis of an administrative review that there is good cause for the continued imposition of such duties, countervailing duties shall not be collected on imports made after five years from the date of publication of the notice of the final determination under section 10.

Enforcement, Including Rules to Prevent Circumvention of Orders
Section 37 of the Act allows the Government to take such action as may be prescribed to prevent circumvention of the application of countervailing duties. However, the Regulations do not prescribe any specific form of action.

Procedures for review and revocation
Administrative reviews and appeals are governed by sections 13 and 14 of the Act and Part VI of the Regulations. The circumstances and procedures applicable in countervailing duty cases are virtually identical to those applicable in antidumping cases.

INJURY ANALYSIS

The injury analysis is part of the investigation. No separate procedure is specifically provided for.

Material injury

Injury determinations are covered by the Regulations. The Regulations do not define the meaning of 'material.'
   Regulation 19 states that injury means:
(i)   material injury to a domestic industry producing a like product;
(ii) threat of material injury to a domestic industry producing a like product; or
(iii) material retardation of the establishment of such domestic industry.
   Regulation 20 provides that in determining injury to the domestic industry, the Government shall base its evaluation of the relevant economic factors and indices having a bearing on the condition of such industry.

Threat of Material Injury

Regulation 22 provides that the Government shall base its decision on facts and not merely allegation, conjecture or remote possibility. The Government will consider, among other factors:
(i)   contracts for future shipment of the subject merchandise to Malaysia;
(ii) capacity utilization in the foreign country under investigation;
(iii) price undercutting;
(iv) recent import trends;
(v)   the existence of significant inventories in the country under investigation.

APPENDIX A

GENERAL TIMETABLE FOR ANTIDUMPING AND COUNTERVAILING DUTY INVESTIGATION

1. Submission of countervailing or antidumping duty petition by petitioner.
No time period.

2. Determination by the Government as to the adequacy of the countervailing or antidumping duty petition.
Fourteen days from the date of receipt, by the Government, of a properly submitted petition.[16]

3. Publication by the Government of a notice of initiation of investigation.
No time period stipulated either in the Act or the Regulations.

4. Preparation and distribution by the Government of questionnaires to any party relevant to the countervailing or antidumping duty investigation.
Within a reasonable period from the publication of the notice of initiation of investigation.[17]

5. Reply to questionnaire.
Parties to be given at least thirty days to reply.[18] Any period granted by the Government may be extended upon receipt of a written request, if, the Government is satisfied with the reasons given for the request.[19]

6. Receipt of questionnaire.
A party is deemed to have received a questionnaire one week from the day on which it was sent to the party or to the appropriate representatives of the interested foreign government in Malaysia.[20]

7. Preliminary determination by the Government.
The Government shall make a preliminary determination within ninety days of publication of the notice of initiation of investigation.[21] In special circumstances this period can be extended by an additional thirty days.[22]

8. Publication by the Government of a notice of affirmative preliminary determination and application of provisional measures.[23]
No period is stipulated.

9. Institution of provisional measures.

May only be taken after the publication of the notice of affirmative preliminary determination and shall not be applied earlier than sixty days from the date of the initiation of the investigation.[24] Unless the Government grants an extension of time that is consistent with Malaysia's international obligations in such matter, the period for the application of provisional measures shall not exceed 120 days from the date of publication of the notice of the affirmative preliminary determination.[25]

10. Request by petitioner for retroactive imposition of countervailing and antidumping duties.

At any time prior to thirty days before the final determination for the imposition of countervailing and antidumping duties[26].

11. Final determination of countervailing and antidumping.

Within 120 days from the date of the publication of the notice of preliminary determination.

12. Correction of administrative errors.

Within ten days from the date of publication of the notice of Final Determination.[27] If the Minister is satisfied that an administrative error exists, then the final determination shall be amended within thirty days from the date of publication of the notice of final determination.

13. Appeals to the Tribunal.

The appropriate interested parties shall have the right to appeal to the Tribunal against an affirmative or negative final determination or any final administrative review determination. Appeals must be filed within fourteen days from the date of the notice of affirmative or negative final determination under section 25 or from the date of the final administrative review determination.

References

1. Countervailing and Antidumping Duties Act (Act 504), 1993 (Malaysia) (hereinafter the "Act 504").
2. Countervailing and Antidumping Regulations, P.U. (A) 223, 1994, (hereinafter "Regulations").
3. A 'producer' is defined under section 2 of the Act as ". . . a producer, manufacturer or processor;"

4. By virtue of section 45 of Act 504, all notices which are required to be published under Act 504 shall be published in the *Gazette*, unless otherwise specified.
5. Subsection 2(6) of Act 504 states that: ". . . One party shall be deemed to control another when the first-mentioned party is legally or operationally in a position to exercise restraint or direction over the latter."
6. Regulations, *supra* n.2, paragraphs (e) & (f) of regulation 32(1).
7. Regulations, *supra* n.2, paragraph (g) of regulation 32(1).
8. Regulations, *supra* n.2, regulation 32(2) & (3).
9. Regulations, *supra* n.2, regulation 29(2).
10. See also Regulations, *supra* n.2, regulation 27.
11. Act 504, *supra* n.1, sections 27(3) & (4).
12. The request must contain factual information as prescribed in regulation 14(2) of the Regulations.
13. Regulations, *supra* n.2, regulation 34(1).
14. This is a reference to the Tribunal established pursuant to section 32 of Act 504 to perform the functions specified in sections 14 and 29 of Act 504. The Tribunal is appointed by the Minister and consists of a Chairman and not more than two other persons. The Chairman and members of the Tribunal hold office for a period not exceeding three years after which they are eligible to be reappointed.
15. The request must contain factual information as prescribed in regulation 14(2) of the Regulations.
16. Subsection 6(1).
17. Subsection 9(1).
18. Subsection 9(2).
19. Subsection 9(3).
20. Subsection 9(5).
21. Subsection 10(1).
22. Subsection 10(2).
23. Subsection 12(1).
24. Subsection 13(1).
25. Subsection 13(2).
26. Subsection 15(1).
27. Subsection 16(1).

Mexico

Juan Francisco Torres Landa R.
Barrera, Siqueiros y Torres Landa, S.C.
Mexico City, Mexico

INTRODUCTION

History

Mexico has a rather short history of foreign trade legislation. The reason for that is simple. As with many other Latin American countries, and clearly during several decades after World War II, the economy was centered on an import substitution model. The foregoing meant that upon establishment of a local industry, the latter was shielded from foreign competition through direct tariff or nontariff barriers. The logic behind this system was that the incipient economies of these countries needed incentives and a series of protectionist measures for the creation of national industries.

The import substitution system must be recognized for having developed industries that otherwise may not have been created. However, almost none of the countries involved, and certainly not Mexico, were able to graduate from that system at the proper time (at which they should have joined the world standards of quality and pricing) with the result that these economies did not open to foreign trade until the second half of the 1980s.

Mexico's entrance into full foreign trade was not formalized until 1986 when it became a party to the General Agreement on Tariffs and Trade (GATT). Therefore, it was not until then that the need for a foreign trade law was fully realized. The Mexican Congress in that year enacted the Regulatory Law of Article 131 of the Constitution in Foreign Trade Matters,[1] a statute that was repealed with the publication of the current Foreign Trade Law and its Regulations.[2]

Therefore, the history of significant foreign trade legislation in this country is only ten years old. Nonetheless, it must also be emphasized that in this rather short period Mexico has experienced one of the most, if not the most, dramatic changes towards openness to foreign trade in the entire world. Aside from the North American Free Trade Agreement (NAFTA),[3] Mexico now has similar Agreements in place with Venezuela, Colombia,[4] Costa Rica,[5] Bolivia,[6] and Chile[7] and is actively negotiating new accords with countries located in Central America, the Caribbean, and the European Union.

Parallel to this growth in trade arrangements, geometrical growth in the interaction with other countries has obviously exposed the local industry to the perils of international unfair trade practices. Hence, Mexico has had a significant rise in the number of cases where foreign trade practices have been investigated and, in many instances, sanctioned through the corresponding antidumping or countervailing duties.

In this article we will present a global view of the Mexican foreign trade remedy legal system.

General Overview

The Mexican foreign trade legal framework is based primarily on the provisions of Article 131 of the Federal Constitution, which in turn is regulated in detail by the Foreign Trade Law (FTL) and the Regulations to the Foreign Trade Law (Regulations). In addition to those statutes, there are a number of both domestic (for example, the Federal Tax Code—FTC) and international instruments that contain important provisions that are relevant for the determination of specific rules that apply in the trade among Mexico and certain trade partners. Among those instruments of the latter category, the following are the most important:

(i) the documents creating the World Trade Organization;[8]
(ii) the applicable agreements of the GATT—the Antidumping Code, the Subsidies Code, the Safeguards Code, and so forth;
(iii) Chapter XIX of the NAFTA;[9]
(iv) Chapter IX of the Free Trade Agreement between Mexico, Colombia, and Venezuela - (the "G-3 FTA");[10]
(v) Chapter VIII of the Free Trade Agreement between Mexico and Costa Rica (the "Costa Rica FTA");[11] and
(vi) Chapter VIII of the Free Trade Agreement between Mexico and Bolivia (the "Bolivia FTA").[12]

All of the foregoing legal instruments must be considered to analyze the rules that govern foreign trade remedy laws in Mexico. Evidently, the application of the different international instruments will depend on the specific countries involved in particular cases.

THE FOREIGN TRADE LAW AND ITS REGULATIONS

Purpose

The FTL is a pubic policy statute that, therefore, may not be waived by private individuals and that the Mexican government must strictly enforce.[13] The Ministry of Trade and Industrial Promotion *(Secretaría de Comercio y Fomento Industrial*—SECOFI) is in charge of enforcing the FTL, and in the area being analyzed does so through a specific agency known as the International Unfair Trade Practices Unit *(Unidad de Prácticas Comerciales Internacionales*—UPCI).

The main purposes of the FTL are:
(i) to regulate and promote foreign trade;
(ii) to increase competitiveness of the national economy;
(iii) to foster the efficient use of the productive resources of the country; and
(iv) to integrate adequately the Mexican economy into the international economy contributing to the general increase of the population's well-being.[14]

International Unfair Trade Practices

The FTL contemplates and restricts two general types of international unfair trade practices: (i) dumping and (ii) subsidies.[15]
(i) *Dumping:* This practice is defined as the importation of goods into national territory at a price below their normal value.[16]
(ii) *Subsidies:* The FTL defines subsidies as an incentive improperly granted in a direct or indirect manner by a foreign government to producers, reprocessors, sellers, or exporters of goods to strengthen their international competitive position, unless they derive from generally accepted international trade practices.[17]

In addition, for these practices to be actionable, the FTL requires an injury test (or threat thereof) affecting national production.[18] The injury test is not required in the event that no reciprocity exists in the trade legislation of the exporting country.[19]

In brief, the elements of unfair trade practices under the FTL and its Regulations are:

Dumping
(i) *Conduct:* Importation of goods that are similar[20] or identical[21] to those of the national industry[22] at a price lower than their normal value.
(ii) *Effect/Consequence:* That such conduct results in, or threatens to cause, injury to the national industry.[23]

(iii) *Causal Link:* That the importation at the dumped price constitutes the direct cause of the injury or threat thereof to the national industry.

Subsidies

(i) *Conduct:* A benefit granted by a foreign government to producers, reprocessors, or exporters of goods.[24]
(ii) *Purpose/Effect:* The benefit is granted to improperly strengthen the competitive international position of such producers, reprocessors, or exporters of goods and results in, or threatens to cause, injury to the national industry.
(iii) *Causal Link:* That the importation at the subsidized price constitutes the direct cause of the injury or threat thereof to the national industry.

With respect to the indicated elements of the dumping and subsidies practices, they are broken down into several concepts that must be individually analyzed.

Dumping

Dumping margin

The dumping margin is determined by calculating the difference between the normal value and the export price of the investigated good.[25] The margin calculation will involve freight, insurance, and financing cost adjustments to allow for a calculation for both items on an "ex-factory" basis (a price at the manufacturer's plant for both products).

The FTL sets forth two methods to determine the dumping margin:
(i) *Type of Goods:* When the investigated product encompasses goods that are not identical, the dumping margin is determined by employing similar goods, and using the normal value and export price of such analogous goods.
(ii) *Using a sample model:* In the event that the types of goods or the number of the transactions to be investigated are extremely large, the dumping margin may be determined by using a sample of the goods.

Normal value

To determine the normal value of an investigated product, there are several methods that are employed, in the following order of priority:
(i) When sales exist in the country of origin[26] the FTL provides that the normal value shall be that of a similar or identical good that is destined for the internal market under normal commercial operations.[27]

(ii) If no sales of an identical or similar good are made in the country of origin, or such sales do not allow a valid comparison,[28] the normal value must be calculated based on the export price to a third country.
(iii) If the third country sales do not allow a valid comparison, the normal value must be calculated by determining the "reconstructed value," which is based on the sum of the production costs and the general expenses required to manufacture a good, plus a reasonable profit, all of which are to be based on normal commercial operations.[29]
(iv) When the country of origin has a centrally planned economy, the FTL requires a procedure whereby a third country with a market economy is selected as a surrogate for purposes of the antidumping investigation and the normal value determination.[30]
(v) If the good comes from an intermediate country and not directly from the country of origin, the normal value shall be deemed to be the comparable price of similar or identical goods in the country the good comes from. However, if the good:
   (i) is just transiting through a country;
   (ii) is not produced in said country; or
   (iii) lacks an export price in such country;
   the normal value shall be determined using the price of the country of origin.[31]

Injury or threat of injury

The FTL defines:
(i) *Injury* as the economic loss or detriment, or loss of any normal or lawful profit, and/or the barrier to establishment of a new industry; and
(ii) *Threat of Injury* as the imminent and clearly foreseeable injury to national production.

The FTL requires that the alleged threat of injury be based on facts and not simple allegations, speculation, or remote possibilities.[32]

Determination of injury or threat of injury

The FTL sets forth, among others, the following criteria to determine if injury or threat of injury exists as a result of an international unfair trade practice.[33]
(i) Injury:
   - Import Volume. Increase in the volume of imports of the investigated product in comparison to the similar or identical products of national production.
   - Effect on Prices. That is, if the investigated products sold in the internal market under dumping conditions result in an abnormal

price reduction, or thwart a reasonable increase that may otherwise have occurred.
- Effect on Producers. The appreciable or potential decrease in the production volume, sales, market share, profits, productivity, investment earnings, or use of the installed capacity, employment, stock, salaries, capital saving capacity, investment, and production increase, among others.
- Impact of the imports on national production or the national producers that jointly constitute the main share of total national production of the investigated good.

(ii) Threat of injury:
The following elements are considered to determine the existence of a threat of injury:[34]
- Increase in the import volumes that indicate that a future and significant surge of imports may be present shortly.
- Available excess capacity of the exporter.
- If the price of the imports is at a level that may negatively impact national prices.
- The currently available inventory levels of the investigated product.
- Current impact of the imports over the national production.
- Expected impact on earnings of possible investments.
- Current rate of growth of the imports of the investigated product.
- Any other economic factor or trend that may validly lead to the conclusion that the imports under investigation may cause injury to the national production.

Causal link

In addition to proving the elements that may constitute the international unfair trade practice, the FTL requires that the relationship between the conduct (the unfair trade practice) and the result (the injury or threat thereof) be directly linked, and that such connection be proven beyond a reasonable doubt. In other words, even if the conduct and the result are proven, but are not clearly linked one to the other, the trade practice cannot be sanctioned and thus no antidumping duties may be imposed.[35]

Period of investigation

The information about the sales made to Mexico, the analysis of the injury or the threat thereof and the causal link must refer to a period that covers at least six months prior to the start of the investigation.[36] However, that period may be expanded by the UPCI if it deems it convenient or necessary to better understand the particular circumstances of the alleged international unfair trade practice.

All data filed by the interested parties in the case will need to refer to the period of investigation. Although parties may wish (or are required by the UPCI) to file information about different periods of time, the basic data that the UPCI will use to resolve the case will be that relevant to the specific period of investigation determined at the time the initiation resolution is published.

Subsidies

The FTL does not contain a lengthy regulation regarding subsidies, but rather applies some of the same principles covering dumping investigations. Subsidies may take the form of incentives, grants, allowances, premiums, or any other kind of aid provided in a direct or indirect manner by a government or governmental entity to producers, sellers, or exporters. Furthermore, the FTL establishes that SECOFI shall issue a limited list of what measures are to be considered as unauthorized subsidies.[37]

Safeguard measures

Safeguards are defined as extraordinary measures that are set in place to temporarily block imports under circumstances that threaten or are causing serious injury to national production. Their purpose is to facilitate the adjustment of the national products to the opening of the Mexican market and the globalization process. The FTL defines safeguard measures as those that regulate or temporarily restrict the imports of identical, similar, or any goods that compete with those of the national industry.[38]

Types of safeguards

The following are the kinds of safeguards regulated by the FTL:[39]
(i) *Tariffs:* Duties imposed upon imports and exports. Two kinds of tariffs exist: (i) Specific tariffs, which are those set forth in fixed monetary amounts; and (ii) Ad valorem tariffs, which are those expressed in percentage terms.
(ii) *Licenses:* As defined by the FTL, a license is a permit issued by SECOFI that is required to allow the entrance or exit of goods to/from the national territory.
(iii) *Quotas:* Measures that translate into setting a limited quantitative amount of goods that may be imported or exported. Accordingly, SECOFI issues a "quota certificate" whereby it assigns a maximum quota or tariff/quota to imports or exports.

Safeguard measures may be imposed by SECOFI when it finds that imports of a specific product cause or threaten to cause serious injury to the national industry of a similar or identical product.[40] The existence or threat of serious injury shall be determined by virtue of an administrative procedure pursuant to the FTL and is only allowed in extraordinary circumstances and for a limited time.[41]

Duration

The duration of the safeguards shall not exceed four years and shall be subject to the adjustment programs that national producers must commit to upon SECOFI's determination to impose the safeguards.[42]

Safeguard measures procedure

The determination of specific safeguards must be carried out in a period not to exceed 260 days after publication of the initiation notice. The scope of the investigation must be limited to the existence of imports in such quantities and/or conditions that cause or threaten to cause serious injury to national production of identical or similar goods, or goods that directly compete with the investigated product, and that may have been imported within a period of six months prior to the initiation of the investigation.[43]

Critical circumstances[44]

The Executive may impose temporary safeguard measures within twenty days after the initiation of the investigation provided that:
(i) Critical circumstances exist such that the delay of temporary measures would cause injury that is difficult to repair.
(ii) Evidence exists that the increase of the imports has caused or threatens to cause serious injury.
(iii) That the increase of the imports was substantial in a relatively short period and that any delay in the application of the measures would result in serious injury that is difficult to repair.
(iv) In the event that a threat of serious injury has been determined, temporary measures may only be assessed if the investigated products are perishable agricultural products and the threat of serious injury cannot be avoided by waiting for the usual investigation period.

Duration. SECOFI shall determine the period such measures shall be in force, provided it does not exceed six months. After such date, said measures may be confirmed, modified, or revoked by SECOFI. If such temporary measures are revoked, the interested parties shall be entitled to be reimbursed for the amounts spent, including the applicable interest.[45]

ADMINISTRATIVE PROCEDURES FOR UNFAIR TRADE PRACTICES

The administrative procedures whereby the existence and effects of international unfair trade practices are verified is carried out by the UPCI.

Initiation

The antidumping procedure may be initiated by:
(i) SECOFI:
SECOFI may commence on its own initiative an international unfair trade practices investigation when it becomes aware of the existence of certain acts or conduct, or of consequences in the national market and/or economy that lead it to believe that an international unfair trade practice exists.
(ii) By the national industry:
A physical or legal entity that manufactures goods that are similar or identical to the goods that are purportedly being imported under unfair trade conditions, or that produce goods that directly compete with goods that are being imported under unfair trade conditions, may request that SECOFI open an investigation of such products to determine if in fact they are being exported under unfair trade conditions.

Furthermore, for the national industry to request the initiation of the antidumping investigation, it must prove that it represents at least 25 percent of the domestic industry which produces that similar or identical product, or that manufactures a product that competes directly with the investigated product.[46]

Initiation Resolution

Within a thirty-day period after the petition to initiate an antidumping investigation has been filed by the national industry, SECOFI must take one of the following steps:[47]
(i) Publish in the Federal Official Gazette (FOG) the initiation resolution whereby the basic facts of the investigation are established, and, if such is the case, the temporary antidumping duty that is to be imposed upon the investigated products during the investigation period.[48]
(ii) Publish in the FOG an initiation resolution whereupon the UPCI requires from the petitioner(s) additional evidence or information required to confirm the appropriateness of initiating such investigation.

The requested information shall be delivered to the UPCI in a period not to exceed twenty days. If such information is not submitted in the referred term, the UPCI shall deem the petition to be abandoned and, therefore, shall proceed to dismiss the investigation.
(iii) In the event that the petitioner does not comply with the applicable requirements, the UPCI shall publish in the FOG a resolution whereby the investigation is dismissed.

Under the first and second scenarios, and once the initiation resolution has been published in the FOG, the interested parties[49] will have thirty days to file their defenses and allegations before the UPCI.

The UPCI may request from the interested parties any information or evidence that it deems convenient for the purposes of the investigation. In the event that the foregoing information requested by the UPCI is not produced by the interested parties, SECOFI may use the best information available to elucidate the facts of the investigation (whatever exists in the file that was filed by the other parties).[50]

Preliminary Resolution

No later than 130 days after Publication of the initiation resolution, the UPCI shall issue a preliminary resolution whereby this agency may:[51]
(i) impose a temporary antidumping duty;
(ii) continue the investigation without imposing an antidumping duty; or
(iii) Terminate the antidumping investigation in the event that insufficient grounds or evidence exists to determine if an international unfair trade practice is being performed.

Final Resolution

No later than 260 days after the initiation resolution is published in the FOG, the UPCI must issue the final resolution, whereby it must decide on one of the following options:[52]
(i) impose a final antidumping duty;
(ii) revoke the temporary antidumping duty established in the preliminary resolution; or
(iii) conclude the antidumping investigation without fixing an antidumping duty.

Once a final antidumping duty is set in place, any of the interested parties may request the UPCI to determine/clarify if a specific good is included under the scope of the specific antidumping procedure, or if such product is beyond the reach of the final antidumping duty.[53]

Conciliation Hearing

An interested party may request from the UPCI during an antidumping investigation that a conciliation hearing take place in which a solution to the conflict may be proposed to end the antidumping investigation. Such a hearing may be requested at any time during the antidumping investigation, but no later than fifteen days before the evidence period of the investigation ends.[54]

The UPCI may hold a conciliatory hearing even if it has not been requested by the interested parties. Assistance to such conciliation hearings does not mean that the interested party is obliged to agree to any of the terms being proposed. The covenants or agreements being taken in the conciliatory hearings must not result in an obstacle to free competition and/or trade.[55]

Public Hearing

After the preliminary resolution is published, but before the final resolution, a public hearing must be scheduled by the UPCI.[56] The purpose of the public hearing is for the interested parties to have the opportunity to discuss their arguments and positions directly before the UPCI. The interested parties will have the opportunity to question and rebut each others' contentions, evidence, and information rendered throughout the investigation, and will cross examine each other before the UPCI officials.[57]

Public, Confidential and Reserved Commercial Information

As a general rule the FTL sets forth that any interested party will have access to the information filed by other parties and, thus, an opportunity to review all data submitted. Furthermore, all parties participating in an investigation must serve notice to all others with a public version of any document that is filed by delivering a copy by messenger service on the same date that it is submitted with the UPCI.[58]

The above notwithstanding, public access shall not be granted vis-à-vis the following types of information:[59]
(i) Confidential information
   Confidential information includes, among others, production processes, costs, identity of components and pieces, terms and conditions of sales, distribution costs, transaction costs, description of clients, distributors and suppliers, variable costs, adjustment quantities,

volumes, and any other specific information that, if disclosed, could result in damage to the company's competitive advantages.[60]

The corresponding interested party must request from SECOFI that such information be considered as confidential by submitting a summary thereof that may be understood by any person that consults it, and by explaining the reasons for its petition.

The preceding information may only be accessed by the legal representatives of the corresponding interested party, provided that they may not use such proprietary information for their personal use, nor disclose it to any other person.

(ii) Reserved commercial information

This type of information is defined as information the disclosure of which would result in an irreversible economic or financial injury upon the owner of such information, which may include, among others, secret formulas or processes with a commercial value, exclusively known to a small group of persons that employ such information in the production of a commercial product.[61]

(iii) Governmental confidential information

Governmental Confidential Information is data as to which disclosure or access is prohibited by any legislation or any other international treaty to which Mexico is a party. It includes proprietary data, information, statistics or documents regarding national security or strategic activities for the scientific or technological development of the country, as well as any other communication between governments qualified as confidential.[62]

Technical Meetings

An interested party may request from the UPCI that a technical meeting be held within five days after the preliminary or final determination has been published in the FOG.[63]

The purpose of the technical meeting is to explain to the interested parties the methodology employed to determine the dumping margins or the calculation of the subsidies, as well as the injury or threat thereof and the causal link.

The interested parties that requested the technical meeting shall have the right to obtain the calculation sheets and the computer printouts that the UPCI used and based its conclusions on when issuing the corresponding resolutions.

Verification Visits[64]

Once the information has been submitted by the interested parties, the UPCI is empowered to conduct a visit at the place of business to verify the accuracy of said information. Accordingly, verification visits may be performed by the UPCI at the interested party's headquarters address, or any other place where the sources of the information filed are located. The UPCI may undertake the procedures it deems necessary to verify the accuracy of the information. In the event that the interested parties refuse to permit a verification visit, the UPCI shall not consider that party's data and shall use the best information available (information filed by other parties[65]), unless other facts that may support its conclusions exist.

Verification visits must be performed during business days and hours by duly authorized personnel of the UPCI. If necessary, and as agreed upon with the visited party, such verification visits may be made or continued during nonbusiness days and/or hours.

The UPCI may request from third parties that may have had a business relation (or other) with the visited interested party to supply information that may help in proving the accuracy of the information submitted.

Imposition of Duties

As mentioned above, as a result of an antidumping procedure, the UPCI may impose an antidumping duty upon the investigated product, assuming of course that the corresponding international unfair trade practice and its respective consequences have been verified as a result of the investigation performed. The duty will be imposed based on the margin determined for each individual producer, and an all-others rate will be imposed for any other producer of the involved product coming from the same country or countries subject to the investigation.[66]

The exact percentage of the antidumping or countervailing duty will be equal to the following:

(i) *In a Dumping Investigation:* The difference between the normal value obtained from the investigation, and the export price of the investigated product.[67]
(ii) *In a Subsidies Investigation:* The amount of the benefits granted by the government.[68]

The duty may be less than the foregoing amounts if they are enough to dissuade the importation of goods under dumping or subsidy conditions.[69]

The importers of identical or similar goods to those on which are levied a duty shall not be obliged to remit such duty if they can prove that the country of origin or transit is not the country that exports the goods under the determination.[70]

The duties shall remain in force during the time necessary to counter the effect and consequences upon the national industry of the unfair trade practice. However, if after five years from the date on which they were imposed, no interested party has requested their revision, nor has the UPCI on its own motion revised the duties, they shall be eliminated.[71]

Annual Revision. An interested party may request every year the review of the duty during the anniversary month of the date on which the duties were imposed by the UPCI. Likewise, the UPCI may on its own, at any time, order the review ex-officio of the duties.[72]

The FTL establishes two scenarios for the revision of antidumping or countervailing duties imposed by SECOFI as a result of an investigation:
- *SECOFI's Revision Procedure:*[73] Duties may be revised, on its own motion, at any time by the SECOFI; or
- *The Annual Revision Procedure:* Duties may be annually revised by the SECOFI upon request made by a party to the investigation, or any other party that, notwithstanding the fact that it did not participate in the investigation, proves to SECOFI that it has a legal interest in the outcome of the resolution deriving from the annual revision procedure.[74]

In the event that a change in the circumstances that led to the imposition of the final duties takes place, the UPCI is obliged to self-initiate a review of the final duties.[75]

The annual revision procedure shall be carried out in the same manner, observing the same procedural steps, that are followed in investigations: i.e., there shall be an initiation resolution, a preliminary resolution, a final resolution, a conciliation hearing, a public hearing, submission of evidence, technical meetings, verification visits, and so forth, all as necessary in the specific case and given the products involved.[76]

The petitioning party may request that the UPCI examine the following:
(i) If the petitioners are foreign producers or exporters or the importers of the product, the petitioners may request that:[77]
- The individual dumping margin be examined.
- The duty be modified or eliminated.
(ii) If the petitioners are national producers, the petitioners may request that:[78]
- The normal value and export price fixed for one or several foreign exporters in a representative period, during the course of normal commercial operations, be examined.
- The antidumping duty be confirmed or increased.

The outcome of the Revision Procedure may be any of the following:[79]
(i) *Revocation:* SECOFI may determine that the dumping margin does not exist any longer. In this case SECOFI will annually review this resolution during the following three years.
(ii) *Substitution:* When as a result of the revision different dumping margins are found to exist, the new final antidumping duties shall substitute for the former antidumping duties.
(iii) *Return:* If, from the revision procedure, it is found that the importers paid excessive antidumping duties, the difference in favor of the petitioner shall be reimbursed with the applicable legal interest.
(iv) *Confirmation:* In the event that, from the revision, it is determined that the importers paid during the revision period an antidumping duty less than the amounts determined by the final revision resolution, the antidumping duty of lesser amount shall be confirmed; that is, no additional duties need be paid.

Voluntary Settlements with Exporters and Governments

SECOFI may suspend or terminate the investigation without the imposition of a duty if, at any time during the investigation prior to the closing of the evidence period (i.e., after the public hearing):[80]
(i) *In Antidumping Investigations:* The exporter of the goods accused of unfair trade practices voluntarily agrees to modify its prices or discontinue/limit its exports.
(ii) *In Subsidies Investigations:* The government of the investigated product eliminates or limits the subsidy.

The settlement formulas will require SECOFI to examine whether the negative effects of the unfair trade practice are eliminated. To do so, the FTL requires that the following factors be considered:[81]

- The impact of the settlement on the final prices of the product vis-á-vis the consumer, and the availability of the goods involved.
- The impact of the settlement on the international economic interests of the country.
- The impact of the settlement on the national industry's competitiveness, employment and investments.
- The fact that such exporters and/or governments are subject to unfair trade practice investigations or countervailing duties in said country or other countries.

Compliance with the terms of settlement must be periodically examined by SECOFI.[82]

REMEDIES AVAILABLE TO CHALLENGE INTERNATIONAL UNFAIR TRADE PRACTICE INVESTIGATION RULINGS

National Remedies

Revocation action[83]

An interested party affected by an act or resolution of SECOFI must challenge such act or resolution by means of a revocation action, which may be filed within forty-five days following the effective date of said act or resolution.[84] Through this action the challenged act or resolution may be revoked, modified, or confirmed. This action is not optional and must be exhausted before proceeding with the nullification action.[85]

Nullification action

The nullification action is processed by the Federal Tax Tribunal. This action may be filed by an interested party within a forty-five-day period to challenge SECOFI's ruling on the revocation action previously filed. This action may result in the challenged resolution being annulled, confirmed, or partially annulled.[86]

Constitutional suit (Amparo)

The affected interested party may challenge the final judgment of the Federal Tax Tribunal through a constitutional suit (an "amparo directo") before the competent Collegiate Circuit Court within fifteen days following issuance of the Tax Tribunal's decision.[87]

International Remedies— Alternate Dispute Settlement Mechanisms

In addition to the remedies provided under Mexican domestic laws, there are other options that may be used based upon the trade instruments to which Mexico is a party.

World Trade Organization

The WTO and the GATT implementing legislation include several codes that set forth the specific guidelines and rules to be followed in antidumping and subsidies investigations. These guidelines must be observed in any instance where a SECOFI resolution is being analyzed to confirm that they were duly applied. The WTO does not provide private parties, however, with the ability to bring a supranational challenge to combat SECOFI's decisions; such actions may be initiated only by WTO member governments.

NAFTA and other trade agreements

Chapter 19 of the NAFTA covers the matter of "Review and Dispute Settlement in Antidumping and Countervailing Duty Matters." This chapter sets forth an alternative dispute settlement mechanism whereby resolutions issued by SECOFI regarding international unfair trade practices are reviewed by a panel that seeks to examine the legality of such resolutions in the same manner that the internal reviewing authority would. In other words, the Chapter 19 panel substitutes international review panels composed of experts from the two countries involved for the domestic judicial review that otherwise would apply. Once a party elects to use this alternate dispute settlement mechanism, the review mechanisms provided by domestic laws cannot be resorted to.[88]

An interested party may challenge a resolution issued by SECOFI within thirty days after it was issued,[89] and the panel shall issue its decision no later than 315 days thereafter.[90] Chapter 19 of the NAFTA and the Rules of Article 1904 set forth the details of the procedure conducted by this binational panel mechanism.

Other trade agreements to which Mexico is a party incorporate similar mechanisms that are obviously usable only when products of the respective countries are involved.

References

1. "*Ley Reglamentaria del Artículo 131 de la Constitución Política de los Estados Unidos Mexicanos en Materia de Comercio Exterior,*" which was published in the Federal Official Gazette ("FOG") on Jan. 13, 1986.
2. The Foreign Trade Law was published in the FOG on Jul. 27, 1993; and the Regulations of the FTL were published in the FOG on Dec. 30, 1993.
3. See note 9 *infra*.
4. See note 10 *infra*.
5. See note 11 *infra*.
6. See note 12 *infra*.
7. Technically speaking, the Agreement signed with Chile is not a Free Trade Agreement, but rather an Economic Complementation Agreement; it was published in the FOG on December 23, 1991.
8. Published in the FOG on Dec. 30, 1994.
9. Published in the FOG on Dec. 20, 1993.
10. Published in the FOG on Jan. 9, 1995.
11. Published in the FOG on Jan. 10, 1995.
12. Published in the FOG on Jan. 11, 1995.
13. The FTL § 2.

14. The FTL § 1.
15. The FTL § 28.
16. The FTL § 30.
17. The FTL § 37.
18. The FTL §§ 29 and 39 *et seq.*
19. The FTL § 29.
20. The FTL sets forth that products are similar when, even if not alike in every aspect, they have similar characteristics and composition and, therefore, serve the same functions and are commercially interchangeable with others with which they are compared.
21. The FTL establishes that a product is identical to the investigated product when it resembles the latter in every aspect.
22. The term "national industry" or "national production" under the FTL must be understood as comprising at least 25 percent of the domestic production of the investigated product (FTL § 40).
23. The FTL § 28.
24. The FTL § 37.
25. The FTL § 62.
26. The FTL § 31.
27. The term, "normal commercial operations," has been defined by the FTL as those operations that reflect the market conditions in the country of origin and that are carried out in the ordinary course of business (with profits), or within a period that is representative between independent sellers and purchasers. (The FTL § 32).
28. That is, when they are not representative (if they represent less than 15 percent of the total sales of the product) or lack prices that are determined under normal commercial operations (the Regulations § 42).
29. The FTL § 31.
30. The FTL § 33.
31. The FTL § 34.
32. The FTL § 39.
33. The FTL § 41.
34. The FTL § 42.
35. The FTL § 29.
36. The Regulations § 76. This section has been interpreted in a very lax manner by the UPCI to reflect that that six-month (or longer) period can cover any time before the start of the investigation (which could result in investigations covering old periods, say during the 1980s or even earlier). A different interpretation would result in the investigation needing to cover a period that is recent and covers at least six months. This latter interpretation is reinforced by the second paragraph of the referred provision which says that the period may be modified by the UPCI to cover a period that exceeds the initiation of the investigation, something that clearly could not happen if the period were a remote one dating to many years before the initiation of the investigation.

37. Despite this prescription by the FTL, such list has not been published by SECOFI.
38. The FTL § 45.
39. The FTL § 45.
40. The FTL § 45.
41. The FTL § 47.
42. The FTL § 77.
43. The FTL §§ 75 and 76.
44. The FTL § 78-79 and § 128-131 of the Regulations.
45. The FTL § 79.
46. The FTL § 50.
47. The FTL § 52.
48. Unless very clear circumstances and evidence exist, usually the UPCI does not impose antidumping duties at the beginning of the investigation.
49. The term "interested parties" has been defined in the FTL § 51 as the petitioning producers, the importers and exporters of the investigated product, and the foreign legal entities that may have a direct interest in the outcome of the investigation. This definition is important, particularly as to the exporters and the foreign entities that were not given standing in these investigations under the old Regulatory Law of Article 131 of the Constitution and that resulted in those parties not being able to challenge SECOFI's decisions.
50. The FTL § 54.
51. The FTL § 57.
52. The FTL § 59.
53. The FTL § 60 and § 91 of the Regulations.
54. The FTL § 61 and the Regulations § 86.
55. The Regulations § 86-88. The UPCI will usually request the assistance of a member of the Federal Competition Commission to guarantee that no violation of the antitrust statutes takes place either during the hearing or in the settlement proposal.
56. The FTL § 81 and the Regulations §§ 165, 166 and 170.
57. The FTL § 81.
58. The FTL § 56.
59. The FTL § 80 and the Regulations § 147-157.
60. The Regulations § 149.
61. The Regulations § 150.
62. The Regulations § 154.
63. The Regulations § 84-85.
64. The FTL § 83 and § 173-176 of the Regulations.
65. The FTL § 54.
66. Regulations § 89. This criterion has been the subject of many interpretations. The UPCI has decided that unless an exporter files information about its commercial operations during the period of investigation, that the all-others rate should be applied. However, this criterion appears to be unfounded and illogical in the case of exporters that did not make any commercial sales to Mexico during the period of investigation (this approach would only appear to be appropriate if the

exporter fails to appear in the investigation, but not if it does and shows that it did not make any export to Mexico during that period). The latter case is being analyzed by the Federal Courts in Mexico to determine what is the correct interpretation of the FTL and its Regulations.

67. The FTL § 62.
68. The FTL § 62.
69. The FTL § 62.
70. The FTL § 66.
71. The FTL §§ 67 and 70.
72. The FTL § 68 and the Regulations § 101.
73. The Regulations § 108.
74. The Regulations § 100.
75. The Regulations § 99.
76. The Regulations § 100.
77. The Regulations § 101.
78. The Regulations § 101.
79. The Regulations § 105-107.
80. The FTL § 72 and § 110 of the Regulations.
81. The Regulations § 114.
82. The FTL § 74.
83. It is worth mentioning that on December 24, 1996, the Federal Administrative Procedure Law (the "FAPL") was amended in order to exclude from its scope matters related to international trade practices. Before such amendment came into force, in lieu of the revocation action, an interested party could challenge a resolution issued by SECOFI by means of a revision action, pursuant to articles 83 to 85 of the FAPL, within a fifteen-day period after notice of the resolution had been made. As a result of the revision action, the challenged act or resolution could be declared nonexistent, annulled, confirmed, avoided, or modified. Currently, and as a result of the exclusion of international trade practices matters from the FAPL's regime, it is unclear whether the FTL §§ 94 et seq. that contemplated the revocation action was given effect again despite the express derogation when the FAPL was originally issued. Therefore, the affected party must decide whether to file the revision action (under the Federal Tax Code § 121) or the revocation action (under the FTL § 94) as the appropriate remedy to challenge acts or resolutions issued by SECOFI. The selection of the remedy is an important decision because in the case of the revocation action under the FTL it must be filed before the matter is taken to the Federal Tax Court, whereas in the case of the revision action filing it is optional.
84. The Federal Tax Code § 121.
85. The FTL § 95.
86. The Federal Tax Code § 121, and § 95 of the FTL.
87. The "Ley de Amparo" § 21 and 158.
88. The FTL § 97.
89. The NAFTA § 1904(4).
90. The NAFTA § 1904(14).

New Zealand

Robert Fardell
Russell McVeagh McKenzie Bartleet & Co.
Auckland, New Zealand

INTRODUCTION

Since the mid-1980s, the New Zealand Government has increased domestic competitiveness by a policy of eliminating import licences and tariff barriers that have previously protected domestic industry. With the almost complete removal of tariff protection, the primary means by which New Zealand industry can protect itself against unfair trade practices is dumping and countervailing duties law, the basic principles of which are embodied in statute form.

The legislation has been recently amended to take into account the Agreement on Antidumping Measures and the Agreement on Subsidies and Countervailing Measures as a result of the Uruguay Round of Multilateral Trade Negotiations.

DUMPING AND COUNTERVAILING DUTIES ACT 1988

Background

Dumping of goods occurs where the export price of the goods imported or intended to be imported into New Zealand is less than the normal value of the goods. The normal value of goods is the price that would be paid for like goods, in the country of export, if the like goods are sold at arm's length for home consumption in the ordinary course of trade.

A transaction is not regarded as being at arm's length if the consideration paid for the goods exceeds the price, if the price is influenced by the relationship between the buyer and the seller, or if, in the opinion of the Secretary of Commerce, the buyer will be reimbursed, compensated, or otherwise receive a benefit for the whole or part of the price.

Where the goods are imported into New Zealand and are purchased by the importer from the exporter and the Secretary of Commerce is satisfied, after considering the price paid for the goods by the importer and importation costs, that the importer either directly or indirectly has sold those goods in New Zealand at a loss, then the Secretary of Commerce may treat the sale of those goods as indicating that the importer will receive a benefit for the whole or any part of the price.

Subsidized goods are goods in respect of which a specific subsidy has been or will be paid, either directly or indirectly by a foreign government. Subsidy is widely defined as including any benefit that has accrued or will accrue, directly or indirectly, to persons engaged in the production, manufacture, growth, processing, purchase, distribution, transportation, sale, export, or import of goods as a result of any scheme, program, practice, or thing done, provided, or implemented by a foreign government. It does not include the amount of any duty or internal tax imposed on goods by that government.

The amount of subsidy is the sum that the Secretary of Commerce considers is the benefit conferred on the recipient of the subsidy. Benefit is not conferred by a foreign government by the provision of equity capital, a loan, a loan guarantee, or goods or services, unless it is inconsistent with the usual practice of investment in the export country. Application fees, export taxes, or other charges levied on the export of the goods are not included in the amount of subsidy.

Export Price

The export price of the goods is the price paid by the importer in an arm's length transaction less an amount that represents both the costs involved in preparing the goods for shipment and the costs incurred in exporting the goods to New Zealand.

Where the purchase of goods is not at arm's length and the goods are subsequently sold by the importer, then the export price is the price at which the goods were sold by the importer less duties, exportation costs, and the amount of profit made by the importer. If the goods are sold by the importer in a condition different from that when they were imported then the export price is a reasonable price as determined by the Secretary of Commerce.

Normal Value

The normal value of goods is the price paid for like goods sold in the ordinary course of trade for home consumption in the country of export. If the Secretary of Commerce cannot determine the normal value of goods in this way, then he or she may determine normal value in two ways:
(i) normal value may be the sum of the cost of production or manufacture of the goods in the country of export, plus such amounts as would be reasonable for administrative, selling, and delivery costs together with the profit normally realized on the sale of such goods; or
(ii) the price paid for similar quantities of the goods sold in the country of export for export to a third country.

Where the normal value of the goods is determined to be the same price paid for like goods in the country of export, then the Secretary of Commerce must compare the subject goods with the like goods at the same level of trade, at contemporaneous time periods, and with allowance for any difference in the terms and conditions of sale, or any other differences that affect price comparability. If the country of export of the goods is not the country of origin, then the Secretary of Commerce may direct that the normal value of the goods be ascertained as if the country of origin were the country of export. Where the seller has sold the goods at a loss, the Secretary may deem the price paid for the goods to be paid outside the ordinary course of trade, and so not to be the normal value.

Material Injury

The determination of material injury, for the purposes of the Dumping and Countervailing Duties Act 1988, involves considering the volume of dumped or subsidized goods, the effect of the dumping or subsidization on prices in New Zealand for like goods and the consequent impact on the relevant New Zealand industry. The Secretary of Commerce also must consider whether there has been a significant increase in the dumped or subsidized goods, the extent to which those goods undercut the prices of like goods in New Zealand, whether or not the goods depress prices in New Zealand or prevent price increases for like goods that would have occurred were it not for the dumped goods, the economic impact on the industry, and the value, quantity, frequency, and purpose of the importation of dumped or subsidized goods.

Investigation

The Dumping and Countervailing Duties Act 1988 is administered by the Ministry of Commerce. Within the Ministry is a section known as the Trade Remedies Group, which receives complaints and conducts investigations. If a New Zealand industry considers itself materially injured by dumped or subsidized imports it may complete a questionnaire providing evidence of dumping, subsidisation or injury, and file this questionnaire with the Trade Remedies Group. Applications must be made by or on behalf of New Zealand producers of like goods.

Before initiating an antidumping or contervailing duty investigation, the Secretary of Commerce must be satisfied that goods are being dumped or subsidized, and that this practice has caused or threatens to cause material injury to an industry, or has materially retarded the establishment of an industry.

In addition, no investigation can be initiated unless the Secretary is satisfied that the application for an investigation is supported by New Zealand producers that collectively produce 25 percent or more of the goods for domestic consumption in New Zealand and more than 50 percent of the total production of such goods.

The application must include evidence of dumping or subsidization and establish a link between the dumping and injury to the industry. Once the Secretary of Commerce initiates an investigation, he must give notice of the investigation and will proceed to consider both the evidence of dumping and or subsidization and the material injury to an industry. Interested parties to the investigation are given an opportunity to present relevant evidence in writing. Information that is confidential may not be disclosed by the Secretary without the express permission of the party that would be adversely affected by the release of such information. The Secretary is empowered to treat information as confidential where disclosure would give a competitor a significant advantage or would otherwise have a significant adverse effect upon the supplier of the information or the party from whom the information was acquired or to whom the information relates. Disclosure is dealt with on a case-by-case basis. The Secretary can request parties to provide a nonconfidential summary of information, or if that is not possible, reasons for keeping the information confidential. If the nature of the information is such that it should be kept confidential, the Secretary will do so.

The nature and extent of the evidence necessary to show dumping or subsidization at the initiation stage must be determined with a view to the subsequent investigation. In this respect the quantum of evidence necessary cannot be any higher at the initiation stage than at the time of the preliminary determination, where the Secretary has wide discretion to determine whether goods are being dumped or subsidized and whether there has been a material injury. Nevertheless, in light of the potential international consequences, an investigation is not embarked upon lightly.

Prior to initiating an investigation, the Secretary must notify the governments of the countries of export of the goods and, where subsidization of the goods is an issue, give the relevant governments an opportunity to clarify the situation and to reach a solution.

The Secretary of Commerce cannot initiate any investigation in relation to the alleged dumping of goods that originate from Australia.

An initial determination must be given to the parties to the investigation within 150 days of initiation.

Termination of Investigations

If the Secretary of Commerce determines that there is insufficient evidence of dumping or of injury to the industry, or, in the case of subsidization, where the imposition of a countervailing duty would be inconsistent with New Zealand's obligations under the World Trade Organization Agreement, then the Secretary shall terminate the investigation and give notice of such termination. He may also terminate the investigation where the application is withdrawn by those people who made the application or where enough producers withdraw their support.

Evidence of dumping or subsidization is deemed to be insufficient where, in the case of dumping, the margin is less than 2 percent of the export price or, in the case of subsidization, the amount of the subsidy is less than 1 percent of the value of the goods at the time of importation. Where the volume of imports as a percentage of total imports of like goods into New Zealand is negligible, then the evidence of dumping or subsidisation is also deemed to be insufficient. "Negligible" is not defined in the Dumping and Countervailing Duties Act 1988, but is determined by the Secretary on a case-by-case basis. A subsequent investigation can only be initiated where it is found that the information supplied affecting the original investigation is later found to be incorrect or does not disclose material facts.

Final Determination

Final determinations must be made within 180 days after the initiation of an investigation but not less than thirty days after an initial determination. The Secretary must decide whether the goods are being dumped or subsidized and whether or not there has been injury to an industry.

Imposition of Antidumping and Countervailing Duties

Once the Secretary has made a final determination, he may levy an antidumping or countervailing duty on the goods to be paid on demand after notice has been published in the Gazette.

The purpose of dumping duties is to protect a New Zealand industry from price discrimination. Thus, dumping investigations primarily involve private industry. Countervailing duty investigations, on the other hand, are more political in nature than antidumping investigations because they call into question the actions of a foreign government.

An antidumping duty may not be imposed where goods have been subsidized. The legislative purpose of the Dumping and Countervailing Duties Act would be distorted if, instead of a countervailing duty, the Secretary could elect to impose a dumping duty, thus enabling a levy exceeding the amount of the subsidy. It would also mean that the Secretary could circumvent the provisions for consultation that are applicable in the case of countervailing action.

The rate of duty is determined by the Secretary of Commerce. For dumped goods, the duty must not exceed the difference between the export price of the goods and their normal value and, for subsidized goods, the duty must not exceed the subsidy on the goods. For both antidumping and countervailing duties, the Secretary must ensure that the duty is not greater than is necessary to prevent material injury or a recurrence of material injury to an industry.

The Secretary of Commerce may, by notice, terminate the imposition of any antidumping or countervailing duty that he imposes. The Secretary is not required under the Act to give reasons for the termination of any antidumping or countervailing duties.

In New Zealand, there is no administrative review or appeal to an independent tribunal. Consequently, New Zealand dumping laws remain subject to the exercise of wide discretion on the part of the Trade Remedies Group. If parties are dissatisfied with findings that are made, recourse is to seek judicial review before the High Court on traditional administrative law grounds.

The Secretary of Commerce, on his own, or on the application of an interested party providing evidence to justify a review, may review the duties or reassess the rate or amount of the duty. A review of the duties must be carried out within 180 days.

All antidumping duties or countervailing duties cease to be payable after five years from the final determination, or the reassessment of the duties, whichever is the later date. For example, if a reassessment takes place in the fourth year after final determination, the duty will remain for a further five years unless a further reassessment is made. If, following a reassessment, the amount of duty payable is lower than that of the final determination, then the balance is refunded by the Collector of Customs.

Price Undertakings

If the Secretary of Commerce has initiated an antidumping or countervailing duty investigation, the Secretary may terminate consideration of a particular consignment of goods if he receives undertakings from either the government of the country of export or from the exporter of the goods that, in the future, the government or the exporter, as the case may be, will conduct its trade to New Zealand of like goods in a way that will avoid injuring an industry or materially retarding the establishment of industry. The undertaking will automatically lapse if an investigation is completed and it is found that there is no injury to an industry or material retardation of the establishment of an industry. However, where the findings of no injury are due to the existence of the undertaking, the Secretary may require that the undertaking be maintained. Notice must be given if the investigation is terminated. The Secretary of Commerce may review any undertaking on his own initiative or, at the request of an interested party that submits positive evidence justifying such a review. A review of an undertaking must be completed within 180 days of its initiation.

Any undertaking automatically lapses five years after the acceptance of the undertaking, or, where a review has been carried out, five years after the date of the initiation of that review.

Provisional Measures

Provisional measures to counteract dumping may be taken at any time after 60 days from the commencement of an investigation by the Secretary of Commerce if the Secretary has reasonable cause to believe that the dumping or subsidization of goods is threatening or causing material injury to an industry or retardation of its development. The Secretary must be satisfied that material injury will occur during the period of investigation and may direct that a security be given to protect local industry. However, an importer may seek an interim restraining order, preventing the imposition of duties or security measures, by making a prima facie case challenging the validity of such measures. A security must not exceed the difference between the export price of the goods and their normal value, or the amount of the subsidy as determined by the Secretary as a result of the investigation.

Once the Secretary has initiated an investigation, he may direct that the duty, payable on the goods that are the subject of the investigation, be secured.

A provisional direction will cease to have effect following the Secretary's final determination and any security given will then be released, except to the extent that duties are for any amount payable on goods imported prior to the final determination. Where the amount of antidumping duty or countervailing duty imposed under a provisional direction exceeds the amount determined by the Secretary of Commerce, then the excess is remitted by the Collector of Customs. Where the duty imposed pursuant to a provisional direction is less than the amount of duty determined by the Secretary, then the difference is not collected on any importation subject to the provisional direction.

Retrospective Measures

Where the Secretary has made a final determination, the antidumping or countervailing duty is payable on the day after the date of the final determination. Where a provisional direction is imposed, the duty is payable on the day after the date of the decision of the Secretary to give notice of the provisional direction.

Where the Secretary determines that there is a history of dumping or that the importer should have been aware that the goods were dumped, and material injury is caused by substantial dumped imports of a product in a relatively short period, then the Secretary may retrospectively impose antidumping or countervailing duties on goods delivered for home consumption or removed for home consumption not more than sixty days prior to the date of application of provisional measures. In the case of subsidized goods, the Secretary must be satisfied that material injury is caused by massive imports of goods, in a relatively short period, that have benefitted from subsidies.

Where a price undertaking has been breached and provisional duties are imposed, the Secretary may impose retrospective duties for the same sixty-day period before the application of the provisional measures. However, the Minister may not impose such measures where the goods have been entered for home consumption before the date of the breach of the undertaking.

Third Country Antidumping and Countervailing Duties

Antidumping and countervailing duties may be imposed on goods where the Secretary is advised by the government of a third country that goods imported or intended to be imported into New Zealand were produced in another country, have been dumped or subsidized, and where material injury is caused to the domestic industry of a third country or the establishment of the industry in that country is materially retarded. The third country must be a country other than New Zealand and must not be the country in which the goods were produced. There is no obligation on New Zealand to accept a third country complaint. However, New Zealand has accepted one third country complaint against plaster of paris bandages exported from Germany to New Zealand. It was established that material injury was being caused to the producer of plaster of paris bandages in Australia.

TEMPORARY SAFEGUARD AUTHORITIES

Introduction

Safeguard actions are different from antidumping and countervailing actions in that they are available to deal with any situation in which imports increase to such an extent and in such a way that serious injury is caused or threatened to a domestic industry.

Investigations into whether safeguard action should be taken are carried out by temporary safeguard authorities whose functions are defined under the Temporary Safeguard Authorities Act 1987.

Safeguard action may be taken against imports from all countries supplying the goods in question whereas antidumping and countervailing actions are taken only against the individual suppliers of the specified dumped or subsidized goods.

To give the domestic industry time to adjust to the changing conditions of international competition, safeguard measures are applied temporarily whereas antidumping and countervailing duties may stay in place as long as the imported goods are being dumped or subsidized and are causing injury.

Imposition of Safeguards

Where it appears to the Secretary of Commerce, either as a result of his or her own inquiries or following a request from producers of like goods or directly competitive goods, that the importation of any goods has caused or threatens serious injury to an industry, then the Secretary may request that an inquiry be held. The Safeguards Authority will then consider the matter and report on whether the industry has suffered, or is likely to suffer, a serious injury as a result of the importation of the goods, whether urgent action is needed to protect the industry from such injury, and what form any such action should take.

The factors that the Authority must take into account in carrying out an investigation are the rate and amount of imports as well as the economic impact of the increase on the industry, including any actual or potential decline in output, sales, market share, profits, productivity, employment, and utilization of production capacity. The Authority must also consider the nature and extent of importations by New Zealand producers of like goods including their value, quantity, frequency, and the purpose of the importation. Before giving its report to the Secretary of Commerce the Authority must take into account any statements of government policy that are given to it.

The Authority must report the results of its inquiry within thirty days of receiving a request. Upon reporting to the Secretary, the Authority may recommend that urgent action be taken and may also report on the rate, extent, and duration of any measures it recommends. If the Authority reports that urgent action is necessary to protect the industry from serious injury then the Authority may recommend the imposition of a duty, the restriction of the importation of the goods, or any other action it considers appropriate. The Authority must act consistently with New Zealand's obligations as a party to the agreement establishing the World Trade Organization.

Norway

Trond S. Paulsen
Heggemsnes & Paulsen
Oslo, Norway

HISTORY AND OVERVIEW OF TRADE REMEDY LAWS AND REGULATIONS SINCE 1947

Norway's Accession to GATT/WTO and Antidumping and Subsidies Codes

Norway has been a party to the General Agreement on Tariffs and Trade since its entry into force on January 1, 1948, as well as to the agreements resulting from the subsequent multilateral GATT negotiations.

Norway was thus a party to the original Antidumping Code (AD) that entered into force on July 1, 1968, to the revised Code in force since January 1, 1980 and to the Uruguay Round 1994 Agreement on dumping. Norway also acceded to the 1979 Subsidy Code and to the present GATT 1994 Agreement on Subsidies and Countervailing Measures (CVD).

Evolution of Trade Remedy Rules

Norway had no specific laws or regulations relating to antidumping or countervailing measures until 1954. The lack of such rules must be seen in the context of the general import and export regulations provided by the respective provisional Acts of December 13, 1946. According to these Acts, licenses were required for all imports and exports. The Norwegian Parliament (The Storting) in 1997 replaced the provisional Acts with a new Act (See OTHER TRADE REMEDIES, below).

The first Norwegian rules on antidumping and countervailing duties, adopted by the Storting, were given effect in November 1954. The rules were enshrined in the Introductory Provisions of the Customs Tariff (IPCT). These rules were very general in character, consisting of a total of five or six short paragraphs. The Storting adopted a couple of minor additions to the rules in 1966 in accordance with the Norwegian accession to the AD Code. The Norwegian rules thereafter remained unaltered until the fall of 1994 when the Storting adopted further additions, in conformity with the Agreement on Dumping of the same year. The following year the new rules were subject to one amendment, which entered into force on January 1, 1996. That amendment added a clause specifying that the imposition both of AD and CVD must be in conformity with the 1994 GATT and WTO Agreements.

The present Norwegian rules are based on the former provisions, and they are still quite general in character, as well as very succinct (less than two pages). The rules are found in section 3 of IPCT. The provisions are supplemented by the Customs Act of June 10, 1966, sec. 16 and sec. 17, concerning the competence of the authorities to conduct investigations in dumping and subsidy cases. Interested parties are required to give any relevant information requested by the investigating authority. The Public Administration Act of February 10, 1967 regulates in general the rights of interested parties to the case, including their right to obtain and to present information. Provisions concerning confidentiality in trade remedy cases are covered by the Customs Act, sec. 8.

In 1992 the Ministry of Finance prepared a four-page memorandum (a guide) concerning Norwegian AD and CVD procedures. A questionnaire for AD requests is annexed to the guide. In the introduction to the guide, it is stressed that the text is not legally binding, and that the Ministry may handle issues differently than stated in the guide. The guide is basically a reproduction of the main provisions of the GATT 1979 Codes, with many specific references to the English text of the two Codes. The Ministry of Finance is expected to update the guide for the 1994 Agreements. The Ministry has announced that it will consider whether the Government should promulgate a regulation concerning AD and CVD procedures.

The rather general character of the Norwegian AD and CVD rules should be seen in the context of the very rare recourse to such measures in Norway. Since 1970, there has been only one case, in 1984, where any kind of protective measures were introduced. In that case an AD was applied for about a year and a half.

The Norwegian trade remedy regulations have been tailored on the GATT rules. The Norwegian government has in practice applied the same rules also to countries that are not party to the GATT Agreements.

Norway is not a member of the European Union. Norway's trade relations with the EU are governed by the European Economic Area Agreement. According to this Agreement (section 26) antidumping measures and countervailing duties cannot be used in respect of trade between the parties. Exception is made for products that are not covered by the Agreement, i.e., agricultural and fisheries products. According to Protocol 13 of the Agreement, antidumping and countervailing duties can, unless the parties agree to other solutions, also be used to prevent circumvention by third countries.

Summary Listing of Trade Remedies, with Statutory/ Regulatory References and Administering Agency

- The Norwegian rules on AD and CVD, as last amended by the Storting, effective January 1, 1996, are included in Section 3 of the IPCT, published annually by the Directorate of Customs.
- The 1992 Ministry of Finance memorandum (guide) has not been published as an official document. The guide is supplied by the Ministry to anyone requesting information about the Norwegian AD and CVD procedures. The guide was updated on February 9, 1993. (AT-Notat nr.4 - 1992, ajourført pr 9.2.1993).

AD and CVD measures are adopted by the "King in Council" (term for the formal procedure for decisions made by the Government, and not by a sole Minister). The Storting shall be informed of any decision to impose AD or CVD duties and be provided with a detailed account of the matter.

The rules are administered by the Ministry of Finance. The Ministry has established an Antidumping Committee (ADC) having at present nine members. The members of ADC are appointed from the Ministry of Finance, the Foreign Ministry, the Ministry of Industry, the Directorate of Competition, the Council for Consumer Affairs, the Norwegian Confederation of Trade Unions, the Confederation of Norwegian Business and Industry and the Federation of Commerce, and the present Chairman represents the academia (being a professor at the Bergen College of Business Administration and Economics). The Secretariat of ADC is in the Ministry of Finance.

The Ministry may conduct an investigation itself, or it can ask the ADC to do so. As there have not been any dumping or subsidy investigations in Norway since 1984, there are few established procedures. If the Ministry of Finance should choose to conduct a future investigation itself, it would in any case ask for the ADC's recommendation as to any trade remedies.

Decisions concerning AD and CVD can be appealed by bringing legal proceedings in the courts. There are no specialized courts for trade issues that are consequently dealt with by the ordinary courts of law. To ensure a speedy procedure for such cases, the Storting in 1997 amended the Customs Act. Sec. 16 AD and CVD cases will accordingly have to be brought before the City Court of Oslo, which shall give such cases priority.

Norway has acceded to the WTO 1994 Agreement on Safeguards. The statutory rule is given in IPCT, Section 4, as amended, effective January 1, 1996. Safeguard measures can be taken by the King in Council. The Storting shall be informed without delay and be given background information about such measures.

The Norwegian provisions on antidumping measures, countervailing duties, and safeguard measures also apply to agricultural products. In addition, there are particular provisions authorizing additional duties for agricultural products in accordance with the GATT 1994 Agreement on Agriculture, article 5. The King in Council is authorized to set additional duties on agricultural products pursuant to IPCT, Section 6.

ANTIDUMPING INVESTIGATIONS

The present Norwegian rules explicitly state that the imposition both of AD and of CVD must be made in conformity with the provisions set by the 1994 GATT and WTO Agreements. These clauses incorporate the 1994 Agreements into Norwegian law, and consequently fill the gaps in the very succinct Norwegian rules on trade remedies. The Government has published extensive preparatory works for the Storting, including translations into Norwegian of the Uruguay Round Agreements in connection with the Norwegian accession. (Ot prpr. nr. 68 (1995-96).

Dumping Determination
Initiation of investigation
By petition

There is no mention in IPCT about petitions from industry for AD. The general reference in IPCT that decisions must be made in conformity with the GATT 1994 Agreement certainly applies. An AD investigation following a petition will thus not be initiated unless there is a written application by or on behalf of the domestic industry concerned (as defined in paragraph 4 of Article 5 of the 1994 Agreement).

By government

In IPCT there is a specific provision giving competence to the Government to impose AD if requested by another state in cases where dumping causes injury or threatens to cause material injury to a domestic industry in the country in question.

Timetable

In IPCT it is laid down that investigations shall normally be completed within one year of their initiation, and in no case more than eighteen months thereafter.

Participation of parties and their counsel

IPCT states that:

> parties shall be notified of the information that has been obtained, and shall be given the opportunity to produce further relevant evidence.

In the Ministry of Finance guide it is stated that if the Antidumping Committee finds it appropriate, a hearing can be held for the parties who will be given the opportunity to present evidence beforehand.

Access to information developed in proceedings

The relevant rule in IPCT is worded as follows:

> Any information given to the authorities in confidence shall be subject to the duty of secrecy unless otherwise provided by statute.

The statute in question is the Customs Act of 1966, which states (in sec. 8) that confidential information can be made known to the parties to the case or to those representing the parties. In sec. 19 of the Public Administration Act of February 10, 1967, it is stated that interested parties cannot demand information which by its nature is confidential. Even if interested parties cannot demand such information, the authorities may at their own discretion disclose such information on certain conditions, as provided for in the GATT 1994 Agreement. The Agreement states that such information shall not be disclosed without specific permission of the party submitting it.

Definitions

The Norwegian rules do not contain any specific provisions concerning like products, period of investigation, domestic industry and petition requirement for industry support, viability of markets, or related parties.

The calculation of dumping margins is provided for in IPCT as follows (Section 3, paragraph 1):

> For the purpose of this section, dumping means the import or marketing of a product from another country:
> (a) at a price that in the ordinary course of trade is lower than the comparable sales price of the like product when destined for consumption in the exporting country, or

(b) if no such price exists in the exporting country, at a price that is either
   (1) lower than the highest comparable export price in the ordinary course of trade for the like product when exported to any other country, or
   (2) lower than the cost of production in the product's country of origin plus a reasonable amount of selling costs and profits. When prices are compared, due allowance should be made for differences in terms of sale and delivery, transport costs, taxation and any other differences which affect price comparability.

There are no specific provisions as to export price, normal value, treatment of sales through related parties, currency conversion, sampling, cost of production and constructed value methodology, nonmarket methodology, use of facts available, price undertakings and other agreements to suspend investigations, or effect of Antidumping Order.

Effective date

Retroactivity, if any

There are no detailed provisions about retroactivity. However, AD measures cannot be given retroactive effect, as this would be contrary to paragraph 97 of the Constitution of Norway.

Duration

IPCT, Section 3, has a provision stating that AD may be imposed as a provisional measure until further information is available. There are no additional rules on such provisional measures.

According to IPCT, duties:

> shall remain in force only as long as is necessary to counteract the injury resulting from dumping or subsidies. The duty shall be terminated at the latest five years after the date on which it was imposed, unless a review indicates that the injury will probably continue or recur.

Scope determination

Duties may be imposed pursuant to section 3:

> for one or more types of products, for goods from one or more specified exporters, or for goods from one or more specified countries.

The Norwegian provisions do not contain any specific rules concerning enforcement, including rules to prevent circumvention of orders; procedures for new shippers; or procedures for review and revocation of order.

Even though there are no specific Norwegian provisions concerning, for example administrative reviews, it is quite clear an interested party can ask for such reviews on conditions foreseen by the GATT 1994 Agreement. Norwegian provisions specify that the imposition both of AD and CVD shall be within the limits set by the 1994 GATT Agreement.

COUNTERVAILING DUTY INVESTIGATIONS

The general comments made in the introductory paragraph to the preceding chapter on AD investigations also apply to CVD investigations.

Section 3 of IPCT covers both dumping and subsidies and the rules of procedure of the investigation apply to both. The only provision relating specifically to CVD briefly states that such duties may be imposed when the Government considers that a subsidy is granted in another country on production or export, including special transport subsidies. The provisions presented above for dumping investigations concerning the initiation of investigation, timetable, participation of parties and their counsel, and access of parties also apply to subsidy investigations.

There are no provisions defining what are countervailable or non-countervailable subsidies. Neither are there provisions on the calculation of subsidies.

INJURY ANALYSIS

Section 3 provides that protective duties may be imposed, if dumping:

> causes injury or threatens to cause material injury to domestic industry or causes substantial delay to the establishment of such industry.

There are no further provisions concerning injury in the Norwegian rules on trade remedies. In the standard Questionnaire it is specified that the party asking for an investigation shall provide information as to all Norwegian producers of the product in question, both as to those asking for the investigation as well as the others. Statistics (or estimates) of production, domestic sales, and exports shall be given for each of the last three years, in respect of every Norwegian producer. Statistical data (or estimates) shall also be given for the imports of the product from the most important exporting countries and from every country alleged to have dumped. The producers who have made the dumping complaint shall provide information regarding the injury (actual or potential). The information should comprise information relating to sales and prices in recent years with explanations, as well as other data, e.g., concerning employment, orders, production capacity, and investment plans.

OTHER TRADE REMEDIES

Until 1994, Section 2 of IPCT authorized the King in Council on certain conditions to impose a supplementary duty of up to 100 percent of the value of the merchandise ("The battle duty") if Norwegian exports were subject to discriminatory measures. The provision had been part of the Norwegian trade remedy laws for almost 100 years. But in practice the provision had never been the basis for any trade measures, and it was consequently repealed in 1994.

The legal basis for import licensing and quantitative import restrictions was until 1997 found in a Provisional Act of December 13, 1946. The new Act of June 6, 1997, relating to the regulation of imports and exports authorizes the Government, in conformity with international obligations, to promulgate regulations that prohibit or set license requirements for imports.

Specific rules on customs-related safeguard measures were laid down by the Storting with effect from January 1, 1995. The rules are found in IPCT, Section 4, which reads as follows:

> Section 4. Customs-related safeguard measures
>
> Customs-related safeguard measures may be applied if, as a result of unforeseen developments, a product is imported in such increased quantities and under such conditions as to cause or threaten to cause serious injury to Norwegian producers of like or competitive products.
>
> The King [in Council] may, in conformity with the provisions of GATT 1994 and the WTO Agreement, apply such safeguard measures. A decision to apply safeguard measures pursuant to this section shall be notified without delay to the Storting. The notification shall include a detailed account of the matter.

To date, no safeguard measures have been taken. As there are neither detailed rules nor any administrative practice, it is uncertain which administrative procedures will be followed if safeguard measures are taken.

The particular provisions authorizing additional duties for agricultural products summarize Article 5 of the GATT 1994 Agreement on Agriculture. The Norwegian provision briefly states that such duties may be set if the volume of imports exceeds a trigger level, or if the import price falls below a trigger price, in accordance with article 5 of the GATT Agreement. The King in Council is authorized to provide more detailed rules.

Peru

Diego Calmet Mujica
Estudio Aurelio Garcia Sayan
Lima, Peru

DUMPING AND SUBSIDIES LEGAL REGIME

Discussion of Peru's Accession to GATT/WTO and Antidumping and Subsidies Codes

The Republic of Peru became a contracting party of the GATT in 1951 during the negotiations of the Torquay Round. At the time of its accession Peru was the 35th country to enter the GATT.

Peru did not subscribe to the Antidumping and Subsidies codes, nor any of the GATT 1947 codes.

Evolution of Trade Remedy Laws and Regulations

The ECLA (Economic Commission for Latin America) import substitution programs in vogue in the 1970s required Latin American countries to close their borders to foreign trade to promote regional industrial development. In accordance with this development model, Peru restricted—and in some cases prohibited—imports, imposing tariffs and customs duties at an extremely high level relative to those in open-economy countries throughout the world.

The current Government's policy of opening the Peruvian market to international trade, implemented at the end of 1990, gradually, but dramatically, reduced import tariffs to an average of 16.5 percent C.I.F. as of June 1994. With this new policy arose the need for mechanisms for controlling unfair trade practices, such as dumping or subsidies. Prior to the new policy, these trading practices did not significantly affect domestic producers because the importation of goods competitive with domestic goods had been restricted and/or encumbered by tariff and customs duties so high as to outweigh whatever advantage might have been derived from dumping or subsidies.

The regulations on dumping and subsidies established in 1991 also created the Commission for the Control of Dumping and Subsidies (the "Commission"), which is an administrative agency authorized to oversee compliance with these laws. These regulations were based on the premise that businesses must compete with foreign producers for their own benefit, as well as for the benefit of the country as a whole.

Commission for the Control of Dumping and Subsidies

The Commission's function is to supervise and facilitate compliance with the new legislation regulating dumping and subsidies. In carrying out this task, the Commission may impose antidumping or compensatory duties in cases involving unfair trading practices. The Commission, however, is not an instrument that local producers may use to control the local market for their own benefit by impeding the entry of foreign products that may compete with local goods.

Originally, the Commission was composed of five members representing the Ministry of Economy, the Ministry of Industry, Tourism, and Integration, the Ministry of Agriculture, the Ministry of Foreign Relations, and the Confederation of Private Business Institutions (*Confederacion Nacional de Empresas Privadas*, CONFIEP). The Commission's task was limited to communicating the results of its investigations to the Vice Minister of Economy and Finance, and had no authority to rule on antidumping or compensatory duties complaints.

The Commission has since been absorbed by the National Institute for the Defense of Competition and the Protection of Intellectual Property (*Instituto Nacional de Defensa de la Competencia y de la Proteccion de la Propiedad Intelectual*, INDECOPI), and is composed of four full members and two substitute members, all appointed by the Directorship of INDECOPI. Currently two of the full members are lawyers and two are economists. Similarly, one of the substitute members is a lawyer, and one an economist. INDECOPI's Directorship itself has three members: two are appointed by the Ministries of Industry, Tourism, and Integration and International Trade Negotiations, and the third is appointed by the Ministry of Economy and Finance.

In 1991, The Andean Pact approved Decision 283, which established specific rules against trade distortions caused by the use of dumping or subsidies practices in the Andean market. According to the Peruvian Constitution, the Andean Decisions are considered national Law in Peru and are, thus, self-executing.

WTO AD/CVD Agreements

The Republic of Peru participated actively in the Uruguay Round negotiations. The Marrakech Agreement, which established the World Trade Organization (WTO), and the multilateral agreements that have been negotiated in the Uruguay Round, were approved by the Peruvian Congress in December 1994 through Legislative Resolution No. 26407. These agreements were promulgated by the President and published in their entirety in the Official Gazette.

The Agreement on Implementation of Article VI (Antidumping Agreement) and the Agreement on Subsidies and Countervailing Measures of the Uruguay Round Final Act, have been incorporated into national legislation and are accorded the highest standing in the Peruvian legal system. These agreements went into force on January 1, 1995.

The government of Peru has conformed Peruvian law and practice with WTO standards and rules. On April 29, 1997, it enacted Supreme Decree No. 043-97-EF as Peruvian main regulation of WTO Antidumping and SCM Agreements.

Notwithstanding, the antidumping and subsidies agreements have been applied directly to current cases as of January 1, 1995, relying on current national legislation to the extent consistent with the WTO.

Summary Listing of Each Trade Remedy, with Corresponding Statutory/Regulatory References and Agency Responsible for Administering such Remedy

Antidumping and subsidies

Substantive law and procedural framework

Legislative Resolution No. 26407—WTO agreements.
Legislative Decree No. 668 (Article 15)
Supreme Decree No. 043-97-EF
Supreme Decree No. 133-91-EF
Supreme Decree No. 277-91-EF
Supreme Decree No. 051-92-EF

Investigations

Law Decree No. 25868 (INDECOPI)
Legislative Decree No. 807 (INDECOPI)
Supreme Decree No. 025-93-ITINCI
Supreme Decree No. 001-94-ITINCI

Andean community law
Cartagena Agreement
Decision 283-Cartagena Agreement Commission

Safeguards
WTO Safeguards Agreement
WTO Textiles Agreement

ANTIDUMPING AND COUNTERVAILING DUTY INVESTIGATIONS

Under Peruvian law, the power to investigate dumping and subsidies cases falls upon the Antidumping and Subsidies Commission of INDECOPI (the Commission). The Commission has the authority to investigate dumping and subsidy practices and material injury caused by unfairly traded imports. This Commission is the only authority with the power to impose antidumping and countervailing duties in Peru.

In cases of dumped or subsidized imports originating from the Andean Community countries, the Peruvian domestic industry affected by those imports has the choice of requesting an investigation either in the Junta of the Andean Community or in the Commission. Because these are alternative proceedings, the petitioner must sign a sworn declaration agreeing not to initiate any other proceeding regarding the same case within alternative fora, once the competent authority is chosen. Since July 31, 1997, the General Secretariat of the Andean Community is the competent authority to investigate dumped or subsidized imports originating from Andean countries.

Initiation of Investigation

An investigation of dumping and subsidy practices shall be initiated upon written request by the domestic producers of identical or like products that account for a major proportion of the domestic industry, according to the standards established by law. In exceptional situations, the Commission may self initiate an investigation in cases of national interest and when, in the view of the Commission, the domestic industry is unable to make such a request, and where there is significant evidence that dumping or subsidy practices are being used and are causing material injury to domestic industry.

Timetable

The Commission has thirty days after the petition is filed to decide whether or not to initiate an investigation.

An investigation is opened after a publication of the Commission's decision to initiate in the Official Gazette. The Technical Secretary of the Commission notifies all interested parties that, within thirty days, each exporter shall present its response to the evidence presented by the petitioner and provide information required by the Commission in the questionnaire enclosed for that purpose. The Commission will consider extensions requests.

Investigations are to be concluded within a period of nine months from the date of publication in the Official Gazette. If, in the judgment of the Commission, there exist reasons for an extension, the period may be extended once, for an additional three months.

These time frames apply to both antidumping and countervailing duty investigations.

Petition Requirement

A petition filed with the Commission must detail evidence of the alleged dumping or subsidy. The complaint must also include documentation demonstrating the injury incurred by the dumping or subsidy, including historical data on domestic output, the current capacity of the affected firm or industry, the total value of sales in the domestic market, inventory, local and export prices, productivity, profits, employees, and salaries.

In addition, the Commission requests the producers, distributors, or traders of the like product, as well as the customs officers, agents, representatives, and persons receiving the imported goods, or any other persons it deems appropriate, to provide information and data which they have at their disposal to support their interest in the case.

Once an antidumping or countervailing duty investigation is initiated, the Commission issues a questionnaire to exporters requesting general information about the operations of the foreign producers. Foreign exporters, as well as the importers of the product that is subject to the investigation, may present to the Commission any information they consider useful to support their case, at any stage of the investigation. Such information must be officially translated into Spanish.

Access to Information Developed in Proceedings

All interested parties have access to the files containing documents with nonconfidential information developed in the proceedings.

All information for which "confidential" status is requested, shall be accompanied by nonconfidential summaries, and a justification for the request for confidentiality. The nonconfidential summaries must be in sufficient detail to permit a reasonable understanding of the substance of the information submitted in confidence.

The Commission will consider requests for confidential treatment when these prerequisites are met.

Definitions

Like products

Although the term "like product" is not specifically defined in Peruvian law, its concept and meaning is widespread in Peruvian law and practice, particularly in the determination of domestic industry. Like goods means, in relation to any other goods:
(i) goods that are identical in all respects to the goods subject to an investigation; and
(ii) similar goods, which are those possessing characteristics that resemble the imported product, taking into consideration its nature, quality, use, and function.

Period of investigation

The period of investigation covers at least six months prior to the initiation, and generally an investigation shall conclude within nine months from the date of publication of the notice of its initiation. If, in the judgment of the Commission, there exist reasons for an extension in the period, it may be extended once, for three additional months.

Domestic industry and petition requirement for industry support

The term "domestic production" includes all national producers of like products, or those among them whose collective output constitutes a major proportion of the national production of said products.

The Commission, according to the WTO Agreements, shall consider that a petition is made on behalf of the domestic industry if it is supported by domestic producers whose collective output constitutes more than 50 percent of the total production of the like product. However, no investigation shall be initiated when domestic producers expressly supporting the application account for less than 25 percent of the total production of the like product produced by said domestic industry.

Related parties

Peruvian law contains special provisions dealing with related parties, specifically in the determination of the domestic industry. Such provisions take into account if the producers are associated with the exporters of the product subject to investigation and whether the producers act as importers of the dumped good.

These rules apply both in investigations carried out by INDECOPI to determine the existence of dumped or subsidized imports as well as for evaluating the existence of injury caused by such imports to the domestic industry.

Calculation of Dumping Margins

Under Peruvian law, an imported good is dumped if the export price of the product is less than the market price of that same good, or of a similar product, destined for consumption or use in the country of origin in an arm's-length transaction. A similar product is one possessing characteristics that resemble the imported product, taking into consideration its nature, quality, use, and function.

Export price

The export price is the actual price paid or to be paid for the product exported to Peru. When, in the judgment of the Commission, no reliable export price can be determined due to the relationship, partnership, or compensatory arrangement between the exporter and the importer or a third party, the export price may be calculated based on the retail price at which the imported products or the similar products are first resold to an unrelated purchaser in Peru. If the products are not so resold, or if the products were not sold in the same condition in which they were imported, the price may be calculated on a reasonable basis determined by the Commission.

To determine the export price, all expenses incurred up to the date of the first resale must be taken into account, including duties, taxes, and a reasonable profit margin. Expenses to be considered include, among others, insurance, transportation, maintenance and unloading, import duties and export taxes owed the country of origin, a reasonable margin for general, administrative and sales expenses, a reasonable profit margin, and any customary commissions.

Market price (normal value)

Peruvian law defines market price as the price actually paid or to be paid for an identical or similar product in the exporting country in an arm's-length transaction for consumption or use in the domestic market of the exporting country. Business transactions between related parties or a partner or pursuant to a compensatory arrangement at prices similar to those applicable to transactions between independent parties meet the arm's-length transaction test.

If a market price cannot be determined by these methods, the Commission may determine market price by:
(i) considering a third country export price in the country of origin of an identical or similar product, provided this price is considered to be representative; or
(ii) calculating the price of an identical or similar product. This price shall be based on production costs incurred in the course of ordinary business in the country of origin, plus a reasonable margin for administrative and sales expenses, and a reasonable profit margin. As a rule, this profit margin will not be greater than that ordinarily available in the sale of a product of the same type in the domestic market of the country of origin.

Adjustments to prices

Adjustments to prices are made to ensure comparisons are made of prices at an equivalent level of trade, normally at the ex factory level. These comparisons must take into consideration the condition of the product at the time of the commercial transaction following the product's manufacture, and must be based on the most recent transactions.

Following are additional adjustments which must be considered:
(i) differences in the product's physical characteristics;
(ii) differences in quantities, considering discounts freely agreed upon in arm's-length transactions during a representative period, and the production costs of different volumes;
(iii) differences in the conditions of sales, including differences in indirect duties and taxes, credit conditions, guarantees, types of technical assistance, post-sale services, commissions, packing, transport, maintenance, insurance, freight charges and additional costs; and
(iv) other criteria that affect these differences.

Sampling

Although Peruvian law contains no specific sampling provision, the Commission uses sampling, for example, to determine the normal value of a product with different kinds of designs, which makes it impossible to get a reliable average domestic price.

Cost of Production and Constructed Value Methodology

Peruvian practice follows the methodology established by the Antidumping Agreement.

Nonmarket Economy Methodology

In cases against nonmembers of the WTO, the Commission is allowed to apply the Supreme Decree 133-91-EF, which establishes a specific antidumping procedure for goods exported from nonmarket economies.

Therefore, in the case of nonmarket economy countries, the Commission will determine the market price on the basis of a comparable price for the same or a similar product sold in the ordinary course of business for domestic consumption or use in a third country whose economic development is at a level similar to Peru's. Should no such comparable price exist, the market price may be calculated on a reasonable basis as determined by the Commission.

Effect of Antidumping Order

Upon completion of an investigation, the Technical Secretary prepares and submits a report for the case with its recommendations to the Commission. The imposition of provisional or final antidumping duties is approved by a majority vote of the members of the Commission.

The Commission will impose a final antidumping or countervailing duty when the Commission finds the existence of dumping or a subsidy, and that those duties are necessary to prevent injury to domestic producers.

The Commission's final determination will be published in the Official Gazette, which must include the margin of dumping, the description of the method used to calculate it, and the basis of the injury finding. The final determination constitutes an order to Customs to start collecting the duties, and the determination enters into force on the day following its publication.

Effective date
Retroactivity

In exceptional cases, the Commission may impose antidumping duties on those imports entered for consumption up to ninety days before the provisional determination.

In cases of subsidies, retroactive duties may be imposed when irreparable damage exists caused by a massive increase in imports over a relatively short period of time, and when, to prevent further damage, the Commission considers it necessary to retroactively apply countervailing duties.

No antidumping or countervailing duty shall be applied retroactively upon goods entered for consumption before the date of initiation of the investigation.

Duration

Duties remain in place as long as they are needed to eliminate the damage caused by dumped imports, but expire automatically after five years pursuant to the Sunset Clause rule established by the Antidumping Agreement. The Commission may initiate a new investigation to extend this period.

The same standard applies to countervailing duty investigations.

Enforcement, including rules to prevent circumvention of orders

In cases where there is evidence of circumvention of antidumping duty orders, the Commission may ask the Ministry of Industry, Tourism, Integration, and International Trade Negotiations to require certificate of origin for all imports of those goods included in the tariff codes subject to antidumping duty order.

In such cases, all importers of goods similar to those subject to antidumping duties must produce before Customs authorities the certificate of origin above mentioned for the goods imported, or otherwise pay or establish guarantees for the corresponding antidumping duties.

The Peruvian Antidumping Commission has applied this Certificate of Origin requirement once in a case of a Chinese textiles antidumping duty order in which it found evidence of circumvention.

This procedure also applies for countervailing duty investigations.

Procedures for review and revocation of order

The annual review of final antidumping or countervailing duty orders established by the Commission, as well as the reviews related to the need of maintaining said orders, are based on the rules and standards established by the Antidumping and Subsidy and Countervailing Measures Agreements.

In regards to the administrative review of the Final Resolution of The Commission, the party who deems itself aggrieved by a Determination of the Commission may appeal therefrom to the Tribunal for the Defense of the Competition and Intellectual Property Rights of INDECOPI whose determination finishes the administrative VIA. It is important to mention that this tribunal is a superior independent body, and thus it can change the decision taken by the Commission on establishing the antidumping duties or not, taken by the Commission.

The Final Resolution of said Tribunal may be appealed therefrom to the Supreme Courts of the Jurisdictional Body Power as the last possible instance in Peruvian Legal System.

COUNTERVAILING DUTY INVESTIGATION

Countervailing duty investigations are carried out by INDECOPI applying the same procedures and standards used for antidumping cases.

Calculation of Subsidies

The Commission applies the rules established in WTO Agreements to determine the specific amount of a subsidy.

INJURY ANALYSIS

Determination of injury is carried out by the same authority that determines the existence of dumping and subsidy in the Peruvian administrative justice, INDECOPI's Antidumping and Subsidy Commission. Therefore, the same procedural framework is applied for injury as well as definitions such as domestic industry, like product, etc.

Material Injury and Threat of Material Injury

As mentioned above, Peruvian producers, trade associations or unions that consider themselves injured or threatened within the previous six months by the dumping or subsidizing of goods similar to those they produce, and claim that the dumping or subsidies may have a significant effect on domestic output, may request the Commission to investigate the imports and to impose antidumping or compensatory duties.

A complaint to the Commission must be made in the form of a filing detailing evidence of the alleged dumping or subsidy, and it shall also include documentation demonstrating the damage incurred by the dumping or subsidy, including historical data on domestic output, the current capacity of the firm or industry affected, the total value of sales in the domestic market, inventory, local and export prices, productivity, profits, employees, and salaries.

The Commission may consider other factors it deems to be relevant to a determination of injury. No single factor, however, is enough to make a definitive determination.

As part of its efforts to determine injury to domestic production by imports, the Commission may consider imported goods deriving from, or native to, two or more countries, for the purpose of evaluating the volume and effect of such goods on domestic output, as long as one of the following conditions is met: (i) source countries for the imported goods have been under investigation for dumping practices or subsidies within the preceding twelve months; or (ii) the imported products are in competition with a similar Peruvian-made product. However, the accumulated effect of those imports must be significant to be considered a factor in the determination of injury.

Slovak Republic

Katarina Cechová
Cechová, Rakovsky
Bratislava, Slovak Republic

HISTORY AND OVERVIEW OF TRADE REMEDY LAWS AND/OR REGULATIONS SINCE 1947

Accession to GATT/WTO and Antidumping and Subsidies Codes

The Slovak Republic (SR) entered into existence on January 1, 1993 after a division of the Czech and Slovak Federate Republic (CSFR). The SR has acceded to most of the international conventions and treaties concluded by the former CSFR.

The CSFR, known at the time as the Czechoslovak Republic (CSR), was a founding member of the General Agreement on Tariffs and Trade (GATT), which entered into force on April 20, 1948 (Governmental Decree No. 59/1948 Coll., as amended, published on April 15, 1948). After the split of the CSFR, the SR acceded to the GATT and has assumed all rights and obligations of the former CSFR toward member states of the GATT since April 20, 1948, i.e., from the date the GATT entered into force in the CSR. The SR is a founding member of the World Trade Organization with the Schedule of Concessions of the SR (No. XCIII) issued by the Secretariat of the GATT. The SR took part in the Uruguay Round of Multilateral Trade Talks and its Minister of Economy signed the Final Act at the Ministerial Meeting in Marrakech in 1994.

Discussion of Trade Remedy Laws and Regulations

The former CSFR was a signatory to the Treaty on Application of Article VI of GATT 1967 (Antidumping Code) and also to the revised treaty signed after the Tokyo Round of Multilateral Trade talks in 1979. Because the economy of the former CSFR was based on central planning (including pricing) until 1989, the application of the foreign trade remedy regulations was very limited. Imports as well as any other issues connected with foreign trade relations were subject to state planning. After 1989, negotiations on competence issues between the Czech and Slovak Republics, the two members of the federation, and other issues prevented the passage of any relevant domestic trade legislation. Thus, with respect to antidumping or countervailing duties, no legal regulations implementing relevant GATT provisions were adopted in the former CSFR. With the Slovak accession to the GATT on January 1, 1993 and its membership in the WTO since January 1, 1995, the Ministry of Finance of the SR (Ministerstvo financií Slovenskej republiky, or MFSR; "the Ministry") has prepared a draft of "Governmental Proposition of Principles of Law on Antidumping" ("the proposition"). This proposition was prepared in accordance with the GATT, the Antidumping Code and relevant European Union Directives (No. 3283/1994 European Journal, No. 384/1996 EJ).

However, this proposition was only the first stage of the legislation process in the SR. A new Act on Protection from Dumping on Import of Goods (the Act No. 59/1997 Coll., "the Act") has been adopted and is effective as of July 1, 1997.

It should also be mentioned that the SR and the Czech Republic form a customs union (No. 199/1993 Coll.), which allows the parties to levy antidumping duties in accordance with Article VI of the GATT.

Summary Listing of the Trade Remedy Regulations

Section 18 of Customs Law No. 180/1996 Coll., contains brief definitions of the terms of antidumping duty, countervailing duty and retaliatory duty:
- Antidumping duty refers to a duty levied upon any product that is imported for sale at a dumped price.
- Countervailing duty refers to a special duty levied for the purposes of offsetting a subsidy or subvention that has been granted directly or indirectly on the manufacture, production, or export of a relevant imported product.
- Retaliatory duty refers to either a surcharge to a normal duty charge, or the application of a special duty to an imported product that is not subjected to duties regularly, temporarily levied upon an imported product originating from a country that discriminates against the SR in mutual trade relations.

Moreover, the Act No. 226/1997 Coll. on Subsidies and Countervailing Measures has been adopted and is effective as of September 1, 1997.

At the present time, there is no other domestic legal regulation relating to the application of the relevant provision of the GATT.

ANTIDUMPING INVESTIGATION

Initiation

An antidumping investigation may be initiated:
(i) following a petition of a natural person capable to do legal acts with a domicile in the SR; or
(ii) following the petition of a legal entity with its seat in the SR.

The petition shall contain the precise identification of the petitioner, the manufacturer, exporter and importer of the imported product, and the Slovak producers affected by the relevant import and other data. The petition shall also contain the express consent of the Slovak producers producing more than 25 percent of the like product for the initiation of the investigation and proof of dumping injury.

The investigation is initiated on the day a notification in the Commercial Bulletin is published.

Timetable

The investigation is to be completed within nine months, or, in some especially demanding cases, within twelve months. In cases where other governmental authorities (having some relationship with the product or domestic industry involved) are requested to present their position with regard to the Ministry's decision, they must express their position within fifteen days, otherwise their consent with the proposal is presumed.

Participation of Parties

The Ministry shall request producers of the relevant like product to present their statements in favor of or in opposition to the petition within one month of initiation. The Ministry shall also request a statement from the Ministry of Economy of the SR or the Ministry of Agriculture of the SR (based on the kind of product imported), the Ministry of Foreign Affairs of the SR, the Slovak Chamber of Commerce and Industry, the Antimonopoly Office of the SR, and other related authorities.

The Ministry shall notify all parties (petitioner, producer, exporter, and importer of the relevant product) and the embassy of the country of origin or of the country of export of the product regarding the initiation of the investigation.

In the course of the investigation, the Ministry shall request necessary information from the parties, related Ministries, other governmental bodies, and other entities, as the case may be. If the party/parties refuses to submit the requested information, or submit it after inadequate delay, or protracts the proceeding in any other way, the Ministry may proceed on the basis of facts that it has at its disposal. The act contains neither detailed provisions regarding the submission of information nor the methodology for analyzing the submitted information.

After a notification to a relevant foreign government (without any objection being expressed) and the consent of the relevant foreign entity, the Ministry may request that foreign entities also submit any information necessary for the investigation.

The Ministry shall inform all parties of all relevant facts constituting the basis for the Ministry's decision and the parties shall be provided one month to present statements regarding the Ministry's decision.

The Ministry may summon a hearing (always closed to public) to have each party explain any contradictory statements; however no party is obliged to take part in this hearing.

Access to Information Developed in Proceeding

Any information is considered to be confidential:
(i) if its disclosure could result in an injury to the provider or source of such information; or
(ii) if its disclosure could result in a material advantage to other persons.

Access to the confidential information is limited to the parties, attorneys to the case, and Ministry officials. All persons coming into contact with confidential information are obliged to keep such information confidential. Any request for disclosure of the confidential information shall contain an explanation for the request. Confidential information cannot be published or provided for the use of other parties.

The Ministry shall require the provider of the confidential information to produce a nonconfidential extract thereof.

The Ministry shall disregard any confidential information where the provider's request for confidentiality is unreasonable.

Definitions

All definitions contained in the Act originate from the relevant provisions of the GATT and the Antidumping Code.

"Product" means any tangible thing imported into the SR.

"Like product" is understood to mean any product comparable in all aspects with the imported product. If there is no such product, it shall mean another product that has similar characteristics as the above-mentioned product, even though it is not comparable in all characteristics.

"Dumping at import" means import of products whose imported price is lower than the price of the same or like products in the usual trade in the country of origin and which is able to cause a dumping injury to the domestic industry.

"Dumping injury" means material damage to the domestic industry caused by import of dumping products, threat of such material damage or substantial postponement of implementation of production of same or like products in the SR.

"Domestic industry" (*vyrobné odvetvie*) is understood to mean:
(i) all domestic producers of the like product in the SR; or
(ii) a share thereof, which represents more than 25 percent of the production of the like product by producers that presented a statement in support of initiation of the investigation.

Calculation of Dumping Margins

The Act contains the precise methodology for calculating dumping margins and basic definitions relating thereto.

"Export price" is understood to mean the price actually paid or the price that is due to be paid for the product sold from the country of origin or a country of export to the SR. If there is no export price or it is not reliable (due to an agreement between the exporter and importer or third party affecting economic competition), the export price shall be defined on the basis of the price that is paid by the first independent purchaser of the imported product.

"Normal value" (value of products in case of usual trade) is understood to mean the price actually paid or the price that is due to be paid for the product among persons who are not in any relation in the country of origin.

If there is no sale of the like product in the country of origin or in the country of export, or if such sale does not allow due comparison, the normal value shall be understood to mean:
(i) the price of the like product exported to a third country; or
(ii) the calculated price—a sum of production costs in the country of origin and other allowed costs plus reasonable profit.

There is no time limitation regarding which sales are taken into account in examining the prices of the relevant products.

If the relevant product is only transloaded in the country of export or such product is not produced in the country of export or there is no comparable price for the relevant product in the country of export, the comparison shall be made using the production costs in the country of origin plus other allowed costs and reasonable profit. A dumping margin is defined as a sum by which the normal value exceeds the export price.

Price Undertakings

The Ministry may issue a decision accepting an exporter's price undertaking containing the exporter's obligation to:
(i)   modify the price of the products previously sold at dumped prices; or
(ii) terminate the exportation of such products.

If the Ministry, after issuance of such decision, finds out that the import of dumping products was realized, that the dumping injury was caused, and that satisfaction of price undertakings was sufficient for the elimination of such injury, the investigation shall be terminated. If the satisfaction of price undertakings does not eliminate the dumping injury, the ministry cancels such decision.

The price undertaking is valid for a period not exceeding five years. Any resulting price increase shall not exceed the dumping margin.

Effect of Antidumping Order

The Ministry may:
(i)   terminate the investigation without levying any antidumping duty;
(ii) issue a decision levying an antidumping duty; or
(iii) issue a decision levying a temporary antidumping duty.

Effective date

Temporary antidumping duty

If the Ministry determines that the importation of dumping products causes the dumping injury to the domestic industry or threatens to cause injury, and such injury would be difficult to remedy and the importer does not agree to a price undertaking or violates the same, the Ministry shall issue a decision levying a temporary antidumping duty without undue delay.

Such temporary antidumping duty shall become effective sixty or more days after the investigation has been initiated. The antidumping duty shall be effective for a period not exceeding four months.

However, if the producer requests a more extensive investigation to be done by the Ministry, the temporary antidumping duty shall be applied for a period not exceeding six months. If the current phase of the investigation indicates that a final antidumping duty will be lower than the dumping margin (i.e., if a lower antidumping duty will be sufficient to remedy the injury to the domestic industry), the temporary antidumping duty shall be applied for a period not exceeding six months. If the producer requests a more extensive investigation, the period shall not exceed nine months. The temporary antidumping duty is imposed for a limited period of time which cannot be longer than a period ending by the day when a final decision on the antidumping duty, termination of the investigation, or the price undertaking becomes valid.

Antidumping duty

If the Ministry determines that the products are being imported at a dumped price, are causing injury or threatening to cause injury to the domestic industry, and the exporter has not agreed to a price undertaking or has violated the same, the Ministry shall issue a final decision levying an antidumping duty. The antidumping duty shall not exceed the dumping margin, although it may be lower than the dumping margin if it is sufficient to remedy injury.

The antidumping duty is levied for a period not exceeding five years.

Scope determination

The temporary antidumping duty and the antidumping duty may be levied only on the products that were subject to the antidumping investigation. The duty is effective throughout the whole territory of the SR.

Enforcement

The relevant provisions of Customs Law No. 180/1996 Coll. apply to the collection of antidumping duties.

This Law stipulates the structure and competencies of customs authorities authorized to collect regular duties as well as other duties imposed in compliance with the Law. It also stipulates procedures for determining the amount of a duty and for collection thereof.

Procedures for review and revocation of order

Antidumping duties or price undertakings may be revoked or lowered (following the party's application, or on the Ministry's own initiative), if the Ministry decides that facts leading to the decision have changed substantially.

All investigations are conducted by the officials of the Ministry. An appeal of the decision to levy temporary antidumping duties or antidumping duties is brought before the Minister of Finance of SR within fifteen days of the final decision. However, an appeal does not suspend the validity of the decision.

If any party to the investigation, after appeal has been brought and decided upon by the Minister of the Finance, feels the decision to be unfavorable, the party has the right to appeal this decision to the Supreme Court of the Slovak Republic. Such proceeding shall be ruled by the relevant provisions of the Civil Court Order (No. 99/1963 Coll., as amended).

COUNTERVAILING DUTY INVESTIGATIONS, INJURY ANALYSIS, AND OTHER TRADE REMEDIES

At the present time, there are no other regulations regarding the above-mentioned issues, except for those mentioned above in this article.

South Africa

Cecil Steinhauer
Edward Nathan & Friedland Inc.
Johannesburg, South Africa

HISTORY AND OVERVIEW OF TRADE REMEDY LAWS AND/OR REGULATIONS SINCE 1947

South Africa's Accession to GATT and the WTO

South Africa was one of the founding members of the General Agreement on Trade and Tariffs (GATT) in 1947. It also participated in the negotiations leading to the formation thereof. Nevertheless, owing to South Africa's previous racist policies, the country became increasingly isolated from the international community, eventually becoming known as a pariah state. Internationally applied sanctions provoked the government of the day to attempt to transform South Africa into a totally self-reliant country, to counter the effect of sanctions. This required the then South African government to pursue a protectionist policy toward its trade and economy in general. As a result, the Government paid little regard to compliance with the provisions of GATT, even though South Africa was a signatory thereto and its representatives attended many international conferences relating thereto.

From the early '90s, when South Africa began its advent to democracy and attempted to rid itself of its apartheid image, the Government changed its established isolationist policies to a policy of mutual understanding and cooperation. When, in 1994, the World Trade Organization was formed, South Africa was again a founding member.

Evolution of Trade Remedy Laws

No significant trade law remedies existed in South Africa prior to 1964. In that year, the Customs and Excise Act, 91 of 1964 was promulgated ("the Customs Act") to make provision, inter alia, for antidumping and countervailing remedies and measures. However, in addition to the antidumping and countervailing measures contained therein, the Customs Act also imposed import duties calculated in accordance with a complex formula as well as a host of import controls. As the import duties were, generally speaking, higher than the antidumping and countervailing measures, local producers found ready protection from international competition through the heavier customs duties and very few dumping investigations were undertaken prior to 1992.

The Board on Tariffs and Trade Act 107 of 1986 ("the Tariffs Act") provided for the establishment of a Board on Tariffs and Trade, the object of which was stated to be the promotion of industrial growth within the framework of the economic policy of the Republic. This object was to be achieved "by conducting investigations into any matter that affects or may effect the trade and industry of the Republic or the common customs area of the South African Customs Union, and to advise the Minister in this regard."

Section 4 of the Tariffs Act, provides that for the purpose of achieving its objectives, the Board may:

(a) (i) of its own accord investigate dumping, subsidized export, or disruptive competition in or to the Republic and, if authorized thereto by an agreement, in or to the common customs area of the South African Customs Union;

(ii) of its own accord investigate the development of industries in the Republic and, if authorized thereto by an agreement, in the common customs area of the Southern African Customs Union by the levying of customs and excise duties;

(iii) by order of the Minister investigate any other matter that affects or may affect the trade and industry of the Republic and, if authorized thereto by an agreement, the common customs area of the South African Customs Union; and

(b) report and make recommendations to the Minister in respect of any investigation referred to in paragraph (a).

The South African Customs Union consists of Botswana, Lesotho, Namibia, the Republic of South Africa, and Swaziland.

Owing to the wide powers given to the Board, local producers relied heavily on the Board to impose antidumping and countervailing measures to protect local industries. Not surprisingly, therefore, the Board (which is appointed by the State President) was seen by foreign exporters to South Africa as a continuation of the protectionist policies of the Government of South Africa. As a result, the Tariffs Act did not cause South Africa to become an accepted player in the international community and its isolation continued into the early '90s.

Summary of Responsible Agencies

Currently, the agencies administering trade remedies are:
(i) the Department of Customs and Excise, which implements the Customs Act with its systems of customs and excise duties; and
(ii) the Board on Tariffs and Trade, which implements the Tariffs Act with its system of antidumping duties and countervailing duties.

Reconstruction

Government Notice 294 of 1996, published March 15, 1996, invited interested parties to submit substantive recommendations relating to the restructuring of the antidumping and countervailing remedies applied in South Africa, with a view to securing compliance with the requirements of WTO. Clearly, South Africa does not at present conform with international agreements and principles relating to antidumping measures and countervailing duties. However, it is anticipated that once submissions have been made and reviewed, new legislation will be promulgated to bring South Africa's practices and procedures into line with accepted international principles.

ANTIDUMPING INVESTIGATIONS

Dumping Determination

Initiation of investigations

Section 4 of the Tariffs Act (quoted above) makes it clear that the Board may initiate investigations either of its own accord or by order of the Minister. The Tariffs Act does not, in its terms, provide for the initiation of an investigation at the instance of other interested persons. Nevertheless, the Board on Tariffs and Trade in September 1995 issued a *Guide to the Policy and Procedure with Regard to Action Against Unfair International Trade Practices: Dumping and Subsidized Export* ("the Guide") which provides as follows, in paragraph 18 thereof:

> An investigation by the Board to determine the existence, degree, and effect of any alleged unfair trade practice, as contemplated above, may be initiated by way of a written petition based on a questionnaire prescribed by the Board, requesting such an investigation by or on behalf of the domestic industry concerned.

Paragraph 19 of the Guide interprets the term "domestic industry" as referring to the domestic producers as a whole "of the like products or to those of them whose collective output of the products constitutes a major proportion of the total domestic production of those products."

In paragraph 23 of the Guide, it is provided that the petition must contain such information as is reasonably available to the petitioner on the following:

> (i) The identity of the petitioner and details of the volume and value of production of the like product by the petitioner.
>
> (ii) Where the petition is submitted on behalf of an industry, the identity of the industry on behalf of which the petition is made and a list of all known producers of the like product plus, to the extent possible, details of the volume and value of domestic production of the like product accounted for by each producer.
>
> (iii) A complete description of the imported product, the name(s) of the country or countries of export or origin of the product, the identity of each known exporter or foreign producer of the product, and the identities of known importers of the product.
>
> (iv) In respect of dumped products, information on prices at which the product in question is sold when destined for consumption in the domestic market of the country or countries of origin or export or, where applicable, information on the prices at which the product is sold by the countries of origin for export to a third country or countries or the estimated cost of production in the country or countries of origin or export plus any other cost and profit deemed reasonable. In the case of exports from a country without a free market economy, a third country must be nominated to be used to determine the normal value of the product under investigation, on the above-mentioned basis.

It should be noted that the Guide is not a piece of subordinate legislation. It is, as its name suggests, merely a guide as to the procedures, principles, and practices to be adopted by the Board in carrying out its functions.

Numerous petitions have already been directed to the Board so that it can safely be said that, as a matter of practice, investigations by the Board may be initiated by the Board itself, on order by the Minister of Trade and Industry, or by way of petition from an affected industry.

Timetable

If, on the evidence before it, the Board decides to initiate an investigation, a general notice will be published in the Government Gazette, in which will be set out the name of the petitioner, a description of the product covered by the petition, the countries of origin or export of the products in question, a summary of the evidence submitted to the Board, the procedure to be followed, and the time limit for response to the notice.

At the same time, the governments of the countries concerned and all the parties known to be concerned with the relevant product will be informed in writing of the Board's decision to conduct an investigation of alleged dumping or subsidized exports as the case may be. The parties known to be concerned will simultaneously be supplied with relevant questionnaires. According to paragraph 30 of the Guide, the questionnaire will be deemed to have been received seven days after the date of the letter accompanying the questionnaire.

A period of thirty days after receipt of the questionnaire will be allowed for comment and response to the questionnaire. If comments and evidence are not submitted by the end of the thirty days, the Board may make a preliminary or final finding on the basis of the evidence available to it. See the Guide, par. 31.

No time limits are laid down within which the Board is either to commence or complete its investigations. Nor is any time limit set for the Minister to respond to the Board's recommendations or impose any duties recommended by the Board. It follows that there is no definite time span between the lodging of a petition or the commencement of an investigation by the Board, on the one hand, and the recommendations of the Board and consequential action by the Minister, on the other hand.

In practice, the Board strives to complete investigations on the basis of twenty-five days for merit assessment, 100 days for preliminary determination and 125 days for the definitive determination. In a document produced by the Trade and Industry Working Group of the National Economic Forum, pursuant to an investigation into antidumping and countervailing measures, it is recommended that rigid time frames be introduced one year after introduction of new legislation and that the time limits be set as follows:

(i) 100 days from publication of the notice indicating acceptance of the case until publication of the preliminary determination;
(ii) 125 days from the publication of the preliminary finding until the publication of the final finding: provided that the 125 days may be extended by a maximum of a further sixty days when it is so requested by the exporters.

Participation of parties and their counsel

Paragraph 33 of the guide provides that "should any of the interested parties wish to be represented in the investigation they must provide the Board with a letter of appointment of the representative detailing the identity of the representative and the scope of the representation." In practice, this means that legal representation will be allowed provided the legal representative has been properly appointed by a letter of appointment.

Access to information developed in the proceedings

Section 17 of the Tariffs Act provides that confidential treatment will be accorded to information which discloses the business affairs of any person. Pursuant to paragraph 51, interested parties are entitled to have access to all evidence except that information whose disclosure could be prejudicial to the competitive position of a firm.

In practice, therefore, a party submitting evidence will indicate that the evidence being submitted by it is confidential and that disclosure thereof could be prejudicial to its competitive position, to prevent third parties having access thereto.

Definitions

Like product

Paragraph 15 of the Guide defines "like product" as "a product which is identical, i.e. alike in all respects to the product under consideration or in the absence of such a product, another product which, although not alike in all respects, has characteristics closely resembling those of the product under investigation".

Domestic Industry

The term "domestic industry" is interpreted in paragraph 19 of the Guide as "referring to the domestic producers as a whole of the like products or to those of them whose collective output of the products constitutes a major proportion of the total domestic productions of those products. When producers are related to the exporters or importers or are themselves importers of the allegedly dumped product, the term "domestic industry" may be interpreted as referring to the rest of the producers."

Other definitions

There are no definitions of minimum level of industry support, period of investigation, related parties or viability of markets.

Calculation of dumping margins

In the Guide, it is provided that no antidumping duty shall exceed the lower of either:
(i)   the margin of dumping; or
(ii) the difference between the price of similar products produced in the Customs Union and the landed cost, inclusive of normal duties, of the dumped product.

In practice, the Board uses the Australian concept of the price disadvantage or the "non-injurious f.o.b."[1] although there are no clear guidelines as to how this is calculated by the Board.

Under the Tariffs Act, "Dumping" means "the introduction of goods into the commerce of the Republic or the Common Customs Area of the Southern African Customs Union at an export price that is less than the normal value of the goods."

"Export price" is defined as the price "actually paid or payable for goods sold for export net of all taxes, discounts and rebates actually granted and directly related to the sale under consideration."

"Normal value" means:
(a) the comparable price actually paid or payable in the ordinary course of trade for like goods intended for consumption in the exporting country or country of origin; or
(b) in the absence of a price contemplated in paragraph (a) -
   (i) the highest comparable price at which like goods are being exported to any third country in the ordinary course of trade; or
   (ii) the constructed cost of production of the goods in the country of origin plus a reasonable addition for selling costs and profit:
Provided that due allowance shall be made in each case for differences in conditions and terms of sale, for differences in taxation, and for other differences affecting price comparability.

Based on the above definitions, it appears that the dumping margin would be the difference between the normal value of the goods and the export price.

Price undertakings and other agreements to suspend investigations

Paragraph 54 of the Guide provides that if, during the course of an investigation, exporters against whom an allegation has been made offer an undertaking to put an end to the dumping or subsidized export, the Board will consider the matter and will submit is recommendation to the Minister. It will also recommend that the investigation either be terminated or continued. The Minister's subsequent decision is then published in the Government Gazette and the interested parties will be informed accordingly. Under paragraph 55 of the Guide, if the exporter does not honor his undertaking, the Board will be entitled to recommend the imposition of relevant duties immediately, retroactive to the date of violation of the undertaking.

Effect of an Antidumping Order

Effective date

If the Board recommends action and its recommendation is accepted by the Minister of Trade and Industry (and by the Minister of Agriculture in the case of primary agricultural products), the Minister of Trade and Industry requests the Minister of Finance to impose the relevant duty by notice in the Government Gazette. If the antidumping duty is to apply prospectively only, the effective date of the duty will be the date of publication of the Government Gazette concerned. In a case where the relevant duty is imposed retroactively, the notice will specify the date from which such duty is payable.

The Minister of Finance may, when publishing notice of the imposition of the duty in the Government Gazette, fix a time schedule for the phasing out of the duty. Alternatively, in accordance with the provisions of paragraph 56 of the Guide, the exporter against whom the duty was imposed, representatives of the country of export or origin or any other person or organization concerned with the relevant product may request that the matter be reviewed by the Board, provided that twelve months shall have elapsed since the imposition of the duty. The Board would in each case decide whether such review is justified, after carrying out a preliminary investigation of the request. The Board may also, on its own initiative, at any time decide to review an antidumping or countervailing duty. The antidumping duty may be withdrawn or reduced by notice in the Government Gazette, pursuant to section 56(2) of the Customs Act.

Scope Determination

The scope of an antidumping order is defined by the terms of the notice imposing the antidumping duty to be paid. The notice contains, in particular:

(i) an accurate description of the dumped product;
(ii) the harmonized system tariff subheading applicable to the product;
(iii) the names of the suppliers of the product or, where this is impracticable, the country of origin or export of the product;
(iv) in the case of dumping, the antidumping duty to be paid;
(v) in the case of subsidized export, the countervailing duty to be paid;
(vi) in a case where the relevant duty is imposed retrospectively, the date from which it is payable; and
(vii) where applicable, the time schedule for phasing out of the duty.

SOUTH AFRICA

Enforcement

Antidumping duties are imposed by amending Schedule 2 of the Customs Act. The antidumping duty will thereafter be enforced by the Department of Customs and Excise in the same manner as any other customs duty imposed by the Customs Act.

Procedures for new shippers

There are no provisions relating specifically to "new shippers."

COUNTERVAILING DUTY INVESTIGATIONS

Subsidy Determination

Initiation of investigations

The same procedures apply as those set out above regarding antidumping investigations with respect to initiation, timetable, participation of parties and their counsel, and access to information.

Definitions

There is no definition in the relevant legislation of the terms "countervailable subsidies" or "noncountervailable subsidies" (green light). The only relevant definition is that of "subsidized export" appearing in the Tariffs Act. The definition provides that:

> Subsidized export means the export or the proposed export of goods to the Republic or the common customs area of the South African Customs Union from any country where the authority of that country or any other country provides any form of financial aid or other assistance in respect of those goods, including assistance in respect of the production, manufacture, transport, or export thereof.

Application to nonmarket economies

There is no provision in the Tariffs Act dealing with this topic. In a dumping investigation, the Tariffs Act provides that if the Board is of the opinion that the normal value of the goods concerned is, as a result of Government intervention, not determined in the exporting country or country of origin according to free market principles, a comparable price of a third country may be applied to the goods of the exporting country or country of origin concerned. There is no comparable provision regarding subsidized exports.

Calculation of subsidies

No guidelines are laid down as to the manner in which the Board will calculate the extent of any subsidy. Paragraph 23 of the Guide merely requires that a petitioner complaining of a subsidized export must provide the Board with information concerning "the nature, source, and amount of subsidy granted and the nature and extent of other Government assistance measures and their effect on the export price of the subsidized product."

Effect of Countervailing Duty Order

The provisions are the same with respect to effective date, scope determination, enforcement and review and revocation, as that set out above regarding antidumping orders.

INJURY ANALYSIS

Introduction

There is no definition of injury in the Tariffs Act. Accordingly, a strict reading of the Act suggests that the Board may exercise its functions without any reference to injury being caused by dumping or subsidized exports. This notwithstanding, the Guide provides that the Board will consider the introduction of an antidumping or countervailing duty or any other action it deems necessary whenever it finds the existence of dumping or subsidized export, provided that:

(i) such export is the cause of material injury to an industry in the Customs Union;

(ii) the threat exists that material injury may be caused to an industry in the Customs Union by such export; or

(iii) such export materially retards or prevents the establishment of a domestic industry in the Customs Union.

Consideration of material injury includes an evaluation of all relevant economic factors and indices having a bearing on the state of the industry, including actual and potential declines in sales, profits, market share, productivity, return on investments, or utilization of capacity; factors affecting domestic prices; the magnitude of the margin of dumping; actual and potential negative effects on cash flow, inventories, employment, wages, growth, and the ability to raise capital investments.

The Guide provides that "for the injury to be material, the decline and the negative effects must be substantial to the point where the affected industry cannot combat the impact of the dumped or subsidized imports from its own resources."

The Guide further states that "a determination of a threat of material injury is based on facts not merely on allegations, conjecture, or remote possibility. The change in circumstance that would create a situation in which the dumping or subsidized export would cause material injury must be clearly foreseen and imminent."

Initiation of Investigation

The Board does not investigate injury per se. Accordingly, there is no procedure for the initiation of an investigation into injury. Injury is one of the factors to be considered when a complaint of dumping or subsidized exports is under consideration.

Definitions

As indicated earlier, there are no definitions relating to injury. It follows that the term "injury" or "material injury" will be given their ordinary meanings. To prove material injury or potential material injury, the Board requires information relating to the current year and the three years prior thereto in respect of:
(i) Customs Union production of the product and similar products, expressed in quantity and value;
(ii) capacity utilization of Customs Union producers;
(iii) imports, in quantity and value, of the product that is the subject of the petition and of like products from other countries;
(iv) exports out of the Customs Union, in quantity and in value, of the product or similar products;
(v) the consumption of the product and similar products in the Customs Union;
(vi) the market share of the Customs Union product and the market share of the imported products;
(vii) prices charged by Customs Union producers and a cost analysis of representative products;
(viii) resale prices of imported products;
(ix) turnover and profit, and projections of future turnover and profit;
(x) employment of labor; and

(xi) factors, other than imports, affecting Customs Union producers detrimentally.

With respect to threat of material injury, the following information must be supplied regarding the extent of the threat:
(i) the rate at which imports are increasing;
(ii) the size of foreign exporters relative to local producers;
(iii) the state of the relevant industry in the foreign country; and
(iv) the extent of the material injury foreseen and the rate at which it will be caused.

See paragraphs 24 and 25 of the Guide.

OTHER TRADE REMEDIES

The only other legislation in South Africa that impacts directly on international trade with South Africa is the Import and Export Control Act, 45 of 1963 ("the Import Act"). The Import Act empowers the Minister of Trade and Industry, in his sole discretion, to prescribe that no goods of a specified class or kind, or no goods other than goods of a specified class or kind, may, inter alia, be imported into South Africa. Goods may be classified according to source or origin. The provisions of the Import Act are extremely broad, conferring an almost unfettered discretion on the Minister. Accordingly, the Minister may prohibit the import of goods into South Africa for any reason. Although the provisions of this Act are clearly out of line with the Government's present policy of international reintegration, the Import Act is still binding law and can be used as a trade remedy.

CONCLUSION

It is apparent that South Africa's trade remedy laws are unsatisfactory, outdated, and out of step with the requirements of the World Trade Organization. That South Africa's trade remedy laws need to be substantially overhauled has been recognized by the Minister of Trade and Industry, who has ordered an urgent investigation into the restructuring of the antidumping/countervailing system in South Africa in order to:
(i) ensure compliance with the requirements of the World Trade Organization;
(ii) take forward the proposals of the Trade and Industry Working Group of the then National Economic Forum (which conducted an investigation into antidumping and countervailing measures); and

(iii) transform the existing dispensation into a system that is, and is seen to be, credible, efficient, professional, and equitable.

Accordingly, new legislation is likely to be promulgated in the not too distant future that will bring South African trade remedy legislation into line with international standards and that will enable South Africa to discharge its obligations under the relevant ancillary agreements to the General Agreement on Tariffs and Trade 1994.

Switzerland

Felix W. Egli, L.L.M.
Hartmann & Meyer and Partners
Zurich, Switzerland

HISTORY AND OVERVIEW OF TRADE REMEDY LAWS AND/OR REGULATIONS SINCE 1947

Switzerland's Accession to GATT/WTO and Antidumping and Subsidies Codes

In 1959, Switzerland acceded to GATT on a "provisional basis" (without member status), because its agricultural trade legislation (mainly its quantitative import restrictions) was found to be incompatible with GATT. The country did not join GATT until August 1, 1966, after a compromise on agricultural trade issues had been reached.

The GATT's Kennedy Round Antidumping Code of June 30, 1967, was acceded to by Switzerland in December 1967, effective January 1, 1968, and the Tokyo Round's revised Antidumping Code of April 12, 1979, was acceded to by Switzerland in December 1979, effective January 1, 1980. Likewise, the GATT's Tokyo Round Subsidies Code of April 12, 1979 was acceded to by Switzerland in December 1979, also effective January 1, 1980.

Finally, Switzerland acceded to the WTO Agreement of April 15, 1996 on June 1, 1996, effective July 1, 1996 and, accordingly, to the respective Uruguay Round Antidumping and Subsidies codes, both effective July 1, 1996.

Evolution of Trade Remedy Laws and/or Regulations in Switzerland

Switzerland's accession to all above-mentioned Antidumping and Subsidies codes was politically undisputed.

Apart from its agricultural trade regulations, post-war Switzerland had, given its comparatively small domestic market and, conversely, the importance of its export markets, no national antidumping and countervailing duty legislation within the scope of GATT. Because agricultural trade was not covered by the GATT Antidumping and Subsidies Codes, there was, basically, no Swiss legislation that could have been affected by such codes.

Outside the scope of GATT, Switzerland had a procedure akin to countervailing duty legislation for certain textile imports (allowed under the Arrangement Regarding International Trade in Textile, MFA), which, however, was recently entirely abolished. (For further discussion, see section II).

ANTIDUMPING AND COUNTERVAILING DUTY INVESTIGATIONS

Switzerland has not enacted any substantive domestic law (such as regulatory acts or ordinances) implementing the GATT/WTO Antidumping and Subsidies Codes.

However, in a particular case, antidumping or countervailing measures may be imposed based on the Federal Act on Foreign Trade Measures of June 25, 1982 (as amended) (FTM-Act), generally authorizing the Federal Council (the Swiss cabinet council) to impose, *inter alia*, temporary import and/or transit restrictions or bans and/or antidumping or countervailing duties, if, and as long as, foreign measures or extraordinary circumstances materially impair Swiss trade. The pertinent Article 1 FTM-Act reads as follows (unofficial translation):

> Art. 1 Protection Against Effects of Foreign Measures or Against Extraordinary Circumstances Abroad
>
> If foreign measures or if extraordinary circumstances abroad affect Swiss trade in goods or services or payments from or to Switzerland to such a degree that material Swiss economic interests are impaired, the Federal Council may, as long as such circumstances persist,
>
> a. license, restrict by quota or otherwise, or ban the import, export or transit of goods and trade in services;
>
> b. control payments to and from certain countries and, where appropriate, impose duties to countervail price or currency induced distortions of the trade in goods or services or of payments to and from Switzerland.
>
> The notion "duties to countervail price induced distortions" includes, without limitation, countervailing and antidumping duties.

According to the Federal Council's implementing Ordinance on Foreign Trade Measures of March 7, 1983 (as amended), the Federal Ministry for Economic Affairs is to define and implement trade licenses and quota restrictions decided upon by the Federal Council.

If the Federal Council imposes trade licensing (as opposed to quota restrictions), the Federal Ministry for Economic Affairs is authorized to limit such licensing to imports from or exports to certain countries and/or respective quotas. In the latter case, or if the Federal Council itself imposes quota restrictions rather than trade licensing, the Federal Ministry for Economic Affairs normally allocates the quota licenses among the applicants in proportion to their historical trade volumes.

Within the Ministry for Economic Affairs, the Section on Import and Export is normally the competent agency to grant such licenses, issued, however, on behalf of the Federal Office on Foreign Trade.

Any such licenses are granted to applicants established within the Swiss customs territory and professionally engaged in the import, export, or transit business in the field for which the license is applied for. Note, however, that, as a rule, no licenses will be granted to applicants themselves protected by such licensing. Moreover, licenses will always be granted revocably (i.e. revocable if the law is changed or if the legal prerequisites are no longer fulfilled), strictly limited to the personal use of the applicant and issued for a duration of at most—including all possible extensions—one year.

License holders violating or infringing their license conditions may be sanctioned by revocation or nonextension of the license and/or by a temporary license ban. In addition, any frustration of official information requests (for control purposes) will be fined by the Federal Office on Foreign Trade up to CHF 5'000.

Nevertheless, the FTM-Ordinance does not provide any precise or detailed substantive law in respect of the trade remedies available under Article 1 FTM-Act, including antidumping and countervailing measures. With respect of the latter, the federal administration is even divided on the issue of whether or not such measures could be directly based on the rather vague FTM-Act, i. e. without an implementing ordinance.

It is, however, noteworthy that until recently Switzerland had, as mentioned above, a single specific countervailing duty ordinance in the field of textile imports, the Federal Council's Ordinance on Textile Imports, based on Article 1 FTM-Act.

Under this ordinance, certain textiles were subject to import licensing. Nevertheless, although the ordinance remained unaffected by the Uruguay Round Agreement on Textiles and Clothing, Switzerland chose to abolish it as part of the implementation of its so called "economic revitalization program" in 1995, effective January 1, 1996. Ever since, textile imports to Switzerland are no longer subject to any import restrictions.

Switzerland notified to GATT on February 28, 1995 (still under the Tokyo Round's Antidumping and Subsidies Codes), that Art. 1 FTM (and the Customs Tariff Act which is of minor importance here) was the only Swiss antidumping and countervailing duty legislation, that the Federal Council was not making use of these powers, and that in the event these powers were used, Switzerland would notify WTO/GATT.

Switzerland's February 28, 1995 notification was filed with WTO/GATT on May 4, 1995, and was discussed and accepted in the competent WTO/GATT committee's meeting in October 1995. Because the situation reported has remained unchanged ever since, no further notification was made when Switzerland acceded, trough its membership to the WTO Agreement, to the Uruguay Round's Antidumping and Subsidies Codes, effective July 1, 1996.

OTHER TRADE REMEDIES

The above quoted Article 1 FTM-Act also serves as the general statutory basis for escape clause measures in the field of foreign trade.

Taiwan

Sui-Yu Wu
Perkins Coie
Taipei, Taiwan

HISTORY AND OVERVIEW OF TRADE REMEDY LAWS AND/OR REGULATIONS SINCE 1947

Taiwan's Accession to GATT/WTO and Antidumping and Subsidies Codes

The Republic of China on Taiwan (Taiwan or the ROC) is not yet a contracting party to the GATT and, for that reason, did not take part in either the Tokyo Round or the Uruguay Round of Multilateral Trade Negotiations held under the auspices of the GATT. As a result, Taiwan has never formally adopted the Antidumping Code (Old Antidumping Code) or the Subsidies Code (Old Subsidies Code) agreed to in the Tokyo Round negotiations (collectively, Old Codes), or their respective successors in the Uruguay Round, i.e., the Agreement on Implementation of Article VI of GATT 1994 (New Antidumping Code) and the Agreement on Subsidies and Countervailing Measures (New Subsidies Code) (collectively, New Codes). However, the Implementing Regulation on the Imposition of Countervailing Duty and Antidumping Duty of Taiwan (Implementing Regulation), first promulgated in July 1984 and amended in November 1994, claimed to have patterned itself after both the New and Old Codes, with simultaneous references being made to the established practices of the United States and the European Union as an aid to enforcement of the Implementing Regulation.

Evolution of Trade Remedy Laws and Regulations of Taiwan

The Implementing Regulation, first promulgated by the Ministry of Finance (MOF) on July 3, 1984, is an administrative regulation and not a legislatively-adopted Statute. It was enacted by the MOF with authority delegated under the Customs Law. The Customs Law itself contains only three Articles, i.e., Articles 46, 46-1 and 46-2, which deal, respectively, with the definition of dumping and subsidies, the methods of determining normal value, and the definition of material injury. All other substantive elements and procedural requirements are addressed by the Implementing Regulation, which has consequently become the mainstay of Taiwan's antidumping and countervailing systems. On November 17, 1994, the MOF published a revised version of the 1984 Implementing Regulation that should be taken as an interim measure in advance of a more extensive revision. The amendment aims to align Taiwan's antidumping and countervailing regime with the New Codes hammered out in the Uruguay Round.

Legislative history aside, the New Codes' authority and their continued influence on the operation of the domestic antidumping and countervailing systems have been well recognized. Indeed, Article 31 of the Implementing Regulation provides:

> The terms "subsidy" and "dumping" prescribed in this Regulation, in addition to those provisions in the Customs Duty Law and this Regulation, may refer to or be defined in accordance with international common practices.

The effect of this Article has not been confined simply to aiding the definition of "subsidy" and "dumping," although its literal interpretation may point to such a conclusion. Rather, the said Article has been relied upon as the bridge linking both the Antidumping and Subsidies Codes and the established practices of the major trading powers with the enforcement of the Implementing Regulation. This bridging function of Article 31 must not be underestimated as a way of keeping the domestic antidumping and countervailing systems efficient and effective.

In short, although Taiwan has not acceded to the Antidumping and Subsidies Codes concluded in the Tokyo Round or the Uruguay Round, its antidumping and countervailing systems, by and large, have followed both the Old and New Codes. Nevertheless, the systems that grew out of the Implementing Regulation adopted in 1984 and revised in 1994 remain incomplete and immature. In large part, the shortcomings are attributable to the small number of cases that Taiwan has tackled and their relative simplicity. Also, the government's resolve to use the existing systems to counter unfair trade practices has offered little incentive for change.

The Implementing Regulation contains only thirty-two Articles to deal with the subjects of both antidumping and countervailing duties, so lacunas and loopholes abound. As a result, administrative discretion has been called upon to fill the gap, adding to the difficulty of introducing judicial review into the antidumping and countervailing systems and diminishing the impetus to upgrade them. These factors have combined to sideline new antidumping and countervailing measures and keep the field dormant for the past decade.

To date, there has been no countervailing duty case in Taiwan. On a handful of occasions where antidumping investigations have actually been pursued, the agency appeared to have conducted the investigations solely with a view to solve the disputes between the conflicting private interests, as opposed to enforcing a trade policy. A notable illustration of the MOF's assumed role as an amicable mediator can be found in Nitrocellulose from Brazil (1989).[1] Thus, in a total of twelve cases filed with the MOF before 1990, no antidumping duty was ever imposed.

The year 1992 marks a watershed in Taiwan's antidumping history. Thirteen cases were filed during the 1992-1993 period, equal to the number of cases on docket in all the prior years combined. In November 1992, the MOF, defying widespread skepticism over the government's resolve to apply Taiwan's antidumping law, levied the first ever antidumping duty against sodium dithionite from Japan. In the first half of 1994 alone, the MOF followed suit five more times, imposing antidumping duties on various imports from Brazil, South Korea, and Japan. These actions have effectively put to an end the dormancy and heralded a new era featuring the active use of antidumping measures against unfair trade practices.

So far, the MOF has not published its internal rules (if any) or defined its practices in handling antidumping complaints, although Article 14 of the Implementing Regulation prescribes a publication requirement for all determinations, negative or affirmative.[2] Because so much of the process is undisclosed, the related laws and regulations provide only a partial understanding of how antidumping matters are handled in Taiwan. Reference to actual disposition of the procedural and substantive issues commonly seen in the investigation process is necessary to round out the picture. But even with such additions, areas of uncertainty remain.

Agencies Responsible for Administering Trade Remedy

It should be noted that Article 19 of the Foreign Trade Act, promulgated on February 5, 1993, assigns to the Ministry of Economic Affairs (MOEA) the authority to investigate and determine whether the material injury requirement has been met. The MOEA set up an agency, the International Trade Commission (ITC), to assume responsibility for such investigations starting July 1, 1994. From that date onward, the investigation of both antidumping and countervailing duty cases has been handled through a dual-track procedure, largely along the lines of the U.S. system; that is, the MOF handles the dumping aspect of the investigation and ITC handles the injury aspect. Articles 3 and 9 of the Implementing Regulation also support the bifurcation of investigation process.

In brief, the MOF submits the complaint to the Commission on the Tariff Rate (Tariff Commission) for evaluation within forty-five days from the day following receipt of the complaint. The Tariff Commission is an inter-ministry agency formed by the mandate of the Customs Law; it operates as an advisory body to the MOF on a wide range of subjects falling within the domain of the MOF's competence. On antidumping and subsidies matters, the Tariff Commission takes on the role of a decision-making body, with the Customs Directorate under the MOF providing the secretariat service.[3] The Customs Directorate, in its capacity as secretariat of the Tariff Commission, examines complaints to determine whether the evidentiary requirements set out in Article 5 of the Implementing Regulation have been satisfied. It can dismiss unqualified complaints in accordance with Article 7 of the Implementing Regulation.

If the determination of the Tariff Commission is affirmative, the case is then referred to the ITC for a preliminary determination on injury. The ITC must notify the MOF of its preliminary determination within forty-five days from the day following receipt of the case. The MOF will then make its preliminary decision on dumping within seventy-five days of receipt of the ITC decision. After the preliminary determination and possible imposition of provisional duty, the MOF will continue the investigation and conclude it within sixty days with its definitive determination. The case is then transferred back to the ITC for a final determination on injury within forty-five days. Within ten days from the receipt by the MOF of ITC's notice of final determination on injury, the MOF must submit the case to the Tariff Commission for its definitive determination of duties.

Pursuant to Article 13(II) of the Implementing Regulation, the imposition of the definitive antidumping or countervailing duty must be sanctioned by the Executive Yuan before it can be enforced. Article 13(II) provides:

> Where the Tariff Commission has examined and resolved to impose countervailing duty or antidumping duty, the MOF shall immediately submit the case to the Executive Yuan for sanction of the countervailing duty or antidumping duty. . . .[4]

Under current legislation, the review by the Executive Yuan is not subject to any time limit. In addition, there is no express constraint on the Executive Yuan in regard to the scope of the review, although, in practice, it is expected to endorse all recommendations made by the MOF, which undertakes the investigation. These shortcomings could compromise the efficacy as well as the efficiency of Taiwan's antidumping and countervailing systems unless the Executive Yuan's action is statutorily circumscribed.

In its proposal to amend the Implementing Regulation (the Proposed Amendment), the MOF intends to abolish the requirement of Executive Yuan approval. However, it also proposes to grant the Tariff Commission the right to review the merit of imposing definitive duties, taking into account, in addition to the dumping or subsidies, the interests of consumers, the interests of industrial users, the employment impact on relevant industries, the competition conditions of domestic market, and trading relationships with other countries.

ANTIDUMPING INVESTIGATIONS

Dumping Determination

Initiation of investigation

The MOF may initiate investigation of an antidumping or subsidies case, *ex officio,* or by petition of the complainant or upon the request of another government agency.

By petition

Only a domestic industry, as defined below, the trade or industrial associations related to the affected industry, and labor and farmer groups can file a complaint (Article 5(I) of the Implementing Regulation). Article 5(III) of the Implementing Regulation defines the term "domestic industry" as all domestic producers of a like product or those domestic producers whose collective output is determined by the Tariff Commission to constitute a major portion of total domestic production. This Article 5(III) also reflects the position adopted in the Old Antidumping Code that producers related to exporters or importers, or that are themselves importers of the allegedly dumped product, will be excluded from the scope of domestic industry in evaluating the standing of the complainant.

By government

Current legislation contains no provision dealing with the requirements for the government's initiation of an investigation.

Timetable

Under Articles 7, 10, 12, and 13 of the Implementing Regulation, the following time limits shall be applied to the dual-track investigation process:
(i) Forty-five days from receipt of a complaint, the MOF shall submit the case to the Tariff Commission for evaluation of the complaint.[5] Where the Tariff Commission has resolved to proceed with the investigation, the MOF shall immediately submit the case to the ITC for investigation of injury.
(ii) Forty-five days from receipt of the request for injury investigation, the ITC shall notify the MOF of its preliminary determination on injury.
(iii) Seventy-five days from receipt of ITC's preliminary determination on injury, the MOF shall make its preliminary determination on dumping.
(iv) Sixty days from MOF's preliminary determination, the MOF shall make and notify the ITC of its final determination on dumping.[6]
(v) Forty-five days from MOF's notice to ITC of its final determination, the ITC shall make and notify the MOF of its final determination on injury.
(vi) Ten days from ITC's notice of final determination, the MOF shall submit the case to the Tariff Commission for the definitive determination of duties.
(vii) The MOF shall immediately submit the case to the Executive Yuan for sanction of the definitive duties.

It should also be noted that Article 15 of the Implementing Regulation allows the extension of the foregoing time-limits by up to 50 percent.

Participation of parties and their counsel

The interested parties in an antidumping investigation will be given notice of the information that the MOF requires and an ample opportunity to present in writing all evidence that they consider relevant in respect of the investigation (Articles 8 and 16 of the Implementing Regulation). The minimum "thirty-day" period provided for response for exporters or foreign producers, as required under Article 6.1.1 of the New Antidumping Code, has yet to be incorporated in the current Implementing Regulation. In practice, parties receiving the questionnaire are asked to complete and return it to the MOF within a month, but the MOF has the discretion to grant an extension.[7]

Pursuant to Article 8 of the Implementing Regulation, the term "interested parties" refers to already known producers (of the allegedly dumped goods), the exporters, the importers, and the government of the exporting country. The trade or business association of the producers, exporters or importers, domestic producers of the like product in Taiwan, and the trade or business association of the domestic producers, as permitted under Article 6.11(III) of the New Antidumping Code, are encompassed within the current definition of interested parties.[8] In practice, the MOF does not give the industrial users of the product under investigation or the representative consumer organizations opportunities to provide information.[9]

Access to information developed in proceedings

Pursuant to Article 17 of the Implementing Regulation, the complainant and interested parties shall, upon request, be given access to all information relevant to the investigation of countervailing or antidumping duty unless the information is deemed confidential in accordance with laws and regulations.

Regrettably, the reference to "laws and regulations" is an amorphous concept in the present context. In previous MOF practice, access to files in the course of investigation was rarely granted. Thus, the goal of keeping the investigation process transparent has not advanced beyond disclosing the rationale for MOF's determinations.

On the subject of confidential information, Article 18 of the Implementing Regulation contains a provision similar in effect to Article 6.5 of the New Antidumping Code. Specifically, Article 18 of the Implementing Regulation provides for the following rules:

(i) The complainant and interested parties shall identify separately which information they submit may be disclosed and which may not; and shall provide a nonconfidential summary of the information for which confidential treatment is sought.

(ii) The MOF or the ITC may reject the request for confidential treatment if it is made without good cause, and may disregard such information when the required nonconfidential summary is not provided. In either case, the party submitting the information may withdraw the submission within seven days.

(iii) The MOF and the ITC may not disclose information submitted as confidential without the consent of the party submitting it.

Definitions

Like products

With regard to the definition of "like products," the Implementing Regulation contains a provision similar in the effect to Article 2.6 of the New

Antidumping Code (Article 5 of the Implementing Regulation). Specifically, Article 5(II) of the Implementing Regulation reads:

> The term "like products" referred to in this Article shall mean a product which is identical to, or is composed of the same material and has the same features or characteristics, as the product imported. A product which is composed of the same material but has different features or packing shall be deemed the "like product."

Period of investigation

In the absence of legislation, the MOF has opted for a shorter period of investigation, usually six months, compared with the practice in other jurisdictions, which often have a reference period not longer than twelve months. However, in its investigation of the antidumping of certain pharmaceutical products from South Korea, the period of investigation set forth in the questionnaires was extended to twenty-seven months.[10]

Domestic industry and petition requirement for industry support

Article 5(III) of the Implementing Regulation defines the term "domestic industry" as referring to either all domestic producers of the like product or those domestic producers whose collective output is determined by the Tariff Commission to constitute a major portion of total domestic production. In addition, this Article 5(III) subscribes to the position adopted in the Old Antidumping Code that producers related to exporters or importers, or that are themselves importers of the allegedly dumped product, will be excluded from the scope of the domestic industry in evaluating the standing of the complaint. The rules regarding regional domestic industry has virtually no applicability to Taiwan, given the relatively small size of the country's domestic market.

As currently written, the Implementing Regulation does not incorporate the numeric standards established in Article 5.4 of the New Antidumping Code for reckoning "a major portion." In a case determined in 1993 *(Aluminum Foil from South Korea)*, the complaint was rejected on the grounds, among others, that the production output of the complainant was only an unrepresentative 20 percent.

Further, the numeric standards set out in Article 5.4 of the New Antidumping Code, by which the standing issue is resolved, has no parallel in the present Implementing Regulation.

> In the Proposed Amendment (Article 5), the MOF intends to adopt Article 5.4 of the New Antidumping Code, that is, a complaint must be . . . supported by those domestic producers whose collective output

constitutes more than 50 percent of the total production of the like product produced by that portion of the domestic industry expressing either support for or opposition to the application. However, no investigation shall be initiated when domestic producers expressly supporting the application account for less than 25 percent of total production of the like product produced by the domestic industry.

Viability of markets (the 5 percent rule on the viability of domestic sales)

Currently, the MOF's practice in determining whether the volume of domestic sales is sufficient to permit a proper comparison has been vague. The guideline furnished in footnote 2 to Article 2.2. of the New Antidumping Code, i.e., 5 percent or more of the sales of the product under investigation to the importing country, will provide the needed certainty.[11]

This being said, however, it should be noted that the new viability test will probably be of less significance to Taiwan than to other countries, because the size of the Taiwanese market, for most imports, will not be substantial, especially imports from major trading countries that have larger domestic markets than Taiwan. Thus, it will not be difficult for imports to satisfy the 5 percent viability test if the volume of domestic sales is to be measured against the volume of imports to the Taiwanese market.

Related parties

As described above, Article 5(III) of the Implementing Regulation excludes those producers related to exporters or importers, or that are themselves importers of the allegedly dumped product, from the scope of domestic industry in evaluating the standing of the complaint.

In the Proposed Amendment (Article 5(IV)), the MOF intends to subscribe to the position adopted in footnote 11 to Article 4.1(i) of the New Antidumping Code that producers shall be deemed to be related to exporters or importers if legally or operationally, (1) one of them directly or indirectly controls the other, or (2) both of them are directly or indirectly controlled by a third party, or (3) both of them directly or indirectly control a third party and are in a position to exercise influence over the producer.

Calculation of dumping margins

Export price

Article 24(I)(1) of the Implementing Regulation authorizes the MOF to use the "representative export price" for comparison with the normal value. Article 24 (I)(1) reads:

> Where the prices of the product imported into the Republic of China vary, the dumping margin may be established on a transaction-by-transaction basis or by reference to the representative or weighted average prices as the price of the product imported into the Republic of China.

Article 24(I)(2) as quoted below, which follows Article 2(5) of the Old Antidumping Code, deals with export sales to related importers to reconstruct export price. It reads:

> Where there is a special relation between the exporter and importer, or where, for other reasons, the price of the product imported into the Republic of China is unreliable, the price at which the imported product is resold to an independent buyer may be construed as the price of the product imported into the Republic of China. In such cases, allowance for the following costs incurred between importation and resale shall be made:
> (1) insurance, transportation, handling, loading and other fees;
> (2) customs duties and other taxes payable for the importation or sale;
> (3) a reasonable margin for overhead and profit or any commission paid.

The method for reconstructing the export price, as contemplated in Article 24(I)(2), often gives rise to a lower export price at the ex-factory level. This is because the adjustment made for the overhead and profit margin of the related importer could be based on an arbitrary standard, often higher than the reality.

Normal value

Article 46-1 of the Customs Law defines the term "normal value" to mean the comparable domestic price in the country of export or origin in the ordinary course of trade. Article 25 of the Implementing Regulation further stipulates that the following two circumstances are outside the ordinary course of trade and sales prices of such transactions shall therefore not be construed as normal value:
(i) there is a special relation or a compensatory arrangement between the buyer and the seller, and the price or sales price has thereby been affected; or
(ii) sales in substantial quantities have been made over an extended period of time and are at prices that do not permit recovery of all costs.

In its Proposed Amendment, the MOF intends to adopt the guidance given in footnotes 4 and 5 to Article 2.2.1 of the New Antidumping Code to the effect that the "extended period" shall be no less than six months and that "substantial quantity" shall mean that the volume of sales below unit cost represents at least 20 percent of the volume sold in all transactions.

If the "comparable domestic price" is not available, the comparable highest export price to an appropriate third country or the constructed value (production cost plus the amounts for administrative, selling and general costs and normal profit), may be used instead. Although current legislation is vague on the "unavailability" issue, prospective changes to the Implementing Regulation will remedy the shortcoming by referring it to any one of the following situations:
(i)   there are no sales of the like product in the domestic market (of the exporting country);
(ii) such sales are less than 5 percent of the sales of the product to Taiwan; or
(iii) in particular market situation.

The standard questionnaire used by the MOF requires that information be provided on both the cost of production, for computing constructed value, and sales to third countries, so it is difficult to draw any conclusion as to which surrogate value the MOF prefers. At any rate, the prospective change from the "highest" export price, the position taken in the current Customs Law, to the "comparable" export price to an appropriate third country, as mandated in Article 2.2 of the New Antidumping Code, will cause the MOF to revise its practice in this area.

Fair comparison

The current Implementing Regulation provides very broad, sketchy guidance on fair comparison of the export price with normal value, as seen above (Article 24). Article 24(II) of the Implementing Regulation instructs:

> In comparing the price of the product imported into the Republic of China and the normal value referred to in the preceding paragraph, the differences in factors such as physical characteristics of the product, level of trade, transaction time, quantity and terms of sale shall be adjusted properly.

No specific rules have been published by the MOF indicating how such differences should be quantified and factored into the formula of comparison, except for the following guidance extracted from standard questionnaire language:

> 1) For the physical characteristics difference, the adjustment is restricted to the difference in cost of production, not inclusive of the effect of prices. The cost of production mentioned in this context refers to variable production cost only, i.e., raw material cost, direct labor, and variable manufacturing cost. Fixed manufacturing overhead, profit, and marketing expenses should not be included in the cost adjustment.

2) For the difference in condition of sales, the questionnaire limits the adjustments to credit costs for domestic sales, after-sale technical service; and guarantee or warranty expenses. No adjustment is allowed for salary, warehousing, and administrative outlay. There are two prerequisites for such adjustment:
i. the factor(s) for which adjustment is made bear a direct relationship to the particular transaction; and
ii. the factor(s) for which adjustment is made brought direct benefit to the buyer of the particular transaction.

Other than the foregoing, the existing regulatory framework leaves the interested parties with little guidance as to how to pursue the most favorable results from the investigation. It is therefore a useful exercise to examine adjustments actually granted by the MOF.

A couple of points should be noted in regard to Article 2.4. of the New Antidumping Code. First, the adjustment for profit on the part of the related importer when the export price is constructed in accordance with Article 2.3 of the New Antidumping Code is allowable under the existing Implementing Regulation, so the present system needs no further legislative action to give effect to this rule in the New Antidumping Code. As for the symmetric application of adjustments to both the export price and the domestic price in the case of related-party issue, the MOF's disposition of a similar issue seems sufficient to allay concerns that the MOF sometimes has not conformed with the discipline set up in the New Antidumping Code.

In certain cases, the enforcement agency (i.e., the MOF) did not, or had not learned to, maximize the dumping margin by choosing the most favorable method. For one thing, the MOF did not compare the export prices with the normal value on a transaction-by-transaction basis, as permitted by Article 24(I)(1). The transaction-by-transaction comparison often results in a higher dumping margin than comparison on the basis of weighted average prices, due to the exclusion of the "negative" dumping margins from the calculation.

The MOF intends to subscribe to the requirement for currency conversion adopted in Article 2.4.1 of the New Antidumping Code in calculating the dumping margin (Article 33(I)(4) of the Proposed Amendment).[12]

Sampling
The Implementing Regulation contains no provision dealing with technical issues such as sampling. To date, the MOF has not opted for strict standards to carry out sampling of the sales data to be reported. It, how-

ever, intends to adopt the new rules framed in Article 6.10 of the New Antidumping Code.[13] Article 6.10 covers the sampling of various subjects of different natures, allowing sampling to be applied to exporters, importers, and producers; to the types of the products under investigation, and to the number of export sales. Once adopted, these provisions will add certainty to MOF's future practice in this area.

Cost of production and constructed value methodology

Although current legislation does not contain the methodology in determining the cost of production and constructed value, the guidelines set forth in Article 2.2.2 of the New Antidumping Code will provide useful guideline to the MOF.

As a matter of fact, the prospective change of the Implementing Regulation will subscribe to the guidelines set forth in Article 2.2.2 to the effect that in determining the constructed value, the amounts for administrative, selling and general costs, and for profits shall be based on actual data pertaining to production and sales in the ordinary course of trade of the product under investigation by the producer.

In the event that such amounts cannot be determined on the above basis, the MOF will also adopt the priorities set forth in Article 2.2.2 in selecting surrogate figures for sales, general and administrative expenses, and for profits when constructing the normal value. The requirement enshrined in Article 2.2.2 that such surrogate figures have to be derived from the domestic sales of either the like product or the same general category of products will also be adopted by the MOF in dealing with the same issue in the near future.[14]

Nonmarket economy methodology

The current Taiwan system does not address this issue. Nevertheless, the nonmarket economy methodology adopted in the Antidumping Codes may provide useful guideline for MOF's future practice.

Price undertakings and other agreements to suspend investigations

Article 21(I) of the Implementing Regulation allows the submission of price undertakings to suspend the investigation. The way that Article 21(I) is drafted, i.e., "Where the government of the country of export or the exporter submits a guarantee or undertakings . . . the Ministry of Finance may terminate the proceeding . . . ," suggests that offers of undertaking must be tendered before the investigation is terminated. The MOF follows such interpretation in practice. Although not confirmed by the MOF, the MOF does not seem to favor price undertakings, due to the ensuing burden of continuously monitoring compliance with the undertakings.

However, as mentioned above, Article 13 of the Implementing Regulation gives the Executive Yuan the final say in imposing antidumping duty. In practice, the MOF used to terminate an antidumping action by accepting price undertakings offered by the foreign manufacturer/exporter under investigation after the agency had concluded the investigation but before completion of the Executive Yuan's review.

The Proposed Amendment will transpose to the Taiwanese system the condition for considering undertaking offers specified in Article 8.2. of the New Antidumping Code, i.e., price undertakings shall not be sought or accepted prior to a preliminary affirmative determination of both dumping and injury.

Violation of a price undertaking shall trigger a reopening of the investigation and the immediate imposition of provisional antidumping duty up to ninety days prior to the date of provisional duty, according to Article 27 of the Implementing Regulation.

Provisional Measures

While the Implementing Regulation provides for the imposition of provisional duties in the course of investigation (Article 11), it casts such action as an emergency measure rather than a regular remedy.[15] For this reason, the enforcement agency, i.e., the MOF, for a long time avoided granting appeals for provisional duties. It was not until early 1993 that Taiwan saw its first provisional duty.[16] It was widely expected that the specific authorization in Article 10 of the Old Antidumping Code and the entrenched practices of the United States and the European Union would inspire the MOF to streamline its practice consistent with the prevailing international practice despite the emergency requirement in the Implementing Regulation. Whether the MOF will, by discretionary practice, begin to apply provisional duties to a regular remedy available to the domestic complaint during the course of an investigation remains to be seen.[17]

As for the duration of provisional measures, the Implementing Regulation specifies a four-month maximum period (Article 11). The Proposed Amendment would raise the maximum to six months (Article 11(III) of the Proposed Amendment).

Effect of Antidumping Order

Effective date and retroactivity

The current Implementing Regulation is silent on the retroactivity of the antidumping duties, except that Article 27 allows the antidumping duty to be levied on goods imported up to ninety days prior to the date of preliminary antidumping duty in any of the following events:
(i) the antidumping has existed for a considerable period and the injury is caused by the importation of a substantial amount of the dumped product within a short period;
(ii) the importers are aware or have reason to be aware of the dumping by the exporters and still import a substantial amount of the dumped product within a short period, causing injury to the industry of Taiwan; or
(iii) there is any violation of a price undertaking previously submitted.

The practice of the MOF has been to assess antidumping duties on a prospective, as opposed to retroactive, basis. However, there is no mechanism under the Implementing Regulation to ensure a prompt refund, as required under Article 9.3.2 of the New Antidumping Code.

In the Proposed Amendment (Article 29), the MOF intends to give effect to Article 10.2 of the New Antidumping Code and permit antidumping duties to be levied retroactively for the period for which provisional measures have been applied if:
(i) a final determination of injury is made; or
(ii) in the case of a final determination of a threat of injury, the effect of the dumping would, in the absence of the provisional measures, have led to a determination of injury.

The prospective change will also incorporate the rule under Article 10.4 of the New Antidumping Code that where a determination of threat of injury or material retardation is made but injury has not occurred, a definitive antidumping duty may be imposed only from the date of the determination of threat of injury or material retardation. It will also give effect to the requirement of the refund of the provisional duties and release of any bonds.

It should also be mentioned that Article 9.3.3. of the New Antidumping Code, which prohibits the deduction of paid antidumping duties in determining the constructed export price to be used in calculating a refund, would also be incorporated into Taiwan's system (Article 25(III) of the Proposed Amendment), which, at present, does not have a legal basis for dealing with the refund issue.

The MOF will also subscribe to a 12- to 18-month refund mechanism similar to the one that Article 9.3.2 of the New Antidumping Code makes available when the amount of the antidumping duty is assessed on a prospective basis. However, the ROC's anticipated provision will accept a refund application from an importer only when the duty has been imposed for at least one year.

Duration

The current Taiwan system does not have a sunset provision. The MOF will incorporate in the Proposed Amendment a provision similar to Article 11.3 of the New Antidumping Code to the effect that any definitive antidumping duty shall be terminated not later than five years from its imposition.

Enforcement, including rules to prevent circumvention of orders

The current Taiwan system has yet to incorporate rules to prevent circumvention of orders.

Procedures for new shippers

The Implementing Regulation does not adopt any rule for review of new shippers. However, the prospective change (Article 35(III) of the Proposed Amendment) would incorporate the rule of Article 9.5 of the Antidumping Code allowing a review to determine individual margins of dumping for new shippers.

Procedures for review and revocation of order

The Implementing Regulation contains a mechanism for reviewing definitive antidumping duties. Article 28 of the Implementing Regulation provides in part:

> After the imposition of countervailing duty or antidumping duty, if the reason for the imposition has been eliminated or changed, the Ministry of Finance may reopen the proceedings and conduct an investigation. . . .

Article 28 however does not explicitly require the lapse of a reasonable period before a review can be requested, as does Article 11.2. of the New Code. In the case of polystyrene and polypropylene resins imported from Japan and South Korea, the MOF opened its review within four months of the imposition of duties and announced that the review would be completed within one month to placate angry downstream industries that had been vexed by the global shortage of supply and the subsequent price hikes.

Nevertheless, the MOF intends to add to the Proposed Amendment (Article 41) a minimum lapse of one year before a review is requested. It would also rule that the review be completed within twelve months, with the possibility of extending the review period by up to 30 percent.

COUNTERVAILING DUTY INVESTIGATIONS

As mentioned earlier, there has been no countervailing case in Taiwan to date. Under the current Taiwan system, all the guidelines in the Implementing Regulation applicable to antidumping cases, as stated above (except for the determination of dumping margins), would also apply to countervailing cases. It is worth noting that in the Proposed Amendment, the MOF intends to incorporate the consultation rule in Article 13 of the New Subsidies Code (Article 7(III) and (IV) of the Proposed Amendment).

It should also be noted that the current Implementing Regulation does not define to the term "subsidies." However, as indicated in Paragraph I. B., Article 31 of the Implementing Regulation has fully recognized the New Subsidies Code's authority and influence on the operation of the domestic countervailing system, including the definition of "subsidy." The prospective changes would further adopt the definition of "subsidy" in Article 1 of the New Subsidies Code. Article 26(I) of the Proposed Amendment would read in part:

> A subsidy shall be deemed to exist if any of the following supports is provided . . .:
> 1) there is a financial contribution by a government or any public body (collectively, the Government), whereby a benefit is conferred, i.e., where:
>   a. there is a direct transfer of grants, loans or equity, or a potential direct transfer of funds or liabilities (e.g., loan guarantees);
>   b. there is an exemption from taxes, or tax otherwise due is foregone or not collected;
>   c. (the Government) purchases goods, or provides goods or services other than general infrastructure;
>   d. (the Government) carries out, through a third party, any type of functions illustrated in (a) to (c) above;
> or
> 2) there is any form of income or price support in the sense of Article XVI of GATT 1994, whereby a benefit is conferred.

In terms of the "benefit" mentioned above, Article 26(II) of the Proposed Amendment would also adopt the guidelines in Article 14 of the New Subsidies Code to disqualify certain benefits from constituting a subsidy. It reads:

The following shall not be considered as conferring a benefit:
1) If Government provision of equity capital is consistent with the usual investment practice of private investors in the territory of that country;
2) If there is no difference between the terms under which the Government provides the loan and the terms under which the firm could actually obtain a comparable commercial loan on the market;
3) If there is no difference between the amount that the firm pays on a loan guaranteed by the Government and the amount that the firm would pay on a comparable commercial loan absent the Government guarantee;
4) If the provision of goods or services by a Government is made for not less than adequate remuneration, or the purchase of goods by a Government is made for not more than adequate remuneration.

INJURY ANALYSIS

As mentioned above, in the Taiwan antidumping and countervailing systems, the investigation of both antidumping and countervailing duty cases has followed a dual-track procedure. The MOF handles the dumping aspect of the investigation and the ITC handles the injury aspect.

The review mechanism currently available in the Implementing Regulation determining the injury caused by dumping or subsidies is sketchy. Article 26 of the Implementing Regulation simply adopts the rules of Articles 3.1, 3.2 and 3.4 of the New Antidumping Code and Articles 15.1, 15.2 and 15.4 of the New Subsidies Code, which require that in determining the injury caused by dumping or subsidies, the investigating authority, i.e., the ITC, should examine the following factors:

(i) the volume of the dumped imports, including the increase in dumped imports, either in absolute terms or relative to domestic production or consumption;
(ii) the effect of the dumped imports on the price of a like product of Taiwan, including whether it is to depress the price or prevent a price increase of a like product in Taiwan, or there has been price undercutting by the dumped imports; and
(iii) the impacts on the domestic industry in question, based on an evaluation of all relevant economic factors, including production, utilization of capacity, inventories, sales, market share, export ability, sales prices, profitability, return on investments, employment, and other relevant factors.

In its prospective changes, the MOF intends to incorporate the rules of Articles 3.5 and 3.7 of the New Antidumping Code and Articles 15.5 and

15.7 of the New Subsidies Code as follows (Articles 36(II) and 37 of the Proposed Amendment):
(i) In determining the injury caused by the dumped or subsidized imports, the ITC should also examine any factors other than the dumped or subsidized imports that are injuring the domestic industry in question, including the following:
 (a) the volume and prices of imports not sold at dumping or subsidized prices;
 (b) contraction in demand or changes in the patterns of consumption;
 (c) trade restrictive practices of and competition between foreign and domestic producers; and
 (d) developments in technology and the export performance and productivity of the domestic industry.
(ii) In making a determination regarding the existence of a threat of material injury, the ITC should, in addition to the factors mentioned above, further examine the following factors:
 (a) the nature of the subsidy in question and the trade effects likely to arise therefrom;
 (b) the rate of increase of (dumped or subsidized) imports into the domestic market indicating the likelihood of substantially increased importation;
 (c) the adjustability of foreign exporters' capacity and the availability of other markets to absorb the exports, as indicators of the likelihood of substantially increased dumped or subsidized exports to Taiwan's market;
 (d) the likelihood that prices of the imports in question will have a significant depressing or suppressing effect on domestic prices and increase demand for imports; and
 (e) the exporting country inventories of the product being investigated.

The MOF would also adopt the rule of *de minimis* in Article 5.8 of the New Antidumping Code and Article 11.9 of the New Subsidies Code. New Article 13 of the Proposed Amendment would require the termination of an investigation if:
(i) the evidence of dumping or subsidies is not sufficient;
(ii) the amount of subsidy is less than 1 percent, expressed as a percentage of the export price;
(iii) the margin of dumping is less than 2 percent, expressed as a percentage of the export price of a like product of the country of export or origin; or
(iv) the volume of dumped imports from a particular country is less than 3

percent of imports of the like product, unless countries collectively account for more than 7 percent of imports of the like product.

In assessment of the cumulative effect of imports from various countries, the prospective change would adopt the specific conditions in Article 3.3 of the New Antidumping Code and Article 15.3 of the New Subsidies Code:

(i) the margin of dumping or the amount of subsidization is more than *de minimis;* and

(ii) a cumulative assessment of the effects of the imports is appropriate in light of the conditions of competition among the imported products and the conditions of competition between the imported products and the like domestic product.

References

1. In 1989 the MOF found that nitrocellulose from Brazil had not been dumped in the ROC. It nevertheless accepted the price undertakings offered by the importer of Brazilian nitrocellulose, which appeared to have resulted from a settlement deal between the complainant and the said importer made prior to the offer; as reported in K.Y. Lee, "Analysis of Implementation of ROC's Anti-Dumping System" (unauthorized translation from the Chinese title), *Journal of Import Injury Relief* (Taiwan), vol. 2, (Jun. 1992), at 58.

2. In practice, almost all of the published determinations summarize only the findings of the MOF without disclosing the details of the parties' arguments or the MOF's reasoning on specific issues. The publication requirement as set forth in Article 14 of the Implementing Regulation, therefore, does not satisfy the demand for transparency. The present practice of the MOF offers a perfect occasion for the new rules framed in the New Anti-dumping Code to be applied; *see infra* text of III.15 for details. Moreover, Article 17 of the Implementing Regulation provides:

    The applicant and the Interested Parties may request to review of [sic] the information relevant to the investigation of the countervailing duty or antidumping duty, except for that information which shall be kept in confidence in accordance with pertinent provisions.

    In practice, disclosure of the MOF's investigation to the interested parties has not been implemented to the satisfaction of the interested parties; *see infra* text III.8. Besides, it is impossible for the counsels of the interested parties to gain access to confidential information under any form of undertaking to protect the confidentiality thereof.

3. The Tariff Commission is composed of representatives from various ministries and agencies, including the Central Bank of China, the Economic Development Council, the Board of Foreign Trade and the Industrial Development Bureau.

4. Article 2 of the Implementing Regulation states: "The recommendation for the imposition of countervailing duty and anti-dumping duty shall be referred to the Executive Yuan for approval after an investigation and examination have been made by the Ministry of Finance." Articles 11 (provisional duty), 13 (imposition of definitive duty), 27 (critical circumstances) and 28 (administrative review) all make specific reference to approval by the Executive Yuan, the highest executive agency under the ROC Constitution, as a necessary prerequisite for action thereunder. Although not specified in Article 21, the MOF's acceptance of price undertakings is still, in practice, subject to approval by the Executive Yuan.
5. The forty-five-day time-limit applies to the processing time from receipt of the complaint by the Customs Directorate to its submission by that agency to the Tariff Commission. In other words, the process of the Tariff Commission's evaluation is neither subject to, nor included in, the forty-five-day time-limit (Article 7 (II) of the Implementing Regulation).
6. There is no specific time limit for the Tariff Commission's final determination based on the result of the investigation carried out by the Customs Directorate; *cf.* Article 12 of the Implementing Regulation. In the event that the MOF makes a definitive determination that there has been no dumping, the MOF shall notify the ITC immediately, terminate the investigation, and publish an official notice of the termination.
7. In the Proposed Amendment, the MOF intends to rectify this shortcoming by giving not only the exporters but also the complainant and all other interested parties at least thirty days to reply (Article 18 of the Proposed Amendment).
8. The MOF is considering including such parties in the definition of interested parties (Article 8 of the Proposed Amendment).
9. Article 8 of the Proposed Amendment contains a catch-all phrase including parties deemed by competent authorities to be "interested".
10. The ITC intends to revise the format of the questionnaires to extend the period of investigation to four years.
11. The MOF is considering adding the 5 percent viability test in the Proposed Amendment.
12. Article 33(I)(4) of the Proposed Amendment reads: "When the price comparison requires a conversion of currencies, such conversion should be made using the rate of exchange on the date of sale; if a sale of foreign currency on forward markets is linked to the export sale into the ROC, the rate of exchange in the forward sale shall be used. Fluctuations in exchange rates shall be ignored, and in an investigation, exporters shall be given at least sixty days to adjust their export prices, extendable for another sixty days if the fluctuations in exchange rates continue."
13. Article 34(I) of the Proposed Amendment reads: "The dumping margin referred to in Article 32 shall be determined on an individual basis for each known exporter or producer. If the number of exporters, producers, and importers or types of products involved is too large to make such determination, the competent authority may conduct the investigation either by selecting a reasonable number of investigation objects by using samples that are statistically valid based on the in-

formation available to the competent authority, or on the exporters/producers who have the largest percentage of the volume of the exports in the exporting country."
14. *See* Article 31 of the Proposed Amendment.
15. Article 11(I) of the Implementing Regulation provides:
    "Where the Ministry of Finance makes a preliminary determination that there is subsidy or anti-dumping in existence and there is *an emergent necessity* to provide provisional protection for the domestic industry concerned, the Ministry of Finance may, prior to the completion of the examination and resolution for the imposition of countervailing duty or antidumping duty, consult the relevant agencies and submit to the Executive Yuan for approval of the provisional imposition, in which the scope, subject parties and amount of the countervailing duty or antidumping duty on the importation of the subject product shall be specified; provided, however, that the period of such provisional imposition shall not be longer than four months." (emphasis added)
16. *PEs from South Korea, 1992* Official Gazette of the Ministry of Finance, Vol. 32, No. 1582, at 32561 et seq.
17. It is noteworthy that the emergency character of the provisional duty is retained in the Proposed Amendment (Article 11).

Thailand

Nopadol Intralib
Nopadol & Khaisri Law Office Ltd.
Bangkok, Thailand

HISTORY AND OVERVIEW OF TRADE REMEDY LAWS AND/OR REGULATIONS SINCE 1947

Thailand's Accession to GATT/WTO and Antidumping and Subsidies Codes

The Kingdom of Thailand became a Contracting Party to GATT 1947 in 1982 by virtue of its Cabinet's approval granted on December 22, 1981. As a contracting party, Thailand was a participant in the Uruguay Round, whereas it was prior to that an observer in the Tokyo Round, which ended in 1979. Upon completion of the Uruguay Round, the designated Ministerial Representative of Thailand concluded the initialing of the Final Act Embodying the Results of the Uruguay Round of Multilateral Trade Negotiations (hereinafter referred to as the "Final Act" and the "Uruguay Round" respectively) at Marrakech, Morocco, on April 15, 1994.

Signing of the Final Act clearly indicated Thailand's recognition of the results of the Uruguay Round, including its annexes, *inter alia*, and the Antidumping and Subsidies codes. However, at the domestic level, for such signing to be given effect in law, confirmation and approval of the signing was required by Parliament. For this purpose, the World Trade Organization Operation Protection Act B.E. 2537 (1994) was promulgated by Parliament in conformity to Thailand's international obligations.

In this connection, the Ministry of Commerce initiated and appointed, amongst others, the Committee on Antidumping Practices and the Committee on Subsidies and Countervailing Measures, to consider Thailand's international obligations under the Final Act and evaluate what measures were needed to implement or revise domestic laws in compliance with its international obligation prior to submitting them to Parliament.

Evolution of Trade Remedy Laws in Thailand and Summary Listing of Each Trade Remedy, With Corresponding Laws and Agencies Responsible for Administering Such Remedy

The pioneering Thai law in the field of trade remedy laws is the Antidumping Act B.E. 2507 (1964). This Antidumping Act has been subsequently complemented by various other laws invoking, either directly or by analogy, trade remedy law principles. These complementary laws are the Customs Tariff Decree B.E. 2530 (1987), the Investment Promotion Act B.E. 2520 (1977), the Import and Export of Commodity Act B.E. 2522 (1979), the Notification of the Ministry of Commerce B.E. 2534 (1991) as has been replaced by the Notification of the Ministry of Commerce B.E. 2539 (1996) as amended on August 6, 1997, on "the Imposition of Antidumping and Countervailing Duties" (hereinafter referred to as the "Notification").

The significance of the Antidumping Act in terms of its applicability to currently practiced trade remedies pursuant to, amongst others, GATT 1994, is severely undermined as it is generally considered to be an outdated law whose structure only reflects, in general, provisions regarding antidumping but in fact, falls short of providing an effective trade remedy mechanism. The Antidumping Act primarily stipulates provisions for the establishment of a Committee to carry out investigations on unfair trade practices. Apart from their passive investigatory role, these Committees however fail to provide any 'policing' or enforcement functions necessary to render effective any trade remedy regulations as described in the Final Act.

Procedures for determining injury caused by dumping are not comprehensively addressed. The Minister of Finance under the Antidumping Act is authorized to appoint an official to implement and enforce any Ministerial Regulations under the Antidumping Act. However, as there has never been a corresponding Ministerial Regulation, the Antidumping Act has effectively been rendered impotent. For these reasons, in practice, no antidumping duty has yet been collected in Thailand.

This shortcoming has been recognized and appropriate changes are currently being drafted. While waiting for the new revised Antidumping Act, the following regulations currently in force rely on international trade remedies in the absence of directly relevant antidumping laws.

Collection of special countervailing duty under the Customs Tariff Decree B.E. 2530 (1987)

Section 13 of the Decree provides that, where it appears to the Minister of Finance that any imported goods have been subsidized by any country or person by any means other than the drawback or compensation of duties and/or taxes, and that such subsidy causes or may cause damages to Thailand's agriculture or industry, the Minister of Finance, with the approval of the Cabinet, is empowered to levy, by notification, a countervailing duty (CVD) upon those goods at the rate he thinks fit, in addition to the normal import duty. The rate of this CVD shall not be in excess of the amount of subsidy deemed by the Minister of Finance to be granted.

Special fee under the Investment Promotion Act B.E. 2520 (1977)

Under Section 49, in case it is necessary to protect the business of a promoted juristic person, the Board of Investment (BOI) has the power to prescribe special fees for the import of products or commodities that are of the same or similar type or that can be used instead of those produced or assembled by the promoted person at a reasonable rate, which must not exceed 50 percent of the cost, including insurance and overseas freight, of such products or commodities.

Special fees under the Import and Export of Commodity Act B.E. 2522 (1979)

Pursuant to Section 5, under necessary and appropriate circumstances deemed to be for the good of economic stability, public interest, public health, national security, public peace and morality or for other interests of the State, the Minister of Commerce, with approval of the Cabinet, shall have the power "to prescribe the category and kinds of goods on which import or export duties shall be levied."

The Notification

The Notification is aimed at protecting domestic industry from being unjustly affected by products imported at unfair prices or by subsidized imports. The Minister of Commerce is authorized under the Import and Export of Commodity Act B.E. 2522 (1979) to implement this Notification. The Notification provides measures in antidumping and countervailing duties comprising 19 clauses, primarily focusing on the following: definitions, dumping margin, subsidy rate, criteria of injury determination, investigation, preliminary and final retaliatory measures, and related provisions. In this respect, the Notification by and large embodies the trade remedy concepts of the Final Act.

This Notification, which contains provisions reflecting the Antidumping and Subsidies codes, is, therefore, the most effective and up-to-date trade remedy law currently in force. Indeed, the purpose of this Notification was to replace existing and relatively inadequate trade remedy provisions to enable Thailand to retaliate against dumping and subsidies from the Contracting Parties until a new or revised Antidumping Act has been enacted.

Due to the reformation of the government agency responsible for antidumping and/or countervailing investigations, the Department of Foreign Trade and the Department of Internal Trade of the Ministry of Commerce are primarily designated to administer such remedy and report directly to the Committee established under the Notification. However, the Customs Department of the Ministry of Finance is responsible for collecting antidumping or countervailing duties or other specifically imposed fees as provided for in the above-mentioned laws.

ANTIDUMPING INVESTIGATIONS

Dumping Determination

Initiation of investigation—by petition

Thailand has, for the most part, adopted the provisions for initiation and investigation as laid out in the Agreement on Implementation of Article VI of GATT 1994. The procedures applicable to antidumping and countervailing duty investigations are virtually identical.

A petition for the committee to conduct an antidumping proceeding may be submitted by or on behalf of the domestic industry to the Department of Foreign Trade.

The petition referred to in the preceding paragraph shall be supported by those domestic producers whose collective output constitutes more than 50 percent of the total production of the like product produced by that portion of the domestic industry expressing either support for or opposition to the petition and provided further that those domestic producers expressly supporting the petition account for not less than 25 percent of total production of the like product produced by the domestic industry.

The submission of the petition shall be in compliance with the rules and procedures prescribed by the Department of Foreign Trade. If the petition is not supported by sufficient or accurate evidence, the petitioner shall be notified to complete or correct the petition within the time period specified. When the petition is supported by sufficient and accurate evidence, the Department of Foreign Trade shall submit that petition to the Committee for consideration.

The petitioner may withdraw the petition. However, if the notice of antidumping and injury investigation has been made correctly, the Committee may terminate or continue with the investigation as it deems appropriate.

In cases in which the Department of Foreign Trade deems it appropriate to initiate the antidumping investigation or when the Committee determines that the petition is supported by sufficient grounds, the Department of Foreign Trade shall notify the Department of Internal Trade. The Department of Foreign Trade and the Department of Internal Trade shall promptly carry out their duties under the Notification.

If the Committee determines that the petition is not supported by sufficient grounds, the Department of Foreign Trade shall notify the petitioner of such determination as soon as possible.

Timetable

The evaluation of the complaint should take no longer than forty-five days, at which time the Committee will either terminate the investigation should it determine the complaint without merit, or continue with the preliminary investigation should it determine that the complaint is substantive.

Upon a decision by the Committee to further investigate, the Committee will proceed as follows:

Preliminary investigation

- The Committee will issue a public notice specifying the product items and the exporting country to be investigated, the date of initiation of the investigation, the summary of the preliminary information, as well as the time limit within which relevant parties can present their views or their opposition.
- It will inform the exporter, the importer, the complainant, and the representative of the exporting country of the initiation of the investigation.
- It will send a copy of the complaint to the exporters and the representative of the exporting country.
- A questionnaire formatted by the Department of Foreign Trade will be sent to the exporters or the producers which are accused of exporting the products at unfair prices or having subsidized imports and likewise a questionnaire will be sent by the Department of Internal Trade to the domestic industry concerned requesting them to respond to and return the questionnaires within thirty days after having received them. The period can be extended for another fifteen days. If the investigation shows that the products were imported at an unfair price and had caused or threatened to cause injury to domestic industry, and it is considered that a provisional measure is needed to prevent further injury during

the investigation, the Departments will submit their investigation results to the Committee for a decision regarding the application of a provisional measure to be approved by the Minister of Commerce within thirty days.

The application of such provisional measures typically involves the levy of a provisional special duty, which shall not exceed the dumping margin or the rate of subsidy as determined by the Committee. The provisional special duty should be determined after sixty days from the start of the investigation and will not ordinarily be enforced past four months, although upon request by exporters representing a significant percentage of the trade involved, the period may be extended to a maximum of six months. If, in the course of an investigation, the question of whether a duty lower than the dumping margin would be sufficient to remove injury is examined, the above periods may be extended to six months and nine months respectively.

As soon as a provisional measure is adopted, or the Committee decides to drop the investigation, all relevant parties will be notified.

Final investigation

Upon completion of the preliminary investigation and the decision to continue with further investigation, the Committee will conduct a final investigation to verify all information received and gather more information to determine whether to impose a "definitive special duty."

Should it be found that there had been an importation of unfairly priced products or the importation of subsidized products that had caused or threatened to cause injury to the domestic industry, the Committee shall submit the results of the examination to the Minister to impose a definitive special duty.

This final investigatory period should end within one year from the date of the initiation of the investigation, although it can be extended as necessary.

Participation of parties

At any time during the investigation, the Committee will provide opportunities for the concerned parties to present their argument to protect their interests.

The parties may examine any document that does not contain confidential information. The parties may submit documents and request confidentiality if they submit the documents to the Committee—in any case, a summary (to be prepared by the parties) containing sufficient substantive content of the information in the documents can nevertheless be disclosed. No information will be disclosed without approval by the relevant parties.

Definitions
Like products
Like product means a product which is identical to the subject goods or in the absence of such product, another product which has characteristics closely resembling those of the subject goods.

Period of investigation
The period of investigation consists of two parts, the "preliminary investigation" and the "final investigation." The entire investigation should be completed within one year of its initiation, although it may be extended for up to a total of eighteen months.

Domestic industry
The domestic industry is interpreted as referring to the domestic producers of the like products whose collective output of the products constitutes more than half of the total domestic production of those products, except that:
(i) when producers are themselves importers of the dumped product or are related to the exporters or importers, the term "domestic industry" may be interpreted as referring to the rest of the producers; who are deemed to be related to exporters or importers only if one of them directly or indirectly controls the other; or both of them are directly or indirectly controlled by a third person; or together they directly or indirectly control a third person, provided that there are grounds for believing or suspecting that the effect of the relationship is such as to cause the producer concerned to behave differently from nonrelated producers; and
(ii) the territory of Thailand may, for the production in question, be divided into two or more competitive markets and the producers of the like products within each market may be regarded as a separate industry if the producers within such market sell all or almost all of their production of the product in question in that market, and the demand in that market is not to any substantial degree supplied by producers of the product in question located elsewhere in Thailand.

Calculation of dumping margins
Export price
The export price is the price actually paid or payable for the product exported from the exporting country to Thailand.

In a case where there is no export price or where it appears that the export price is unreliable because of an association or a compensatory arrangement among the relevant parties, the export price is constructed on the basis of the price at which the imported products are first resold to an independent buyer or, if the products are not resold to an independent buyer or are not resold in the condition in which they are imported, any reasonable basis adjustment for all costs and expenses including duties and taxes, incurred between importation and resale, and for profits accruing, is made so as to establish an export price.

Normal value

Normal value is based on the prices paid or payable for the like product in the ordinary course of trade by independent customers in the exporting country. Sales of the like product destined for consumption in the domestic market of the exporting country shall normally be used to determine normal value if such sales volume constitutes five percent or more of the sales of the product exported to Thailand from that exporting country. However, a lower ratio may be used when the prices charged are considered representative in the market of the exporting country.

Adjustments

Where there are no sales of the like products or where the price is unreliable because of an association or a compensatory arrangement among the relevant parties or because of the particular market situation in the domestic market of the exporting country, such sales do not permit a proper comparison, the normal value is determined as follows:
(i) on the basis of the export prices, in the ordinary course of trade, to an appropriate third country, provided that those prices are representative; or
(ii) on the basis of the cost of production in the country of origin plus a reasonable amount for administrative, selling, and general costs and for profits.

Such sales made at prices below production costs plus administrative, selling, and general costs are treated as not being in the ordinary course of trade and may be disregarded in determining normal value if it is determined that such sales are made within an extended period of time in substantial quantities and are at prices which do not provide for the recovery of all costs within a reasonable period of time. If prices which are below costs at the time of sale are above weighted average costs per unit for the period of investigation, such prices shall be considered to provide for recovery of costs within a reasonable period of time.

Imports from nonmarket economy countries are determined by comparison with information in a comparable market economy third country or where that is not possible, on any reasonable basis, including the price of the like product sold in Thailand.

When products are not imported from the country of origin but are exported to Thailand from an intermediate country, information existing in the exporting country is normally used as the basis for establishing the normal value. However, the price in the country of origin may be used in determining normal value if the products are merely transshipped through the exporting country, or such products are not produced in the exporting country or there is no comparable price for them in the exporting country.

A fair comparison is made to determine a dumping margin based on the same level of trade and time. Due allowances are made for differences which affect price comparability. In the case where the export price and normal value are not at the same level of trade or are not from nearly the same time, due allowances, in the form of adjustments, are made for differences in factors which affect price comparability.

Price undertakings and other agreements to suspend investigations

Antidumping proceedings may be suspended or terminated with respect to any exporter without the imposition of provisional measures upon the receipt of satisfactory undertakings by the Department of Foreign Trade from such exporter to revise its prices or to cease exports of the dumped products in question.

The Department of Foreign Trade may accept an undertaking only if it is satisfied that, by accepting such undertaking, the injurious effect of the dumping will be eliminated. Undertakings may be sought by the Department of Foreign Trade or proposed by exporters. However, price increases under such undertakings shall not be higher than necessary to eliminate the dumping margin. The undertakings, to become effective, must be approved by the Committee only after the Committee has made a preliminary determination.

The Department of Foreign Trade may reject the undertakings offered by the exporters for any reason including general policy and where practicable, shall provide to the exporter the reasons which have led it to consider acceptance of an undertaking as inappropriate.

The fact that exporters do not offer the undertakings, or do not accept an invitation to do so shall in no way prejudice the consideration of the case.

An exporter from whom an undertaking has been accepted shall provide information within the time period specified by the Department of Foreign Trade and shall permit the verification of such information. In case of a violation of an undertaking, provisional measures may be applied and the antidumping proceedings may be continued.

Upon acceptance of an undertaking, the antidumping proceedings may nevertheless be completed by the Committee if the exporter so desires by indicating its intention in the undertakings or if undertakings are accepted in respect of some but not all of the exporters or if such undertakings are subsequently violated or if the Committee so decides upon the completion of the final determination, if:

(i) a negative final determination is made, the undertaking shall automatically lapse, except in cases where such a determination is due in large part to the existence of an undertaking. In such cases, the Committee may require that an undertaking be maintained for a reasonable period;

(ii) an affirmative final determination is made, the undertaking shall continue; and

(iii) an affirmative final determination is made in case of violation of an undertaking, the Committee may levy an antidumping duty retroactively on products entered for consumption not more than 90 days before the application of a provisional measure, except that any such retroactive assessment shall not apply to imports entered before the violation of the undertaking.

Effect of Dumping Order

Effective date

Retroactivity

If the final investigation shows that the rate of definitive special duty is higher that the provisional duty already imposed, the difference will not be collected retroactively.

Duration

A special duty will remain in effect only as long as is necessary to counteract injury. In no case will it last longer than five years from either its imposition or its last review.

Enforcement

In the event that by virtue of the Notification anyone is convicted of importing or exporting products without paying the imposed antidumping duty or pays less than the required amount, a fine of Baht 20,000, a prison term of one year, or both may be imposed pursuant to the provisions of the Import and Export of Commodity Act B.E. 2522 (1979).

Procedures for review and revocation of an order

The parties, with the support of reliable information, may request the Committee to review the special duty. At that time, the Committee may change or remove the duty if it deems it no longer appropriate. The Committee may also initiate this action on its own.

Refund

Thai law allows for a prompt refund of any provisional duty paid if the results of the final investigation show either no unfair price or subsidy, or no injury.

If the final investigation shows that the rate of definitive duty is lower than the provisional duty, the difference will be refunded.

COUNTERVAILING DUTY INVESTIGATION

Subsidized imports are deemed to exist where the government of the country of origin or exporting country is engaged in the following activities and a benefit is thereby conferred:
(i) granting of a financial contribution including:
 (a) any activities which will eventually result in a transfer of funds or liabilities being reduced or terminated;
 (b) foregoing or noncollection of government revenue that is otherwise due;
 (c) purchase of goods or provision of goods or services other than general infrastructure; or
 (d) making of payments to a funding mechanism, or the acts of entrusting or directing a private body to carry out one or more of the types of functions illustrated in (a), (b), or (c);
(ii) giving of any form of income or price support, whether direct or indirect, in order to increase an export or reduce an import of any product.

The following types of subsidies are deemed to be specific:
(i) a subsidy to which access is limited to certain enterprises, whether in law or in fact;
(ii) a subsidy which is limited to certain enterprises located within a designated geographical region. However, the setting or change of generally applicable tax rates by all levels of government entitled to do so shall not be deemed to be a specific subsidy;
(iii) a subsidy contingent, in law or in fact, upon export performance in a manner prescribed by the Department of Foreign Trade; and
(iv) a subsidy contingent upon the use of domestic over imported goods.

The Department of Foreign Trade applies special rules and procedures in regard to agricultural products.

Countervailing duties do not apply to subsidies which are prescribed by the Department of Foreign Trade and for which the benefit is provided through programs that grant assistance for research activity; assistance to disadvantaged regions; or assistance to promote adaptation of existing facilities to new environmental requirements imposed by law and regulations.

INJURY ANALYSIS

During the investigation, the Department of Internal Trade will examine the available information and determine what injury has taken place, plus what injury may take place in the future. Injury includes material injury, threat of material injury, or material retardation which is based on positive evidence of the following:
(i) the volume of dumped imports and the effects of the dumped imports on prices of the like product in the domestic market of Thailand; and
(ii) the consequent impact of these imports on domestic industry.

A determination or threat of material injury to domestic industry are to be based on facts and not merely on allegation, conjecture, or remote possibility. The change in circumstances which would create a situation in which the dumping would cause injury must be clearly foreseen and imminent or indicate the imminent likelihood of further dumped exports and that, unless protective action is taken, material injury will occur. In making a determination regarding the existence of a threat of material injury, consideration is given to factors such as:
- a significant rate of increase of dumped imports into the domestic market of Thailand indicating the likelihood of substantially increased imports;
- sufficient freely disposable capacity of the exporter or an imminent and substantial increase in such capacity indicating the likelihood of substantially increased dumped exports to Thailand, considering the availability of other export markets to absorb any additional exports;
- whether imports are entering at prices that would significantly depress prices or prevent price increases which would have occurred, and would probably increase demand for further imports; and
- inventories of the product.

In order to determine whether material retardation of a domestic industry exists, factors which may lead to a material retardation, including the possible viability and time period for the establishment and development of such domestic industry must be present.

OTHER TRADE REMEDIES

Aside from the provisions concerning countervailing duties under the Customs Tariff Decree, special fees under the Investment Promotion Act, and the Import and Export of Commodity Act, Thai law is silent on any other trade remedies such as an escape clause, national security exception, and customs sanctions.

Trinidad & Tobago

Petal Sue Roopnarine
in conjunction with Olive Angela Tibbetts Ramchand
Fitzwilliam, Stone, Furness-Smith & Morgan
Port-of-Spain, Trinidad

HISTORY AND OVERVIEW OF TRADE REMEDY LAWS AND/OR REGULATIONS SINCE 1947

Trinidad and Tobago is a member of the World Trade Organization (WTO) and adheres to the WTO Antidumping and Subsidy Codes, which establish procedures for dealing with dumped and subsidized imports. Responsibility for applying the provisions of the Code rests with the Antidumping Authority and the Ministry of Trade and Industry. The governing legislation is:
- Act No. 11 of 1992 (the Antidumping and Countervailing Duties Act) and;
- Act No. 23 of 1995 (an Act that amends the Antidumping and Countervailing Duties Act). (The Amendment Act is hereinafter referred to as "the Act").

Action in this field and the circumstances in which it may be exercised are outlined in the Antidumping and Countervailing Duties Regulations 1996 (the Regulations) (Legal Notice No. 25 of 1996) and the Antidumping and Countervailing Duties (Subsidies) Regulations 1996 (Legal Notice No. 26 of 1996).

The legislation conforms generally with Trinidad and Tobago's obligations under its membership in the General Agreement on Trade and Tariffs (GATT) and is broadly consistent with the provisions of the GATT Agreements relating to the implementation and interpretation of Articles VI, XVI, and XXXIII (1980; 1994) and the Agreement on Subsidies and Countervailing Measures (1994).

The introduction of domestic legislation to combat dumping and subsidization in Trinidad and Tobago in the 1990s has coincided with extensive tariff reductions, the result of the government's initiatives to liberalize trade and its desire to ensure that any trade liberalization be placed on a secured footing. In fact, the major concerns of developing countries such as Trinidad and Tobago in the Tokyo and Uruguay Rounds of GATT were to seek improved and predictable conditions of access for a diverse range of exports and to seek an improved framework for the conduct of international trade, while at the same time taking into account the development of the country, the financial and trade needs of the country, and the desire for preferential tariff treatment where possible and appropriate.

The statutory measures have only recently been introduced and manufacturers as a whole have yet to fully utilize these existing statutory measures for their protection. Because no investigation has been completed since the introduction of the new legislation, the success and/or shortcomings of the statutory measures have yet to be determined.

Under the basic Trinidad and Tobago legislation, the codified remedy against two elements of unfair competition, dumped or subsidized imports, is the imposition of antidumping or countervailing duties as provided for in Part II of the Act. These duties can be imposed only after a formal investigation has shown that:
- dumping or subsidization is or has been taking place;
- this dumping or subsidization is causing or threatening material injury to a local industry; and
- the imposition of such duties would be in the local interest.

The Act provides that it shall be the duty of the Antidumping Authority, as appointed by the Minister:

(a) to investigate the existence, degree, and effect of the alleged dumping, or grant of subsidy of any goods;

(b) to ascertain in accordance with the Regulations whether any goods imported in Trinidad and Tobago cause or threaten to cause material injury to any industry established in Trinidad and Tobago or materially retard the establishment of any new industry in Trinidad and Tobago;

(c) to identify goods liable for any duty or additional duty chargeable under this Act;

(d) to submit his findings to the Minister as to the margin of dumping or the nature and amount of subsidy in relation to such goods; and

(e) to make recommendations to the Minister regarding directions and determination.

ANTIDUMPING AND COUNTERVAILING DUTY INVESTIGATIONS

Initiation of Investigation

The Act provides that the Authority may initiate an investigation to determine the existence and effect of any alleged dumping or subsidizing of any goods at the direction of the Minister, on his own initiative or on receipt of a complaint in writing by or on behalf of an industry producing like goods, provided that the Authority shall not initiate an investigation where the members of such industry who support the complaint do not account for more production of the like goods in Trinidad and Tobago than do the members, if any, of such industry who signify to the Authority in writing their opposition to the complaint.

A complaint for these purposes must allege that the goods have been or are being dumped or subsidized; specify the goods; allege that dumping or subsidizing has caused, is causing, or is likely to cause material injury or has caused or is causing material retardation; state the facts on which such allegations are made; and make such other representations as the complainant deems relevant.

Timetable

Section 18(3) provides that when the Authority initiates an investigation, notice to that effect will be given. Where the Authority decides not to initiate an investigation it shall give notice specifying reasons therefor. Section 18 (3a) provides that the investigation shall normally cover a period of not less than six months immediately prior to the initiation of the investigation.

The preliminary examination

In order to decide whether a full investigation is warranted, the Authority will examine the complaint to ensure that it is in an acceptable form.

The Authority must also be satisfied that there is sufficient prima facie evidence of dumping or the giving of the subsidy and of the quantum; actionable injury; and a causal link between such imports and the alleged actionable injury. Consultation may be held with the government of the exporting country. The Authority will hold a preliminary hearing of all interested persons and such experts and other witnesses as it thinks fit and may require any of those persons to complete a questionnaire.

Where the Authority has requested the completion of a questionnaire, it shall allow thirty days to provide the information.

Participation of Parties and Their Counsel

Section 19(1) of the Act provides that the Authority shall ensure that all interested persons are given reasonable opportunity throughout the investigation to present in writing all evidence relevant to the investigation, to have access to all nonconfidential information relevant to the presentation of their case and use by the Authority in the investigation, and to present opposing views and offer rebuttal arguments.

Industrial users of the product under investigation and representative organizations, where the product is commonly sold at the retail level shall not be considered interested persons under this Section but shall be entitled to submit to the Authority information that is relevant to the investigation of dumping, subsidization, injury, and the causal link between injury and dumping or subsidization.

Exporters, foreign producers, and importers of the product subject to investigation, and in the case of subsidization, the representative of the country of origin, may request that the Authority inform them of the essential facts and the basis upon which the Authority recommends that the Minister impose a duty or a provisional duty.

The Act makes specific provision for the treatment of confidential information. Any information provided to the Authority on a confidential basis during the course of an investigation shall not be disclosed by the Authority to any other person without the specific authorization of the person providing such information. Persons supplying confidential information may be requested to furnish a nonconfidential summary of information or reasons why such summary is not possible. Where satisfactory reasons for confidentiality are not supplied or a summary not provided, this information may be disregarded. The Act provides that all interested parties to an investigation may be represented by an Attorney at Law or by an agent.

During the course of the investigation, the Authority shall seek to obtain all relevant facts from importers, local producers, traders, and exporters and, when necessary, from member states and foreign suppliers. The Authority may arrange meetings between these parties so that conflicting views and arguments may be exchanged and heard.

Effect of the Antidumping and Countervailing Order

Preliminary determination

Within three (3) months after an investigation is initiated, the Minister may make a preliminary determination and by notice give directions to the Comptroller of Customs & Excise ("the Comptroller") to assess provisional duties pursuant to Section 25. Payment shall be secured in accordance with Section 31.

Securities for payment of duties

The Comptroller may require and take securities for payment of duties payable under this Act. Pending receipt of the required security, the Comptroller may refuse to pass any entry or do any other act in relation to any matter for which security is required. The security in question may be by bond with sureties or guarantees, or by a deposit of cash or any method satisfactory to the Comptroller. The security may be provided in relation to any particular transaction or generally with respect to all transactions and for such period and amount as the Comptroller may think fit and under such conditions regarding forfeiture, penalty, or otherwise as the Minister may direct.

Following the final determination, where provisional duties are collected and they are lower in relation to the duty to be imposed, there shall be no requirement to pay the difference; if the provisional duty is higher the difference shall be refunded. A direction shall cease to have effect following a final determination made by the Minister. Any security given pursuant to the direction shall be released except to the extent that the duties are payable pursuant to an order under this Act.

The final determination

The final determination is given by notice. The notice shall be published no later than four months after the date of the preliminary determination.

Where the Minister makes a final determination, he may by Order impose a duty to be known as an Antidumping Duty.

Under Section 9 of the Act, the Minister may include in the final determination other provisions as may be required by the Order. These provisions may:
(i) limit the description of goods by reference to the particular persons or organizations who produced the goods or who received the goods;
(ii) define the rate of duty by reference to value or weight or other measured quantity;
(iii) direct that the duty be assessed for any period or periods, whether continuous or not, or at different rates for different periods or parts of periods;
(iv) impose retrospective duties under Section 30; or
(v) authorize repayment of duties in connection with the commencement, variation or termination of a duty where it is shown that the prescribed conditions are fulfilled.

The Minister's discretion under Section 9 must be read in conjunction with Section 29 and Section 29 A, which deal with the duration of duties.

Duration of duties

The Minister shall review the need for the continued imposition of a duty where warranted on his own initiative, on the recommendation of the Authority, or if an interested person so requests and submits prima facie evidence substantiating the need for review. A duty shall remain in force only so long and to the extent necessary to counteract the injurious effect of the dumping or subsidization and may be reduced or withdrawn at the Minister's discretion.

Duties shall expire on the fifth anniversary of their entry into force or their last review unless an investigation for review pursuant to the Act is in progress. At least one month prior to the fifth anniversary, where an interested person submits to the Authority prima facie evidence that expiration of the duties would again lead to actionable injury, the Authority shall immediately initiate an investigation with duties remaining in force pending the outcome of the investigation. Procedures that apply to investigations under Section 18 shall also apply to an investigation under this provision.

Undertakings

The Minister may cause an investigation to be terminated or suspended if he is given and accepts an undertaking by the Government of the country of export or by the exporter of the goods. Pursuant to the undertaking, the Government, or the exporter as the case may be, agree to so conduct future export trade to Trinidad and Tobago of like goods as to avoid causing actionable injury to the domestic industry. The Minister may refuse to accept an undertaking if he considers its acceptance impractical or for public policy reasons. The Minister shall communicate the reasons for such refusal in writing to the person offering the undertaking and shall allow that person to make comments thereon before the refusal takes place where practicable. The Authority may suggest an undertaking but no person may be obliged to enter into such an undertaking. The fact that a person does not offer such an undertaking shall in no way prejudice the consideration of that person's case.

The price increase in the undertaking should not exceed the margin of dumping or the amount of the subsidy as the case may be.

Retrospective duty

Under Section 30 (2) of the Act the Minister has powers to impose retrospective duties. Generally, duties and provisional duties shall only be applied to goods that are entered for home consumption after the date of an order imposing the duty.

Retrospective duties may be imposed in several situations:
- Where a final determination of material injury to an industry (but not of a threat of material retardation to the establishment of an industry) is made by the Minister, or in the case of a final determination of a threat of material injury where the effect of the dumped or subsidized import would, in the absence of provisional duty being paid or security being taken under Section 31, have led to a finding of material injury, duty may be imposed retrospectively for the period for which duty was paid or security was taken.
- Where the Minister determines, with respect to dumped goods either:
  (i) that there is a history of dumping causing material injury or that the importer was or should have been aware that the goods were dumped and that such dumping would cause injury, or
  (ii) that the material injury is caused by substantial dumped imports of a product over a relatively short period of time the Minister may impose dumping duties retrospectively to preclude the injury from recurring.
- Where, in the case of subsidized goods, in critical circumstances, the Minister determines that material injury which is difficult to repair is caused by massive imports, over a relatively short period, of goods benefiting from export subsidies paid or bestowed inconsistently with the provisions of the GATT, the Minister may impose a countervailing duty retrospectively to preclude such material injury.

The Minister may impose duties on goods that were entered for home consumption not more than ninety days prior to the date of the provisional direction except that an antidumping duty may be imposed with retrospective effect prior to the date of the investigation.

Retrospective duties shall not apply to goods that have been entered for home consumption before the date of the violation of an undertaking.

Procedures for review and revocation of order

The Minister may review the imposition of the duty where warranted on his own initiative, or on the recommendation of the Authority.

Where an interested person so requests and submits evidence of changed circumstances sufficient to warrant a review, the Authority may make a recommendation for a review if at least one year has elapsed since the duty was imposed or last reviewed.

Where warranted by the review, the Minister may amend or revoke the order imposing the duty, except that the duty may be maintained or confirmed to the extent necessary to counteract the injurious effects of dumping or subsidization.

Appeals

A person aggrieved by an Order imposing a duty may appeal to the Tax Appeal Board in accordance with the Tax Appeal Board Act.

Newcomer duties

Where a person satisfies the Authority, in relation to a product that is the subject of an Order under Section 7, that:
(i) it did not export the product to Trinidad and Tobago during the investigation period used for determining the facts on the basis of which the Order was made;
(ii) it is not an associate of any person whose products are subject to an Order upon importation into Trinidad and Tobago; and
(iii) it has exported the product to Trinidad and Tobago after the investigation period;

the Authority shall initiate an investigation that shall be carried out as expeditiously as possible but shall be limited to verifying the matters in paragraphs(i) and (ii) above in order to determine the dumping margin of the person in question. During the investigation, the goods exported by the person in question shall be exempt from antidumping duties. However, any Order imposing such duty shall have retroactive effect to the date of initiation of the investigation.

ANTIDUMPING DETERMINATION

Calculation of Dumping Margin

The margin of dumping in relation to an article is defined in the Act as "the amount, if any, by which the normal value of such article exceeds the price at which it is exported."

Imported goods shall be regarded as having been dumped:

(a) if the export products from the country in which the goods originated is less than the normal value of goods in that country; or
(b) in a case where the country from which the goods were exported to Trinidad and Tobago is different from the country in which they originated:
 (i) if the export price from the country from which the goods originated is less than the normal value of those goods from that country; or

(ii) if the export price from the country from which the goods were so exported is less than the normal value of those goods in that country.

Ascertainment of Normal Value

The Act provides that the normal value of any goods exported or intended to be exported to Trinidad and Tobago shall be the price paid for like goods sold in the ordinary course of trade for home consumption in the country of export in sales that are "arm's length" transactions by the exporter or, if like goods are not so sold by the exporter, by other sellers of like goods.

Cost of Production and Constructed Value Methodology

Where the Minister is satisfied that the normal value of goods cannot be determined for the reasons set out in this Act, then the normal value shall be the sum of:
(i) such amount as determined by the Minister to be the cost of production or manufacture of the goods in the country of export; and
(ii) (assuming the goods have been sold for home consumption in the ordinary course of trade in the country of export) such amount as the Minister determines would be reasonable for administrative, selling and general costs, and profits.

The Minister may in his discretion determine that the normal value shall be the price that is representative of the price paid for sales made in the ordinary course of trade of like goods from the country of export to a third country.

Non Market Economy Methodology

In cases where the Government of a country of export has a monopoly or substantial monopoly of the trade of that country, or determines or substantially influences the domestic price of goods, the foregoing provisions that are based on market economy concepts are not appropriate. Therefore, normal value may be established by reference to the price or cost of similar goods in a comparable market economy country.

Use of Facts Available

Where any interested person refuses access to, or otherwise does not provide necessary information within a reasonable period, or significantly impedes the investigation, the Minister may make determinations on the basis of the facts available. Costs are calculated on the bases of available accounting data, normally allocated when necessary, in proportion to the turnover for each product under consideration.

Adjustment and Currency Conversion

Section 12(7) provides that:

> [W]here the normal value of goods exported or intended to be exported to Trinidad and Tobago is the price paid for like goods, to effect the fair comparison, the normal value and the export price shall be compared by the Minister—
> (a) at the same level of trade, preferably at the ex-factory level or as near to that level as possible;
> (b) in respect of sales made at or as nearly as possible the same time;
> (c) with due allowances made as appropriate for any differences in terms and conditions of sale, differences in taxation, and any other differences that are demonstrated that affect price comparability.

Under Section 12 (7A), comparison which requires conversion of currency shall be made using the rate of exchange prevailing on the date of sale except that where foreign currency is sold on forward markets in a transaction directly linked to an export sale, the currency of the export sales shall be converted at the rate of exchange used in the forward sale. Movements in exchange rates need not be taken into account until they have been sustained over a substantial period.

Export Price

The export price of any good shall be determined in accordance with the following:

(i) where the purchase of the goods by the importer was an arm's-length transaction, the export price shall be the price paid or payable for the goods by the importer, other than any part of the price that represents:
   (a) costs, charges, and expenses incurred in preparing the goods for shipment to Trinidad and Tobago that are additional to those costs, charges, and expenses generally incurred on sales for home consumption; and
   (b) any other costs, charges, and expenses resulting from the exportation of the goods or arising after their shipment from the country of export; or

(ii) where the purchase of the goods by the importer was not an arm's-length transaction, and the goods are subsequently sold by the importer in the condition in which they were imported to a person who is not an associate of the importer, the export price may be determined as the price at which the goods were sold by the importer to that person less the sum of the following amounts:
   (a) the amount of any duties and taxes imposed under the Act or any other Act;
   (b) the amount of any costs, charges, or expenses arising in relation to the goods after exportation; and
   (c) the amount of the profit, if any, on the sale by the importer or, where the Minister so directs, an amount calculated as the rate of profit that would normally be realized on the sale by the importer, having regard to the rate of profit on the sales of goods of the same general category by the importer where such sales exist.

COUNTERVAILING DUTY DETERMINATION

A subsidy is deemed to exist where a benefit is conferred through the making of a financial contribution by a government or a public body or through the granting of any form of income or price support. A government or public body makes a financial contribution where:
(i) it makes a direct transfer of funds or enters into a transaction involving a potential direct transfer of funds or liabilities;
(ii) it foregoes or does not collect revenue that is otherwise due;
(iii) it provides goods or services other than general infrastructure, or purchases goods; or
(iv) it makes payment to a funding mechanism, or entrusts or directs a private body to do any of the things described in paragraphs (i), (ii), and (iii).

A finding of actionable injury shall be made when the subsidized imports are found to be causing or threatening to cause material injury to the industry producing like goods or are materially retarding the establishment of the production in Trinidad and Tobago of like goods.

Having made such a determination, the Minister may, by order, impose a countervailing duty which shall be at a rate that is not greater than is necessary to prevent actionable injury. The amount of the duty shall not exceed the amount of the subsidy given on the goods.

Definitions

Countervailable subsidies

A subsidy shall be subject to countervailing measures only if it is specific to an enterprise. A subsidy shall be deemed to be specific where the granting authority, or the legislation pursuant to which the authority operates, explicitly limits access to a subsidy to a particular enterprise. Specificity shall not exist where the granting authority establishes neutral and objective criteria governing the eligibility for and the amount of the subsidy, provided that the eligibility is automatic and that such criteria is strictly adhered to.

The Authority may consider other factors if it has reason to believe that a subsidy is specific, notwithstanding that it appears to be nonspecific.

Noncountervailable subsidies

Under Regulation 7 of the Subsidies Regulations, the following subsidies shall not be subject to countervailing duties: (a) subsidies that are not specific within the meaning of the regulations; (b) subsidies that are specific but are research subsidies, subsidies to disadvantaged regions and regional subsidy programs; and (c) any of the Domestic Support Measures listed in the Schedule to the Subsidies Regulations, provided to promote the adaptation of existing facilities to new environmental requirements imposed by law.

Calculation of Subsidies

The amount of countervailable subsidies is calculated in terms of the benefit conferred to the recipient which is found to exist during the investigation period.

Calculation of the benefit to the recipient shall be subject to the following principles:
(i) provision by a government of equity capital shall not be considered as conferring a benefit, unless the investment can be regarded as inconsistent with the usual investment practice (including the provision of risk capital) of private investors in the territory of the country of origin or the country of export;
(ii) a loan by a government shall not be considered as conferring a benefit unless there is a difference between the amount that the firm or enterprise would pay for a comparable commercial loan which the firm or enterprise can actually obtain on the market and the amount received, in which case the benefit shall be the difference between the two amounts;

(iii) a loan guarantee by a government shall not be considered as conferring a benefit unless there is a difference between the amount that the firm receiving the guarantee pays on a loan guaranteed by the government and the amount that the firm would pay for a comparable commercial loan in the absence of the government guarantee, in which case the benefit shall be the difference in fees; and
(iv) the provision of goods or services or purchases of goods by a government shall not be considered as conferring a benefit unless provision is made for less than adequate remuneration. The adequacy of remuneration shall be determined in relation to prevailing market conditions for the product or service in question in the country of provision or purchase (including price, quality, availability, marketability, transportation, and other conditions of purchase or sale).

Allocation of Subsidies Over Time

Where a subsidy can be linked to the future acquisition of fixed assets, the amount of the countervailing subsidy shall be calculated by spreading the subsidy across a period that reflects the normal depreciation of such assets in the industry concerned. The amount so calculated, which is attributable to the investigation period, shall be allocated over the level of production, sales, or exports of the products concerned during the investigation period.

Where a subsidy cannot be linked to the acquisition of fixed assets, the amount of the benefit received during the investigation period shall in principle be attributed to this period and allocated as described above unless special circumstances arise justifying attribution over a different period.

INJURY ANALYSIS

Definitions

Section 3 of the Act defines "industry" as such Trinidad and Tobago producers of goods whose collective output constitutes at least 25 percent of the Trinidad and Tobago production of like goods, except that:
(i) where certain Trinidad and Tobago producers of like goods are associates of the exporters or importers, or are themselves importers of the relevant goods, the Minister may make a determination that such producers shall not be taken into account in applying the foregoing definition;

(ii) Trinidad and Tobago may, for the production in question, be divided into two competitive markets with all the producers within one such market regarded as the industry, if the producers within such market sell all or almost all their production of the goods in question in that market and the demand in that market is not to any substantial degree supplied by producers of the goods in question located elsewhere in Trinidad and Tobago.

"Like goods" in relation to goods under consideration, means goods that are identical in all respects to the goods under consideration, or that, although not alike in all respects to the goods under consideration, have characteristics closely resembling those under consideration.

Finding of Actionable Injury

Where a complaint of actionable injury is made, the authority shall examine all relevant facts and shall duly consider:
(i) the volume of dumped or subsidized imports as assessed, either in absolute terms or relative to production or consumption in Trinidad and Tobago; and
(ii) the effect of dumped or subsidized imports on prices with reference to:
   (a) whether there has been significant price undercutting by the subsidized imports as compared to the price of like goods produced in Trinidad and Tobago;
   (b) whether the effect of such imports is to depress or prevent price increases, which would otherwise have occurred; and
   (c) the consequent impact of dumped or subsidized imports on the industry that produces like goods as assessed by reference to all relevant economic factors and indices having a bearing on the state of the industry, including sales, profits, production, market share, productivity, return on investment, rate of use of production capacity, inventories, cash flow, employment, wages, growth, ability to raise capital, and investments.

The Authority is not bound to give priority to any of these factors in making an injury finding.

A Threat of Actionable Injury

A determination of threat of actionable injury is made where a particular situation is likely to develop into actionable injury. In making a determination, the Authority shall consider such factors as:

(i)   the rate of increase of dumped or subsidized imports into Trinidad and Tobago;
(ii) the export capacity in the country of export, either already in existence or which will be operational in the foreseeable future with the likelihood that the resulting production will be exported to Trinidad and Tobago;
(iii) the depressing or suppressing effect of the prices of imports and the likelihood that such prices will increase the demand of further imports;
(iv) the inventories of the product being investigated; and
(v)   the nature of any subsidy or subsidies and the trade effects likely to arise therefrom.

Injuries caused by other factors such as volume and prices of imports that are not dumped or subsidized, contraction in demand, or changes in the patterns of consumption, trade restrictive practices of and competition between foreign producers and the industry, developments in technology and the export performance and productivity of the industry, which individually or in combination also adversely affect the domestic industry, shall not be attributed to the dumped or subsidized imports.

In exceptional cases, the Authority may find actionable injury even where a substantial potion of the industry is not so injured if there is a concentration of the dumped or subsidized imports into an isolated market, and the dumped or subsidized imports are causing actionable injury to the producers of all of the production within such market.

Tunisia

Mohamed Zaanouni
Zaanouni Law Firm
Tunis, Tunisia

HISTORY AND OVERVIEW OF TRADE REMEDY LAWS AND REGULATIONS

The economic development process pursued in Tunisia for the last three decades has brought major changes to the country's economic structure, a transformation that has been marked by three stages:

1960-1970: Large public investment in basic sectors.

1970-1985: Development of national entrepreneurship through a liberal policy of openness and encouragement of private initiative.

1986 to date: Integration of the Tunisian economy into the world market, through GATT membership and the signing of the agreement to establish a Free-Trade Zone between Tunisia and the European Union.

Therefore, Tunisia approaches the fourth decade of its development since independence with a liberal program of economic reforms, allowing it to better integrate into the international market. The entrance of Tunisia into a market economy occurred after a period of collectivization experienced during the 1960s, similar to that of other developing countries that were former colonies. Although the state had the essential role in reconstruction, its influence has lessened rapidly since the end of the sixties.

The Tunisian economy is a liberal economy, open to the outside world. For example,

- Investment is free in most sectors.
- 92 percent of production is subject to international competition.
- 87 percent of producer prices are governed by market mechanisms.
- Tunisian currency is convertible for current transactions.
- Exchanges of goods and services with other countries represented 93 percent of GDP in 1995.
- Annual growth in the GDP was 4.2 percent (at constant prices) from 1987 to 1995, and is expected to reach 6.7 percent by 1996.

- Throughout this period, exports have been an important growth sector.
- Exports of goods and services increased by an average of 8.8 percent per year (at constant prices) from 1987 to 1995.

The sectors making the greatest contribution to GDP were manufacturing industries (12 percent per year) and tourism (6.5 percent per year). In 1994, these two sectors represented nearly 76 percent of all exports.

Tunisia gives special encouragement to foreign investment, which is considered complementary to Tunisia's domestic development effort.

Foreign investors can benefit from the advantages of the investment law, and may hold up to 100 percent of the project capital without needing to seek authorization, except for:
- partially exporting services, for which authorization is required when the foreign capital share exceeds 50 percent; and
- ownership of agricultural lands, which may, however, be leased on a long-term basis for as long as 40 years.

Foreign investors in activities devoted solely to export can benefit from an off-shore status that entitles them to full exemption from duties and taxes for all equipment and inputs.

Foreign investors are allowed free transfer of their profits. They also benefit from a range of multilateral and bilateral guarantees, thanks to Tunisia's endorsement of MIGA and of the New York Convention regarding the execution of arbitration sentences and the signing of agreements on investment protection and exemption from double taxation.
- Since 1994, Tunisia has lifted quantitative restrictions on most products, with the exception of luxury goods, consumption subsidized goods, and certain textile products.
- Tunisia has also established trade laws to ensure a smooth transition from protectionism to free trade. In the course of international competition, these laws aid in the struggle against the unfair practices of international commerce and include antidumping legislation, and other appropriate procedures to fight such trade practices followed by certain foreign suppliers.

In November 1959, Tunisia was admitted provisionally to the GATT, and remained a provisional member until 1986.

Beginning in 1987, Tunisia engaged in tariff negotiations to become a contracting party to the GATT.

Tunisia actively participated in the Uruguay Round negotiations, both in global negotiations and in the various working groups.

ANTIDUMPING INVESTIGATIONS

Dumping Determination

Initiation of investigation

Petitions regarding imported products that are claimed to be dumped or subsidized may be presented to the Minister in charge of Commerce either by individuals or by legal entities or by competent institutions.

The petition must be sent in writing to the Minister in charge of Commerce and must present sufficient evidence establishing the existence of dumping or subsidizing practices that cause or threaten to cause serious prejudice to products locally produced that are similar to those imported.

When a preliminary evaluation of the petition establishes that the evidence presented is valid, the Minister in charge of Commerce shall order an immediate investigation of the claim and shall officially inform the petitioner or petitioners of the initiation of the investigation.

The initiation of an investigation shall not delay procedures for the product to clear customs.

Timetable

When an investigation is initiated, the Minister in charge of Commerce shall send to the petitioners appropriate forms requesting information necessary for the investigation. The petitioners shall fill out the forms and return them to Commerce within thirty days following their receipt. This deadline may be extended by fifteen days if necessary.

Participation of parties and their counsel

The exporters and the importers of the product under investigation, as well as the petitioners, are regularly informed about the development and the results of the investigation. Exporters or foreign producers have thirty days to reply to the questionnaires used in an antidumping inquiry. Parties may request an extension of this time limit and the Minister in charge of Commerce shall grant the extension for good cause shown. Each party has access to all documents regarding the procedure of the investigation and all other documents produced by the adversary. The investigating authorities may hold hearings either on their own initiative or upon the request of the parties concerned; the latter may be heard together or individually. To verify information generated during the investigation, representatives of the Ministry in charge of Commerce or any other official duly appointed to that effect shall have the right to enter and examine work and production areas belonging to individuals or legal entities affected by the investigation.

Access to information developed in proceedings

The investigation shall proceed on the basis of information available. When it appears that one of the parties concerned, for any reason whatsoever, is unable or unwilling to supply information or attempts to supply false information or attempts to obstruct the investigation, then the Minister shall use the information available to reach a determination of dumping or subsidies. Information obtained during the investigation shall not be used for any purpose whatsoever other than carrying out procedures relating to dumping and subsidizing practices.

Definitions

Like product

The expression "like product" means an identical product, that is to say, similar in all respects to the considered product, or, in the absence of such a product, of another product which, if not similar to it in all respects, has similar characteristics to the considered product.

Period of investigation

The period of investigation extends from its initiation by the Minister in charge of Commerce until its termination without any provisional or definitive measure being adopted, or when there is acceptance of alternative settlements offered, or when there is no longer any grievance to redress. All decisions to terminate investigations shall be published in the Tunisian Official Gazette. When an alternative settlement is accepted during the course of the investigation, the investigation may be terminated. The termination of an investigation shall not prevent a definitive retention of funds deposited as a guaranty for the payment of provisional compensatory taxes.

The Tunisian National Production Branch

The expression "national production branch" means all national producers of the similar product, or the producers who constitute a major portion of the total national production of these products. Thus, when the producers are linked to the exporters or to importers, or are themselves importers of the alleged product that is the subject of a dumping investigation, the expression "national production branch" can be interpreted to mean the remaining producers.

Calculation of dumping margins

Export price

A product shall be considered to be offered at a dumped price when it is exported to Tunisia at a price that is lower than its normal price or lower than the price of a similar product sold in the ordinary course of trade in the exporting country or in the country of origin of the product.

The price at export is the price indicated in the export contract plus an amount for administration and marketing expenses. When there is no price at export, or when it appears to the concerned authorities that the export price is not the result of an arm's-length transaction, the export price can be construed on the basis of the price at which the imported product is resold for the first time to an independent buyer, or, if the product is not resold to an independent buyer or is not resold in the same state as it was imported, on any reasonable basis that the authorities can determine.

Normal Value

The normal value of a product is its marketable value when it or a similar product is sold in the ordinary course of trade for domestic consumption in the exporting country.

The sales of a similar product destined for consumption in the internal market of the exporting country will normally be considered to be in sufficient quantities for the determination of normal value if the sales constitute 5 percent or more of the sales of the considered product to the importing country. A lower proportion of sales may be acceptable where the sales are of sufficient importance to enable a valid comparison.

A comparison between export price and normal value will be made at the same commercial level, which will normally be the ex-works stage. Sales must be made in as contemporaneous a time period as possible. The Minister will take into account in each case, according to its particularities, any differences affecting the comparability of price, including differences regarding the conditions of sale, taxation, levels of trade, sales quantities, physical characteristics, and any other differences shown to affect the comparability of prices. The Minister must also take into account any fees, duties, or taxes, that are incurred between the importation of the product and the sale. By taking these factors into account, the authorities can establish normal value at a commercial level equivalent to the commercial level of the price at export. The authorities will indicate to the concerned parties what information is necessary to ensure an equitable comparison. The burden of proof with respect to these adjustments must not be unreasonable.

Currency conversion

When the comparison between export price and normal value requires a currency conversion, said conversion must be made using the exchange rate in force at the date of the sale. Fluctuations in the exchange rate will not be taken into consideration. However, the authorities allow exporters

60 days to adjust their export prices to take into account any lasting movements in the registered exchange rate during the period covered by the investigation.

Although the Central Bank of Tunisia continues to monitor the value of the Tunisian Dinar against other foreign currencies, generally the exchange positions are taken in Dollars as the Dollar is the reference currency of all quotations and the first currency of payment.

Use of facts available

All interested parties in an antidumping investigation will be advised of any information required by the authorities and are provided an opportunity to produce in writing any information they deem necessary for purposes of the investigation.

Except for information requiring confidential treatment, any information produced in writing by an interested party will be made available to other interested parties participating in the investigation.

The temporary compensatory tax

The temporary compensatory tax shall be finalized in one of the following manners:
(i) If the amount of the definitive compensatory tax is equal to that of the temporary tax paid in the form of a provisional guaranty, the latter shall be considered as final payment of the tax due.
(ii) If the amount of the definitive compensatory tax is higher than that of the temporary tax paid in the form of a provisional guaranty, the difference becomes due and must be paid.
(iii) If the amount of the definitive compensatory tax is less than that of the temporary tax paid in the form of a provisional guaranty, the excess amount shall be reimbursed.

Price undertakings and other agreements to suspend investigations

Alternative settlements shall be understood to mean any act or action by which:
(i) the government of the country in which the considered product is produced or from which it is exported while enjoying subsidies eliminates or limits such subsidies or implements measures to end the prejudice that such subsidies cause; or
(ii) the exporter concerned revises his prices or renounces exporting the considered product so that the dumping margin or the nefarious effects thereof are eliminated.

If alternative settlements are accepted but not implemented, the investigation shall follow its normal course and the nonimplementation shall be deemed to mean that the parties concerned recognize that dumping or subsidizing practices do exist and do have the nefarious effects on national production that are attributed to them.

Effect of Antidumping Order

The decision to impose or not impose an antidumping compensatory tax in a case where all required conditions are met, and the decision to determine the amount of the antidumping compensatory tax at a level that equals the whole or only part of the dumping margin are the duty of the authorities of the importing country. The amount of the duty may be less than the dumping margin if the duty is sufficient to eradicate the damage caused to the national production branch.

Effective date

Retroactivity

The compensatory tax may be applied retroactively provided, however, that a period of not more than ninety days has elapsed since said products have cleared customs to be offered for sale.

Duration

The temporary compensatory tax is valid for a maximum period of four months starting from the date on which it goes into effect. However, the period of validity may be extended by two months following a decision by the Minister of Finance upon a proposal made by the Minister in charge of Commerce.

Any definitive compensatory tax will be revoked five years from the date it was imposed unless the authorities determine, during the course of a new investigation undertaken before said date, that it is probable that the dumping and the injury will continue if the tax is revoked. An application for a new investigation may be made, either at the government's own initiative, or following an application duly submitted by the national production branch or in its name, within a reasonable period of time before said date. The tax may remain in force awaiting the result of said new examination.

Enforcement

When an antidumping tax is imposed with respect to a given product, this tax will be recovered without regard to the importer of said product, with the exception of imports coming from sources where an alternative settlement has been accepted. The authorities will inform customs of the name of the supplier or suppliers of the concerned product. If, however, many suppliers from the same country are involved in the investigation and are found to be dumping, the authorities can merely inform customs of the name of the supplier country in question.

Procedures for review and revocation of order

There may be a review of decisions imposing compensatory taxes and of those relating to the acceptance of alternative settlements stipulated in Article 31 of the present law.

Such a review may take place at the request of the parties concerned who shall present evidence establishing that the situation has changed sufficiently to justify that such a review be carried out. Any party may request a review, provided that at least one year has elapsed since compensatory taxes have been imposed.

A request for review shall be addressed to the Minister in charge of Commerce. If a review is deemed necessary, the investigation will be reopened.

Turkey

Yüksel Ersoy
Ersoy Law Office
Ankara, Turkey

HISTORY AND OVERVIEW OF TRADE REMEDY LEGISLATION SINCE 1947

Accession to GATT/WTO and Antidumping and Subsidies Codes

Turkey joined the General Agreement on Tariffs and Trade (GATT)[1] with the approval on December 21, 1953[2] of the Torquay Protocol dated April 21, 1951. According to Article 1 (a) ii through Article 1 (b) of this Protocol, Turkey accepted the application of Article VI of the GATT concerning dumped and subsidized imports with a reservation, pursuant to the so-called "grandfather clause," which obligates the contracting parties to comply with Part II of the General Agreement "to the fullest extent not inconsistent with existing legislation."

However, this reservation did not cause a different application in Turkey of the principles laid down in Article VI due to the lack of a national legislation on the subject matter until 1989.

Turkey's membership in the World Trade Organization (WTO) was authorized by law no. 4067 dated January 26, 1995 approving the World Trade Organization Foundation Document, which was published in the *Official Gazette* no. 22186 dated January 29, 1995, effective December 31, 1994, while the relevant Decree no. 95/6525 dated February 3, 1995 was published in the *Official Gazette* no. 22213 dated February 25, 1995.

The rules related to the protection of imports contained in these documents apply to trade relations between Turkey and other members of WTO.

Association and Customs Union with EU

The European Economic Community (EEC) concluded an "association agreement" with Turkey by which Turkey became an "associate member" of the EEC with the treaty signed in Ankara on September 12, 1963, which came into force on December 1, 1964. The Association Agreement aiming at a customs union between the EEC and Turkey contained rules on protection against dumping during the transitional period similar to those that are contained in Article 91 of the EEC Treaty.[3]

In the relationship between the EEC and Turkey, the EEC Regulation No. 2176/84 and the Decision No. 2177/84/ECSC provided the legal basis for any protective measures taken by the Community against imports from Turkey and *vice versa*. However, these instruments had to be applied within the framework of the special rules contained in the Association Agreement.

During the transitional period, Turkey endeavored to conform its legislation to the requirements of the EEC before entering into the customs union agreement. Up to this period Turkey did not have internal laws regulating the matter of unfair competition, even though there existed previous regulations concerning trade remedies especially through adoption of the texts generated by international organizations. The new enactments created a more detailed body of legislation concerning the subject, consistent with the principles and rules being developed in the international field.

After the establishment of the European Union (EU) with the Treaty of Maastricht on February 7, 1992, the Association Council EU-Turkey adopted Decision No. 1/95 on March 6,1995 establishing the rules for the implementation of the "customs union." The special rules of Articles 31 and 32 confirm the principle of free competition while Article 38 establishes the right of Turkey to be informed of the decisions adopted by the EU in connection with Articles 85, 86, and 92 of the EU Treaty.

Turkey's current position as a customs union associate is not the same of that of full membership in the EU, i.e. Turkish national measures are still applicable during the transition period. Thus, Turkey will be in the same position as the other full members of the EU with regard to the protection against unfair trade practices only after the completion of the period of transition. At the end of the transitional period, the responsibility for application, reviewing, amending, or repealing the national trade measures will be transferred to the Commission.[4]

Turkish National Legislation

Turkey has adopted new legislation in compliance with its commitments under the WTO as well as its association with the EU. The "Statute for the Prevention of Unfair Competition in Imports" (SPUC) No. 3577 adopted on 14 June 1989,[5] the "Decree for the Prevention of Unfair Competition in Imports" (DPUC) issued by the Council of Ministers No. 89/ 14506 dated 8 September 1989[6] and the "Regulation for the Prevention of Unfair Competition in Imports" (RPUC) issued by the Undersecretariat to the Treasury and Foreign Trade[7] on September 27,1989[8] together constitute Turkey's unfair trade remedy laws.

This legislation contains parallel procedures for both dumping and subsidy practices which invites, for purposes of this chapter, a joint treatment of several provisions. Hence, we intend to examine, first, the peculiar aspects to each of these practices and then to treat the aspects that are common to both of them. In relation to dumping, we shall examine its definition, the determination of normal value and export price as well as the margin analysis and in the relation to subsidization, the concept, and calculations of a subsidy. The common aspects include the investigation procedures, price undertakings, and injury analysis.

ANTIDUMPING EVALUATION

Concept of "Dumping"

A product is considered to be dumped if its export price is lower than its normal value. Article 2.a of the SPUC defines dumping as "the entry into Turkey of a product exported from any country to Turkey at an export price which is less than the normal value of an identical or similar product."[9]

Normal Value

Determination of "normal value"

In normal circumstances

In normal circumstances, the normal value is established according to "the comparable price actually paid or payable in the ordinary course of business transactions for an identical or similar product which has been intended for consumption in the exporting country or the country of origin."[10]

Comparable representative price

In the event that, in the domestic market of the exporting country or the country of origin, no similar or identical products are sold in the ordinary course of business transactions, or such sales do not allow an appropriate comparison, then the normal value is the comparable representative price of an identical or similar product when exported to a third country.[11]

Constructed value

Constructed value may be determined by adding a reasonable profit margin on to the cost of production.[12] Therefore, the concepts of "cost of production" as well as the reasonable "profit margin" need definition in order to understand the notion of the "constructed value."

- *Cost of production:* An element to be evaluated for the calculation of the "normal value" according to Article 2 (e.3) of the SPUC is the "cost of production." According to the Regulation, the cost of production shall be computed on the basis of all costs, in the ordinary course of trade, both fixed and variable, in the country of origin, of materials and manufacture, plus a reasonable amount for selling, administrative and other general expenses.[13]
- *Profit:* As stated by the Regulation, the "profit" to be added to the production cost to obtain the normal value should not exceed the profit rates prevailing in the sale of identical or similar products in the domestic market of the country of origin.[14]

Other cases of determination of "normal value"

If a product is not directly imported from the country of origin but is imported from an intermediary country, then "the normal value shall be the comparable price actually paid or payable for an identical or similar product on the domestic market of the country of origin or the exporting country."[15]

If the product is only shipped in transit from the exporting country without being produced there or if there is no comparable price in the exporting country for that product, "the price in the country of origin may serve as the sole basis."[16]

Like (similar) product

Turkish legislation uses the term "the same (identical) or similar product" and defines the term "similar product" as "a product which is alike in all respects to the dumped or subsidized product or, if there is no such product, another product the characteristics of which are alike to the said product."[17]

Ordinary course of trade

The domestic price must be a price that is obtained in the ordinary course of trade and the sales involved are those made at arm's length in normal open market transactions.[18]

The sales shall be deemed not to have been made in the "ordinary course of trade," if it is determined that the actual sale price of an identical or similar product on the domestic market of the country of origin is below its production cost, that such product has been imported into Turkey in great quantities during the period of investigation, and that sales during the period under investigation have not been made at a price that covers all the expenses to be added to the production cost.[19]

In such event, "the normal value shall be calculated on the basis of the export price to third countries, or the price determined by adding a reasonable amount of profit margin to the production cost, or the price on the domestic market that is sufficient to meet production costs at least or the price obtained by adding a reasonable amount for profit to the amount needed to make up for the loss caused due to sales made at prices lower than the production cost."[20]

The provisions examined in the foregoing paragraphs are also applicable in cases where an association or a similar arrangement affecting prices and costs is determined to exist between the parties.[21]

Average and sampling techniques

In cases where the prices under examination vary, the normal value and export price are determined using weighted averages, sampling techniques, or other statistical methods.[22]

Nonmarket economy countries

In the case of imports from those countries which are described as countries with Nationalized Foreign Trade in the Import Regime Decision and from countries without a market economy, normal value shall be determined on the basis of one of the following criteria:[23]
(i) the price at which an identical or similar product is sold
   (a) for consumption on the domestic market of a third country where a market economy prevails, or
   (b) the export price to other countries;
(ii) the constructed price obtained by adding a reasonable profit margin onto the production cost of an identical or similar product in a third county where a market economy prevails; or
(iii) in cases where prices determined as per (a) and (b) do not constitute an appropriate basis, the price actually paid or payable for an identical or similar product in Turkey, adjusted so as to include a reasonable profit margin.

Export Price

To assess whether dumping has occurred, the normal value is compared with the export price. The "export price" is the price "actually paid or payable for a product sold for export purposes."[24]

In cases where there is no export price or where the exporter and the importer or a third party are determined to have an association of interests or a compensatory arrangement, or where the price actually paid or payable for a product for export to the country cannot be relied upon for any other reason, then "the price at which the imported product is resold to a third buyer having no relation with the exporter may be taken as the export price."[25]

If the product has not been resold or not sold with the same quality and conditions of importation to such a buyer "the export price may be calculated on any reasonable basis and in such event allowance shall be made for all costs arising between importation and resale, including customs duties and other taxes and a reasonable profit margin."[26]

In evaluations for the determination of export price, the following elements are to be taken into consideration:
(i) usual transport, insurance, handling and loading expenses, and similar additional expenses;
(ii) customs duties, antidumping duties, compensatory taxes, other taxes and additional charges payable in the importing country by reason of the importation or sale of the goods; and
(iii) overhead and reasonable profit margin and/or commissions usually paid or agreed.[27]

Comparison of Normal Value and Export Price

Certain factors are taken into consideration to enable a fair comparison of prices, provided that the same is demanded and supporting documents are presented by the parties.

These factors are physical properties, import costs and direct taxes, sale expenses such as transportation, insurance, handling and loading expenses, and additional expenses such as packaging, credit cost, warranties, guarantees and other after-sale services, which vary with the conditions of trade.[28]

"Dumping margin" means the amount by which the normal value exceeds the export price.[29]

In the comparison of the normal value and the export price, dates as close to one another as possible are to be taken into account.[30]

SUBSIDY EVALUATION

Concept of Subsidy

As subsidy is defined as "[a] direct or indirect benefit provided by a country of origin or by an exporting country to their companies in the manufacturing, production, export, or transportation of a product exported to Turkey...."[31]

Determination of Subsidy

Subsidies according to GATT list

The evaluation of which cases are to be deemed cases of subsidization and the calculation of the subsidy will take into account the Annex "Illustrative List of Export Subsidies" to the Agreement on Interpretation and Application of Articles VI, XVI, and XXIII of the GATT.[32]

Cases not constituting subsidization

Exemption from or reimbursement of customs duties or other indirect taxes applying to the import of the components incorporated in the identical or similar product that are exported from the country of origin or exporting country shall not be deemed to constitute subsidization.[33]

Determination of subsidy amount

Subsidy amount

Subsidy amount is defined in the statute as "the amount of the benefits, made available to exporters directly or indirectly by the country of origin or exporting country at the stage of manufacturing, production, exportation, and transportation of a product exported to Turkey."[34]

Determination

The amount of the subsidy shall be determined by reasonably spreading the subsidy value over an appropriate period, at the production and export stages of the product in question, if it is determined that subsidies are made available but not in accordance with the quantities manufactured, produced, exported, or transported. Normally, such period is the relevant fiscal year of the party receiving subsidies.

The amount of subsidies shall be determined after deducting normal amounts for wear and tear of such assets, if fixed assets are received, or are to be received, by way of subsidies. If nondepreciable fixed assets are in question, the subsidy shall be considered an interest-free loan.

The amount of subsidy shall be computed on the basis of the quantity and value of the imported quantity and other data, if, during a subsidy investigation, the required information is not furnished on the basis of produced, exported, or transported quantities.[35]

Determination in nonmarket economy countries

For imports from nonmarket economy countries, the amount of subsidy shall be determined pursuant to the provisions related to the determination of normal value and export price in antidumping investigations.[36] Weighted average shall be used where the amount of subsidy is variable.[37] As explained below, in the case of determination of both the dumping and subsidy, the higher rate of the antidumping duty and countervailing duty shall be applied.[38]

Deductions

The calculation of subsidy shall take account of the following deductions:
(i) any application fee or other costs incurred to benefit from the subsidy; and
(ii) export taxes, customs taxes, and similar fiscal liabilities levied on the product exported to Turkey to decrease the subsidy amount and additional financial liabilities other than the above.[39]

INJURY ANALYSIS

Concept of Injury

Dumped and/or subsidized goods are regarded as causing "injury" when they produce material damage or threaten material damage to a production sector, or give rise to market distortion or materially retard the establishment of an industry.[40]

Injury Requirement

Although the law is ambiguous on the requirement that injury be found to impose an antidumping or countervailing duty,[41] Turkish decisions consistently incorporate the injury threshold. The investigations are always terminated where no injury is found.

Concept of Industry (Production Sector)

Industry (Production Sector) shall mean all the producers of an identical or similar product in Turkey or those producers who account for a significant portion of the production of such products in Turkey.[42]

However, as an exception, if producers have business relations with exporters and importers, or are themselves the importers of the products which it is alleged are dumped and/or subsidized, industry shall mean the remaining producers.[43] The producers who are at the same time importers of dumped/subsidized products are not taken into consideration in the determination of the material injury, which is estimated in relation with the remaining producers.

Material Injury

The determination of material injury shall be based on:[44]
(i) the volume of the dumped and/or subsidized imports, including increases, either absolute or relative, in relation to production and consumption in Turkey;
(ii) the import prices of the dumped and/or subsidized products relative to the price of an identical or similar product in Turkey; and
(iii) the effects on the relevant industry of economic indicators such as output, capacity, stocks, sales, market share, prices, profits, returns on investment, cash position and employment.

In practice, the competent authority deems as a material injury the existence of the increase of stocks, the decline in prices, price pressure, the loss of market share and the decreased use of capacity.

Threat of Material Injury

The determination of a threat of material injury shall be based on:[45]
(i) the export capacity existing or that will come into being in the near future in the country of origin or exporting country, and the potential level of exports to Turkey;
(ii) the rate of increase in the dumped or subsidized exports made to Turkey;
(iii) the structural nature of dumping and/or subsidies and their potential commercial effects on the market.

There are very few cases where a threat of material injury has been alleged; in most of the cases the investigation is premised on alleged material injury.

Estimate of Injury

The distortion effect of the dumped and/or subsidized importation on the local production of an identical or similar product shall be determined on the basis of available data.[46]

If no identical or similar product can be identified, the effects of dumped and/or subsidized imports shall be evaluated by reference to the production of the nearest product group for which necessary information can be obtained.[47]

DUMPING AND SUBSIDY INVESTIGATIONS

Competent Authority

Under Article 2 of the SPUC, the authority for conducting both antidumping and countervailing duty investigations, as well as decisions to be taken, is vested in the General Directorate of Imports, which operates under the Undersecretariat of Foreign Trade and to a special committee, the Committee for Evaluation of Unfair Competition in Imports,[48] created within the structure of the General Directorate.

Dumping and Subsidy Determination Procedure

Initiation of inquiry

By petition

The filing of a petition with the Directorate General initiates an antidumping or countervailing duty investigation.

The petition must be based on sufficient evidence for an investigation to be initiated. All relevant documents are to be attached to the petition.[49] The party filing the complaint will be notified by the competent authority if evidence presented with the petition is not sufficient to begin an investigation.[50]

By government

Although the Directorate General may begin a dumping or subsidization inquiry on its own initiative, no investigation has been initiated by the Directorate General, as all inquiries having been started upon a petition from an interested party.

Initiation of investigation

Within a maximum sixty days from the beginning of the inquiry upon a complaint or by the initiative of the Directorate General, the Committee shall decide on whether to open an investigation.[51]

The matter shall be pursued no further and those concerned shall be notified to this effect, if, at the end of the inquiry, the decision is against the initiation of an investigation.

If the decision is to start an investigation, such decision shall be published in the *Official Gazette* and the pertinent questionnaires shall be sent to the importers and exporters of the product in question.[52]

Timing of investigation

Those concerned are required to submit to the Directorate General in writing the information asked for in the questionnaires and such other information and documents as they will deem useful for the investigation, within thirty days of the date of dispatch of the questionnaires. This may be extended by a period not exceeding fifteen days if an application is presented in due time.[53]

The final decision on a complaint related to dumped or subsidized imports shall be taken within one year of the date of commencement of the investigation. This period may be extended up to six months by the decision of the Committee.[54]

Participation

Even though the law does not explicitly enumerate them, interested parties include real and legal persons or professional associations filing the petition and importers, exporters, and producers of the allegedly dumped or subsidized goods and their professional associations, as a result of the provision concerning the persons having right to present complaints and the parties against which an investigation for dumping or subsidization may be initiated.

The parties to an investigation are allowed to participate in the investigation, first, by presenting evidence supporting their claim or defenses. During the course of the investigation, the parties may be granted, upon written request to the General Directorate, the right to examine "non-confidential information remaining outside the scope of the work being carried out in connection with the investigation".[55] Always during the investigation, the Directorate General may hear the parties separately or together upon the demand of the parties or on its own initiative.[56]

All parties involved in an investigation are allowed to be assisted by legal or financial counsel even though such a possibility is not clearly mentioned in the legislation.

Gathering and verification of information

For the purposes of verifying the information obtained during investigation or completing any missing information, inspections may be conducted of the interested parties. It is also possible for such inspections to be carried out abroad, where necessary. Depending on the subject of the investigation, information may also be obtained from related public agencies.[57]

In the event that one of the parties fails to furnish the information required, furnishes wrong information, refuses to furnish information within the time granted, or is understood to be obstructing the investigation, the decision shall be taken on the basis of the information available.[58]

With regard to the prices to be examined in relation with a dumping or subsidy investigation, Turkish legislation does not refer to any specific period. Therefore, the competent authority has substantial discretion in defining the period of investigation.

Access to information developed in proceedings

Nonconfidential information

Parties may be granted the right to examine nonconfidential information remaining outside the scope of the work carried out in connection with the investigation, provided that they apply to the Directorate General in writing. Because there is not definition of information carried out in connection with the investigation," it is not clear what nonconfidential information is available.

Confidential information

Although confidential information submitted in antidumping or countervailing duty investigation is not to be disclosed to other parties, the party requesting confidentiality must state the reasons for such request and provide a nonconfidential summary of the information be furnished or, when a summary is not provided, provide a document explaining the reasons therefore "with the purpose of achieving transparency and protecting the mutual interests of the parties vis-à-vis one another to the maximum extent possible in the investigation."[59]

The competent authority may disregard the information if it considers that a demand for confidentiality is not justified or the party furnishing the information refuses to disclose the information in part.[60]

It is to be noted, however, that no party presenting information in these investigations has asked for confidentiality since the inception in 1989 of these provisions.

SUSPENSION OF INVESTIGATION

Acceptance of Undertaking

During an investigation, undertakings may be offered by the country of origin, the exporting country, or the exporter spontaneously,[61] or upon the proposal of the General Directorate.[62] The General Directorate may refuse an undertaking offered by the exporting country or the exporter if it deems that price undertaking is unacceptable due to the high number of actual or potential exporters or for other reasons.[63]

The Committee may suspend the investigation, if, during the course thereof, the exporter agrees and undertakes to raise prices to a level that would eliminate the injury or eliminate the dumping margin and/or subsidy amount, or states and undertakes that it will comply with a quantitative restriction on its exports, or if it is determined that the harmful effect of the dumped or subsidized imported goods ceases to exist.[64]

The acceptance of undertakings shall not always imply the end of an investigation. The investigation may be completed upon the request of the exporter, the exporting country or country of origin or by decision of the Committee.[65]

Undertakings shall be valid until the dumping and/or subsidization has come to an end.[66]

Compliance with Undertaking

The Directorate General may seek information from the exporter, or the country of origin or the exporting country, to determine if the undertaking is being complied with and may verify such information. Failure of the exporting country, or country of origin or exporter to furnish information or comply with a request to examine such information shall be deemed noncompliance with the undertaking.[67]

If it is determined that an undertaking has not been complied with, the Committee may take provisional measures on the basis of available information.[68]

ANTIDUMPING AND COUNTERVAILING MEASURES AND DUTIES

In conformity with the traditionally accepted principles, the protective measures and duties in this area are remedial, rather than punitive. It is because of this concept that the legislation provides that the amount of the measure or duty be limited to an amount less than the full margin of dumping, or the total amount of the subsidy, if the lesser amount would be sufficient to remove the injury caused to the domestic market by the dumped and subsidized imports.[69]

Evidence of dumping or subsidization and injury are to be considered simultaneously during the investigation, which must be terminated on a finding of no injury.

Although the statute does not specify that an injury finding is a prerequisite to the imposition of duties, Turkish investigations have consistently treated the injury finding as a prerequisite to the imposition of an antidumping or countervailing duty.

Provisional Measures

Adoption of provisional measures

If it is determined, during the investigation, that circumstances justify the adoption of provisional measures, a security deposit must be made in an amount equal to the dumping margin or subsidy amount, or sufficient to compensate the injury. This decision is to be published in the *Official Gazette*.[70]

Timing

The period of validity of provisional measures is four months. This period may be extended for two months when deemed necessary by the Ministry.[71]

Conversion of provisional measures

Any provisional measures taken during the investigation shall become definitive "if it is determined, at the end of an investigation, that a definitive measure should be taken."[72] Definitive measures may be different from provisional measures.

Definitive Measures: Duties

Adoption of definitive measures

If definitive measures are decided upon, the decision shall be published in the *Official Gazette*.[73]

Nature of antidumping and countervailing duties

The Decree imposing antidumping or countervailing duty must specify the exporters of the goods and the country of origin or exportation. In cases where several exporters of a single country are involved and it is impossible to determine all of them, provisional and definitive measures may be imposed on all imports of the product that is under investigation from that country.

Incompatibility of duties
Antidumping and countervailing duties may not be applied simultaneously in cases where there are both dumping and subsidy claims for the same or similar product. In such cases, only the duty with the higher rate shall be applied.[74]

Duration of duties
There is no maximum period for the validity of duties. Definitive measures taken against dumped and/or subsidized imports remain in effect for such time as will be sufficient to eliminate the effects of the losses caused by such imports.[75]

Retroactivity of duties
The period of retroactive application may not exceed ninety days from the date upon which provisional measures are taken;[76] the Council of Ministers has discretion to decide appropriate cases for retroactive application of provisional duties.

The circumstances calling for retroactive antidumping duty
The circumstances calling for the retroactive application of an antidumping duty are as follows:
(i) cases where the imports causing injury have also been made in the past and the importer is aware of, or should have known, that the exporter is engaged in dumping and that this practice leads to injury; and
(ii) cases where dumped goods are imported in such quantities as to cause injury are made over a short period of time and it becomes necessary for the antidumping duty to be applied retroactively to prevent recurrence of such injury.[77]

Circumstances calling for retroactive countervailing duty
Circumstances calling for the retroactive application of a countervailing duty are as follows:
(i) cases where imports have benefited from export subsidies provided in violation of the provisions of the Agreement concerning the Interpretation and Application of Articles VI, XVI, and XXIII of GATT, cause injury that is difficult to remedy and it becomes necessary for the countervailing duty to be applied retroactively to prevent a recur-

rence of such injury; and
(ii) cases in which there is a breach of an undertaking regarding subsidized goods. However, such retroactive application may not be earlier than the date of breach of the undertaking.[78]

Procedures for review and revocation

Decisions relating to definitive measures may be reviewed, either upon the demand of one of those concerned or automatically, no earlier than one year after the completion of the investigation. In such an event, new evidence to justify such review must be submitted to the Directorate General.[79]

The reopening of an investigation shall not prejudice the enforcement of measures previously taken that are in effect.[80]

Duty liability

The liability to pay antidumping duty or countervailing duty belongs to real or legal persons importing the dumped or subsidized products.[81]

Collection agency

The Customs Administration is empowered to collect antidumping duty or countervailing duty imposed by the competent authority, separately from other tariffs on imports.[82]

Release and refund

If the definitive antidumping or the countervailing duty is higher than the amount of security taken previously, the difference shall not be collected, while if it is lower than the security, the difference shall be refunded.[83]

If, as a result of the investigation, dumping and/or a subsidy is found not to exist, then the provisional measures shall be revoked and the security refunded.[84]

The antidumping or countervailing duty already collected in relation with the products destined to be returned or destroyed on grounds of noncompliance with the terms of the purchase agreement shall be refunded.[85]

OTHER TRADE REMEDIES

Supervision and Protection Measures

Turkish legislation contains a series of other trade remedies, apart from antidumping and countervailing provisions, in the form supervision and protection measures concerning importations.

The government has the authority to impose supervision or protection measures, including tariffs or quotas, against products whose importation may cause injury or threaten serious injury to the domestic producers, or against products of the countries that discriminate against Turkish exports.

A series of decrees and regulations, including the Decree for Supervision and Protection Measures and the Quota and Tariff Management, the Decree for the Protection of the Trade Rights of Turkey and the Regulation on Supervision and Protection of Imports, which created a system of supervision and protection for unfair trade practices, has been adopted on the basis of the WTO agreements as well as the Treaties signed for the association of Turkey with EU.

Commencement of inquiry

According to the Regulation on Supervision and Protection Measures of Imports,[86] issued pursuant to the Decree for Supervision and Protection Measures and the Quota and Tariff Management,[87] all concerned real and legal persons, or their professional associations, may request the General Directorate to conduct an inquiry as to whether any product is being imported in such increased quantities and under such conditions as to cause or threaten serious injury to domestic producers of like or directly competitive products. The Directorate may also initiate an inquiry on its initiative.

Investigation

The results of the inquiry are presented to the Committee of Evaluation of Supervision and Protection Measures in Imports, which decides whether to initiate an investigation or not. If an investigation is initiated, it must be completed by the General Directorate within nine months. This period may be extended by up to two months.

Supervision or protection measures

After the completion of the investigation, the results are presented by the Directorate to the Committee, which decides whether a supervision or protection measure is to be applied. In both cases the decisions are published in the *Official Gazette*. The decision to apply a supervision or protection measure is subject to the approval of the Minister before publication.

Supervision measures

Supervision measures can be applied retrospectively and prospectively. The aim of the prospective supervision is to closely follow the trends in the importation of a product. In the case of a supervised product, importation is accompanied by the submission of the "supervision document" which is obtained from the Undersecretariat. The "supervision document" is valid during the period that the supervision measures are valid unless otherwise specified. Supervision measures are provisional and loose their validity automatically at the end of one year, unless decided otherwise by the Committee.

Protection measures

Protection measures include limitations on the validity period of the "supervision document" or requiring of importation of the product under "import license" or "permit," which is tantamount to the quota.

The protection measures are applied for the period that is sufficient to prevent or remove the serious injury and permit adjustment by the local industry. This period can not exceed four years, including the duration of the provisional measures. It may be extended after a new investigation, but may not, in any case, exceed ten years.

Retaliatory authority

The Committee for Evaluation of Turkey's Commercial Rights is authorized to take commercial measures to remove foreign obstacles to Turkish trade.[88] Commercial measures may be applied after an inquiry and they may not be in conflict with Turkey's international obligations and procedures. Authorized measures include suspension or withdrawal of the concessions given through commercial negotiations and adoption of any measure that limits the importation of products from the offending country or countries.

References

1. General Agreement on Tariffs and Trade, October 30, 1947, 61 Stat. A-11, T.I.A.S. 1700, 55 U. N.T.S. 194 [hereinafter "GATT"].
2. Accession of Turkey, Law No. 6202, December 20, 1953 (entered into force with the publication in the *Official Gazette*, December 31, 1953, No. 8597).
3. J.F. Beseler - A.N. Williams, *Anti-Dumping and Anti-Subsidy Law - The European Communities*, 34 (1986).
4. *Id.* at 36.
5. *Official Gazette*, No. 20212 (July 11, 1989).
6. *Official Gazette*, No. 20295 (September 27, 1989).
7. This Undersecretariat was later divided into two departments: the Undersecretariat to the Treasury and the Undersecretariat to Foreign Trade.

8. *Official Gazette*, No. 20295 (September 27, 1989) (amended November 5, 1992).
9. The same concept is repeated in Article 14 of *Ithalatta Haksiz Rekabetin Önlenmesi Hakkinda Yönetmelik (RPUC)*.
10. *Ithalatta Haksiz Rekabetin Önlenmesi Hakkinda Kanun* (SPUC), art. 2.e.1, and RPUC, art. 15, para. 1.
11. SPUC, art. 2.e.2, and RPUC, art. 15, para. 2.
12. SPUC, art. 2.e.3, and RPUC, art. 15, para. 3.
13. RPUC, art. 16.
14. SPUC, art. 2.e.3 and RPUC, art. 16, para. 1.
15. RPUC, art. 19, para. 1.
16. RPUC, art. 19, para. 2.
17. SPUC, art. 2, para. d. This definition is inspired by Commission Decision No. 2177/84/ECSC of July 27, 1984, On Protection against Dumped or Subsidized Imports from Countries not Members of the European Coal and Steel Community, Article 2.F which states: "'like product' means a product which is identical, *i.e.*, alike in all respects to the product under consideration, or in the absence of such a product, another product, which has the characteristics closely resembling those of the product under consideration."
18. Beseler-Williams, *supra*, n.3 at 54.
19. RPUC, art. 17, para. 1.
20. RPUC, art. 17, para. 2.
21. RPUC, art. 17, para. 3.
22. RPUC, art. 23.
23. RPUC, art. 18.
24. SPUC, art. 2 (c); RPUC, art. 24, para. 1.
25. RPUC, art. 20, para. 2.
26. RPUC, art. 20, para. 3-4.
27. RPUC, art. 21.
28. RPUC, art. 22, para. 2.
29. SPUC, art. 2.g.
30. RPUC, art. 22, para. 1.
31. SPUC, art. 2 (b) and RPUC, art. 24, para. 1.
32. RPUC, art. 24, para. 2.
33. RPUC, art. 24, para. 3.
34. SPUC, art. 2.h; RPUC, art. 24, para. 1.
35. RPUC, art. 25, para. 1-3.
36. RPUC, art. 25, para. 4.
37. RPUC, art. 25, para. 5.
38. SPUC, art. 13, para. 3.
39. RPUC, art. 26.
40. SPUC, art. 2.i; RPUC, art. 27, para. 1.
41. SPUC, art. 2.a and 2.b; RPUC, art. 14 and 24; *see also* SPUC, art. 4, 13 and RPUC, art. 10.
42. RPUC, art. 27, para. 2.

43. RPUC, art. 27, para. 3.
44. RPUC, art. 28.
45. RPUC, art. 29.
46. RPUC, art. 30, para. 1.
47. RPUC, art. 30, para. 2.
48. The Committee is chaired by the General Director of Imports or one of his deputies and includes the relevant Department Head of the General Directorate and one authorized representative each from the Ministry of Finance and Customs, the Ministry of Agriculture, Forestry and Rural Affairs, the Ministry of Industry and Trade, the Undersecretariat of the State Planning Organization, the Union of the Chambers of Commerce, Industry, Maritime Commerce and Product Exchanges and the Union of the Agricultural Chambers of Turkey.
49. *See* RPUC, art. 3, and the form attached thereto as Annex-A.
50. RPUC, art. 3, para. 2.
51. RPUC, art. 5, *as amended* on November 5, 1992.
52. RPUC, art. 5, *as amended* on November 5, 1992, includes in Appendix-2 the inquiry form to be sent to the importers, and in Appendix-3, the inquiry form to be sent to the exporters.
53. RPUC, art. 5, para. 3.
54. RPUC, art. 11. The result of the investigation is to be published in the *Official Gazette*.
55. RPUC, art. 9.
56. RPUC, art. 8.
57. RPUC, art. 6, para. 1.
58. RPUC, art. 6, para. 2.
59. RPUC, art. 7, para. 2.
60. RPUC, art. 7, para. 3.
61. SPUC art. 11; RPUC, art. 12, para. 1.
62. RPUC, art. 12, para. 3. Neither the exporter, the country of origin, or the exporting country is obliged to accept such a proposal.
63. RPUC, art. 12, para. 2.
64. SPUC, art. 11. *See also* RPUC, art. 12, para. 1.
65. RPUC, art. 10, para. 2.
66. RPUC, art. 12, para. 4.
67. RPUC, art. 13, para. 1.
68. RPUC, art. 13, para. 2.
69. SPUC, art. 7, para. 1 and art. 12, para. 1.
70. SPUC, art. 12, para. 1-2.
71. SPUC, art. 12, para. 3.
72. *Ithalatta Haksiz Rekabetin Önlenmesi Hakkinda Karar* (DPUC), art. 4, para. 1.
73. DPUC, art. 5, para. 1.
74. SPUC, art. 13, para. 3.
75. DPUC, art. 5, para. 2.
76. SPUC, art. 7, para. 2; DPUC, art. 2, last para.

77. DPUC, art. 2, para. a.
78. DPUC, art. 2, para. b.
79. DPUC, art. 6, para. 1.
80. DPUC, art. 6, para. 2.
81. SPUC, art. 8.
82. SPUC, art. 9.
83. SPUC, art. 14, para. 1.
84. SPUC, art. 14, para. 2.
85. SPUC, art. 14, para. 3.
86. Regulation No. 95/6814, *Official Gazette*, No. 22300 (June 1, 1995).
87. Decree No. 95/6814, *Official Gazette*, No. 22300 (June 1, 1995).
88. Decree for the Protection of Turkey's Commercial Rights, No. 95/7608 (Dec. 20, 1995).

Uruguay

Daniel M. Ferrere
Estudio Ferrere Lamaison
Montevideo, Uruguay

HISTORY AND OVERVIEW

Uruguay is one of the original signatories of the 1947 GATT Agreement, and at the beginning of the GATT system, the country placed high hopes in the operation of its rules on subsidies. Because Uruguay is a producer of basic agricultural goods, it had the expectation that the GATT Agreement would eventually produce a gradual and progressive elimination of agricultural subsidies.

The subsequent evolution of trade policies around the world, and in particular the inclusion of the provision allowing the sale of subsidized agricultural surpluses resulting from the establishment of minimum internal prices for agricultural commodities as an exception to the application of Article VI of the GATT, led the country to a general disillusionment with the effectiveness of the GATT 1947 Agreement as an effective tool for establishing a reasonably fair system of trade policies. In fact, Uruguay only participated diligently in the Annecy and Torquay rounds, and, after that, it withdrew to observer status until the start of the Uruguay Round in 1986.

Three elements defined the conceptual conflict between Uruguay and the essential rules of the GATT.

First, the belief that the GATT system as a whole was unfair to developing countries was strengthened by what was later called the "Uruguayan Recourse to Article XXIII." In the early sixties Uruguay initiated a procedure under the GATT claiming that eight major developed countries consistently applied trade practices contrary to GATT provisions that injured Uruguay, and asked for an investigation under Article XXIII. The investigation concluded with a finding indicating that six of these countries were effectively violating the Agreement in relation to Uruguayan exports, and made recommendations directed at the elimination of such practices.

Two years later Uruguay informed the Contracting Parties that only one of the eight countries—Sweden—had modified those of its practices contrary to the Agreement, and asked for a "declaration" by the GATT members stating that the remaining countries continued to violate the Agreement. The committee appointed to analyze the situation stated that the Agreement did not foresee the making of "declarations" of this type, but indicated its willingness to consider a request by Uruguay for the application of retaliatory measures under Article XXIII. Faced with the prospect of a trade war against five of the major developed countries of the world, Uruguay considered it prudent to drop the issue.

A second relevant element that led Uruguay to the virtual abandonment of any adherence to the GATT rules was the widespread adoption by Latin American countries in the late sixties, of the "developmentalist" theories of the Argentine economist Raúl Prebisch, by then in charge of the Economic Commission for Latin America of the United Nations, and later ideologist of the United Nations Conferences on Trade and Development. Under Prebisch's ideas, subsidies were a perfectly reasonable instrument to be used by developing countries in their effort to offset the long-term deterioration of the terms of their trade with developed market economies.

Finally, the policy of import substitution that the country had applied since early in the century made antidumping rules virtually unnecessary. If a product was produced locally, competitive imports were either totally forbidden or taxed at rates of as much as 450 percent. Antidumping duties became clearly irrelevant in this context, and Uruguay did not even consider the possibility of adhering to the GATT antidumping code.

The situation was different however, with respect to subsidies. In 1964 (Act 13.268, passed in July, 1964) Uruguay adopted a system of undisguised subsidies applicable to virtually all its exports, with the sole exception of agricultural products, that could go up to 50 percent of the CIF value of the exported goods when they were shipped and insured by local companies. These subsidies produced a drastic increase in exports, but at a very significant cost for the government of the time, and also at the expense of successive conflicts with the United States, which repeatedly applied countervailing duties to Uruguayan leather and textile products in the late eighties and early nineties.

The conflicts with the United States did not affect the decision of the government to maintain these subsidies. In fact, in 1979 a statute (Decree Law 14.868) was passed allowing the creation of a "tax on products subject to countervailing duties" whose only purpose was to offset the effect of the subsidies exclusively in the country applying those duties, while maintaining them in force for all other destinations. Under this system, every time the United States applied or seriously threatened to apply countervailing duties to a Uruguayan product, Uruguay would impose a tax on that product at a rate equal to the rate of the subsidy, thus eliminating the risk of a countervailing duty in the United States.

What countervailing duties did not do, budgetary problems finally did, and by the early eighties, the government was already facing severe deficits that would eventually lead to a major crisis in 1982. The GATT Subsidies Code was seen by the government at that time as an instrument to persuade local exporters of the need to eliminate the existing subsidies. The elimination of subsidies was justified s an unavoidable consequence of the approval of the GATT Subsidies Code. The adoption of that Code was, in turn, justified as the only feasible way to maintain the existing subsidies during a "phaseout" period agreed to with other member countries under Section V.6. of the Agreement on the Interpretation of Articles VI, XVI, and XXIII (the Agreement), which provided that developed countries would not apply countervailing duties against subsidies applied by developing countries that were complying with a commitment to progressively eliminate those subsidies.

Uruguay ratified the Subsidies Code by act of Parliament in 1980, and the Minister of Economy undertook to eliminate, pursuant to the Agreement, all subsidies in force by January 1, 1983. The same act also adopted the rules of the GATT on dumping, and one year later (on February 25, 1981) Decree 86/81 established a detailed procedure for conducting antidumping or countervailing duty investigations.

As in the case of subsidies, however, the reasons for adopting these rules had more to do with internal politics than with substantive issues. By that time the government started dismantling the system of tariff protection that had made virtually impossible any competition between imported and locally manufactured products. In fact, by the time of the approval of this statute, the maximum tariff had been reduced from 375 percent to a mere 103 percent, producing a shock in certain traditionally-protected sectors that claimed that this policy would turn them into an easy prey for foreign exporters.

The passage of an act on subsidies and dumping was, in this context, not the result of a long-term economic policy, but a short-term response to the opposition of local producers against tariff reductions. When it became evident that local producers were not going to be appeased by these measures, however, the attention of the government drifted somewhere else and the act and its system were forgotten for more than a decade.

During 1984 and 1985, a succession of meetings between developed and developing countries took place, generating for the first time in developing countries the hope that a change in trade policy rules could eventually occur. The prospect of effectively including the treatment of agricultural subsidies in the GATT discussions made all the difference for Uruguay, which again became a bona fide participant in the meetings of the Contracting Parties. Uruguay adopted by law the WTO Agreement, its Annexes, and all the components of the Declaration of Marrakech on December 13, 1994, by Act of Parliament No. 16.671.

By this time, however, Uruguay had become a member of the MERCOSUR Agreement with Brazil, Argentina, and Paraguay, which has its own agenda and problems with respect to subsidies. The adoption of the Annexes to the WTO Agreement, therefore, led the current government to approve a detailed Decree (Decree 142/96, dated April 24, 1996) enacting the rules of the Antidumping Code, while it simultaneously avoided any provision related to subsidies. The previous rules on subsidies were not repealed, but absence of any subsidy provision in the Decree evidences the problems related to the treatment of subsidies amongst MERCOSUR countries, which are discussed below.

LISTING OF TRADE REMEDIES

Following is a list of Uruguayan trade remedies:

Statute	Purpose	Authority of Application
Decree-Law 15.025	Turns into domestic law the principles of Article VI of the GATT	Executive Power, Ministry of Economy
Decree 86/81	Regulates the procedure for countervailing duty investigations under Decree-Law 15.025	Executive Power, Ministry of Economy
Decree 315/93	Provides for the application of alternative measures against unfair trade practices	Executive Power, Ministry of Economy
Decree 142/96	Regulates the investigation of dumping	Executive Power, Ministry of Agriculture (OPYPA) and Ministry of Industry (DNI)

ANTIDUMPING INVESTIGATIONS

Dumping Determination

Initiation of investigation

No antidumping investigations have ever been initiated in Uruguay. Pursuant to Decree 142/96, investigations are to be initiated by written request directed to the Agriculture Department's Office of Programming and Policy (OPYPA) or the Ministry of Energy, Industry, and Mining's National Industrial Administration (DNI), depending on the type of product involved.

The petition must identify, inter alia, the product claimed to be dumped, its country or countries of origin or exportation, known exporters and importers, price information, the volume and value of national production of similar products, and the claimed effect of the imported goods on the local production. In exceptional circumstances with sufficient evidence of dumping and resulting damage, the petition process may be dispensed with, and the Government may self-initiate the investigation.

Timetable

The government is required to make an initial determination of whether the complaint is in proper form within twenty days of its receipt. It may request additional information, however, in which case the time for its assessment may be extended an additional twenty days. Assuming that the complaint contains the required information and preliminary verification of the facts alleged, the authority will, within an additional thirty days, conduct a preliminary review the available evidence and provide its recommendation concerning the opening of an investigation to an Advisory Commission composed of representatives from the Ministry of Economy and Finances, Ministry of Foreign Relations, Ministry of Agriculture, Ministry of Industry, Energy, and Mining, and Executive Office of Budget and Planning

The Advisory Commission then decides within another thirty days whether a formal investigation will be initiated, or the petition will be rejected. A decision of the commission to open a formal investigation is published in the Official Registry. Interested parties are given twenty days from the date of publication to be recognized as such and have the right to participate in the proceeding.

Prior to making a decision as to the existence of dumping, injury, and causal relation, the authority is required to call a hearing on the essential facts to be included in its statement. Interested parties are given a period of fifteen days to present final allegations. The investigation phase of the proceeding is then considered terminated. The authority then has an additional thirty days to make its finding. The investigation should be concluded within one year. In exceptional cases the term may be extended to eighteen months.

Participation of parties and their counsel

The party requesting the investigation must file copies of its petition, or a nonconfidential summary thereof to be distributed to interested parties, including authorities of the exporting country, within five days of the initiation of the investigation. Interested parties may be requested by the Advisory Commission to provide relevant information in response to written questionnaires, and may submit any other information which they deem important.

During the course of the investigation, all interested parties are to be given the opportunity to defend their interests in writing or at a meeting of the Commission. Interested parties shall be given thirty days prior notice of any hearings and the subjects to be considered in such hearings. Attendance is not required, but those who wish to make presentations must present written text of their proposed comments at least ten days prior to any hearing, and must identify any legal counsel who will be present at least five days prior to the hearing.

Access to information developed in proceedings

Confidential information may be provided to the Commission and will be treated as such at the request of the provider if it is previously established that such treatment is justified. No precedent exists on this matter, but confidential information is not to be disclosed to the legal counsel to the other interested parties.

Definitions

"Like product" means an identical product, or one that is equivalent in all aspects, or if such product does not exist, a product with characteristics very similar to the original.

"Domestic industry" is the total number of local producers of like products, or those producers whose combined production constitutes a significant proportion of the total domestic industry. In the event that a local producer is the importer or connected to the importer of a subject product, "domestic industry" may be defined as the remaining local producers of like products.

Calculation of dumping margins

The "export price" is defined as the price actually paid or to be paid for a product exported to Uruguay, net of taxes, discounts, and deductions actually given and directly related to the sale.

The "normal value" of an item is considered to be the comparable price of a like product for local consumption in the normal course of trade in the exporting country.

Adjustments in comparisons of export price and normal value will be made on a case-by-case basis for differences in conditions of sales, taxation, quantities, level of trade, and other factors reasonably shown to influence the comparability of prices.

Currency conversion, when necessary, is normally conducted as of the date of the sale, which is generally established as the date of the purchase order or contract.

In the case of products exported from a country with a nonmarket economy, normal value is calculated on the basis of the actual price at which like products produced in a selected market economy country are sold for domestic consumption or to other countries, including Uruguay. If this is not possible, any other reasonable basis may be used, including the actual price paid for like products in the Uruguayan market, with appropriate adjustments.

Treatment of sales through related parties

When the export price cannot be reliably measured in the normal way due to a relationship or compensatory agreement between the parties involved, the export price may be determined on the basis of the price of the first resale of the goods imported to an independent purchaser, or if there is no such resale, on any reasonable basis.

Price undertakings and other agreements to suspend investigations

By joint resolution of the Ministries represented on the Advisory Commission, investigations may be terminated or suspended based on voluntary agreement of the exporter to revise its prices to end dumping and the injury to the domestic industry.

Effect of Antidumping Order

Normally, antidumping orders are effective only as of the date of the order. Orders may be made retroactive for a maximum period of ninety days prior thereto. An antidumping order shall only remain in effect during the time and in the form necessary to neutralize the harmful effects of the dumping. The maximum duration of an order is generally five years. This period may be extended in certain cases. The amount of the antidumping order may not exceed the dumping margin.

COUNTERVAILING DUTY INVESTIGATIONS

Subsidy Determination

Initiation of investigation

Only one investigation was started under Decree-Law 15.025. This investigation had barely started when the Decree 5/983 was approved, and the government and the party that had requested the investigation agreed on dropping the investigation under Law 15.025 and to impose "variable levies" under Decree 3/83 instead.

Decree-Law 15.025 grants investigative power of subsidies to Ministry of Economy and Finances. Investigations may be initiated on the petition of an interested private party or on the initiative of the Ministry.

Timetable

The Ministry of Economy makes a preliminary evaluation of the complaint within forty-five days of its presentation. A decision in favor of opening an investigation is published in the Official Registry and communicated directly to the parties involved. The initial investigation period is twenty-one days, with ten additional days to respond to the Ministry's questions in person. The Ministry then has a further ten days to take action. If no action is taken during this time, the petition is considered dismissed. These time limits are, however, only indicative, because no consequences are attached to their violation.

Participation of parties and their counsel

Parties must respond in person at the hearing conducted by the Ministry of Economy and Finances. The Ministry may require production of evidence or the posting of bonds or provision of guarantees to allow for the continuation of imports during the proceedings. Parties may be represented by counsel, provided the Ministry is notified of such representation at least five days prior to the hearing.

Access to information developed in proceedings

Confidential information provided by a party in the course of an investigation will be treated as such with respect to third parties. If such information is relevant to the decision, however, it must be made available to counsel of the other interested parties.

Undertakings which suspend investigation

The Ministry of Economy and Finances may suspend any investigation on agreement with the exporter to revise its prices so as to eliminate any injury.

Effect of Countervailing Duty Order

Orders may have retroactive effect for up to ninety days if the subsidies are found to be severe, or if there are other circumstances that justify a harsher treatment of such imports. Orders may not be for amounts greater than the calculated dumping margin. A provisional antisubsidy order may be imposed for four months. Fines of up to five times the price of the merchandise are allowed if it is determined that goods were imported with false declarations aimed at avoiding antidumping or countervailing duty laws.

OTHER TRADE REMEDIES

Variable Levies not Depending on Injury Analysis

In 1983, Uruguay was deeply affected by the payments crisis of the eighties, and by then most local exporters and industrialists were either in technical bankruptcy or very close to it. Under these circumstances, the government decided to "make antidumping legislation more effective," a phrase repeated in the initial paragraph of Decree 5/983.

This Decree assumed that proving dumping by some producers, and particularly providing evidence of subsidies by some countries, was a task that exceeded the capabilities of local businessmen, and that accordingly the government should be allowed to act on the basis of belief in the existence of unfair trade practices, even if hard evidence of such practices was not available.

This system was favored by businessmen not only because it reduced the burden of proof, but also because it did not include any requirement related to the injury to a domestic producer. Both exporters and importers were able to use the decree to their benefit, the former against their foreign competitors, and the latter against their local competitors importing from other sources. The government, for its part, also liked the system because its application was not mandatory, and, accordingly, it could not be pushed into applying countervailing duties against a friendly country, or against a country that was simultaneously tolerating Uruguayan subsidies on other products.

Under Decree 5/983, investigations could be initiated at the request of an interested party, or directly by the government. The government was not required to investigate claims by private parties, and was not obliged to explain the reasons for not following, or for abandoning, an investigation. Investigations were conducted by the Ministry of Economy, although an Advisory Committee in which other Ministries, the Central Bank and the state-owned bank that at that time controlled imports, had permanent representation. The parties interested in the importation into Uruguay of the products under investigation had no formal right to participate in the procedure, and the fact of the initiation of an investigation was not required to be made public.

The investigation did not require any evidence of injury to local industry, nor any substantive evidence of actual dumping or subsidy. Unfair trade practices could be found on the basis of a comparison of the actual import prices with the prices of similar or identical products in the market of the exporter, or of third countries or, particularly, by comparison with "export prices of other countries that normally export the product (investigated)..." (Art. 3.D. of the Decree 5/983).

Decisions were adopted directly by the Executive Power through the determination of a "minimum export price" against which all FOB imports were compared. If the product for which a minimum export price existed was imported into Uruguay at a lower FOB price, it became automatically subject to a variable levy whose amount was equal to the differential between the minimum export price and the actual FOB price. The variable levy was also included in the basis for calculating the customs duties and the value added tax applicable upon importation. This was the only system applied in Uruguay against real or presumed unfair trade practices following its creation in 1983, until its first significant change in 1990.

By 1990, the system created by Decree 5/983 had lost any connection to its original purpose of offsetting unfair trade practices, and had become a blatant nontariff barrier applied against hundreds of different products, many of which were not even produced locally. A new government, which had recently taken office, then decided to review this situation, and passed a new Decree that substantially maintained the rules of the previous Decree, but required "... elements of proof of the damage caused ... not only to the interested party but also to all the national production, if possible ..." (Art. 6.C of Decree 523/990).

The new Decree also imposed a higher burden on the party requesting the investigation, providing that the failure by such party to submit the evidence required by the Decree would result in the cancellation of the investigation, signaling the unwillingness of the government to pursue these investigations by its own means. This situation however, was a transitory one, and only lasted until a new and more complicated Decree was passed in 1993.

Variable Levies Requiring Injury Analysis

The purpose of Decree 315/993 was to establish a system of variable levies directed at offsetting unfair trade practices that would comply with the substantial criteria of the GATT, and in fact terminate with the use of variable levies as a regular protectionist tool.

The Decree accordingly strengthens the burden of proof of injury, using very explicit language to indicate that "the determination of injury shall be based on indisputable evidence . . ." (Art. 8), and that ". . . the determination of the existence of a threat of injury must be based on facts and not simply on allegations . . ." (Art. 9).

The Decree was not intended, however, to accommodate fully the GATT rules, which would deprive the Government of the possibility of applying trade remedies in cases where insufficient evidence exists, or to use these duties as disguised nontariff protection.

The Decree still allows, then, for the determination of "minimum export prices," now called "normal prices," by comparison with export prices from countries considered to be "normal exporters of the product," as opposed to the actual exporter, thus allowing the application of variable levies to prices considered abnormal, but resulting from market events and not from dumping or subsidies.

Additionally, the Decree allows for the possibility of discarding the declared import price altogether, when ". . . the competent authorities consider that there exists an association or an offsetting agreement between the exporter and the importer or a third party, or if, for other reasons, the price paid or to be paid may not be treated as a valid reference . . ."

This provision clearly refers to situations in which, taking advantage of the freedom of international payments now available in Uruguay, the importer could decide to declare and pay to an associated exporter an import price higher than the real one, to avoid the variable levies, and later receive back the difference, or apply it to future purchases of unregulated imports.

On the basis of this rule, paper imports from Brazil have been subject to variable levies based on an assumed price, irrespective of the FOB price declared by the exporter and importer. Application of this rule to other imports has, however, been resisted by the Government.

Legality of These Decrees

The legality of the Decree 5/983 was never disputed, not only because it was approved by a military dictatorship, but also, after the return to democracy, because virtually all affected domestic parties had something to gain by its application. The authority of the Government to disregard actual import prices under Decree 315/93 however, was disputed by the importers of Brazilian paper, and the dispute is currently pending in the Court of Administrative Claims, a high level court similar to the French Conseil d'Etat.

It is not clear that these rules are consistent with Article VI of the GATT, or with Uruguayan Law 15.025 that, as previously noted, mirrors the provisions of GATT Article VI.

These Decrees have exactly the same declared purpose as the GATT rules on subsidies and countervailing duties, follow substantially the same procedures, provide for similar remedies by applying duties directed at offsetting the price differential resulting from the dumping or subsidy, and allow for provisional measures subject to confirmation. In general, these Decrees are similar in all aspects to antidumping and countervailing duty investigations under GATT rules, except for the criteria used to determine the actual existence the dumping or subsidy, which are less rigorous than the GATT.

MERCOSUR RULES

The MERCOSUR common market agreement between Argentina, Brazil, Paraguay, and Uruguay became effective in 1991, and since then the member countries have devoted significant attention to unfair trade practices.

All the member countries of MERCOSUR have in effect measures that would qualify as subsidies under GATT rules, and laws that provide for the application of countervailing rules against such practices by others. If the MERCOSUR Countries were to apply these laws to each other, then, the matter would lead very rapidly to a major crisis. To avoid this, the members have implicitly decided not to apply countervailing duties against each other at least for some time.

Brazil is opposed to dealing with MERCOSUR member subsidies by leaving them to private parties to resolve. Brazilian negotiators have taken the position that these situations should be negotiated amongst Governments, and solved through agreements amongst Governments, not through the mechanical application of any law.

In 1992, the Council of the Common Market (the highest multilateral governing body of the MERCOSUR, composed by the Ministers in charge of international trade of the member Countries) established a procedure for complaints about unfair trade practices during the transition period that ended in 1995 leading to the formation of the common market. In 1993, the Council approved a proposal for a common regulation addressing dumping or subsidies by third parties not members of the MERCOSUR. In 1994 the Council approved a Decision (Nr. 10/1994) which provides that the parties shall not grant any export incentive not compatible with the provisions of the GATT. Finally, in 1995 the Commission on Trade of MERCOSUR (the multilateral group in charge of overseeing the application of trade rules and negotiating trade disputes) approved a new procedure for the exchange of information about dumping investigations; and the Council of the Common Market approved a "Program of Action" through the year 2000 that states that the approval of a code on dumping and subsidies applicable to parties not members of the MERCOSUR, is a priority for the group.

In this context, Uruguay has systematically resisted applying countervailing duties against MERCOSUR countries, and has always been able to find a way to appease the affected producers without applying countervailing duties, through what has become known as the policy of "tariffication" of responses against unfair trade practices.

Under this policy, when the government believes that certain imports are benefiting from subsidies by other MERCOSUR countries, it increases—with the consent of the other MERCOSUR Governments—the tariff applicable to the product, up to the value needed to offset the margin of dumping or subsidy. This has been de facto accepted by Argentina and Brazil—which are clearly aware of their own subsidies—and explains the absence of investigations against other MERCOSUR countries under the Decree 381/93.

In sum, all MERCOSUR members know that they will have to eliminate subsidies of products traded amongst themselves, but they are not yet willing to do so, at least until they are sure that other MERCOSUR members will do the same. In the meanwhile, they prefer to confine conflicts to government negotiation, instead of subjecting the issue to dispute resolution contemplated by Article VI of the GATT.

Venezuela

Gonzalo Capriles
Bentata Hoet & Asociados
Caracas, Venezuela
and Jorge Castro-Bernieri, Legal Counsel
Andean Community General Secretariat
Lima, Peru[1]

HISTORY AND OVERVIEW OF TRADE REMEDY LAWS AND REGULATIONS SINCE 1947

Venezuela's Accession to the GATT/WTO.

Venezuela became a contracting party to the GATT in 1990 and is a founding member of the WTO. Venezuela did not subscribe any of the Tokyo Round codes. The Protocol for the Provisional Accession of Venezuela to the GATT does not contain any provision regarding Venezuelan adherence to the Antidumping or the Subsidies codes.

Evolution of Trade Remedy Laws and Regulations

Prior to Venezuelan accession to the GATT, trade remedies were provided mainly through the use of discretionary import licenses or prohibitions. From 1983 to 1989, when a foreign exchange control system was in place in Venezuela, the Government resorted to the denial of foreign currency for those imports that could cause injury to the national production of similar goods. Decisions 46 and 230 of the Andean Community[2] Commission, which contained some vague rules on dumping and subsidies, were never applied in Venezuela. In 1991, the Andean Community Commission approved Decision 283, which substituted Decision 230 and established clearer rules against trade distortions caused by dumping or subsidy practices. This Decision has been recognized as self-executing by the Venezuelan government.

In 1992, prompted by the reduction of trade barriers, the elimination of the foreign exchange control system, the accession to the GATT and the Uruguay Round negotiations, the Venezuelan Congress passed the Unfair International Trade Practices Act, which follows closely many provisions of both the Antidumping and the Subsidies Codes of the GATT. The regulations of this Act were approved by the President of the Republic in April 1993. In December, 1994, Venezuelan Congress passed an act approving the Marrakech Agreement, which created the WTO, and another act approving the Free Trade Treaty of the Group of Three (Mexico, Colombia, and Venezuela), hereinafter the "G-3 Treaty," which has a number of special rules for dumping and subsidies involving trade among its members.

The Act approving the Marrakech Agreement gives the Uruguay Round Antidumping Agreement and the Agreement on Subsidies and Countervailing Measures the force of law in Venezuela. As a result, in the context of investigations regarding exports from WTO member countries, the provisions of these Uruguay Round Agreements would prevail over any contrary or different provisions that may exist in previous laws, such as the Unfair International Trade Practices Act. The antidumping and countervailing duty provisions in the G-3 Treaty are only applicable to trade between Colombia and Mexico and between Venezuela and Mexico, since cases involving exclusive trade between Colombia and Venezuela fall under Andean Community regulations.

As indicated, Andean Community regulations on antidumping and countervailing measures predated the Venezuelan national law. Decision 283 preempts national Venezuelan law in cases of trade between Andean countries.[3] It also applies to certain cases involving third-country imports, namely when:

(i) such imports injure domestic production of an Andean Community Member Country to be exported to another member of that Community; or
(ii) the imports are subject to the Andean Common External Tariff and the measures to prevent injury must be taken in more than one Member Country.[4]

Although all Andean countries are WTO members, the Andean Antidumping/Countervailing Duty regulations have not been updated since conclusion of the Uruguay Round.

Summary Listing of Each Trade Remedy, with Corresponding Statutory/Regulatory References and Agency Responsible for Administering Such Remedy

Antidumping and countervailing duties

The Andean Community regulations

Under Andean Community regulations, antidumping and countervailing duties investigations are conducted by the General Secretariat that serves as the community's technical body and is based in Lima, Peru. The General Secretariat concentrates all powers to decide the cases (including initiation of cases, imposition of provisional and definitive duties, and findings on the issues of unfair trade practices, material injury, and causation). All known interested parties are notified of all such decisions, which are also published in the Cartagena Agreement Official Gazette.

National legislation

The Venezuelan rules on dumping and subsidies are:
- The Act that approves the WTO.[5]
- The Act that approves the G-3 Treaty.[6]
- The Unfair International Trade Practices Act.[7]
- The Regulations of the Unfair International Trade Practices Act.[8]

The five-member Antidumping and Subsidies Commission (*Comisión Antidumping y sobre Subsidios*—CASS) concentrates authority to initiate, conduct, suspend, and terminate investigations; to make determinations on unfair trade practices; to impose antidumping or countervailing duties; and to accept or reject settlements. Under this concentrated system, CASS determines the existence of unfair trade practices, as well as the injury to domestic industries and causation.[9]

Other trade remedies

Subsidies

Countermeasures contemplated in the WTO agreement on this matter, other than countervailing duties (i.e., those prohibited or actionable subsidies which can be challenged in the WTO) are authorized, upon request, by the Ministry for Industry and Commerce. If countermeasures are authorized, the competent body for the establishment of same would depend on their nature.

Safeguards

The General Secretariat of the Andean Community can authorize member countries to adopt safeguard measures to intraregional trade for balance of payment reasons, for import surges, and for monetary devaluations.[10]

Under the G-3 Treaty, its parties may apply bilateral safeguards for import surges due to the tariff reduction program established in that Treaty, and may also extend to parties global safeguards pursuant to the GATT.[11]

Measures for national security reasons, for the protection of human, plants, or animal health, for the protection of public morality, and for matters related to nuclear materials are contemplated in the Cartagena Agreement,[12] the G-3 Treaty,[13] the Treaty of Montevideo 1980,[14] and the Venezuelan customs legislation.[15]

Customs surcharges

Up to 60 percent of the ad-valorem tariff, on the basis of discretionary decisions by the President of the Republic.[16]

ANTIDUMPING AND COUNTERVAILING DUTY INVESTIGATIONS

Dumping and Subsidy Determinations

Initiation of investigation

Venezuelan domestic producers of products that are identical or like those allegedly being dumped or subsidized, can request the initiation of investigations.[17] Under special circumstances, CASS can also initiate an investigation ex officio, whenever it considers that there are indications of unfair trade practices.[18]

Member Countries of the Andean Community, as well as legitimately interested companies—if their respective national legislation permits them—may request that the General Secretariat of said community initiate an investigation.[19]

Timetable

Once formal requirements of a petition are deemed by the CASS Technical Secretariat to be complete, CASS has ten working days to consider whether to open an investigation.[20] After passage of the WTO, the provision that required CASS to impose provisional countervailing duties on imports of agricultural products whose subsidies were established in official publications and budgets of the subsidizing country, as soon as CASS received from its Technical Secretariat the corresponding file,[21] can no longer be applied in investigations involving imports from WTO countries.

After an investigation is opened, interested parties have sixty working days to present their allegations and submit evidence, both to prove their case and to challenge the other party's case.[22] CASS' Technical Secretariat must conclude the investigation within one year from the date of initiation, and send a report to the Commission.[23] The Commission must decide the case within thirty working days after the conclusion of the investigation.[24]

During the course of an investigation, the Commission may impose provisional duties.[25] The imposition of provisional duties must be based on a preliminary finding that unfairly traded imports may be injuring national production of similar goods.[26] Provisional duties are immediately notified to the customs authorities and importers of the goods.[27]

Provisional duties can only be imposed for four months at a time. Importers can decide whether to pay provisional duties in cash or by posting a bond for the full amount. Bonds must be posted through banks or insurance companies domiciled in Venezuela and approved by the customs authorities.[28] During the course of the investigation, CASS may modify and, if necessary, revoke the provisional duties, according to any new information available.

Under Andean Community rules, the General Secretariat must decide on the initiation of the investigation within twenty working days following the request for investigation, if such request complies with all procedural requisites.[29] The General Secretariat must complete its investigation within a four-month period following the publication of its Resolution on the initiation of the investigation in the Official Gazette.[30] This lapse of time can be extended for an additional two-month period. The General Secretariat must issue its decision within the twenty working days following the end of the investigation.

Participation of parties and their counsel

All interested parties can participate in antidumping and countervailing duty procedures, directly or through counsel. In addition to domestic producers, all other parties whose rights or legitimate interests may be affected by the results of an investigation, are considered to be interested parties.[31] Interested parties may present allegations, provide evidence, and have access to the proceedings and to the files containing general information. Such parties include the following:

(i) foreign producers or exporters of the investigated product; governments of such producers or exporters, and their respective embassies in Venezuela;
(ii) Venezuelan importers of the investigated product;
(iii) trade associations of producers, exporters, or importers; and
(iv) industrial users of the investigated product and consumer associations.

In fact, the list of interested parties contained in the Unfair International Trade Act is broader in content than the one contemplated in the

WTO Antidumping and Subsidies Agreements.[32]

There are no provisions in the Unfair International Trade Act regarding consultations with WTO members whose products are under investigation. However, both CASS and the Ministry for Industry and Commerce would enter into such consultations before imposing definitive countervailing duties, in cases involving exports from WTO countries.[33]

Andean Community rules enable producers, exporters, importers, and/or consumers, as well as governments of Member Countries to make allegations, offer evidence, and supply other information.[34]

Access to information developed in proceedings

All interested parties have access to the files containing documents with nonconfidential information developed in the proceedings, and may read and copy such documents.[35]

Parties that provide information in a proceeding may request confidential status for such information.[36] The determination of confidentiality is made by the CASS' Technical Secretariat, on the basis of whether publication of the information would grant an unfair advantage to competitors or would otherwise have a prejudicial effect on its provider or on a third party.[37] The Technical Secretariat also considers whether the information provided is otherwise generally available.

Confidential information is kept in a separate file. Access to that information is restricted to the members and staff of the CASS and its Technical Secretariat, and to the submitting party (or persons authorized by the submitting party). If confidentiality is denied, the providing party may withdraw the documents at its convenience; in such case, CASS will not use that information for its determinations. Otherwise the documents are annexed to the main file of the case, and are then accessible to all interested parties.[38]

Regarding Andean Community proceedings, the General Secretariat can maintain confidentiality of any information provided to it, so long as same is requested by the provider of such information and is otherwise duly justified. A nonconfidential brief must be submitted along with the confidential information, except if the information cannot be presented in a nonconfidential manner.[39]

Definitions

Like products

Under Venezuelan law, like products are defined as either identical, similar (like), or substitutes, to the investigated goods.[40] Identical products are those that have entirely coinciding characteristics. Similar products are those, that although not identical, have a marked likeness in their specific use and in other characteristics. Substitute goods are those that lead to identical results when used.[41] The following elements are taken into account to determine whether the goods are alike: nature, physical characteristics, components, technical attributes, origin, use, function, market performance, quality, commercial brand and prestige, and consumer acceptance.[42]

Parts or components that are being imported separately can be considered like products, if such importation has no commercial purpose and is being done to evade treatment imposed on finished goods.

Andean rules define a like product as a product equal in all aspects to the one that is allegedly dumped or subsidized, or, if such product does not exist, as one with very similar characteristics, taking into account elements such as its nature, quality, use, and function.[43]

Period of investigation

The period of investigation covers at least six months prior to the initiation, and generally extends at least one year.[44]

Andean Community rules do not define the period of investigation.

Domestic industry and petition requirement for industry support

In application of the requirements of the WTO Agreements, CASS verifies that petitions are supported by national producers representing at least 25 percent of the national industry. Similarly, CASS verifies the support from the largest percentage of the national industry, that expresses its opinion on any particular petition.[45]

Andean Community rules do not include general definitions of domestic industry and petition requirements for industry support.

Viability of markets

Under Venezuelan Law, the definition of ordinary commercial operations for the calculation of normal value required, among other things, that the individual volumes of sales to purchasers in the export or origin country be approximate to the volumes of sales of the allegedly dumped good, and that the exporter or producer of similar goods place in the export or origin country an amount equivalent to at least twenty percent of the total volume of its world sales (including those to Venezuela) of the allegedly dumped good.[46] Currently, according to the WTO Antidumping Agreement, CASS would normally have to consider as an acceptable volume of domestic sales for purposes of determination of the normal value, those that are at least five percent of the sales within Venezuela.[47]

Related parties

Related parties can be excluded for purposes of the estimation of dumping and for the determination of injury to the national production. Related parties include relatives, common managers, partners or associates, employed persons, persons who directly or indirectly control a same person or are controlled by it.[48]

Andean Community rules allow transactions among related parties to be excluded from the determination of dumping. Related parties are not defined.[49]

Countervailable subsidies

CASS shall apply the definition of subsidy contemplated in the WTO Subsidies Agreement,[50] which has become the cornerstone of subsidies regulation in Venezuela. The Unfair International Trade Practices Act lists all the export subsidies contained in the Illustrative List of Export Subsidies attached to the Subsidies Code of the Tokyo Round[51] and enables CASS to identify other kinds of subsidies.[52]

The Andean Community considers that an import has been subsidized when the production, manufacture, transportation, or export of the imported product, or of its raw or intermediate materials, has received directly or indirectly any prime, support, prize, or subvention in the country of origin or of exportation.[53]

Noncountervailable subsidies ("green light")

There are no provisions in Venezuelan law, other than the provisions of the WTO agreements (such as those of Part IV of the WTO Subsidies Agreement, regarding non-countervailable subsidies, and the rules contained in the Agreement on Agriculture).

Andean Decision 283 does not have any provision on non-contervailable subsidies.

Application of countervailing procedures to non-market economies

There are no provisions in Venezuelan law or in Andean Community rules, on this matter.

Calculation of dumping margins

Export price

The Venezuelan law defines dumping as the introduction in Venezuelan territory of goods for sale or consumption at a price lower than their normal value.[54]

The export price is defined as the price actually paid or to be paid for the good for its export to Venezuela. This price must be adjusted for any taxes, discounts, or reductions, that have actually been granted and are related to the particular transaction.[55]

CASS must first try to estimate the direct export price. If a direct price does not exist or is inadequate (does not represent the real conditions of the market), due to the existence of associations, agreements, or compensatory arrangements between the exporters and importers of the goods, CASS may estimate an indirect export price.[56] Indirect export prices are calculated based on the price that the importer charges for the goods to the first independent purchaser in Venezuela. An independent purchaser is defined as a purchaser who is not associated or tied to the importer, exporter, or to associations or arrangements that refer to price, sale, profits, or costs of the goods. Finally, CASS may calculate the price of exports for goods that are transformed after importation into Venezuela, such as goods that will be assembled, packaged, or manufactured in Venezuela, before they are sold to the first independent purchaser in Venezuela.[57]

Andean rules define dumped imports as those with an export price that is lower than the normal value of a similar product, destined to its consumption or use in its country of origin or exportation, in normal commercial operations.[58]

Under Andean rules, the export price is the price actually paid or to be paid for the product sold for export to a Member Country.[59]

Normal value

Normal value is defined as the price actually paid, or to be paid, in the course of ordinary commercial operations, for the presumably dumped good consumed in the country of origin or exportation.[60] Normal value is calculated based on information from the country of exportation. If that country serves only as a temporary point of transshipment, normal value is determined based on information from the country of origin.[61]

When there is no domestic market for the goods, prices are fixed by the domestic government, or when the domestic sales have not occurred in conditions of free competition,[62] CASS may calculate a normal value by resorting to a compared export value, i.e., the price of exports made by the exporter of the investigated good to countries other than Venezuela and the countries of export or origin.[63]

If a compared export value is not adequate, CASS must use a constructed value, calculated by the sum of production costs, sale expenses, administrative and other general expenses, plus a reasonable margin of profits.[64]

Under Andean rules, normal value is defined as the price actually paid or to be paid for a product similar to the one imported into the Member Country, when that product is sold for consumption or use in the internal market of the origin or export country, under normal commercial operations.[65]

Adjustments, including those reflecting level of trade

To compare normal value to export prices, CASS introduces adjustments to correct for differences in aspects such as: physical characteristics of the goods; levels of fiscal burdens (e.g., taxes, import duties, etc.); sales at different commercial phases, of different quantities, or under differing commercial conditions.[66]

Adjustments to prices can only be introduced by the request of an interested party. The requesting party must provide CASS with supporting information regarding the validity of the adjustment.[67]

After adjustments, if any, CASS determines an average normal value and compares it to an average export price. The results of these comparisons are then used to determine whether dumping exists, and if so, what is the margin.

Under Andean rules, the export price and the normal value must be examined on a comparable base, in terms of physical characteristics of the product, quantities, and conditions of sale, differences in taxation, and other criteria that may affect the price comparison.[68]

Treatment of sales through related parties

As mentioned above,[69] sales through related parties can be excluded for purposes of the determination of the normal value and the export price. In that case, the authorities can resort to other methods of determination.

Currency conversion

There are no specific rules under Venezuelan law, nor under Andean Decision 283, for currency conversion in comparisons of prices.

Sampling

In cases of a large number of transactions, CASS may use sampling techniques.[70]

There are no provisions in Andean Decision 283 for the use of sampling.

Cost of production and constructed value methodology

As mentioned above,[71] a normal value is constructed by CASS in cases when there is no domestic market for the goods, prices are fixed by the domestic government, or when the domestic sales have not occurred in conditions of free competition, and a compared export value is not deemed adequate.[72]

CASS also may construct a value, when the dumped goods are being sold in their domestic market at a price lower to their production costs.

Production costs include all fixed and variable costs associated with inputs employed and to the production process, in the course of ordinary commercial operations, in addition to sales, administrative and other general expenses.[73] In the case of below-cost sales, the Commission also may opt for either one of two other methods:
(i) disregard below-cost sales and calculate a normal value based on domestic sales at an above-cost price; or
(ii) estimate a normal value based on the price of exports made by the exporter of the investigated good to countries other than Venezuela and the countries of export or origin (compared export value).[74]

Under Andean rules, if a similar product to the one being exported is not sold under normal commercial operations in the internal market of the country of origin or export, or if such sales do not allow a valid determination, and a representative comparable export price cannot be used, the normal value can be assessed through a constructed value. The constructed value will result from the cost of production under normal commercial operations in the country of origin with the addition of a reasonable margin for administrative expenditures, sales expenditures, and profits.[75]

Nonmarket economy methodology

When goods originate from a centrally-planned (nonmarket) economy, CASS calculates a normal value through a compared export value or constructed value, as applicable, based on information from a third (proxy) country. This third country must have a market economy and a level of development similar to that of the investigated country.[76]

Under Andean rules, in the case of imports from centrally-planned economies, normal value will be obtained based on the comparable price for a similar product, under normal commercial operations, sold for use or consumption in a third country with a market economy and a similar degree of development.[77]

Calculation of subsidies

Treatment of loans, grants, and equity investments

In the case of loans granted at lower interest rates or more favorable conditions than those of the market, a distinction will be made between short-term loans (no more than a two-year credit term) and medium and long-term loans. For short-term loans and for longer term loans, the subsidy will be calculated pursuant to the rules for recurrent subsidies and nonrecurrent subsidies, respectively, explained below.[78] The calculation methodology for longer term loans can be applied to short-term loans, it is established that such loans are renewed for a total of two years.[79]

Grants, assignments and any other concessions for the benefit of producers or exporters of the subsidized good, including forgiveness or deduction of debts owed to any governmental entity, shall be considered as subsidies.[80]

Shares subscription, or any other kind of capital contribution by any governmental entity, or by any entity in whose capital there is a governmental participation, in less favorable conditions for these entities than those prevailing in the market will be considered as a subsidy.[81]

There are no rules on these matters in the Andean Community regulation on countervailing duties.

Allocation of subsidies over time

A distinction is made between recurrent subsidies, i.e., subsidies the advantage of which is received each time that conditions occur which repeat themselves periodically, and nonrecurrent subsidies. In the first case, the subsidy amount will be calculated by dividing the benefit received by the total of sales made by the exporter or the producer during the time period for which the benefit was received. In the second case, the number of years during which the benefit is to be distributed must be determined. To this effect, a ten-year period will be used as a reference, except if the benefit consists in the use of a certain asset, in which case a shorter period based on the amortization or depreciation of the asset can be used. Once the period of application is determined, the value of the benefit will be discounted by a rate that reasonably reflects the capital costs for the exporter or the producer at the moment of reception of the benefit.[82]

The Andean Community does not have rules on this matter.

Use of facts available

Interested parties have the burden of promoting evidence to support their claims. If a party withholds information or evidence, does not provide them promptly when requested by CASS or its Technical Secretariat, or in any other way obstructs the course of the investigation, CASS may adopt preliminary or definitive decisions, based on the best information available. Similarly, if CASS finds that information or evidence provided by a party is false or misleading, it will not take such information or evidence into account, and may reject the petitions presented by the providing party.[83]

The Andean Decision 283 does not contain rules on the use of best available information. There are no specific rules on this matter in the Andean Pact regulation, although it is understood that the General Secretariat will take its decision on the basis of the information available to it at the end of the investigation.

Price undertakings and other agreements to suspend investigations

An antidumping investigation or countervailing duty may be concluded or suspended by CASS, as a result of a settlement by the parties.[84] A settlement may include provisions for a revision of prices, a suppression or limitation on the amount of subsidies provided, or a reduction or elimination of the margin of dumping and the injurious effects on Venezuelan production.[85]

Before an investigation can be suspended or concluded, CASS must approve the settlement. CASS may ask for the opinion of the national competition authority (the Superintendency for Promotion and Protection of Free Competition) about the impact of specific compromises to raise prices or limit imports on general competition.[86] Even if parties subscribe to a settlement, CASS may continue with an investigation. On deciding whether to continue an investigation, CASS can act ex officio, or upon the request of foreign exporters or producers, or by the foreign government of the country of origin. If, after such investigation, CASS makes a final negative determination on the case, the settlement will be annulled.[87]

Even after settlements are approved, CASS retains oversight, by which it may solicit parties for information to verify their compliance with the settlement, and to approve or disapprove the settlement based on the parties compliance or noncompliance. Failure to surrender information may be considered an element of a prima facie case of failure to fulfill the terms of a settlement.[88]

Under Andean Community rules, the General Secretariat may convene meetings of interested parties in order to try to get a "direct solution" to the claim. The General Secretariat will determine through a Resolution whether it will suspend the investigation on the basis of the undertakings reached in that meeting, or whether it will continue the investigation at the request of the party against whom the claim was made. If such undertakings are not fulfilled, or the information on their fulfillment is not provided to the General Secretariat, it will restart the investigation and will immediately impose duties at a level determined on the basis of the information available, or if it is not available, at the level requested by the claimant.[89]

Effect of Antidumping or Countervailing Duty Order

At the conclusion of an investigation, CASS issues a final decision in one of two forms. If it considers that one or more of the necessary elements (dumping or subsidization, injury, and causation) are missing, CASS must terminate the investigation without imposing duties. If an investigation is terminated, all provisional duties paid will be refunded and any posted bonds will be released.[90]

CASS may decide to impose definitive duties only if it makes a positive finding on all three issues (dumping or subsidy, injury, and causation).[91] Duties cannot exceed the margin of dumping or the amount of subsidy. CASS can also apply a lesser-duty rule and impose a smaller duty sufficient to eliminate the injury or threat of injury to national production.[92]

If CASS finds the margin of dumping to be de minimis (i.e., under 2 percent as a percentage of the export price), or the volume of dumped imports or that of the injury to be negligible, it shall terminate the investigation without imposing duties.[93] Likewise, investigations will be terminated and no countervailing duty will be imposed when the amount of the subsidy is lower than 1 percent ad-valorem, or the volume of subsidized imports or that of the injury is negligible.[94] Special de minimis and other provisions in favor of developing countries are applied.[95]

Under Andean Community rules, the General Secretariat can authorize the importing Member Country to impose provisional or definitive antidumping or countervailing duties, or can order such imposition to the importing country, in those cases where it is not the claimant.[96] These rules contain a provision similar to the indicated above, regarding the maximum amount of duties.[97]

Effective date
Duration
Duties should only stay in place for as long as they are needed to offset or prevent the injury to national production. They are generally imposed for a period of five years, and can be reviewed yearly. The Unfair International Trade Practices Act includes a sunset clause, by which duties automatically expire after five years, unless a new investigation leads to the extension of the duties. Duties can only be extended once, for a period not to exceed five years.[98] Under the G-3 Treaty, definitive duties will expire after being in force for five years, if no review of same has been requested or initiated ex-officio.[99]

Andean Decision 283 only states that the General Secretariat Resolution must indicate the duration of the duties imposed.[100]

Retroactivity, if any
Venezuelan law does not include any provisions for the application of ret-

roactive duties.

Andean Community rules enable the General Secretariat to impose definitive antidumping or countervailing duties on goods that were imported within the ninety days previous to the date in which provisional duties were established.[101]

Scope determination

Antidumping or countervailing duties must be imposed to all imports of the goods found to be dumped or subsidized and causing injury to national production, regardless of their origin, with the exception of those originated from sources that have become parties of settlements approved by CASS. CASS can identify all suppliers of the like product from a country, or from several countries, if it is impossible for CASS to identify in its Resolution the suppliers that have dumped or received the subsidy.[102]

Enforcement, including rules to prevent circumvention of orders

All importers of goods similar to those being subject to antidumping or countervailing duties must produce before customs authorities a certificate of origin for those goods, or else pay the corresponding duties.[103] Duties must be imposed on products imported as intermediate goods or components when CASS determines that the importation was made in this manner to evade the duties imposed on the finished goods.[104]

Procedures for new shippers

There are no specific rules under Venezuelan law for the treatment of new shippers.

Procedures for review and revocation of order

Antidumping and countervailing duty orders may be reviewed in several ways. First, parties may challenge decisions made by CASS or its Technical Secretariat directly before the Commission for an internal administrative review. CASS decisions cannot be reviewed or overturned by any other authority within the Venezuelan Executive branch, which gives CASS a greater autonomy than that of most government agencies in Venezuela. Second, if a party is dissatisfied with a CASS decision, it can also challenge it before the five-judge First Contentious-Administrative Court.[105]

Decisions subject to potential administrative or judicial challenges include final determinations, as well as any decision that may put an end to a procedure (such as a decision not to open an investigation), prejudgment of a case, or violation of the right of defense of any party.[106]

Even without challenging the original validity of a decision, a party may ask the Commission to revise a duty, whenever the party considers that there is a change of circumstances or that it has paid an amount in excess of the margin of dumping or of the subsidy. A party may ask for such a revision after one year has passed from the date on which the definitive duties were imposed.[107]

Interested parties may challenge the General Secretariat's resolutions in an antidumping or countervailing duty case and request that they are reconsidered. Parties may also challenge such resolutions before the Andean Court of Justice (based in Zuito, Ecuador). The Court may nullify resolutions found to be in violation of the law.

INJURY ANALYSIS

Extension of Injury Test

A so-called mirror-image clause in the Unfair International Trade Practices Act allows CASS to grant injury tests only to imports from countries that grant a similar benefit to Venezuelan exporters.[108]

Timetable and Relation to Dumping and Subsidy Analysis

In addition to the finding of the existence of an unfair trade practice, CASS must find that national production has been injured, to impose duties. CASS can make a positive finding of injury when national production of like products has been materially injured, is suffering a threat of a material injury, or has been significantly retarded in its initial development.[109]

Under Venezuelan law, injury determinations are conducted by the same authority and simultaneously with the antidumping/countervailing duty investigation. Most of the procedural rules mentioned in relation with the antidumping/countervailing duty determinations, including the initiation, timetable, and phases of the investigation, are, therefore, applicable to the injury portion of the proceeding.

Definitions

Domestic industry

Injury must affect at least an important part of the national production, defined as those national producers who represent 30 percent of the national production. In some cases, depending on the structure of the market, CASS may determine that an important part of the national production requires as much as 40 percent or as little as 20 percent.[110]

National producers who are associated with foreign exporters, who are themselves importers of the allegedly unfairly-traded goods, or whose activity does not result in an actual transformation of the inputs into the final goods, are not considered as part of the domestic industry for purposes of injury determination.[111]

Whenever national production represents less than 5 percent of the national consumption of the similar goods, CASS may consider that such production is insignificant, and make a negative finding of injury. Even in cases of insignificant production, however, CASS can make a positive injury determination if it finds that the industry is experiencing a positive growth tendency, as shown by a significant and sustained development during a reasonable period of time.[112]

In exceptional cases, CASS can make an analysis of injury to a regional production comprising only the producers of a limited territory within the country, when most of the regional production is sold within the same region and the regional demand of the good is not satisfied by national producers from other regions of the country.[113]

Material injury

Material injury is defined as a significant and substantial harm to national production.[114] CASS analysis centers on three elements, of which at least two must simultaneously exist, to make a positive finding.[115]

The first element is whether or not the volume of imports of the dumped or subsidized goods is significant and has increased in absolute terms or in relation to the national production of like products. Imports are significant when they represent at least 5 percent of the national production of similar goods and at least 3 percent of the total imports of similar goods into Venezuela,[116] or 4 percent in cases of subsidy investigations of imports from developing countries.[117]

The second element is whether or not the dumped or subsidized goods are sold at prices substantially lower than those of the nationally produced similar goods or have had the effect of depressing or impeding natural and competitive changes in the prices of domestic like products.[118]

The third element is whether or not the importation of dumped or subsidized goods has had a negative effect on the national producers of like products, taking into account factors such as production in units, sales, market share, profits, returns on investment, use of installed capacity, cash flow, inventories, growth, prices of national "inputs," investment plans, and capacity to obtain financing.[119]

Threat of material injury

The threat of material injury must be real and certain, related to an imminent injury. The following factors are taken into consideration when this determination is made:[120]

(i) In the case of subsidized imports, the nature of the subsidy is taken into account. CASS is directed to be particularly concerned with direct and export related subsidies that are higher than 5 percent ad-valorem.
(ii) Increases in productive capacity or in idle capacity in the country of origin are taken into account, when there are indications that such increases may boost exports to Venezuela.
(iii) Accelerated increases in share of the Venezuelan national market by dumped or subsidized goods that have not yet caused material injury are considered.
(iv) Overproduction or accumulation of inventories of dumped or subsidized goods with the probability of exportation to Venezuela are analyzed.
(v) The accumulation of inventories of dumped or subsidized goods in Venezuela, even if they have not been sold yet, are reviewed.
(vi) The potential capacity of a foreign producer to switch the production of goods on which antidumping or countervailing duties have been levied to the production of other dumped or subsidized goods not subject to those duties is taken into account.
(vii) Any tendency in the behavior of sales and exports of dumped or subsidized goods that may lead to an increase of exports of such goods into Venezuela, or other circumstances as determined by CASS, is examined.

All of the above-mentioned indicators may be used by CASS to determine whether or not a threat of injury exists and is not merely based on allegations, conjecture, or remote possibilities.[121]

Other injury findings—significant retardation

To determine whether dumping or subsidies are causing a delay in the initiation of the national production of similar goods, CASS must evaluate the national productive potential when importation of the dumped or subsidized goods began or was imminent. CASS must assess whether the imports are having a negative effect on what should have been the development of that potential. To make this determination, CASS must consider the following factors as referred to the national production: projections of results vis-à-vis actual results; use of productive capacity; situation of orders and deliveries; financial situation; and other circumstances as determined by CASS.[122]

Causation

CASS must evaluate whether a causal relation exists between the importation of dumped or subsidized goods and the harmful impact on national producers. This evaluation includes analysis on whether or not the time of the unfair trade practices coincides with the time of the injurious effects, and whether or not factors other than unfairly traded imports can explain the critical situation of the domestic producers.

OTHER TRADE REMEDIES

History and Rationale

Safeguard clauses

Safeguard provisions have been a staple ingredient of the economic integration agreements to which Venezuela is a party since the inception of the Latin American Free Trade Association (LAFTA) in 1960.[123] The Cartagena Agreement of 1968, which established the Andean Pact—now referred to as the Andean Community—also contains safeguard provisions, which were strengthened as part of the compromises reached when Venezuela joined the Agreement in 1973. LAIA, the Latin American Integration Association, as such, does not have provisions on safeguards, but the bilateral or multilateral agreements reached under LAIA, called "agreements of partial scope" usually contain safeguard clauses. The G-3 Treaty, for example, which is an "agreement of partial scope" under LAIA, does have safeguard provisions. The GATT of 1994 regulations on safeguards, and the WTO Safeguard Agreement are also in force in Venezuela. Venezuela does not have domestic safeguards legislation.

The rationale for safeguard clauses is the perceived need to protect domestic production from injuries due to import surges, monetary devaluation or balance of payments disequilibrium.

Measures for national security, protection of human, plant or animal health, protection of public morality, and measures related to nuclear materials

All economic integration agreements to which Venezuela is a member, as well as the GATT of 1994 and the WTO, contain rules allowing for measures intended to protect the subjects mentioned above. Venezuela has restrictions on imports of weapons for national security reasons. Imports of pornographic goods are prohibited for protection of public morality, and imports of several kinds of goods are prohibited or restricted for sanitary, zoosanitary, or phitosanitary reasons.[124]

Customs surcharges

The presidential capacity to impose customs surcharges in a discriminatory fashion has existed in Venezuelan customs law for many years. Currently it is at least partially intended, apparently, to provide leverage in trade negotiations, as the President can impose the measure merely indicating the reasons for its establishment and can lift said measures "obtaining the advantages he deems convenient, if that were the case."[125] In other instances it has been used for the protection of domestic production of agricultural goods[126] or as a way to counter suspected subvaluation of goods imported by persons related to the exporters.[127]

Procedures

Safeguard clauses

Under the Cartagena Agreement, any member of the Andean Community can:
(i) extend the measures adopted for the correction of balance of payments disequilibrium to intracommunity trade;[128]
(ii) impose corrective measures when its economy or an important sector of same is seriously injured, or threatened of serious injury, as a result of the application of the Agreement's trade liberalization program;[129]
(iii) impose corrective measures against import surges that cause perturbations to the national production of a product in that country;[130] and
(iv) impose corrective measures when a monetary devaluation in another Member Country alters normal conditions of competence.[131]

In cases i and ii, above, a previous authorization from the General Secretariat is required, but the importing country can take urgent measures without such authorization. The General Secretariat must be immediately notified of such measures, which will decide on its maintenance, modification, or abrogation. In case iii, above, the importing country does not require a previous authorization, but the General Secretariat can suspend, modify, or authorize the measures. These measures must guarantee market access for a level not lower than the last three-year average for the product's volume of imports. In case iv, above, once the General Secretariat verifies the alteration of the normal conditions of competition, the importing country can adopt corrective measures, in accordance with the General Secretariat's recommendations. These measures may not reduce imports below its level prior to the devaluation. Any other Member Country may take the matter to the Commission of the Andean Community to get a final decision. A Member Country that devalued its currency may ask the General Secretariat, at any time, to review the situation to suppress or lessen the corrective measures. The General Secretariat's resolution on this matter may be amended by the Commission.

Any party to the G-3 Treaty may adopt either bilateral or global measures. Bilateral measures are intended to prevent or correct serious injury to the domestic production, or its threat, caused by imports from another party, of identical goods, like goods or goods that are in any other way direct competitors of the domestically produced goods. Imports must have been made because of the application of the Tariff Reduction Program of the Treaty. The bilateral measures can be taken in accordance with the following rules:

(i) measures can be taken within the fifteen-year period commencing from the entry into force of the Treaty;
(ii) only tariffs not higher than those applied to imports of that product from nonparties can be applied;
(iii) measures can be applied for a period of up to a year and can be extended once for a similar period; and
(iv) once the measures terminate, the tariff to be applied to the import of the good from a party will be the one indicated in the Tariff Reduction Program.[132]

A mutually agreed compensation must be granted by the party who applies the safeguard measure on the basis of a threat of injury or for an extended period.[133]

Global measures may be taken in accordance with Article XIX of GATT, but can be applied to imports from another party of the G-3 Treaty only if that party has been one of the five main suppliers of the good to be subject to the measure, during the three-year period prior to the imposition of the safeguard, and the imports from that party are considered to contribute in an important way to the serious injury or the threat of serious injury.[134] Compensation must be granted in accordance to the GATT.[135]

The imposition of both bilateral or global safeguards must be preceded by an investigation on the volume and conditions of the imports; an injury test and causation.[136] The initiation of the investigation must be officially published by the importing party and notified to interested parties. If the results of the investigation yield basis for the taking of measures, the importing party must request consultations with the exporting party. The other party can join in the consultations, if it has a substantial interest in its outcome. Safeguard measures can only be taken once the consultations are concluded.[137] Similar procedures must be followed when the extension of the measure is intended.[138]

There are no procedural rules in Venezuelan law regarding other safeguard measures.

Measures for national security, protection of human, plant or animal health, protection of public morality and measures related to nuclear materials

There are no provisions in Venezuelan law that regulate procedures for measures intended to protect national security and public morality. Authorities have wide discretionary powers in this regard. Measures for the protection of human health, including the authorization or prohibition of manufacture, importation or sale of foodstuffs, are taken by the Ministry for Health and Social Assistance. Foodstuff must be registered with this Ministry before its importation. Registration will only be granted if the foodstuff is approved after technical examination.[139] Importation of foodstuff whose consumption is not permitted in its country of origin, is prohibited.[140] Phitosanitary and zoosanitary measures, including the prohibition or restrictions of imports, can be taken by the Ministry for Agriculture and Livestock. The General Secretariat of the Andean Community registers all agriculture and livestock health standards of the Member Countries. Only standards registered with the General Secretariat can be applied to imports from another Member Country. A Member Country which considers that there are no longer scientific reasons for a standard, may ask the General Secretariat to review the matter. The General Secretariat's resolution will be accepted by all interested parties.[141] The General Secretariat can also be asked to determine whether a particular measure applied by a Member Country is an unjustified restriction of another Member's exports. The General Secretariat will take its decision, which will be obligatory for all interested parties, on the basis of a technical report.[142] The G-3 Treaty also contains rules on zoosanitary and phitosanitary protection.[143]

Customs surcharges

There are no procedural rules in Venezuelan law regarding this discretionary power of the President of the Republic, other than the requirement that the decision must be taken in the Council of Ministers, that he must explain his reasons, and that the decision must be published in the *Official Gazette* of Venezuela.

Administrative Framework

Safeguard clauses

All proceedings before the General Secretariat of the Cartagena Agreement, as well as notifications and consultations under the G-3 Treaty are to be made by the Ministry for Industry and Commerce. Other bodies have not been specifically granted jurisdiction on the taking of measures, but if same involve tariffs and/or imports prohibitions or restrictions, the Ministry of Finance would be competent to take such measures.[144]

Measures for national security, protection of human, plant or animal health, protection of public morality, and measures related to nuclear materials

As indicated above, the taking of measures for national security and protection of public morality depends on discretionary decisions by the President of the Republic in the Council of Ministers. If the measures involve import prohibitions or restrictions, the Ministry of Finance would be competent for their enforcement. Imports prohibitions or restrictions for the protection of human health are to be taken by the Ministry for Health and Social Assistance, while measures for zoosanitary and phitosanitary reasons are competence of the Ministry for Agriculture and Livestock. The General Secretariat of the Andean Community has the above indicated powers regarding trade of agricultural products within the Community. A Committee composed of representatives of each party administers the application of zoosanitary and phitosanitary measures under the G-3 Treaty.[145]

Customs surcharges

The competent authority to establish a custom surcharge is the President of the Republic in the Council of Ministers, and the Ministry of Finance will be competent for its enforcement.

Timetable

Safeguard clauses

There is not a timetable for safeguard measures under the Cartagena Agreement for the purpose of balance of payments or for injuries due to the Tariff Reduction Program. The Member Country that imposes corrective measures for import surges must inform to the General Secretariat of them within sixty days of their imposition, and the General Secretariat must issue its resolution on the matter within the sixty-day period following its reception of such information.[146] In the case of monetary devaluation, the

General Secretariat must issue its resolution within one month from the date in which any Member Country requests the General Secretariat's recommendations. If the importing country has unilaterally taken urgent measures, the General Secretariat must decide within seven days.[147]

Under the G-3 Treaty rules, notification to interested parties will be made within the ten working days following official publication of the decision to initiate an investigation. Consultations last for forty-five days, unless the parties agree to another timetable.

References

1. The views expressed herein are personal, and should not be attributed to the Andean Community General Secretariat nor to the Venezuelan Antidumping and Subsidies Commission, where Mr. Capriles served as General Counsel. The authors are responsible for the translations in the text.
2. Formerly known as the Andean Pact. The founding treaty is the 1969 Cartagena Agreement, which establish a Commission composed of one plenipotentiary from each Member Country and a General Secretariat. The Commission's "Decisions" are mandatory and directly applicable in all Member Countries. Venezuela became a member in 1973. The other members are Bolivia, Colombia, Ecuador, and Peru.
3. Unfair International Trade Practices Act, Article 1; Decision 283, Article 2.
4. Decision 283, Article 2. While this currently means that most antidumping and subsidies cases involving Venezuelan imports are subject to national jurisdiction, as the process of regional integration progresses (with a growth in intraregional trade and an incorporation of further products and countries in the Andean Customs Union), more cases can be expected to fall under Andean Community jurisdiction.
5. Published in the Official Gazette of the Republic of Venezuela N° 4,829 Special Edition of December 29, 1994.
6. Published in the Official Gazette of the Republic of Venezuela N° 4,833 Special Edition of December 29, 1994.
7. Published in the Official Gazette of the Republic of Venezuela N° 4,441 Special Edition of June 18, 1992.
8. Approved by Presidential Decree N° 2,883 and published in the Official Gazette of the Republic of Venezuela N° 4,567 Special Edition of April 26, 1993.
9. Unfair International Trade Practices Act, Article 33.
10. Cartagena Agreement, Articles 78, 79, 79-A & 80.
11. G-3 Treaty, Chapter VIII.
12. Cartagena Agreement, Article 42.
13. G-3 Treaty, Chapter XXII.
14. This treaty creates the Latin American Integration Association (LAIA), which

provides a broad umbrella for different integration agreements. All South American countries and Mexico are members of LAIA. The relevant provision on this matter is article 50 of the Treaty of Montevideo 1980.
15. Customs Organic Act, Article 4 (15).
16. Id., at Article 3 (11).
17. Unfair International Trade Practices Act, at Article 37.
18. Id., at Article 38. To date, the Commission has not used this power. However, in the Oil Country Tubular Goods from Argentina and Mexico case, it decided to continue ex officio an investigation, after the petitioner withdrew its petition.
19. Decision 283, Article 10.
20. Unfair International Trade Practices Act, Article 41.
21. Id. at Article 60.
22. Id., at Article 45.
23.. Id., at Article 51.
24. Id.
25. Id., at Article 19 & 60. After passage of the WTO, provisional duties on imports from a WTO country can not be imposed until at least sixty days after initiation of the investigation. WTO Antidumping Agreement, Article 7.3.
26. Id. at Articles 19 & 60.
27. Regulations of the Unfair International Trade Practices Act, Article 81.
28. Unfair International Trade Practices Act, Articles 54 & 61.
29. Decision 283, Article 11.
30. Id., at Article 15.
31. Unfair International Trade Practices Act, Article 2(6).
32. Unfair International Trade Practices Act, Article 2 (6); WTO Subsidies Agreement, Article 12.9.
33. WTO Subsidies Agreement, Article 13.
34. Decision 283, Article 12.
35. Organic Law for Administrative Procedures, Article 59; Unfair International Trade Practices Act, Article 44.
36. Unfair International Trade Practices Act, Article 48.
37. Id.
38. Id., at Article 49.
39. Decision 283, Article 13.
40. Unfair International Trade Practices Act, Article 2 (11).
41. Regulation of the Unfair International Trade Practices Act, Article 4.
42. Id., at Article 2.
43. Decision 283, Article 4.
44. Unfair International Trade Practices Act, Article 43.
45. WTO Antidumping Agreement, Article 5.4. WTO Subsidies Agreement, Article 11.4.
46. Regulation of the Unfair International Trade Practices Act, Article 8 (2) & (3).
47. WTO Antidumping Agreement, Article 2.2.
48. Unfair International Trade Practices Act, Article 2 (16).

49. Decision 283, Articles 5 & 6.
50. WTO Subsidies Agreement, Articles 1 & 2.
51. That list was partially modified by the WTO Subsidies Agreement.
52. Unfair International Trade Practices Act, Article 9.
53. Decision 283, Article 8. The fact that Bolivia does not have sea coast is to be taken into consideration in the determination of the existence of a subsidy on transportation to and from that country. Multiple exchange rates for financial or commercial transactions in the country of origin or the country of exportation can be considered as subsidies.
54. Unfair International Trade Practices Act., Article 2 (4).
55. Id., at Article 6.
56. Id. and Regulation of the Unfair International Trade Practices Act, Article 18.
57. Regulation of the Unfair International Trade Act, Articles 15 & 21.
58. Decision 283, Article 3.
59. Id., at Article 5.
60. Unfair International Trade Practices Act, Article 2 (14).
61. Id., at Article 5.
62. Id., and Regulation of the Unfair International Trade Practices Act, Article 10.
63. Regulation of the Unfair International Trade Practices Act, Articles 8, 10 & 11.
64. Id., at Article 12.
65. Decision 283, Article 6.
66. Unfair International Trade Act, Article 7.
67. Id.
68. Decision 283, Article 7.
69. See Section II.A.5.e above.
70. Unfair International Trade Practices Act, Article 8 (3); WTO Antidumping Agreement, Article 6.10.
71. See Section II.A.6.b above.
72. Unfair International Trade Practices Act, Article 5; Regulation of the Unfair International Trade Practices Act, Article 10.
73. Regulation of the Unfair International Trade Practices Act, Article 12.
74. Id., at Article 13.
75. Decision 283, Article 6.
76. Regulation of the Unfair International Trade Act, Article 10. CASS verifies the similarity of the degree of development of the two countries. In the Blue Jeans from the People's Republic of China case, the normal value was calculated based on the export value of blue jeans from Indonesia to Saudi Arabia. The petitioner's qualification of Poland as a centrally-planned economy was rejected in the Steel Beams from Poland and Romania case.
77. Decision 283, Article 6(d).
78. See Section III,A.(7) (c) below.
79. Regulation of the Unfair International Trade Act, Article 44.
80. Id., at Article 40 (1).
81. Id., at Article 40 (2).

82. Id., at Articles 43 and 45.
83. Unfair International Trade Act, Article 46. In these cases, CASS shall take into account the provisions contained in the Uruguay Round Antidumping and Subsidies Agreement and in Annex II of the Antidumping Agreement on the use of available information.
84. To date, no settlements have been reached in application of the Venezuelan Unfair International Trade Practices Act.
85. Unfair International Trade Practices Act, Article 23.
86. Regulation of the Unfair International Trade Practices Act, Article 58.
87. Unfair International Trade Practices Act, Article 24.
88. Id., at Articles 25 and 26.
89. Decision 283, Article 14.
90. Unfair International Trade Practices Act, Articles 45, 51 & 52.
91. Id., at Article 4.
92. Id., at Article 16.
93. In the Iron and Steel Grinding Balls for Mills from Peru case, CASS terminated the investigation without imposing duties, when the margin of dumping was found to be below 2 percent.
94. WTO Subsidies Agreement, Article 11.9. G-3 Treaty, Article 9-04(1). Under the G-3 Treaty, a volume of imports that represents less than 1 percent of the internal market for the like product of the importing country is considered insignificant, unless the cumulation of these imports with imports of subsidized similar goods from other countries represent more than 2.5 percent of that market.
95. WTO Subsidies Agreement, Article 27.
96. Decision 283, Article 2.
97. Id., at Article 21.
98. Unfair International Trade Practices Act, Article 57.
99. G-3 Treaty, Article 9-11.
100. Decision 283, Article 18.
101. Id., at Article 24.
102. Unfair International Trade Practices Act. Article 18.
103. Joint Resolution of the Ministries of Finance and Development N° 3055 and 321 respectively, dated July 19th, 1996, published in the Official Gazette N° 36,007, of July 25th, 1996.
104. Regulation of the Unfair International Trade Practices Act, Article 54.
105. This court decides challenges to decisions taken by subcabinet level agencies on a broad range of subjects. Its review generally focuses on whether an agency has acted within its legal authority. This includes factors such as whether or not the body was competent, whether or not all procedural formalities were fulfilled, whether or not all legal and factual circumstances were taken into consideration and were reflected in the text of the decision, and whether or not all parties were given adequate opportunity to defend their rights. If a decision is challenged by a party on grounds of violation of any of its constitutional rights (e.g., right of defense), the court decides the case on a special (expedited) procedure.

106. Attempts have also been made by aggrieved parties in several cases to challenge preliminary determinations that decide to impose or not to impose provisional duties. Venezuelan law is silent on whether preliminary determinations can be challenged without waiting to challenge them jointly with the final determination. As this article is being written, the Court is reviewing this question in several cases.
107. Unfair International Trade Practices Act, Articles 55 & 56. In addition to these review mechanisms, some trade agreements provide for other procedures to challenge decisions. WTO member countries, for example, can challenge antidumping decisions that nullify or impair the benefits that they could have reasonably expected under the agreements. The Mexican Government can also challenge decisions under the dispute settlement mechanism of the G-3 Treaty.
108. Unfair International Trade Practices Act, Article 11. This currently guarantees an injury test for at least all WTO member countries. In a preliminary decision in the Blue Jeans from the People's Republic of China case, CASS considered the fact that the People's Republic of China was not a contracting party to GATT as prima-facie evidence that it would not grant an injury test to Venezuelan exporters.
109. Unfair International Trade Practices Act., Article 11. Regulation of the Unfair International Trade Practices Act, Article 46.
110. Unfair International Trade Practices Act, Article 14. Regulation of the Unfair International Trade Practices Act, Article 47. As mentioned above, CASS verifies the support to a petition among the whole national industry, as well as the share of the national industry represented by the petitioner. WTO Antidumping Agreement, Article 5.4 and WTO Subsidies Agreement, Article 11.4.
111. Unfair International Trade Practices Act, Article 14. Regulation of the Unfair International Trade Practices Act, Article 48.
112. Regulation of the Unfair International Trade Practices Act, Article 48.
113. Unfair International Trade Practices Act, Article 14.
114. Regulation of the Unfair International Trade Practices Act, Article 46.
115. Id., at Article 50.
116. Id., at Article 50 (1). WTO Antidumping Agreement, Article 5.8.
117. WTO Subsidies Agreement, Article 27.10 (b).
118. Regulation of the Unfair International Trade Practices Act. Article 50 (2).
119. Id., at Article 50 (3).
120. Id., at Article 51.
121. Unfair International Trade Practices Act, Article 13.
122. Regulation of the Unfair International Trade Practices Act, Article 52.
123. LAFTA was created by the Treaty of Montevideo in 1960. All South American countries and Mexico were members. The failure of LAFTA in the establishment of a free trade zone was one of the main reasons for subregional integration schemes. LAFTA was replaced in 1980 by LAIA. The relevant provisions were contained in Chapter VI of the Treaty of Montevideo.
124. Sanitary measures are regulated by the Ley de Sanidad Nacional (National Health

Act), of July 21, 1938 and by the Reglamento General de Alimentos (General Regulation on Foodstuff), of January 15, 1959; zoosanitary and phitosanitary measures are regulated by the Ley sobre Defensas Sanitarias Vegetal y Animal (Plant and Animal Sanitary Defenses Act), of July 29, 1941. Decision 328 of the Andean Community establishes the Andean System for Agriculture and Cattle Health.

125. Customs Organic Law, Article 3 (11) and (12).
126. Before implementation of the currently in force Andean System of Price Bands for the importation of several agricultural products, the Venezuelan government resorted to measures of this kind for the protection of domestic production of certain cereals and milk.
127. Before Venezuela's accession to the GATT, imports of computing hardware made by Venezuelan subsidiaries of foreign producers of such hardware were subject to a customs surcharge.
128. Cartagena Agreement, Article 78.
129. Id., at Article 79.
130. Id., at Article 79-A.
131. Id., at Article 80.
132. G-3 Treaty, Article 8-03.
133. Id., at Article 8-04.
134. Id., at Articles 8-05 and 8-06.
135. Id., at Article 8-07.
136. Id., at Article 8-09.
137. Id., at Articles 8-12 & 8-14.
138. Id., at Article 8-17.
139. General Regulation on Foodstuffs, Articles 30, 34 & 35.
140. Id., at Article 41.
141. Decision 238, Article 12.
142. Id., at Article 18.
143. G-3 Treaty, Chapter V. Section B.
144. Customs Organic Law, Article 4 (13), (14) & (15).
145. G-3 Treaty, Article 5-29.
146. Cartagena Agreement, Article 79A.
147. Id., at Article 80.

About the Editors

Leonard E. Santos is a partner in the Washington, DC, office of Perkins Coie, where he cochairs the international trade practice group. He was educated at New York University Law School, where he served as Note and Comment Editor of the International Law Journal and clerked for Judge Ozell Trask of the U.S. Court of Appeals for the Ninth Circuit. Before entering private practice, he was Legal Advisor on international matters to the Secretary of the Treasury and was International Trade Counsel to the Senate Committee on Finance. He is a prolific writer and public speaker, serves on NAFTA Chapter 19 dispute settlement panels, and is a member of the Steering Committee of the Trade Committee of the American Bar Association's Section on International Law and Practice.

Stephen J. Powell is Chief Counsel for Import Administration in the U.S. Department of Commerce, the agency responsible for the administration of U.S. antidumping and countervailing duty laws. He also is responsible for legal advice on the Foreign-Trade Zones program and represents Commerce before binding NAFTA dispute settlement panels, as well as litigating challenges to Commerce AD/CVD determinations brought before U.S. federal courts and WTO dispute settlement panels.

Mark T. Wasden is an associate in the Washington, DC, office of Perkins Coie, where he practices in international trade and customs law. He was educated at Brigham Young University (BA, 1990) and George Washington University (JD, 1993). He has represented private parties in antidumping and countervailing duty cases before the U.S. Department of Commerce, the U.S. International Trade Commission, and the U.S. federal courts. He is admitted to practice before the U.S. Court of Appeals for the Federal Circuit and the U.S. Court of International Trade. He is admitted to the bars of Maryland and the District of Columbia and is an active member of the Customs and International Trade Bar Association and the Maryland State Bar Association.

About the Authors

Diego Calmet Mujica is a partner in the firm of Estudio Aurelio Garcia Sayan, located in Lima, Peru. He was educated at the Peruvian Catholic University Peru–Lima. He currently serves as Vice Minister of International Trade Negotiations of Peru and is Chairman of the Competition Policy Group of the Free Trade Area of the Americas (Andean Pact). He formerly served as President of the Peruvian Antidumping and Subsidies Committee.

Gonzalo Capriles is a partner in the firm of Bentata Hoet & Asociados, located in Caracas, Venezuela. He was educated at the Central University of Venezuela (law degree, 1972; master's degree, Law of Integration, 1976) and Cambridge University in England (diploma, International Law, 1979). He was formerly Advisor to the Institute of Foreign Trade and to the Minister of Finance and was Consultant to the Board of the Cartagena Agreement and Latin American Economic System. He is currently Adviser to the Minister of Industry and Commerce. He drafted the Bill of Unfair Practices in International Trade (1992) and the Foreign Trade Bank Bill (1994).

Jorge Castro-Bernieri is Legal Counsel at the *Junta del Acuerdo de Cartagena* (Andean Pact Secretariat), located in Lima, Peru. He was educated at the Central University of Venezuela in Caracas (law degree), where he was Professor of International Trade and Administrative Law, and at the School of Foreign Service, Georgetown University, Washington, DC (master's degree). He was formerly Legal Counsel of the Venezuelan Antidumping and Subsidy Commission.

Katarína Cechová is a partner in the firm of Cechova, Hrbek, located in Bratislava, Slovak Republic. She was educated at Comenius University in Bratislava, Slovak (Juris Doctor, 1984). She has worked in law offices in Bratislava since 1984, became a member of the Slovak Bar Association in 1987, and founded a law firm in 1990.

Dae Yun Cho is a partner in the firm of Kim & Chang, located in Seoul, Korea. He was educated at the College of Law, Seoul National University (LLB, 1973), Yale Law School (LLM, 1976), and Brookings Institute (ROK-US Trade Seminar and Training, 1984). He serves as Consultant for the Korean Trade Commission, a member of the Government Advisory Group on International Economic Affairs, and ROK National Candidate for WTO Panelists.

Felix Egli is a partner in the firm of Hartmann & Meyer and Partners, located in Zurich, Switzerland. He was educated at the University of St. Gallen HSG (JD, 1989) and Southern Methodist University in Dallas (LLM, 1988). He is an author on insurance law (Swiss/EU Insurance Treaty, 1989) and on international debt enforcement among Switzerland, Germany, and Austria (1991); he is coauthor of agency and distribution agreements in Switzerland.

Yüksel Ersoy is a partner in the Ersoy Legal Office, located in Ankara, Turkey. He was educated at the Ankara University Law School (law degree, 1959) and the School of Law of the University of Rome in Italy (PhD, 1964). He formerly was a visiting scholar at the University of California–Berkeley (1975) and at the University of Virginia in Charlottesville (1979). He teaches as a full professor at the University of Ankara and has his own law office in Ankara that specializes in contract law, torts, company law, and national and international commercial law.

Robert Fardell is a partner in the firm of Russell, Mcveagh, McKenzie, Bartlett, & Company, located in Auckland, New Zealand. He was educated at the University of Canterbury in New Zealand (LLB, Hons.). He has acted as Legal Adviser on many customs and trade issues and has appeared as Counsel in a number of leading cases. Between 1980 and 1986, he was a Crown Counsel in cases concerning the customs, excise, and trade.

Daniel M. Ferrere is a partner in the firm of Ferrere Lamaison located in Montevideo, Uruguay. He was educated at the University of Uruguay (Doctor in Laws and Social Sciences, 1974) and Harvard Law School (Master in Laws, 1976). Until 1996, he was Senior Professor of Law of International Trade in the University of Uruguay and Professor of Banking Regulation in the ORT University of Uruguay. He is Director, Uruguay–USA Chamber of Commerce.

Gabriel Ibarra-Pardo is a partner in the firm of Castro, Escobar e Ibarra, located in Santafé de Bogotá, Colombia. He was educated at the Pontificia Javeriana University in Colombia (law degree) and Exeter University in England (LLM, International Business Law). He is a member of the Colombian Society of Specialists in International Trade.

Nopadol Intralib is a partner in the Nopadol & Khaisri Law Office, located in Bangkok, Thailand. He was educated at Chulalongkorn University in Bangkok (LLB, Hons., 1971) and Honorable Society of Gray's Inn in London (barrister-at-law, 1976). He specializes in government contracts, project finance, joint venture, taxation, investment law, and natural resources law.

V. Lakshmi Kumaran is a partner in the firm of Lakshmi Kumaran & Sridharan, located in New Delhi, India. He was educated at the University of Madras (graduate in mathematics and law). He was a member of the Indian Revenue Service, dealing with customs, excise, and other trade-related matters. He represents clients in antidumping and countervailing duty investigations.

Peter A. Magnus is a partner in the firm of Smith Lyons, located in Ottawa, Canada. He has an MBA (1976), LLB (1976), and BA in economics (With Distinction). He is the author of "The Canadian Antidumping System" in *Antidumping Law and Practice: A Comparative Study* (edited by Professor John H. Jackson) and "The North American Free Trade Agreement" in *Anti-dumping under the WTO: A Comparative Review*. He is Editor of *Antitrust and International Trade Law Update*, the newsletter of the International Bar Association's Section on Antitrust and Trade Law. He specializes in international trade law including Canadian trade remedy law, the North American Free Trade Agreement, WTO Agreements, and, generally, matters relating to cross-border transactions.

Osvaldo Jorge Marzorati is a partner with the firm of Allende & Brea, located in Buenos Aires, Argentina. He was educated at the University of Buenos Aires (LLB, *magna cum laude*, 1964), Princeton University, Columbia Law School (MCL, *cum laude*, 1967), University of Buenos Aires (PhD, Commercial Law, 1989), University of Madrid (1967), and Max Planck Institute in Hamburg (1985). He was recipient of a Fullbright Fellowship (1966). He is Professor of Private International Law and International Transactions, University of Buenos Aires and author of *System of Commercial Distribution, The Contract of Franchising, International Business Transactions,* and *Joint Ventures and Strategic Alliances.*

Eduardo Mayora Alvarado is a partner in the firm of Mayora & Mayora, located in Guatemala City, Guatemala. He was educated at Georgetown University (LLM, Common Law Studies, 1982). He specializes in international business law, foreign investment in Guatemala, and international trade matters. He has been a part-time Law Professor at Francisco Marroquin University.

Trond S. Paulsen is a partner with the firm of Heggemsnes & Paulsen, located in Oslo, Norway. He was educated at the University of Oslo, (MA, political science—international relations, 1968; Graduate in Jurisprudence, 1981) and University of Nice in France (Graduate in Business Administration, 1970). He was head of the International Division, Ministry of Fisheries (1975–1982) and Director General of the Ministry of Fisheries (1983–1989). He has published articles and studies of international trade and fisheries management, including "The EC Anti-dumping Rules and Practice" (Oslo, 1990).

Maria Fernanda Pecora is a partner in the firm of Lilla, Huck e Malheiros, located in São Paulo, Brazil. She was educated at the Universidade de São Paulo Law School (LLB, 1984) and New York University Law School (Master's of Comparative Jurisprudence, 1988). She formerly was Trainee, Gide, Loyrette, Nouel, Brussels (antidumping in the EU). She has given the speeches "Dumping" at the Federation of Commerce of the State of São Paulo (March 1994) and "Dumping and Countervailing Duties" at an American Bar Association meeting (November 1995).

Olive Angela Tibbetts Ramchand is a partner in the firm of Fitzwilliam, Stone, Furness-Smith & Morgan, located in Port-of-Spain, Trinidad. She was educated at the Norman Manley Law School in Jamaica. She is the partner in charge of intellectual property and also practices in the areas of conveyancing, commerce, trust, and administration of estates.

Raul Santa María D. is a partner in the firm of Claro y Cia, located in Santiago, Chile. He was educated at Catholic University of Chile. He was Professor of Economic Law, Catholic University of Chile (1966), University of Chile (1976), and University Diego Portales in Santiago (1986). He was Legal Adviser for legislation to the government of Chile in economic law matters (1973–1989), to the Comptroller General (*Contraloría General de la República,* 1968–1973), and to the Central Bank of Chile (1973–1983) and was Chief Legal Counsel of *Banco Central de Madrid España,* Chile Branch (1983–1986).

Quay Chew Soon is a partner in the firm of Skrine & Company, located in Kuala Lumpur, Malaysia. He was educated at the National University of Singapore (Bachelor of Laws, 1987; Master in Laws, 1991). His area of practice includes joint ventures and acquisitions, with emphasis on foreign investment. He has worked in several other jurisdictions, including Singapore and Brunei. He is currently a partner in the Corporate & Conveyancing Department.

Clive Stanbrook is a partner in the firm of Stanbrook & Hooper, located in Brussels, Belgium. He began his career in London and then moved to Brussels and established the trade firm Stanbrook & Hooper, where he was one of the early practitioners in EC antidumping and customs law. He is the author of *Extradition: The Law and Practice* (1989) and coauthor of *Dumping and Subsidies* (3rd ed., 1996). He was President of the British Chamber of Commerce for Belgium and Luxembourg and is a member of the Council of the Belgo–Luxembourg Chamber of Commerce in London. He was awarded the Officer of the British Empire in 1988 and made a Queen's Counsel in 1989.

Cecil Steinhauer is a partner in the firm of Edward, Nathan & Friedland, located in Johannesburg, South Africa. He was educated at University of the Witwatersrand, Johannesburg (BA, LLB *cum laude*). In addition to drafting commercial agreements, he has been involved in major commercial litigation and has represented successfully a major international motor manufacturer in a South African antidumping case.

Ralf Thaeter is a partner in the firm of Gleiss Lutz Hootz Hirsch & Partners, located in Prague, Czech Republic. He was educated at the University of Passau in Germany (State exams, 1987, 1990; Dr. Jur., 1991) and American University Washington College of Law (LLM, 1992). He is a specialist in mergers and acquisitions and international business transactions, with an emphasis on Central and Eastern Europe; an author of a book on Czech business law; and member of the German, Czech, American, and International Bar Associations.

Juan Francisco Torres-Landa R. is a partner in the firm of Barrera, Siqueiros y Torres Landa S.C., located in Mexico City, Mexico. He was educated at the National Autonomous University of Mexico (1988) and Harvard Law School (LLM, 1990). He is Corporate Law Professor at the National Autonomous University of Mexico and the Universidad Iberoamericana, both in Mexico City. He is a member of the International Bar Association and the Mexican Bar Association and is currently the Vice-Chair of the Mexican Law Committee of the American Bar Association. He has represented several foreign companies in antidumping investigations launched by the Mexican Ministry of Trade and Industrial Promotion and is an active member of the Mexican Trade Lawyers Association.

Yasuhide Watamabe is a partner with the firm of Nagashima & Ohno, located in Tokyo, Japan. He was educated at Tokyo University (LLB, 1981), Legal Training and Research Institute of the Supreme Court of Japan (LLM, 1984–1986), and Columbia Law School (LLM, 1991). He is admitted to the bar in Japan (1986) and New York and California (1992). His recent publications include "Various Issues Related to Dispute Resolution by GATT/WTO from a Procedural Viewpoint" (coauthor, Fair Trade Center, 1995) and "Various Types and Dispute Resolution Procedures and Methods—Establishment of New Procedures for APEC" (coauthor, Fair Trade Center, 1996).

Sui-Yu Wu is a partner with the firm of Perkins Coie, Taipei, located in Taiwan. He was educated at National Taiwan University (LLB), Soochow University School of Law (LLM), and the University of Michigan Law School (LLM, SJD). He represents parties to antidumping proceedings in several countries and has authored numerous articles on antidumping laws.

Mohamed Zaanouni is a partner in Zaanouni Law Firm, located in Tunis, Tunisia. He was educated at the University of Tunis (LLB, 1992) and the University of Paris in Sorbone (LLM, International Trade Law, 1993; LLM, Business and Economic Law, 1994). He is author of *Foreign Investment in Tunisia* (1993) and *Settlement of Conflicts in Case of Multiple Assignment of Receivables* (1994). He formerly was in International Practice in London at More, Fisher, Brown and in New York at Walter, Conston Alexander & Green (1993–1995). He is a member of the Tunisian Bar Association and Business Law Association Paris–Sorbone.